WE LIVED
WITH
DIGNITY

WE LIVED
WITH
DIGNITY

THE
JEWISH
PROLETARIAT
OF AMSTERDAM,
1900–1940

Selma Leydesdorff

Translated by
FRANK HENY

 Wayne State University Press   Detroit

Artwork for the maps was prepared by Tony Parillo. These maps are based on maps from Karl Baedeker, *Belgium and Holland: Handbook for Travellers* (Leipzig: Karl Baedeker, 1910).

Originally published as *Wij hebben als mens geleefd*. Copyright © 1987 by Selma Leydesdorff and J. M. Meulenhoff, Amsterdam.

English edition copyright © 1994 by Wayne State University Press, Detroit Michigan 48202. All rights are reserved.

No part of this book may be reproduced without formal permission.

Manufactured in the United States of America.

99 98 97 96 95 94   5 4 3 2 1

Library of Congress Cataloging-in-Publication Data

Leydesdorff, Selma.
    [Wij hebben als mens geleefd. English]
    We lived with dignity : the Jewish proletariat of Amsterdam.
1900–1940 / Selma Leydesdorff : translated from the Dutch by Frank Heny.
      p.   cm.
    Includes bibliographical references and index.
    ISBN 0–8143–2338–3
    1. Working class—Netherlands—Amsterdam—History—20th century.
2. Jews—Netherlands—Amsterdam—History—20th century. 3. Jews—
Netherlands—Amsterdam—Social conditions. 4. Amsterdam
(Netherlands)—Social conditions. I. Title.
HD8518.5.J5L4813   1994
305.5′62′0899240492—dc20

               94-30740
               CIP

CONTENTS

LIST OF MAPS

PREFACE TO THE ENGLISH EDITION

In the Netherlands the question of how the murder of the Jews by the German occupying forces could have proceeded so flawlessly in such a civilized and respectable country is gradually coming to the foreground. How could this happen in a nation where the Jews were a part of the society and seemed so well integrated?

The high percentage of Jews murdered is unique for the "civilized" West and can only be compared with certain regions of Eastern Europe. Answers can be found in the far-reaching competence and obedience of the Dutch civil service and in the early planning by the Germans for deportations, which started in the Netherlands. Answers can also be found in the attitude of the Dutch population, for whom the German victory seemed an accomplished fact, and for whom survival was uppermost.

Jacob Presser reported on the tragedy of the Dutch Jewry between 1940 and 1945 in his book *The Destruction of the Dutch Jews.* Although his is not the only account, it is the one that made the most impression on me at the beginning of my history studies. Presser chose deliberately to write about the *sinaasappeljood*—the fruit peddler, the poor curmudgeon—and he was criticized for it. Many regarded Presser's premise that the lowest classes were the first victims of the Jewish Council as irrelevant.

Whether irrelevant or not—and how this complex of questions is colored by guilt feelings on the part of the Dutch who saw their Jewish neighbors deported, some of whom even worked as the tram drivers or local civil servants who made the deportations possible—this is not an issue that I care to pass judgment on. What interests me more is that these questions are now being debated on a national level in the Netherlands, and that the argumentation has become part of many post-World War II political questions and accusations. What truly interests me is the choice *for* the Jewish proletariat, whose culture was destroyed.

For many years nostalgia was the dominant factor in accounts of this lost world. The poverty and misery of the old Jewish neighborhood were explained and excused. In contrast to this was the heroic fight on the part of the influential Jewish socialism. In this book I tried to look behind and beyond the nostalgia, and at the same time examine the idea that the Jewish proletariat had rejected its cultural past and embraced socialism. Such a cultural transformation would be infinitely too complex to occur in only a couple of years, and it could not take place simply as a conscious political act. In this sense, this book deals with the power of tradition, which is part of our unconscious.

I have been asked whether this book is an expression of my own reevaluation of that tradition, an account of my search for my own Jewish roots (not in a religious but in a cultural sense). Naturally it does express my sense of belonging, even though my family did not belong to the Jewish proletariat of Amsterdam. Except for my father (who was a socialist), the themes in this book have little to do with my family's history. Rather, it was a personal quest for a Jewry that should not be completely overshadowed by the Shoah.

I have also been criticized for focusing too much on the demise of the culture of the Jewish poor and too little on the fact that the rich were also deported and murdered. For an international audience it is of utmost importance to stress that *the genocide spared no one*, even though there are patterns of class, age, and geography to be found among the victims.

My interest was in the special atmosphere and culture that have vanished forever; so I chose to search among the poor. The reactions of the Jewish proletariat to the transformations in their cultural world intrigued me. That was more important to me than delineating their class and placing them in the sophisticated and subtle web of social hierarchy and mobility. Whether the "rosy dawn" that lived in the fantasies of many would have ever become a reality we will never know. The social changes that were in play during the decades I wrote about were broken off by the war.

The present volume was originally published in Dutch in 1987. Because of the length of time between the writing of this book and the publication of this translation, a number of the more theoretical observations have become dated. Oral history and the biographical approach to history have undergone such tempestuous developments that now I would write this book differently. But that does not necessarily mean it would be a better book!

In between the publication of this English translation and the original Dutch version, a more literary and typographically elegant edition was published in German by Suhrkamp. In the German edition, much of the scholarship was left out in order to make it a lovely reader for a more general audience on Jewish Amsterdam.

The theory of memory is retained in this American edition only where it is essential for understanding the rest of the text. The historiographic excursion in which I placed this work in the context of academic debate has also been left out. With regard to the theoretical aspects of memory and oral history, my involvement in editing the *International Yearbook of Oral History and Life Stories* (published annually by Oxford University Press) has kept me abreast of the debates on the innovative manner in which oral history can be written.

Since the original publication of this work in Dutch, another work from my hand has appeared—*Het water en de herinnering* [Water and Memory]. It deals with the 1953 flood in Zeeland, and examines trauma and memory from a somewhat different perspective. But all the above has not broken my deep bond with this book.

This project is the result of many years' work, during which I received much support. In the Dutch edition I listed many by name, and I wish to thank them again here for their help. But I especially want to renew my gratitude and thanks to those I interviewed. When this book appeared in the Netherlands, they told me that they felt it was "their" book; as I write this, I realize how many of them have died since then. When I interviewed them, I knew that time was pressing, but I did not realize how much. I was not fully aware that it was the penultimate moment before the last traces of an old culture would vanish. The words and thoughts of those I interviewed deserve a broad audience, and it is their courage that gave me the strength to endure the laborious process of this translation.

I have Kay Richardson of R & R Associates, who translated the notes and verified, edited, and typeset the translation by Frank Heny, to thank for the fact that there is an English translation. She gave my text the attention and care that it needed. In the Netherlands my book had been praised not only because of its content, but because of its "voice," and this seemed untranslatable into English. As best I can judge, we have succeeded, and this is primarily because of Kay's patience; Kay has become a friend from afar. Before this I had wonderful support from Lee Mitzman, who helped me explain why the same words in different cultures have different emotional values.

This book was written during the time that I taught at the Faculty of Political and Social Sciences at Amsterdam. Since then I work at the Belle van Zuylen Institute (Amsterdam Postgraduate Center for Comparative and Multicultural Gender Studies), which kindly allowed me time for the work necessary for this edition. The translation was subsidized in part by the City of Amsterdam, the Anjerfonds, the Faculty of Political, Social and Cultural Sciences of the University of Amsterdam, the Research Center for Women's Studies, and the Belle van Zuylen Institute.

Special thanks go to my former professor, Arthur Mitzman. I can only dedicate this book to the interviewees—Suze, Sal, Loe, Mirjam, Mordechai, and Annie, to mention only a few—who have become so precious to me. My partner of many years, Siep Stuurman, always knew how to brighten my life even when translations went awry; he often reminds me that life is sometimes more important than memory.

The city, however, does not tell its past, but contains it like the lines of a hand, written in the corners of the streets, the gratings of the windows, the banisters of the steps, the antennae of the lightning rods, the poles of the flags, every segment marked in turn with scratches, indentations, scrolls.
(Cities and Memory 3)

This city which cannot be expunged from the mind is like an armature, a honeycomb in whose cells each of us can place the things he wants to remember: names of famous men, virtues, numbers, vegetable and mineral classifications, dates of battles, constellations, parts of speech. Between each idea and each point of the itinerary an affinity or a contrast can be established, serving as an immediate aid to memory.
(Cities and Memory 4)

Italo Calvino, *Invisible Cities*

INTRODUCTION

THE STORY OF MAURITS

I will call him Maurits. This introduction is about him, yet his story is not merely the introduction to this book, but in a sense the cause of it as well. We met just after I first had the idea of writing a book about the Jewish proletariat of Amsterdam. The subject had attracted me as a research topic from the very beginning of my studies in history, and it seemed inevitable. Actually, I had had the desire to know more about it even earlier. I believe it was related to my mother's stories of the kindergarten where she had worked in the old Jewish neighborhood. Through my acquaintance with the topic, I was well aware how great a role World War II played in the memories of the Jewish survivors, and how those memories overshadowed all else.

Maurits worked at an open-air market stall two days a week. I noticed him because of his unkempt appearance, the language he used, and his way of looking at things. I stood watching him too long to escape notice, and we began a lengthy conversation sitting on orange crates, a conversation that was continued a couple of days later. Over the next few months, we saw each other from time to time, and I tried to persuade him to write his autobiography with my help. Sometimes we met by chance, more often because I went looking for him. Sometimes he yelled at me, but usually he was glad to see me and welcomed me.

Though Maurits clearly wanted to help, he could not tell me what I wanted to know. But he did teach me to listen to endless contradictions. His monologues often lasted hours. There were also long silences. Among the orange crates, in the cafés round Waterloo Square (the flea market that used to be the center of Jewish life and where the police had long since stopped coming), and in his living quarters. Our lives became linked by the silences. Beyond, life continued as before. We remained in contact, fixed in the relationship of listener and storyteller. I was never allowed to record the conversations. Because of that, the reader will have to accept my word; I can prove nothing.

This beginning to a historical treatise may seem odd, although an anthropologist, psychologist, or psychoanalyst would probably find it less strange. An anthropologist is regarded as fully justified in commenting on a society or person (s)he investigates without turning on the tape recorder. The psychological and psychoanalytical literature certainly contains a number of historically oriented accounts of World War II (which is what the tale of Maurits is

1

about) that do not adhere to generally accepted norms regarding research methods.

One of the best accounts dealing with postwar Jews is Claudine Vegh's unorthodox book in which she describes the grief of children whose parents were deported during the war (*Je n'ai lui ai pas dit au revoir*, I Never Said Goodbye to Him). Her book is not a painstaking report of psychoanalytical sessions, nor does it generalize about the various ways people coped. Rather, it is a description of how the *involved listener* came to hear what, in fact, cannot be told and yet eventually was told—as an act of solidarity, as a concession, sometimes just because, for once, the people gave in to the need to speak freely to someone who would not judge (let alone condemn) and to those who tried only to understand. Through her involvement, Vegh succeeded in producing a new kind of knowledge, which her scientific training allowed her to turn into a breathtaking book. In it she added a new dimension to what the psychoanalysts Alexander and Margaretha Mitscherlich referred to in the title of their book, *Die Unfähigkeit zu trauern* [The Inability to Mourn]. I would call her book a form of oral history.

In his postscript to the American translation of Vegh's book, Bruno Bettelheim emphasized the importance of that mourning. In order to begin the process of mourning, Bettelheim believed that it is important to talk. Ultimately the significance of communicating becomes more important than the dreadful experience itself. In the book referred to above, the Mitscherlichs emphasize the meaning of this mourning for society—the ability to cope with what happened simply by acknowledging that it did happen. In this way, such horrors might be prevented from ever occurring again. They were referring, of course, to Germany, which was wrestling with the past. The inability to cope with the past, which can lead to repression, was also dealt with later by Adorno in his masterly essay *Was bedeutet: Aufarbeitung der Vergangenheit?* [What Does Dealing with the Past Mean?] Although Adorno did not give mourning a central role, he did emphasize the fact that people must be able to look their past in the eye, as it were, and thus must find some way of dealing with their mourning for the past if they are to maintain a healthy society.

It will therefore come as no surprise that one of the principles underlying my book is the recognition of the importance of the mourning process for all those who still need to confront the ghosts of World War II in some way. Above all, I have tried to discover the various forms this process has taken and how it has influenced all later experiences.

Maurits taught me a great deal about the ghosts of the past. He made me see that there was no single picture of the Jewish proletariat, but that I would be given a variety of accounts that made up quite distinct histories, all interwoven with one another. Lanzmann's film *Shoah* taught me that it was not simply a matter of studying people's lives and their stories, but that confronting the past also means studying the traces it has left behind in the world around us.

Maurits was weary, but he wanted to tell me his life story, despite the pain this caused him; our conversations often left him upset. Through his emotions he taught me to maintain my distance from him and not to become caught up in his life. I was kept busy dealing with endless contradictions, for what was said one time was denied the next; it was clearly impossible to wrest a "true" story from him. Yet he was not insane. Indeed, he was one of the sanest people I have ever met. The stories almost seemed to have been told by a number of different people; it was precisely this multiplicity that showed me the kind of book I wanted to write.

This book, in the end, contains more than just people's stories. Those who desire to write oral history must bring order into the world they hear about. The stories must be confirmed, the facts verified, the distortions explained by reference to other material. That is the great difference, in my opinion, between this work and mere journalistic interviews designed solely to gather information. I was forced to undertake such explorations.

Maurits was not the only one whose vision of day and night, light and darkness, life and death set him apart, obscured, as it were, by a threatening shadow hovering between the eyes and the external world. Life and death had gained a new dimension for these people—they had been face to face with mortal decisions engineered on a scale so vast that we who were not there can hardly comprehend it. One of the reasons this book took nine years to write is that so little research has been done into the way our perception of life and death can be distorted by such experiences. Scholarly sources shed little light on how they affect our recollections of the past. So the processing of practically every interview, every "fact," involved a struggle between reality, distortion, and myth.

The bizarre tale of Maurits the vagrant can be summarized as follows. Born early in the 1920s in the Jewish Quarter of Amsterdam. Moved to East Amsterdam—the Transvaal area—during adolescence. He had neither education nor a real job until World War II came along, and during the Depression he often lived by peddling and begging. Yet I was not talking to an uneducated man; Maurits had studied—later, after the war. First he went into hiding; he was discovered and deported to Poland. There he was forced to find a way to survive in a world where he was aware of being a Jew for the first time in his life. Then the contradictions started in earnest. Had he not been a Jew back home—the scavenger of the Jewish Quarter? And if he was not a Jew, yet a week later suddenly became one, to what extent did he do so? Was the anti-Semitism he now had to deal with so new because it had not existed before the war, or because it was so much worse? I had no idea how to write about such matters without generalizing on the basis of individual experiences. So I decided to write this book.

After the war, Maurits wandered around, learned more, and then went to

America to study. He unsuccessfully tried psychoanalysis in order to over-come his feelings of guilt at surviving the Holocaust. In short, Maurits was a model interviewee, for he knew well that "I" did not refer to just one person but to various components of the personality, and that during the process of remembering a game begins between the various phases of one's life.

In my attempt to provide a sketch of prewar proletarian Amsterdam on the basis of interviews, I immersed myself in the memories of many people, including those who are not used to dealing consciously with the past. The problem of memory—the creation of historical data through contact with individuals who believe themselves to have been eyewitnesses and thus able to remember everything—is the theme of the methodological discussion that opens this book. I have tried to let that theme resonate again and again. It recurs whenever I try to provide sketches based on a number of stories. Taken together, these sketches yield a more adequate view than we had before of a world that has ceased to exist.

Following this introduction is a global summary of the historical, eco-nomic, and demographic relationships within which the Amsterdam Jewish proletariat lived. In the chapters following that, the changes in living condi-tions and the conscious attempts that were made to help a cultural and relig-ious minority adapt to what was regarded as "modern" or "progressive" are dealt with in more detail. Then I describe the culture of poverty, the strategies for survival that characterized it, and the apparent impossibility of escaping from it. This impossibility is called into question in chapter 6, where I give an account of the great number of opportunities open to precisely that generation of poor Jews I was studying. In short, I try to provide a picture of the diversity of their experiences: disruption contrasts with attachment, a feeling of "Dutchness" with that of always being a foreigner, a sense of security with an increasing awareness of the threat looming from Germany, assimilation with devotion to tradition and at the same time exclusion from the society into which they attempted to assimilate. All this gives rise to the question: What did it feel like to be a member of the Jewish proletariat? How proletarian—and how Jewish—was it?

In this book, the term "ghetto" is used from time to time for the old Jewish Quarter. This usage can be questioned, since it might seem to suggest that the Jews were forced to live there. Maurits used the term in order to convey a feeling of what it was like. Around 1900 the term was commonly used by contemporaries, and in the postwar literature it was quite normal. There is no better word, though I know it will evoke denial among some readers, since people could freely choose that atmosphere and way of life and thus could look back on it with longing.

Perhaps there are contradictions and rebuttals in my discussion that remain partially unresolved. If so, this is because I did not feel it was my place to resolve them. My task was to describe them and make them visible. In the same way, Italo Calvino in his *Invisible Cities* never found it necessary to provide a true and realistic description of the cities he had in mind. He provided us with a quiet tour through parts of a city and through a world of experiences. The changes in the shadows could be glimpsed through the calm.

Despite the war, it surprised me how Maurits and many others I interviewed were able to build a new existence for themselves, in which they could find pleasure in even the smallest of things. To me, this is a remarkable indication of strength and character.

Maurits, my model, is dead, drowned in wine and grief, singing about the happy life—the vagrant who could look so very much like a respectable gentleman. He will never know how much he influenced this book about his people.

Amsterdam 1986

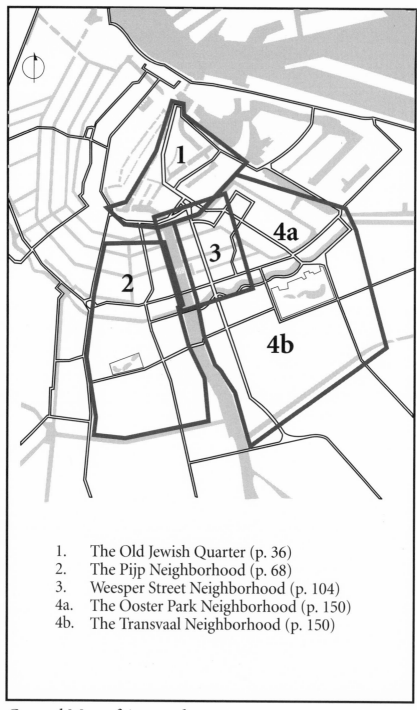

1. The Old Jewish Quarter (p. 36)
2. The Pijp Neighborhood (p. 68)
3. Weesper Street Neighborhood (p. 104)
4a. The Ooster Park Neighborhood (p. 150)
4b. The Transvaal Neighborhood (p. 150)

General Map of Amsterdam

CHAPTER ONE

METHODOLOGICAL CONSIDERATIONS

MARKEN AND ITS SURROUNDINGS

Personally, I knew nothing of the existence of the Nieuwe Grachtje [a street in the old Jewish neighborhood, translated roughly as "New Little Canal"] until a month or so ago when I set out on an expedition with an investigator from that fine association Liefdadigheid naar Vermogen [Charity according to One's Means], which showers so many blessings on the world and would spread yet more if every Amsterdamer would indeed attempt to give charity according to his means. . . .

The investigator was searching for a family whose head, through no fault of his own, had lost his job. This family was said to live on the Nieuwe Grachtje. The Messenger of Charity knew in general terms where that little street had to be, yet when we reached the area and began asking where we could find it, not a single person was able to help.

"Y'want a little canal? What canal? You'd better look someplace else."

We heard that, in many variations, from all sides.

Until my guide, now much in need of guidance himself, stumbled quite by chance through a little cross street and over a bridge. There, around the corner of a little canal with a row of houses—we saw only the backs of houses standing right on the water on the other side—was a small sign-board. When we consulted it, it showed in white letters on blue enamel: Nieuwe Grachtje.

"Well, I'll be darned! Guess it is here! Now if you'd just told me before that y' wanted Marrekeschrachie [colloquially Little Canal on Marken] . . . well!" a man called after us. . . .

We were, then, on Marrekeschrachie. Papa, may he rest in peace, he died there, and Ma—she should live to be a hundred at least—she lives there still. And if Frannie with the help of God gets married, then she, too, will come here to live. But who calls it "Nuve Chrachie"?

Is there any further need for me to say in which part of the city Nieuwe Grachtje can be found?

In the Jewish Quarter of Amsterdam.

The country visitor who, after the obligatory visit to Artis Zoo, goes back again into the city, naturally also sets a visit to the Jewish Quarter high on his agenda. He has heard—and read—so much about it. Especially on Friday afternoons, just as the Sabbath is about to begin. It must be so "picturesque" there! And when he has walked through Jodenbree Street, crossed over the St. Antonie Sluice, and has walked on until he reaches Hoog Street, hears the incomprehensible cries of the fruitsellers, and sees the obvious traces of Semitic origin on people walking by, and the busy bustle and din, then surely he must have seen the Jewish Quarter—hasn't he?

Oh, no!

. . . .

Do not go directly into Jodenbree Street; instead, enter the little square on your right and then the narrow street that runs parallel to it, behind the heavily traveled thoroughfare. That is the Joden Houttuinen [Jewish Timberyards] where one remaining wooden shed recalls how this name came about. Cross the bridge to Valkenburger Street—or as it is called there, Marken—and make your way bravely through Batavier Street and Uilenburg. You will need to be brave if you are to conquer the disgust you feel at the muddy streets and musty hovels, though no one will do you harm or molest you. Now cross Bree Street diagonally—but remember the electric tram and the axle grease of the handcarts—then cross through the complex of streets and alleys around Waterloo Square, which is called Vlooienburg [Bastion of Fleas].[1] The saying *nomen est omen* also applies to the places where people live!

And, assuming that you have feasted your eyes, your ears, and your nose along the way, you have now indeed seen the Jewish Quarter of Amsterdam! Now you know that you are wandering through a place of misery and deprivation and of their faithful companion, uncleanliness. Yet still you do not realize that you are passing through a place of toil and slaving, for that toiling and slaving is actually accomplished for the most part outside the neighborhood itself.

Nor do you yet know anything about the souls of those pariahs. You have read about them in modern books. . . . But, leaving aside their literary worth, to what extent are the conditions sketched in those modern novels manipulated in advance to support the author's own political, economic, and philosophical insights? . . .

As I passed by, I once asked who lived in one of those basements. One room, an animal pen really, sheltered father, mother, grandmother, and seven children—with their own sons and daughters on the way.

There they ate and drank (if there was anything to eat and drink) and slept. . . . There the mother brought her children into the world and did the laundry in the tub; there the father kept his stock in trade, and there was a pail, half covered by a narrow plank, which served as a toilet.[2]

Thus starts the book *Joodjes-leven* [Jewish Life] by the writer van den Eewal. The language he portrayed had the effect of distancing the ghetto people from the rest of the city, as did the confusion over place names that was introduced in the opening paragraphs. The language and the confusion give evidence of a lost culture from the past that contrasts with the "official" descriptions of it. Indeed, explanation and interpretation of such experiences play a central role in the debates regarding contemporary social history. Later in this introduction I will discuss a number of methodological problems related to these questions. For the most part, they are problems that arise when oral description and memory are used as sources for the history of interwoven experiences.

Van den Eewal's account forms a picture of toil, hopeless misery, hunger, and a hand-to-mouth existence. It was probably written around 1902. At that time, the Jewish proletariat of Amsterdam still lived as a poverty-stricken mass within the confines of a small number of streets. Driven together into warehouses, wallowing in dirt and poverty, they differed from other paupers by their speech and mannerisms. During the decades covered by this book (1900 to 1940) these bearers of a distinct culture left for other parts of the city, newer and better districts. This relocation became the cause of politicians, municipal officials, philanthropists, doctors, and social workers who, drawn to the concept of civilizing the mass of paupers and improving their living conditions, all added their cent's worth of input to the debate over the terms and conditions under which it was to occur.

There were many questions. Did being civilized mean living just like everyone else—or was that simply not possible in the case of the Jewish working class? Were they just dirtier, more aggressive, more powerless, and ruder than other workers who had moved from the slums to better housing? Or were they more antisocial? And why were they unwilling to adjust to their new environment? Was that because of their religion? Yet so many of them seemed to have abandoned that religion. Few still attended the local synagogues, and (at least superficially) the socialist lifestyle seemed to represent a break with religious tradition. Moreover, the number of marriages to non-Jews was increasing rapidly, so there was nothing to prevent the total integration of the Jewish working class into the general population of Amsterdam. They had lived there as long as could be remembered and had always been welcome. Or so many thought, and only a few doubted.

Nevertheless, integration did not move ahead quickly, for in the modern housing to which they moved new ghettos kept developing where Jews clung to one another, shutting others out and, in turn, being shut out. In this book, by carefully following the history of four decades, I have tried to shed some light on these conflicting tendencies.

The total integration of Jews into Dutch society and their complete emancipation would have resulted in the loss of much that distinguished the Jewish community, those special characteristics that had held it together for centuries. The distinctive codes and customs had formed a shield against disintegration so that social networks and mutual support could be maintained. Through their strict customs, the Jews were protected against what people in that era considered to be decadence and dissipation, and epidemics, which only rarely raged in the overpopulated Jewish neighborhood. In order to understand these decades of change properly, I have returned to the earlier periods from time to time, just enough to shed light on the later developments.

The attempt to integrate the Jews gradually into Dutch society as a whole grew out of their emancipation, which was officially enacted in 1796, during the period of Napoleonic rule.[3] Jewish intellectuals had been pointing out for half a century before the emancipation how desirable it was to be assimilated into the surrounding non-Jewish population. Before that could occur, it was necessary to obtain legal emancipation. In their eagerness to live just like the others, those in favor of emancipation found themselves in conflict with those who wished to preserve the old community with its unique values, norms, and forms of government. Support for that viewpoint came not only from the Jewish administrators, the religious authorities, and a handful of old-fashioned believers; it was the viewpoint of the majority. The progressives were no more than an elite, but their influence grew steadily throughout the course of the nineteenth century.

In my opinion, the significance of Jewish integration into Western society was and is one of the main concerns of thinking and writing about Jewish history in Western Europe. It is a debate that is both conscious and unconscious, not only in written documents but also in the attitudes adopted toward customs, codes, lifestyles, and interactions with others. In any attempt to assess the situation, it is all too easy to point to the newer and better dwellings of the Jewish working class as indicators of progress and modernization—both of which were viewed as positive developments. Yet modern dwellings can hide great poverty, and "progress" can sometimes be a compulsion and a denial of history. It is also incorrect to write only of disorientation and loss of the community's religious cohesion—there are two sides to the question.

It was not only the Jewish working-class minority culture that disappeared in the twentieth century; many minorities were kept culturally subordinate through the cultural norms regarding how people were expected to speak, to live, and to think. History also teaches us that certain groups claim to be furthering the interests of minorities without considering carefully enough the cultural differences that exist between them and that minority. One example of this certainly was social democracy in Amsterdam, which desired to undertake anything that would benefit the Jewish poor and the working class. Relying on these good intentions, the social democrats interpreted the sociocultural distance between themselves and the Jews as that between the modern and the obsolete. And, of course, the modern was always considered better and integration was an unconditional prerequisite to a better life.

The history of the attempt to "civilize" the Jewish masses, to educate them and guide them toward the "rosy dawn" is simultaneously the history of the struggle to determine the cultural ideas of Dutch social democracy. How much room should there be in a modern, socialist society for people who behave differently, for people who—however much they might like to adapt to the rest of society—are unable to do so? Many members of the Jewish proletariat believed that it was possible to live according to a new socialist morality. They thought of the prewar period as the beginning of the "rosy dawn" of their liberation—only the day itself never dawned.

In this study I have assumed that the memories of those times cannot avoid distortion.[4] Memories, after all, are how one thinks *now* about what happened in the *past*. More important than the distortion introduced by today's perspective, from our point of view, are the distortions caused by what happened between 1940 and 1945. The experiences of World War II make it all too easy to idealize the era before.

AN INTRODUCTION TO THE USE OF MEMORIES

We all possess our own individual memories, but there are some things that we remember *jointly*. History and memories of times past are not objective but are colored by the collective memory, by "how people think things used to be." Any attempt to reconstruct the life of the prewar Amsterdam Jewish proletariat must include an analysis of the factors that determine individual and collective distortions. The images that remain in memory through the repeated telling of stories to one another are important in this respect. Sometimes such images become common property, so that it seems as if the memories really correspond with reality. This book, too, turned into a struggle between the alternatives that are offered to the historian in the course of his/her attempt to describe a lost society and culture.[5] As a result it proved to be impossible to do full justice to every aspect of the situation.

Memories can develop into a collective myth. For this to happen, it is necessary for the individual memories to be shared by others, and for a group of people to have some reason to maintain the myth. It is almost unnecessary to point out that a group like the Amsterdam Jewish proletariat, which was massacred on so vast a scale, would be surrounded by collective myths. Such myths are simply part of the nostalgia for the good old days that will never return. But that is not the only factor. It seems equally important to me that nothing but other memories are left to correct the images now rising to the surface.[6] Everyone can see perfectly well how the accounts all came together to form one nostalgic, sentimental picture that is laid over history like a screen. On rare occasions, however, one can catch a glimpse of something else behind it, but no one who has tried to remember the past can escape from the vacuum of the past. Social forms, survival strategies, norms and patterns of values—all those things that would be needed to correct the memories—no longer exist.[7]

Anyone who attempts to reconstruct the past must recognize that one's view of history is determined by one's view of the present—and vice versa.

And the past never permeates directly through to the present. Political, ideological, and demographic events are inexorably bound to the point in time
when they occurred. Thus, for example, Waterloo Square and its surroundings, e.g. the huge flea market and the Moses and Aaron Church, cannot be
viewed in the same way today as they were in 1930—even by those who are
not primarily interested in the Jewish proletariat.[8] The need for such a perspective is caused not only by demolition and new construction; history is like
a fabric laid over the past, as if bygone times were buried in archaeological
layers.

Our perceptions are different from those that occurred in the past; the lens
through which we filter them is different. Moreover, the people who could tell
of the past have themselves become older and more experienced. Yet there is
a relatively direct connection between our perception of buildings today and
the ways people perceived those buildings in the past, or, for example, between the progressive Christian service held in the Moses and Aaron Church
near Waterloo Square today and the service held in that church during the
1930s. That connection is far more tangible than any between us and the
Jewish proletariat that no longer exists. There are physical links with the past
in the first two cases, but lifestyles and mindsets leave no direct material
traces.

Perhaps the language of the Jewish proletariat with its mordant humor is
the most striking and recognizable remnant from earlier times. Even when
one of the survivors has worked his or her way up to the "better" nonprole-
tarian levels of society, there will be times during a private conversation when
the speech betrays the past. By speech I mean syntax as well as word choice,
but above all I am referring to their pronunciation of Dutch, so that occasionally a singsong tone suddenly takes over in a sibilant.[9] Still, it remains a
matter of looking and reconstructing, regardless of whether we visit the
neighborhoods where they once lived or visit one of the survivors. Although
the interiors of their houses often retain traces of their background, time has
erased the most significant aspects of Jewish life and culture.

More members of the Amsterdam Jewish community (including its proletariat) were murdered than of any other Jewish community in Europe during
World War II. The most integrated proletarian group in any European country
was consciously or unconsciously sacrificed first by those who themselves
would later be murdered.[10] During the Occupation the Germans (as was their
custom) set up a Jewish Council (*Joodse Raad*, in German *Judenrat*), whose
power lay in the hands of upper-class Jews who tended to protect those from
their own social class and those who were useful because of their physical
strength (i.e., young men). Obeying the orders of the Jewish Council, the
Jewish poor and the workers did not put up a fight. Because they were offered
work, and because there was no choice, they obeyed. They seldom went into
hiding, either because they did not have the money to do so, or because they

did not know how to proceed. If they had the chance to hide, they often did not because others would have had to be deported in their place, or because they wanted to remain with their family and face the difficult times together.

The great storyteller André Schwartzbart described how the central character in his novel *Le dernier des Justes* [The Last Just Man] gave himself up at a concentration camp outside Paris because he could not bear to be excluded from the fate that overtook his family and loved ones. Only very rarely was there any fighting when the Weerafdeling (WA, a branch of the Nationaal–Socialistische Beweging or NSB—the Dutch counterpart of the National Socialist Party), disturbed the old Jewish neighborhood. When the Jewish Council ordered this to cease on the grounds that fighting would only make things worse, the Jewish proletariat offered almost no resistance at all. Of course, it was not in a position to put up much of a fight anyway.[11] Although the resistance movement contained a relatively large proportion of Jews, their actual numbers were not very high.

The trains to Eastern Europe took with them a way of life. The people who left had lived from hand to mouth. The war and the lonely return to a destroyed culture overshadowed their former misery, so that the time preceding the Holocaust became, in their own private histories, happy and joyful. Perhaps that is why a sense of gaiety dominates the nostalgic descriptions underlying the current Dutch view of the history of that time.

When I began this research, I assumed that much of the material concerning the Jewish proletariat had probably been destroyed and that I would therefore have to deal with a scarcity of sources and with fragments of material. This was not the case. In addition to the private archives that I was able to consult, the Municipal Archives of Amsterdam contained enough material from which I was able to obtain information (admittedly often indirect) about the Jewish proletariat. To the extent that I used such material for this book, I had to deal with overabundance more often than with shortage.

For instance, there were records of those who applied for municipal welfare. In them, one can find personal data on thousands of families. Not only personal data—various municipal officials added commentaries of their own to official reports resulting from visits to the homes. The people who requested support in this way often had dealings with other municipal authorities. Reports from those authorities concerning the family or other social unit were also added to the file. In this way it is easy to trace thousands of Jewish proletarian families. I made considerable use of such descriptions.

However, I was not even limited to sources of this kind. Many newspapers, pamphlets, and books have been preserved, containing information that sharpens the picture or deals with some particular experience, causing the kaleidoscope to change even more. In 1920 about 70,000 people were living in a fairly homogeneous Jewish society that differed substantially from the rest of the city in belief, lifestyle, and traditions. They had been living like this for centuries, and although their world has disappeared there is nevertheless a great deal to find.

These people had been the target of official strategies and had been studied and investigated. They had been talked about and written about. Sometimes the results yield a penetrating picture of poverty, filth, and the impossibility of living under certain conditions. But can we learn much about the Jewish proletariat from such sources? Or do we simply discover more about what others thought of it? To what degree is one tale of poverty simply a variation of others, and is there any sense in recording yet another? I have chosen to write about memories of experiences, about the interaction between culture and the material circumstances within which it existed. How did these people experience their lives, how did they struggle with the demands of everyday life, and does the picture that emerges correspond with the literary descriptions?

Scholarly research cannot take issue with literature—a writer of fiction has the freedom to place the emphasis where (s)he will. There are passages in the works of the well-known Dutch Jewish author Meyer Sluyser that capture the atmosphere of the time so well precisely because of their nostalgia, exquisite sensitivity, and exuberance.[12] His tales of street life, with its handcarts full of rags, rubbish, and oranges, celebrating the good times before the great slaughter, and full of longing for those times, are rich in character precisely because they are not analytical. Through him we hear the sounds of the street as he believes he heard them as a child, we experience the friendliness of people toward one another, and we listen to the gentle sounds of family gatherings. Thus we make contact all the more vividly with what has vanished and will never return.

Yet it is precisely this intense nostalgia that makes the picture untrustworthy. To what extent do such stories truly depict what they purport to describe, and to what extent do they instead express the bitterness and harshness of life after World War II? Do they not in fact serve principally as a way to show sorrow and lighten the grief felt for those times that now, in retrospect, seem so good? This is true not only of Sluyser.[13] The nostalgia is powerful and is often a way of putting into words feelings that can find no other expression.

The classic example of such a nostalgic storyteller is Kafka in his testimony about the disruption of Jewish culture at the turn of the century. This can be found in his conversations with Janouch, which were published posthumously. Regardless of whether Kafka himself actually said it, the following passage scarcely needs anything added, for in one stroke of the pen it manages to convey his feelings about the assimilation of the Jewish culture in Prague and the modernization of the old Jewish Quarter of that city. Despite the assimilation, he did not believe that the old Jewish culture could disappear:

Look at that synagogue. All the surrounding buildings are taller. Among the modern houses that surround it, the synagogue is nothing but an old-fashioned enclave, a foreign body. Thus it is with everything Jewish. That is the cause of the hostile tensions, which time and again are repressed by aggressive actions. . . . The language and the people must disappear. But you cannot root out by violence that which has itself come forth from the dust of the earth. The original seed of all beings and things remains. The substance itself is eternal.[14]

However, it is the task of the historian to do more than create a sentimental and charming picture in which people can recognize themselves. (S)he must take on the task of determining why people cling to nostalgia while everything that does not correspond to it is hidden away, found unimportant, or simply never mentioned. Moreover, it is necessary to illuminate the structure that underlies the more superficial accounts and to investigate what is not immediately obvious. Eyewitnesses seldom do this, as such an investigation calls for a theory about how events are related to structures. The perceptions of witnesses are as much affected by their personal histories as by the way in which an event is written or talked about. When something lies right before us, evident and real, it is extremely difficult to distance ourselves from it. But this is essential if we are to abstract it and place it in a more general context. Some people can do this on occasion, but usually it is impossible—certainly when the event lies in the distant past and a semiofficial version of that past has developed. If one wants to gain that necessary distance, one must leave the charming picture for what it is and begin to ask questions.[15]

THE USE OF INTERVIEWS AS A SOURCE

Since it was my intention to describe the experience of the Jewish working class, an obvious source was memories of that experience. The method I followed posed some problems. First, it was hard to find people who had lived through and remembered the time. Second, the value of an oral source has to be assessed differently from that of a written source. In this section I deal briefly with these problems.

For the purpose of the study, I interviewed a large number of people in the Netherlands, the United States, and Israel. I talked with more than 90 people. Sometimes the interviews lasted a couple of hours; in other cases there were numerous visits and conversations. Quite a few people believed they came from the Jewish proletariat but closer examination showed that this was not true, no matter how broadly one interprets "proletariat."

In the next chapter I defend my expansion of the term "proletariat" to include not only industrial workers in the strict sense but also all others who were part of a proletarian culture. In other words, those who were unemployed and started small businesses were also included, as was the woman who had a little store in Weesper Street. Despite this broad definition, a number of people I interviewed did not really fit. For example, there was the child of a small businessman who never experienced true poverty. His sisters did not need to learn a trade, and they had some savings in the bank. They did attend school with the proletariat, sharing in brotherly and sisterly fashion their headlice and scabies. And they lived among them and felt themselves bound to them, and they knew them well from contacts with the socialist movement. But they did not belong to the proletariat.

Yet I interviewed them because so few from the true proletariat remained. Moreover, these people often felt themselves to be so closely related to the Jewish proletariat that they were not only an important source of information but also regarded themselves as Jewish proletarians. During interviews they explicitly identified themselves as such.

The "true" Jewish proletariat had an even lower survival rate than other Jews. It was interesting that a number of members of the real proletariat did not wish to be named in this book and refused to let me tape our interviews. These were mainly older people living in nineteenth-century districts of Amsterdam who have "gone into hiding" since the war, living as non-Jews and disguising their Jewishness from their neighbors. Their greatest fear is that their origins might become known and that the threat to minorities which exists in those neighborhoods would also become a threat to them. I respected these feelings in preparing this book; I am not a therapist attempting to change people's attitudes toward life. Before the war, these people often had the greatest confidence in their neighbors' trustworthiness and hoped that the new socialist utopia would make categorizing people into Jews and non-Jews irrelevant. Their confidence was both abused and justified.[16]

The period just after World War II was often more relevant to the present than were the war years themselves. By then, they had lived in a society in which the propaganda machine of anti-Semitism had droned on for five years.[17] Joy over the liberation could not be fully shared by the survivors, because far too many of those who were close to them had disappeared. A large portion of the conversations dealt with the loneliness they felt after the war and the sporadic attempts they made to live on, to deal with what could not be dealt with, and to build a new life. The witnesses of those times showed that the return could be almost as traumatic as the wartime experiences.

One woman, who agreed to my recording her account, said this: "I arrived back with a cotton dress and a pair of soldiers' boots. They never asked me, 'Do you have a dress?' or 'Do you have somewhere to live?' Almost nothing! . . . Nothing, nothing, nothing! Although I came back late. I did not get to Amsterdam until October because I had been terribly sick. [The war had ended in May.] I was in the hospital in Hamburg. So everything was already gone when I got back to Holland. You couldn't get a place because everything was occupied.

Yes, dirty apartments where the NSB [the Dutch branch of the National Socialist Party] had been. But they did very, very little for us. . . .

"They brought me home in an army truck, one with those tiny little windows. First you had to go to the police station here. There was a big board with 'Welcome to your country!' . . . And you had to sit on a wooden bench, which was almost impossible because you were so thin, and it was ten o'clock when we arrived. And they said, 'You must be hungry.' I said 'Indeed, I am.' They brought me a plate of cold gruel. And I said, 'Is this welcome to your country? It's like I'm still in the camp.' They didn't do a thing." [18]

Bitterness over their reception after the war is evident in contemporary autobiographical comments, such as notes in the journal of the Jewish writer Sam Goudsmit. On 24 June 1945 he expressed his alienation from the inhabitants of a country that allowed 80 percent of its Jews to disappear. Everywhere he went, he saw collaborators or people who had turned a blind eye.

> And even now these people cannot hope for redress against the criminal gang that walks their streets, but make a hue and cry over the shameful silence of the graves dug to take their minds off the pillaging and subjugation they have suffered.
> Strange world! . . .
> Patience, patience my heart! Although the loved ones will never return, the Day of Judgment will come.

On 16 July 1945:

> No matter how much I try to adapt my dress, I am too conspicuous. In addition to friendly glances and greetings from strangers, there are also bitter stares, always with unchanged, self-assured, hostile attitudes. This evening my walk was totally poisoned, and it was but a child that did it, a boy of no more than thirteen or fourteen; but he was quick-witted.
> I was walking along with somber thoughts of my dearest one who will never return, when from the side of the road I heard: "That's *famoos*" [a play on words, based on a mispronunciation of the French word *fameux*, meaning "something special" and *van Moos* a common Jewish boys' name]. He was with four friends who merely stared while I was within earshot. The boy could not have thought up this little play on words himself, it must have been something his friends had come across. But the incident drained me emotionally till long after I was back home in my room. How can this disgrace to the Dutch people still be possible, and for no other reason than that this ghastly, stupid, poisoned little piece of garbage feels safe.
> Woe to this people who put up with such treacherous leaders. Perhaps I expect too much. . . .[19]

It was not just the anti-Semites who were disturbed by the fact that the Jews were demanding their old positions and belongings back. Even in "trusted" circles things were said that now seem unbelievable. The story of the return from the camps is now gradually becoming known. Jews who had had everything taken away from them were asking for the restitution of their houses and possessions, yet often failed to get them back.[20] They were penalized by the insurance companies for falling behind with their insurance premiums, and they were prevented from remarrying as long as there was no absolute proof of death of the former spouses. The chaos on the Red Cross lists, the endless visits to stations to meet arriving trains (which some of the people I spoke to made till well into the 1950s, meeting every train that came from Eastern Europe), the difficulty of getting back what they had in their bank accounts (they had sometimes saved a little money before the war)—these experiences seem to have been at least as traumatic as the war itself.

Practically every interview was imbued with the feeling of isolation; it was experienced as the treachery of people whom they had previously naively believed to be friends and fellow socialist party members. Their world view had been profoundly disturbed, and not by the Nazis alone; things never looked quite right again. Even after I had listened to such talk for hours, there was always a lingering fear of talking so openly about those kinds of problems. I might be trustworthy, but the neighbors and Dutch society were not. The true story was seldom told explicitly, and while they were telling it, I was not permitted to make any recording. Yet those stories have their own role to play—they add nuances to the experiences and give us some idea of the pain felt.

Thus it was possible to find the old Jewish proletariat, dispersed as it was over countless networks, united in tiny groups and social organizations. Many had climbed the social ladder, often with each other's help, and had been supported from the end of the 1950s by pensions and other "gifts," such as the *Wiedergutmachung* [restitution payments], which purported to compensate for the suffering in guilders. The more people I interviewed, the more I found to interview. I prepared 50 recorded interviews for this book. The picture may be slightly distorted by the fact that quite a few contacts were made through the help of one Jewish organization or another. This means that the people in question had requested some kind of Jewish care for the elderly or some social service. The reader must realize that good and intensive contacts could not have been made without such help, and must weigh whatever distortion exists against this fact.

Memory as a Source for Writing History

Using the recollections of individual contemporaries as a source of history is not new. They have been used throughout the centuries and have at most fallen somewhat into disuse. In place of memory, emphasis was laid on the use of "real" sources that, analogous to what is customary in the natural sciences, had to be verifiable and hence written. Scholars also distinguish the use of written sources from work with historical events to generate theories that are often dismissed as social studies research.

Oral history—the use of interviews as a historical source—is not limited to the writing of history. As the field that deals with the distortion of memories, oral history need not defend itself against the observation that memories are distorted. It is now assumed that even "objective" written sources are no more than documents set in time, and both kinds of sources demand critical evaluation, both internal and external. By considering the subjectivity of each person engaged in research as the researcher approaches the subject, and by making the subjectivity of each source explicit, the practice of oral history overtly recognizes those aspects of the data that are culture- and time-dependent. This approach to historical research also shows how the writing of history can silence the individual voices. In this sense, the use of oral sources forms part of a tradition of sociohistorical research in which the reactions of individual people to social processes are analyzed.[21]

Another important source of inspiration is the life-history approach in sociology. Culture and historical phenomena can be analyzed not only on the basis of archives—they demand a broader perspective, a crossing of the boundaries set by the institutionalization of scholarship and created in the various faculties and disciplines.

Because it has been limited to the use of written sources, the writing of modern social history often becomes ineffective when faced with difficult and complex entities, such as the changes that occur in a popular culture. Oral history is one of the ways in which it is possible to study such complicated processes, and many great historians have paid careful attention to what their elders said. The French historian Michelet wrote on this subject:

> If ever old age has been respectable, it is when the old have seen and done great things. The old people of today witnessed the revolution and lived through it. They fought the battles of the empire, supported the restoration, and founded representative government. They are living books . . . annals that do not always recognize their own existence but that have thousands of answers. They can teach any who think of consulting them.[22]

In Jewish tradition, oral transmission based on remembering what had been learned has always been important. Indeed, religious laws were in part transmitted orally. Oral transmission is the basis of a culture in which much is narrated and told. People remember their genealogies for generations; they know where they came from and when. It is unthinkable not to use such a tradition as a source in the writing of history when there is such a void without it.

REMEMBERING AND MEMORY

This research deals with various ways in which acts of remembering may be subjective. The following account of the factors affecting memory is influenced by the work of the French sociologists Bertaux and Bertaux–Wiame.[23]

1. Remembering is influenced by the way in which one lives.

All the people I interviewed who had emigrated to Israel remembered their experiences in a totally different way from those who had continued to live in the place where they had experienced so much pain. In Israel they had dealt with the war in a different and often better way; at any rate they were less fixated on it. Their early years and the time before the war were experienced less intensely as a happy time. Geographical distance had helped them to see the past in relative terms.

2. People remember what they are conscious of, but data can be
 processed in the unconscious before being selected for recall.

Certain items in memory seem to have disappeared, and those things seldom recalled may be difficult to access. This repression can be encouraged or prevented by the collective memory.[24] Often people have not thought about the prewar period for years and have clung to an almost mythical picture. In this way, the official nostalgia and the formulas that go with it have replaced individual memories. What remains is a vague notion of better times surrounded by vague ambivalence about security and anxiety.

A trivial occurrence can bring that vague, veiled past back to mind. An elderly lady told me of walks with her grandmother along the canals on the way to where her aunt lived in the Jewish Quarter. "Do you know what the birds say?" asked her grandmother. "They call out 'save, save.'" The grandmother had been well off, as many diamond workers had been for a short time in the *Kaapse Tijd* or Cape Period (1872–1876), when the diamond trade flourished due to imports from South Africa. But that changed with the decline of the diamond. Just as with other diamond families, the money had all been spent. Only poverty remained. "Save" referred to the wealth that was gone and to the poverty of the present.

That word "save" brought us to the visits they made during their walks. And slowly countless members of the Jewish family loomed out of the mists of the past, people who had lived in the slums of the old Jewish ghetto. Suddenly she remembered the stench of the *bedstee* or bed niche[25] in the basement, but she could not put it into words. It was the poverty there that struck her most forcibly, and the fact that it was far worse than at her home in a diamond worker's family in the Pijp, a neighborhood outside the old Jewish area for people who had raised their standard of living. Those were the things that remained sharply etched in her memory.[26]

3. Remembering is deliberate, not instinctive.

To remember something is to include the present, for the course of one's life modifies the memory. In order to remember something, there must be some point in doing so. Some kind of link must be forged between (the emptiness of) the present and the past, and the usefulness of remembering has to be explained time and again.

It turned out to be quite easy to convince Dutch Jews of the usefulness of this undertaking. Everyone was sympathetic to the idea that certain things ought not to be forgotten: "The fascists were able to take everything from us, and posterity has to be told about the atrocities." Yet at the same time, anxiety over the rise of fascism made the richness of experience less accessible. We have already seen how it was impossible to record some of the interviews, either on tape or on paper. One might ask why in such cases it was nevertheless possible to talk. The answer is simple. Every anxiety that is strengthened offers a new perspective on the memory itself, and from the conversations with these people it is clear that they were more conscious of the prewar non-German anti-Semitism than those who allowed themselves to be recorded. (Perhaps they were somewhat *too* conscious of it.) Moreover, much could be learned from an interview that was not recorded, even when the information that emerged could not be checked and does not meet the demands of scholarly research.

4. The media and historical writings affect memories.

As was already pointed out, nostalgia played a considerable role in many interviews. People spoke of miserable poverty, but in the context of a loving account full of symbols. That put the investigator on a false trail, for the stories were often variations on a theme that could easily have been read somewhere. One misleading notion in nostalgic accounts is the idea that before the war it was always possible to recognize a Jew by sight. That was certainly not the case for the Jewish proletariat of Amsterdam.

5. Memories are determined in part by collective memory and by society.

Given the myth that all the Dutch were "good" during the war, it is almost unthinkable to talk about the anti-Semitism of the 1930s. In part, this is caused by guilt feelings about those who were deported.

During the interviews, one of the most persistent myths of social democracy was that being left-wing meant being against anti-Semitism. The February Strike—a massive opposition to deportations of the Amsterdam working class on 25 February 1941—is cited as an example. This strike went down in history and in popular memory as being of almost mythical proportions. Although it was indeed a unique moment of left-wing solidarity, it does not mean that the left before the war was free of anti-Semitism. Confrontations with the ex-members of the Dutch communist party became harsh on occasion when I pointed to Stalin's persecution of the Jews, even during the war. This sometimes led to tension and irritability. Moreover, in writing the history of communist Jews, no one can avoid making value judgments in regard to support for the Jewish colonization project in Siberia, Biro Bidzahn. People would rather not be reminded of that.[27]

6. Remembering is a physical process.

Sometimes, among the lines on cheerful faces, one can see traces of the sorrow that has been experienced. The degree to which a person is able to put up a fight in the face of difficulties, despite old age and sickness, can often be felt as soon as one meets him or her. For various reasons this can be misleading. Concentration camp survivors have often suppressed and overcome so much that they will do anything to look healthy, well cared-for, and robust. Often they were forced to hide weakness—they cannot forget that weakness is associated with death.

METHODOLOGICAL PROBLEMS: HOW VALID IS THE SUBJECTIVE AND UNIQUE PICTURE?

SUBJECTIVITY

An interview is a conversation between two people and thus an interactive happening, even when one person appears to be doing all the talking. Every interview by the historian that searches people's memories reveals as much about the interviewer as about the person being interviewed—even when the interviewer intends to say as little as possible, to interrupt seldom, and to act in such a way as to avoid steering the interview. When the story has to do with the war, however, and survivors sometimes talk about what worried them most—their deepest fear—and the greatest disaster of their lives, it is impossible not to react and to keep one's face from reflecting feelings.

The fact that I am Jewish influenced the research both positively and negatively. It was positive that I could react to a particular kind of war story. It created space within which more could be told, and no one had the feeling that I would not understand. A second advantage was probably that the people I interviewed had fewer questions about my motivation than would have been the case had I not been able to understand the horror. There were certainly problems between those interviewed and myself, but there was always a shared goal; the nature of the project was clear to both parties. And the conversation was often simplified by the fact that it was not necessary to explain Jewish customs and events. Usually I knew their meaning perfectly well.

My involvement could occasionally have led to my not asking enough questions to round out a topic properly. When one knows how painful a topic is, one is more inclined to hold back in order to avoid opening old wounds.

That same involvement can lead to a situation where both partners in the conversation regard things as obvious that would be less so for an outsider, and this could lead to doubt about what has been told.

HOW GENERAL IS THE PICTURE THAT HAS BEEN OBTAINED?

Research projects carried out on the basis of interviews can just as effectively be based on one life as on more than one. In itself, this is not unique to "oral history," though it is usual in the case of oral history to ask oneself how far the interviews are representative. There are a number of books open to this kind of criticism, but at the same time it is generally acknowledged that such studies renew and refresh the practice of history.

A fine example of this is *Les fromage et les vers* [Cheese and Maggots] by the Italian historian Carlo Ginzburg. He tells the tale of a miller in the Friuli who saw maggots coming out of cheese and thereby concluded that life on earth originated in the same way. This opinion got him into trouble with the Inquisition. The book is interesting because the miller's simplistic idea (if you let cheese stand long enough, maggots come out of it, thus the cheese creates maggots) is examined from the perspective of one person clashing with official ideology. The miller is a human being, and the Inquisition is not a distant official body but an official body that can meddle directly in his personal life. The suffering of this one human gives an excellent picture of the daily life and mentality of that given era.

Another objection to my research method is that the sources can be one-sided. However, it is not uncommon for an entire book to be written on the basis of one source. The best-known example of this is Le Roy Ladurie's *Montaillou*. It is based on a carefully used and unique source that details the daily life in a village where witchcraft is suspected. Because the village life is described in such complete detail (including illicit love affairs), it is possible for the reader to experience the reality of that village.

One life or one source can exemplify the situation effectively because it can deepen our knowledge in ways that more generalized study (assuming it is even possible) cannot. The Italian historian Ginzburg had this to say about the problem: "The fact that a source is not 'objective' . . . does not mean that it cannot be used."[28] For research on what can be called the history of every-day life, it is often necessary to resort to this kind of limited and scattered documentation. It is more profitable than to proceed on the basis of a kind of naive empiricism, rejecting certain documents out of hand because they are one-sided.[29]

The interviews that I held can be compared to scattered documents, but at the same time they are more than that. They arise from an artificially created situation, a conversation in which one of the partners is expected to remember something. Thus it is not about a previously structured life history.[30] The person's life is followed from the earliest memory, often preceded by a global discussion of how (s)he had managed to come through the war or, if that was too difficult, how (s)he now felt about life.

THEORETICAL APPROACHES

INDIVIDUAL AND COLLECTIVE MEMORY

Oral history has to conquer a great many problems if it is to reach its goal. A major problem with writing history on the basis of oral sources is that it raises the question of why someone remembers something in a certain way. How much is the individual testimony shaped by major social changes? Second, the formal object of oral history is the past, but this is an illusion. When memory is used to reconstruct the past, the past is reconstructed on the basis of the present.

In *The Voice of the Past*, the English historian Paul Thompson claims we cannot deny that the raw material for oral history is not factual information but consists primarily of ideas. It is an expression of culture and hence contains not only literal accounts of events but also the dimension of memory that comprises ideology and unconscious desires.

Hence the "facts" that are passed on in an interview do not exist as pure facts. A story is woven around them, a story that conveys some message from the person being interviewed, even when (s)he is not conscious of this.[31]

MEMORY: REMEMBERING AND FORGETTING
IS A THEORETICAL PROBLEM

When we do historical research on the basis of interviews, we assume that the person interviewed (or, better, the person who is telling us something about his or her life) is actually remembering it.[32] In the course of an interview we often hear the words, "I remember . . ." and a story follows. In this section we will look at the meaning of that remembering in more detail. Who is the "I" in "I remember," and what does the word "remember" mean?

It has gradually become accepted that an event can be processed by a person in various ways. Thus the same person can remember the same event in different ways, and people also differ from each other in regard to the way they remember. Experiences are overlaid by later events during the course of one's life, and the way in which one remembers also depends on the events at the time of remembering. Confrontations, shocks, signs of the past can often lead to remembering suddenly what had been "forgotten." The same signs do not conjure up the same associations in different persons. One cannot accuse anyone of lying just because the stories contradict each other or are internally inconsistent.

Biographical discontinuities help shape our perception of the past and our memory. Each fact remembered reflects a fleeting moment in a lifetime of change. In the interviews, moreover, experiences are processes that only took shape in a *gradual* fashion. Along with the truly personal experiences there are things we are *expected* to remember. These hegemonic memories can function as a superego and differ according to the environment, the country, and the culture.

Individual experiences/memories are inconceivable without more general experiences embedded within those memories. Yet analytic and individual experience can be distinguished from the more general experience. If we did not do that, we would deny the role of personal subjectivity, which is created in part by individual biography. It is also important not to look only at the social forces created by what the French sociologist Maurice Halbwachs called "collective memory," but to distinguish them from the separate world in which other forces create the individual memory and consciousness. This concerns that area in which the collective and the individual are inseparably bound to each other; they are to be distinguished from each other in the experiences that every individual has undergone separately.

Individual memory (in itself a contradictory and ambiguous expression) is created in part by the way in which relationships of power are experienced in the course of one's life. Through the manner in which we view our own life and our own past, individual consciousness becomes more than just a component of the ruling ideology around it. Unconsciously and without any intention of doing so, individual consciousness can contradict the dominant myths. That is what makes an individual account so difficult to understand. The question is whether the authenticity of individual experience is able to break through the stereotypes that sometimes govern our actions. At the same time, there is no other way available than to appeal to that authenticity if we wish to determine which stereotypes shaped the collective thinking of a period.

Individual Memories

Psychoanalysis is the discipline most concerned with the act of remembering life histories.[33] Oral historians generally find that psychoanalysts have more to contribute to their work than do people in other branches of psychology, in which memory is regarded as a difficult problem.[34] Psychoanalysis uses stories obtained during sessions with patients, and in this respect also exhibits similarities to oral history. Clearly, the historian cannot simply apply the methodology of psychoanalysis to historical interviews. For one thing, the historian is seeking a different kind of knowledge about the past;[35] (s)he is looking for a picture of society in the words and signs encountered during an interview.

In contrast, psychoanalysis strives for free expression by the patients. The stories and free associations throw light on personal identification, a person's relationship with his/her parents, and the development of sexuality. All this is brought to light through a reading of the account that concentrates on its symptomatic content. In that sense, language provides access to and acts as the spokesperson for the unconscious. Historians, on the other hand, look for general ideas, which is not the same thing. Thus hunger is not *in the first instance* taken to be a notion that is linked to sexuality but is understood as a feeling of hunger overshadowed by the war. The analogy does not yield an identical interpretation, though the same framework can easily be used.

Psychoanalytical theory has always asked why people forget something more often than why they remember it. Forgetting is understood to be the result of repression. Ideas and feelings that cannot be understood solely by means of reason are repressed. This cannot be neatly divided into blocks, measurable units and parts, and impressions. Moreover, psychoanalysis postulates that the present is determined by the past, or rather that *events from the past live on in another form, influenced by other events from the mental present.*[36] Psychoanalysis juxtaposes what we remember against what we forget. Nothing that has happened is ever lost, and it is necessary to investigate why certain things rise to consciousness. Conscious thought itself contains an area of resistance. Forgetting is explained as "*failure* to appear in consciousness." Freud's theory of forgetting thus implicitly contains a theory of remembering. (The "Freudian slip" is the classic example of the ever-present past that is there even when the person making the slip wants to forget.)

Freud called the sharp but unimportant memories *Deckerinnerungen* or screen memories, behind which other chains and events that are far more significant hide. The screen memories mediate between what was seen/forgotten and the idea that has appeared in place of them. Because free association can lead to a painful, unpleasant memory, it appears that the remembered event was not forgotten.[37]

A further implication from my interviews is that a spoken word can be linked in memory to nonverbal thought and transposed experience, in addition to the word's meaning in the language system. This kind of memory is often strictly a substituted memory. Fresh observations of specific places can bring the *substituted* memory into discussion. Such memories are usually no longer present because much (if not everything) fades away from childhood. Then the apparently unimportant screen memories are the most direct route to the manner in which the childhood, neighborhood, family, environment, culture, and school were experienced.

Collective Memory

As mentioned earlier, the term "collective memory" is known mainly as the result of the work of Maurice Halbwachs.[38] It concerns those factors that determine the choice by the individual of what is remembered and what is forgotten/repressed. Halbwachs claims that the collective memory is not simply built up as the sum of individual memories, although every individual memory is part of it. Rather, it is a matter of what society (or a particular group within society) expects from history, and thus is ideological. In the collective memory there are fewer discontinuities than in the case of a real individual. Halbwachs regards it as the task of the historian to trace the points where individual histories become disjointed. In this way we can follow the trail back and gain insight into the collective memory. In turn, knowledge of this gives us the ability to understand individual memories better.

My criticism of Halbwachs is that he does not show how important political mechanisms are in determining the creation and existence of a dominant ideology and thus of memory. Because ideology plays a crucial role in the maintenance of relationships and values, it is not neutral but a matter of political struggle. Analogously, memory is shaped by a political force field of the continually changing balance of power within our society. Collective memory is dominated by the ruling ideology, but at the same time tells its own story. This relatively autonomous collective consciousness is crucial for the active process of remembering and for the distortions that occur within it.

THE SIGNIFICANCE OF NOSTALGIA AND THE PAST

Surviving traditions and nostalgia do not carry enough weight to counteract the silence that exists concerning the personal or nonhegemonic past. Raymond Williams, the English cultural historian, calls the hegemonic past the "significant" past,[39] but the other, nonhegemonic picture can lead to a more substantial account of the events. With this in mind, Williams claims that these counter-images are not part of the prevailing historical perceptions, not even as contradictions to them. Thus it is those elements that run counter to the accepted view of the Jewish proletariat which are most important in the interviews. The dominant picture was often contradicted, but at the same time people looked back with sentimentality and nostalgia to former times, to times when their world was easier to grasp.

Every oral historian knows well that when people are asked about how it used to be, their answer tends to be along the lines of, "It was much better then." The protective world of childhood and the safety of the parents' home are unique in the course of a life. In a number of interviews, however, this was not the case. The poverty was so great that the past was not safe at all. A feeling of insecurity permeated many interviews, especially those I was not permitted to record. This was strengthened by the trauma of the war. Very few families of the people I interviewed came through unscathed. This meant that the accounts were told dramatically and emotionally.

In turn, denial for nostalgic reasons is part of the dominant culture. In order to maintain the dominant view of the past, it is necessary to give continual expression to this denial. Thus the people interviewed sought approval from the dominant culture and the pictures of the past associated with that culture by telling about their happy childhood. At the same time, this account functioned as a substitute for memory. It led to stories that were not—and could not be—unraveled further. One's personal memories cannot be made available for public perusal. The memories that bring unpleasant feelings with them remain hidden, while the recurring picture of Friday evenings—candles on the table, good food, and sweet things, nuts, and fruit afterward—express a longing for a happy childhood.

An example of such a romanticized tale came from a woman who said there were not enough chairs for all eleven members of the family to sit at the table in the stuffy little room. Yet those evenings were the happiest memories she had of her childhood. Even more powerful were the tales of Friday evenings when there was not enough money for food. In more than one literary description we find the story of the woman who set a pot of water to boil in order to hide from the neighbors the fact that they had no money for chicken soup. The steam glistening on the windows gave the impression that they were cooking inside. I was told a number of times how the children sat hungrily round the table with their parents. Again and again I was told the story of the water soup as a personal experience. It is interesting that it was always remembered as charming.

Whether or not it was true is not all that important in light of other accounts of how miserable it was to sit at the table with an empty stomach. Even if one managed to bear it, it was horrible. Insofar as we can speak of memories of a happy childhood, this is certainly in accord with the "official" nostalgia. The culture serves as a vengeful and correcting father figure, as a superego. In his writings on mass psychology, Freud pointed out that culture can take over the role of a superego for the experience and consciousness of the individual.[40] As a result, collective and personal memory merge in the individual's story about the past.

Feelings that tended toward romanticizing often dominated the interviews. That does not mean that this book should be regarded as an argument against nostalgia. Precisely where there is nothing else (and there are indeed very few other memories left of the Jewish proletariat), a charming picture has a positive effect. Through the past, people give themselves a place in a world that has often become cold and empty since World War II. It keeps them going, and through it they know how the world should have been. In turn, the pretty stories become an ideological weapon in the struggle against those groups who try to deny the murder of the Jews. They are nice to write, they can be told again and again, and they are often full of humor. If they were music, we would say, "That's a pleasure to listen to!" People can identify with that happy, untidy little world of markets and charming (albeit somewhat dirty) *gezelligheid*, that untranslatable Dutch word for a mood of closeness, coziness, pleasure, and security.

IDENTIFICATION WITH THE PAST

People recognize themselves in symbols from the past, and if the symbols are joyful, then so much the better. In interviews with elderly Jewish residents of Amsterdam, it soon became clear that many of them identified the symbols by which they measured their past with reality. In their relation to reality, they assumed a commonality of interest. I have compared this tendency to identify reality with symbols with Bertold Brecht's ideas about naturalistic theater.[41] In his polemical work, Brecht argued that the accurate portrayal of human suffering (as well as the way in which it is suggested to the public so that one could transport oneself into that suffering) makes it impossible to give a critical evaluation of the truth being represented. He said, "When you depict something, you choose a standpoint that makes real criticism impossible. People identify with you and find their true place in the world. You were as you were and the world remains as it was."[42]

A photograph is never reality—it is a photograph. Faithful representations of flowers in a painting are simply painted flowers, and real ones are different because they have a real existence. A good play must therefore keep some distance from reality in order to penetrate "reality"; it must render visible the laws that underlie the suffering being represented. Thus theater must show more than reality that is "faithful to the truth," namely, it must show what is not seen in representational art. To achieve this, the playwright must distance himself from the obvious, the natural, through a kind of alienation. Only then can anything be made transparent. Identification can trivialize the exceptional. But alienation, according to Brecht, creates the historical; the banal is made exceptional. Moreover, it becomes historical because in this way persons and events become historical and thus accessible. *Speaking in the third person*, Brecht called it. In contrast, identification results in the explosion of the temporary into the eternal, the constant, the inescapable.

According to psychoanalytical theory, identification involves believing in imagined common characteristics, and hence it is in part ideological. In this case, ideology is the combination of people's experiences with the way in which they place those experiences in their pictures of their relationships to reality. Through ideology each individual turns his or her own existence into a meaningful project. In literary theory this complex is called "addressing the subject."[43] In literary descriptions of the past, opportunities for identification are given again and again; in fact, this is an essential part of a certain kind of literary endeavor. Experience, ideology, and reality are treated equally. Recognizing him/herself, the reader is made the subject of the story.

The identification with which we we are dealing here takes place through symbolic, nostalgic narration. It is essential to the construction of the romantic memory. The fact that people chose symbols like Friday evening, chicken soup, the *gezelligheid* of gathering round the white tablecloth, and the chaos at the markets (which was nevertheless regarded as fun) has to do with the fact that people are trying to express something of their feelings through language. Nostalgia has transformed their reduction to poverty, the poverty itself, and hunger into a picture of the past they can look back on with longing. This picture corresponds perfectly with other accepted images of how it used to be, and with their longing for the time before the Holocaust, when Jewish families were still large.

LANGUAGE AND EXPERIENCE

People identify with the existing accounts of the past, whether oral or written. These accounts are framed within existing language systems. People try to use the systems to verbalize the way they miss what no longer exists—the emptiness. But because the emptiness is so great, the attempt is (at least in part) doomed to failure.

The experiences of the old Jewish proletariat had to be related to me—a woman historian, Jewish, of the postwar generation, who had grown up in the affluence of the 1950s and 1960s. That had to happen in a language I could understand. Those who tried to tell me their stories had to search for words to do this—words that were often never found. They looked for roundabout ways of speaking when that was the only way to verbalize what was essential for them. One framework within which they could work was the semi-official reading of the past that was so significant in determining the collective memory. Moreover, the words used in that had acquired a changeable meaning in the course of time, a life of their own.[44]

In order to grasp this more precisely, let us trace step by step the various stages that intervene between an event and recounting the story of this event from memory.

Remembering involves verbalizing events, translating them into language. Fifty years ago—or whatever—an event was translated into the language of that time. It was stored in memory as a story, and as more than that. The words that are added to the summary have a life of their own; they refer to a number of other events that are expressed in language and also to what I will here call, for simplicity, (sensory) experiences. Certain words acquire a different meaning in the course of time. In my research, a good example is the word "hunger," in Dutch *honger*.

Many people I interviewed had to deal with hunger during their early years—not deadly hunger or starvation, but simply always having an empty stomach and never anything nice to eat. This was quite different from what they felt in a concentration camp; compared with the hunger of a camp, childhood hunger was nothing at all. Moreover, hunger in a concentration camp was interwoven with the fear of death, with the knowledge that one could die at any moment. Even after the war, everyone experienced an "empty stomach" occasionally. And after an interview someone might say, "Don't you feel hungry after all that talking?" During the interviews, the concept of hunger encompasses an amalgam of experiences and meanings.

In an interview with C., an elderly lady in Israel, this led to considerable confusion. I sought her out in a home for senior citizens. I had to get up at six o'clock in the morning and arrived there thirsty, dusty, and hungry. We had arranged to meet in the late morning, after which we would go to lunch, and then I would tape her story. It was unlikely that we would have an opportunity for a second meeting. She told me about her early years in a little village, a *medina* or Jewish community outside the big cities. As a teacher she had to walk long distances in order to give lessons to children in a neighboring village. When she arrived she would eat what she had taken with her, so that it would be kosher. If she forgot to take anything, she would get somewhat hungry. While she was still quite young, C. married a man from Amsterdam and they came to live in the old Jewish Quarter. There she noticed the problems of the children and tried to do something for the poorest of them. I asked her about life and the way things were during World War I (1914–1918):

"Can you remember whether there were any other things at that time? The potato riots just after the war in 1919?"

"Oh, yes, there was hunger at that time, but not hunger as I came to know it later . . ."

"Can you remember . . ."

"In Bergen–Belsen I stood by the trash can, and if there were people who just couldn't get their food down their throats, I would ask them, 'Give it to me.' "

"But [during the First World War] there wasn't hunger like in Bergen–Belsen . . ."

"I was in Bergen–Belsen."

"No, but in Amsterdam in 1919, much earlier, was there already hunger? I mean even if it was another kind. . . ."

"Yes, but we didn't know what real hunger was at that time."[45]

She described the poverty of her earlier years, but lovingly, whitewashing the filth, so to speak, and in the light of her camp experiences she could not imagine any real hunger at that time. World War II was the principle experience of her life, and that was what she wanted to talk about.

As we walked to lunch that morning she asked me if I was hungry. After the conversation she planned to nap for a while, but she asked if I didn't want to stay on and eat something that evening, with the hospitable observation that otherwise I might feel hungry on the way back.

In all these cases, C. tried to tell me something through her use of that
word. In one instance, it was concern for others, the neighborhood children
whom she had loved so much. Another meaning was the malnutrition she
experienced in Bergen–Belsen. And finally, her charming, attentive concern
for me was linked to polite usage. Above all, one of those meanings expressed
great feeling and was not just a matter of words for her, but a metaphor for
many repressed feelings. In my attempt to obtain a picture of Uilenburg in the
old Jewish Quarter, the word formed a kind of barrier against the emotions
she had felt during the war and in the earlier years.

UNTOLD STORIES

My approach involves searching for untold stories lurking in the gaps of the
stories that are told overtly. The psychoanalytical concept of *layers* is the
basis for the search.[46] Freud borrowed this concept from archeology to indicate that our perceptions of ourselves and of the past are built up, consciously
and unconsciously, and that new experiences are added to them in turn. These
are then translated into a story. Biographical details are buried by newer
happenings. The researcher, like an archeologist, is continually digging up
new layers of the person, both in the memory and in the personality. This
concept also suggests that certain aspects of the personality overlap each
other. And this in turn suggests that the layers do not just give rise to other
aspects but also influence each other.

The real story is often not told and cannot be told; it is to be found only by
reading between the lines. Thus, at first, I could make no sense at all of a
story told to me by one woman. She really did her best to involve me in her
memories. I admired her and was curious about her work with children, about
the buildings where she had worked, about her ideas on education, and her
interactions and working relationships. She told me a good deal. But not until
I reread the interview did it become clear to me that what she really wanted to
say was: "I loved them, those children I took care of. I gave everything to
them. I protected them, looked after them, nourished them with the best of my
ideals. But one thing I could not prevent: they were all murdered."[47] The
woman told me everything except what she cared about most—the children.
They were the untold story that needed to be traced carefully.

Stories thus have more than one layer. French oral historians call the tellers
of oral history a dynamic source.[48] The problems affecting this kind of research are not immediately solved by recognizing the difficulties of dealing
with the act of remembering. But bringing the stories out into the open makes
it easier to search for why people tell certain things as if they were remembering them accurately. It gives us a way of approaching a better understanding
of the Jewish proletariat between the two world wars.

The individual story is subordinate to the existing nostalgia. Identification with nostalgia is achieved through symbols and spoken formulas. Yet in identifying oneself with formulas that have been spoken by others and are empty of real feeling (or at least distanced from it), one implicitly undervalues oneself and thus creates confusion.

An example of this was Mr. B., a diamond worker I interviewed, who was ashamed of the fact that his parents taught him so very little about Judaism. In his eyes, they had not given him a Jewish upbringing. He had paid no attention to the fact that he was Jewish and now wished that he had been more conscious of his background. This regret was a common phenomenon after World War II. After all, it was during the war that he was recognized as a Jew—by himself as well as by others. Before that, he had not seen himself as different from other people. Suddenly it became clear to him that before the war he scarcely had contact with non-Jews—virtually only when he had run errands for the family. He grew up in East Amsterdam and attended a public school, but in a neighborhood where most of the children were Jewish. His social life centered around the family. When he left school, he started work in the diamond industry, where he saw very few people who were not Jewish. I asked him to describe what he did when he was not at work.

"First we went to the barber, and . . . oh, straight on to the bathhouse, of course, the Boerhaave, and it was easy to spend half a day there. . . . I always went to Blitz, a really well-known barber on Vrolik Street. Well, it was always full of diamond workers and you always had a great time there. And in the evening we'd mostly go to the Kroon, a really big billiard saloon on Rembrandt Square. On Saturdays, but also during the week, sometimes we'd take in a movie or we'd go dancing—there'd be live music!"[49]

This man, who did not feel that his lifestyle had been Jewish, was describing a Saturday spent entirely with Jews. He hardly knew anyone else. Yet only with the rise of fascism did he feel he had become a Jew. Mr. B. was unaware that he was far from being alone in this. During the interview I had to contend with the collective notion that the Jewish proletariat was in the first instance "Jewish." Because he did not know that radical assimilation had been widespread, he felt that the time before the war was not a part of Jewish history. He was a "victim" of a view of history that "forgot" that his behavior pattern was quite normal. And because he could not deny that part of his own past, he tried to use regret to insert himself into the standard view of history. Ultimately he had no reason to be ashamed.

The historian, armed only with a tape recorder and taking away only a transcript to convey the rich and colorful life each individual shows her, is powerless in the face of all these complex interpretations of "I remember."[50]

For the moment, let us regard memory as a street into which main thoroughfares and sidestreets feed. The entrances to those streets can be blocked off or open. We do not know which is the case or why it is that way, but we do know that events in the present seem to determine why we walk between houses down a little alley that leads to a street we already know but for some reason have not walked down before. When and why do we raise barriers? When do particular processes start working in our brains? We have no answer to this; we only know that certain events make the past less accessible to one's conscious memory.

The experiences of the war play an important role in this, as does the way in which one deals with those experiences. Memories associated with going into hiding or imprisonment can give rise to so much distress—sometimes simply because people survived those times—that those associations are better not made. Everyone deals with memory in one's own way, but in the case of the Amsterdam Jewish proletariat there was enormous shared trauma. Jacob Presser, the historian who described the annihilation of the Dutch Jews, wrote about how those who survived no longer believed in a "normal" life after what had happened.[51]

Romanticism and nostalgia blend into each other in the stories. They coincide with the longing for lost childhood, with the feeling that it was better in former times, and to some extent with already existing written memories. Their sweetness also makes them, in part, a survival strategy, for they allow one to identify with what once existed, or to avoid thinking about the war, or to keep from having to contradict existing images.

But the historian is not totally powerless. No method can aim at providing complete historical accuracy. Sometimes I knew for certain that people were just making up stories, without really wanting to lie to me. In other cases, I carefully pieced together the jigsaw puzzles of their lives. This was not always possible, however; the fact that many people never really put the war behind them was a huge problem throughout the study.

Many hours were taken up by tales of suffering and resistance. I was confronted with an endless stream of horrors. The vast amount of time that I needed for these interviews was due to the fact that probably no one can walk unscathed down the steps of Hades with the help of someone living, let alone make it back out again, without great difficulty. One subject told of the cheerful impressions evoked by a scene of a glowing fire in a movie, the fire being a screen memory, a metaphor for the hell of the camps. In several cases, people concerned themselves only with their own resistance activities. Such activities were no doubt estimable, but they so dominated many conversations that the subject we had agreed to deal with was hardly touched upon.[52]

Survival forces one to deal with guilt toward the dead as if one survived at the cost of someone else's death. That can involve as little as the fact that one was unpleasant once or twice to a particular person, or it can be a matter of collective guilt because one survived. The guilt ignores the fact that those who survived were often those who were physically or mentally strong and who had special qualities. Guilt can also lead to an unwillingness to recall particular feelings and events. In cases where these guilt feelings became unbearable during an interview, they were (as far as possible) analyzed and countered.

The historian should not act as a therapist. However, historical analysis can contribute to ways of dealing with the past. Quite a few of the interviews for this research ended in having unexpected emotional consequences. These varied from finding the peace of mind to die, expressed in the form of a farewell letter, to gaining a new perspective on life. There is, however, so much to say about this aspect of oral history that I have chosen not to address it in a direct manner here.

CONFIDENCES AND CONTRADICTIONS

Although the historian is not a therapist and does not have the training to assist people in dealing with the past, (s)he can sometimes help put life in perspective by means of historical corrective.[53] There is no sense in giving people an illusion. The listening ear is no more than the ear of someone who is interested in a story. Because it is impossible to reach across the war to the memories of the time before the great traumas, it is misleading to suggest that an intimate and closer bond exists.

In this work I chose to have the greatest possible respect for memories, even those that are distorted. Based on the fact that a memory, distorted or not, is an account of a life, I searched first for a chronology of the events. This served as a counterbalance to the powerful finality of the telling of a life story. Furthermore, I systematically encouraged those who gained insight into their histories to put such insight into words if at all possible. This in turn breathed new life into the memory.

Facts that came to light during the interviews sometimes led to painful confrontations, but sometimes they led to better understanding and to a lessening of the pain. Sometimes, something that I had never understood became clear. Respect for a life that survived a horrible war was paramount. No one intentionally misled me, and every story-teller worked hard to remember things as accurately as possible. Together we walked down a street where some doors were closed, and behind every door lurked something that had not yet been dealt with, some sorrow not yet embraced. The one who told the story had to determine which doors to open, because when the grief was overwhelming, the historian was powerless. In a number of cases it was only possible to speak sporadically about the joys and tears of a lost childhood.

It is the historian's task to help create a clear, open, and honest relationship. After all, one is dealing with that person's survival, and his or her self-respect. Ultimately that is more important than any historical work.

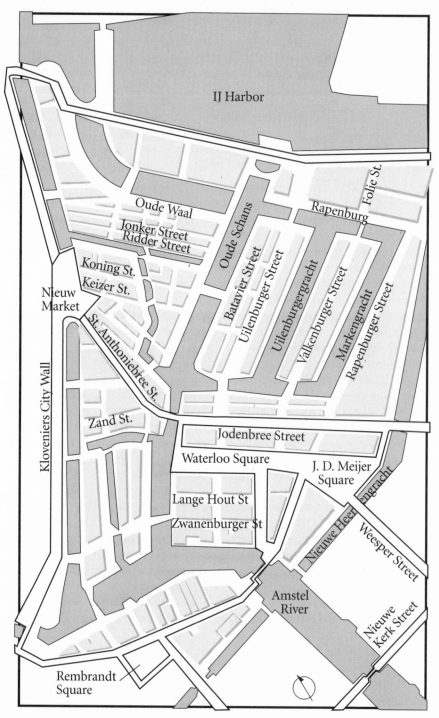

The Old Jewish Quarter

IJ Harbor

Folie St.

Oude Waal

Rapenburg

Jonker Street

Ridder Street

Oude Schans

Koning St.

Keizer St.

Nieuw Market

Batavier Street

Uilenburger Street

Uilenburgergracht

Valkenburger Street

Markengracht

Rapenburger Street

St. Anthoniebree St.

Kloveniers City Wall

Zand St.

Jodenbree Street

Waterloo Square

J. D. Meijer Square

Lange Hout St

Zwanenburger St

Nieuwe Heerengracht

Weesper Street

Amstel River

Nieuwe Kerk Street

Rembrandt Square

CHAPTER TWO

THE JEWS AND AMSTERDAM

HISTORICAL BACKGROUND

SETTLEMENT: PLACE AND PROCESS

When the Amsterdam chapter of the Association for Advancement of Architecture organized a competition in 1865, contestants were invited to develop a plan: "How can Amsterdam be expanded?"[1] One respondent proposed building a city in which the then filthy streets would be replaced by a *cité ouvrière*, a new district, created for the segment of the working class that was in the process of developing a stable existence for itself. This had already happened in other Western European cities. Paris was the best-known example; early in the nineteenth century, the slums had been replaced by substantial (working class) districts through which ran broad boulevards.[2]

Following this model, the association envisaged a situation in which a new, growing class of educated people would live in respectable, albeit small, middle-class houses situated in well-maintained streets. Amsterdam was expanding rapidly at the time and not only needed to build residential districts for the middle and lower middle classes and workers, but also, it was felt, had to expand the harbor, improve railroad connections, fill in canals, and broaden the streets, thus converting the city as a whole into a modern metropolis. In the years that followed, the working-class neighborhood of the Pijp was developed and the city expanded to the south in the direction of the Museum Quarter.[3]

It was not only the aesthetic appearance of the city that needed to be improved; there was also an acute housing shortage. Furthermore, the chaos and filth threatened the very health of the population, just as in other overpopulated cities—an opinion put forward by the pubic health authorities and adopted by local government and its bureaucratic apparatus and by a large segment of the population.

Among other sources, the published entries to the architectural competition show that there was general concern over the filthy conditions then prevalent in the working-class sections of the city, and above all in the Jewish Quarter. The worst misery was in the old Jewish neighborhoods. There, on the islands of Marken, Uilenburg, and Rapenburg, the poorest of the poor lived in narrow alleys in squalid buildings, slums totally devoid of sanitation. The documents relating to the competition raise questions about the reasons for this. Could it be because a different kind of people lived there? Was it really so bad? Why was it worse there than elsewhere? Because of the religious practices of the people? Because of some distinctive properties of the social structure found there? Or because of purely cultural differences of some kind? Those who entered the competition reached no consensus, but their remarks give us some idea of how they approached the problem. Some were judgmental, others sought the cause elsewhere.

One of the contestants described the conditions as follows:

> The grime and filth prevailing in Marken, Uilenburg, and bordering neighborhoods are probably not surpassed in any other place on earth. . . . We do not wish to blame the inhabitants for this evil; rather, we believe that the cause lies in the narrowness of the alleys and passageways, as well as the cramped, poorly organized housing. Moreover, this evil stems in part also from the nature of the work of the inhabitants, most of whom ply their trade in the public streets, despite the fact that a handcart can scarcely pass along the main thoroughfares: Batavier, Uilenburger, and Valkenburger. The inhabitants are forced to carry out their work in the streets because their homes are too cramped.[4]

Yet the situation was not hopeless as a result of the inherent inferiority of the district. Indeed, these neighborhoods were precisely the ones felt to have the greatest potential for future development. After demolition and reconstruction, the proximity of this area to the harbor and to the city center gave it real promise. Moreover, Amsterdam's water supply was regulated in such a way that the ground water pumped up in this area was among the freshest and cleanest in the city. The unsanitary conditions that were prevalent there could easily be combated through other regulations. So, what was necessary to create a true *quartier ouvrière*?

The filthy conditions in the Jewish neighborhood were discussed in other entries to the competition. One author maintained that the poverty and squalor affected the behavior of the inhabitants. In contrast to this opinion, it appeared to many people that the situation in the Jewish area had gotten so out of hand that it almost seemed as if it must somehow result from the specific characteristics of the people who lived there. After all, there was housing desperately in need of modernization elsewhere in the city, and it seemed to be in an equally deplorable condition—yet the poverty and squalor of the Jewish neighborhood were not found anywhere else in the city. Thus the Jews were held responsible.

The result was an attitude of anti-Semitism that was not political but prejudicial in that it assumed a natural linkage between Jews and filth. The following passage admirably exemplifies this widespread popular attitude:

> Watch out for Snoekjes Alley where the excrement of the descendants of Abraham is dumped every Sunday morning before church. And when it is occasionally cleaned up before worship, one often finds the filth has returned by the end of the service. Beware of the intersection of Snoekjes Alley, St. Anthoniebree Street, and Hoog (or Oude) Doelen Street, where— and I must add that I do like and admire a diligent and honest Israelite—a mass of uncouth Jewry blocks the streets with their wares, making you gag with their vile smell. The crowd is augmented from time to time by numbers of ragsellers who set up a thriving trade with their disgusting rags, crawling, of course, with vermin, gathered from hospitals and dirty caverns. It is difficult to creep by without subjecting oneself to the danger of touching them or of exposing oneself to some creeping or crawling thing, with the added risk of becoming entangled in an old or discarded rug. For you, rough merchants, no statues, but a fence to hold you in. You scoff at the police when they give you warnings, and after sputtering abuses and jeering at them, you shuffle down the street a little way at a snail's pace, and as soon as the officer has turned his back, once again defy the police ordinance.[5]

These utterly filthy, impoverished Jewish masses had lived in Amsterdam for ages.[6] Their families had been there since the eighteenth century—some even longer. First came the Jews from Portugal, who during the seventeenth century settled in the area that was later called the Jewish Quarter. The majority of these Sephardic Jews were well-to-do, some even from the nobility; they had money and business contacts at their disposal. They were followed by the Ashkenazim from Eastern Europe who, in contrast to the Portuguese Jews, arrived penniless and were largely dependent on charity. They were hardly able to keep their heads above water.[7]

There were fewer Sephardic Jews than Ashkenazim, and the two groups kept to themselves. Each had its own customs, synagogues, and distinct social networks. Though the two groups occupied the same neighborhoods until late in the nineteenth century, they were still counted separately in the census of 1849.

At the beginning of this century, there was a separate orphanage for Portuguese Jewish boys—and of course one for girls, too—likewise Portuguese Jewish maternity centers, infant care, and charitable institutions. The Sephardim maintained their own social structure. A great difference existed between the education offered in the relatively small Portuguese Jewish boys' orphanage, Aby Jethonim, and the much larger and overcrowded general orphanage for Jewish boys, Megdalé Jethonim.[8] A 1941 pamphlet of the Jewish Council reported that the traditionally greater wealth of the Portuguese Jews had resulted in needy Portuguese Jewish girls obtaining relatively large dowries from charitable institutions. By the 1930s, this wealth had vanished, and with it the basis for the separate social institutions.

Initially, the Jews in Amsterdam were ruled as a "Jewish Nation" within their closed community, with their own governing body, which was tolerated by the non-Jews. The Jews of the city represented the largest segment of the Jewish population in the Netherlands, although relatively speaking their numbers decreased in the course of the nineteenth century.[9] Around the turn of the century, the percentage of Jews living in Amsterdam increased again, until 58 percent lived there in 1941, just before the occupying forces made all Jews live in the city.

These statistics provide a first impression. Later in this chapter, however, they will be called into question since it was precisely at this time that it was unclear exactly what "Jewish" meant. The statistics use a new category, "half-Jew," which was counted separately. Between the wars, the Jews comprised 10 percent of the population of Amsterdam. In 1941, before the Germans forcibly concentrated all Dutch Jews in that city, 79,497 of the 803,073 people living in Amsterdam were Jewish. In that same year, according to a report commissioned by the occupying forces, there were 140,001 Jews living in the Netherlands. These statistics were based on the number of "full Jews"—yet another new term,[10] and one that had significance only in the language of the Nuremberg Laws.

EMANCIPATION, ASSIMILATION, INTEGRATION

During the Napoleonic period at the end of the eighteenth century, the Jews were emancipated in the Netherlands as in other countries occupied by the French. Rather than a "Jewish Nation," they became the "Jewish Dutch," subject to the same laws as the non-Jews and formally given equal rights and duties. Yet in areas not directly subject to legal regulation, equality was not achieved until well into the twentieth century. Some organizations did not admit Jews, and Jews were informally excluded from various official posts and professions.[11]

In the Netherlands, as elsewhere in Europe, the desirability of emancipation was fiercely debated in Jewish circles. A small minority, those of the Enlightenment, followed such leaders as Moses Mendelssohn in striving toward the "rational new person" and advocated integration of the Jews, adoption of non-Jewish lifestyles, abandonment of Yiddish as the mother tongue, and abandonment of all ancient customs. Although only a handful of Jewish intellectuals and leaders debated this question,[12] the integration of Jews into Dutch society was already under way, regardless of any conscious effort.

Integration was a gradual and barely noticed process, the outcome of which filled the opponents of assimilation and integration with concern. For them, integration was the same as assimilation. Partly as a result of the cultural exclusion of Jews, integration often did *not* mean assimilation. Even where traditions were not consciously maintained, "assimilation" was—certainly in the lower social classes around the turn of the century—often no more than a thin layer of varnish—although thick enough to trouble those who cared.

Superficially, assimilation was making good progress. Certainly among the well-to-do there had been great changes in Jewish society since the beginning of the nineteenth century. An increasing number of Jews began to live like non-Jews and were often regarded as "Christians" by their own people. They sought entrance to new professions and to universities, gradually leaving behind the lifestyle of the ghetto and the mentality that went with it. They adapted to a world with a different calendar, where other holidays were celebrated, people lived in a different manner, and, in particular, ate differently.

At first only the elite made the transition, because it was originally a question of having the intellectual or financial wherewithal to break out of the closed environment. Later it became more common, and the Jews mingled increasingly with the rest of the population of Amsterdam. The old, closed ghetto, in which almost all the poor and rich lived in close proximity to one another, no longer existed. Of course, poor Jewish neighborhoods in which Jewish culture was completely dominant remained—little ghettos in the full sense. The poorer residents of these ghettos chose to stay and live together of their own free will. Living outside these familiar surroundings in non-Jewish neighborhoods required taking a giant step.

ATMOSPHERE

The atmosphere in the Jewish Quarter is most strikingly portrayed in the writings of Meijer de Hond, the rabbi of the poor. In baroque language laced with Jewish vernacular phrases, de Hond vividly described the turbulence of Waterloo Square. No other contemporary author wrote more exuberantly about the Jews of Amsterdam; no one was more respectful or had more compassion for the masses of peddlers. Without contempt for those who knew no better, he wrote passages like the following, in which he depicted the hubbub and overcrowding around him. More than van den Eewal (cited in the previous chapter), de Hond immersed himself in the turmoil. He was no outsider:

> Thousands of hardened characters who would fight to kill. A vengeful swarm in ordered ranks. . . .
> The sighs of those falling vie with whispers of others falling. Colors teem in unthinkable mixtures and scream louder than throats—cut sharper than weapons. A veritable war among peoples. Nations approach each other intent on the worst. Countries become bodies rushing together, each seek-

ing the total immolation of the other. Is not screaming pain a universal language? Do not sorrow and sighs exist in all languages?[13]

De Hond's vivid accounts of these people appeared in his articles for the magazine *De Libanon* [The Lebanon], which he published around the turn of the century.

After the war, the historian Jaap Meijer gave a far more nostalgic tour of the neighborhood in his book *Het verdwenen getto* [The Vanished Ghetto], which painted a very different and far more melancholy picture of concern. De Hond's firsthand observations are colored by his love for the world he knew and for the traditions that he wished to preserve. Meijer's work, on the other hand, is lit by his love for that which is no more. The reader who accompanies him in spirit on his tour comes to feel something of what those who knew the neighborhood in former times now miss—the absent heart. In his book, Meijer brought to life the streets and alleys of the neighborhood he knew.[14] Canals and bridges crisscrossed the area so that it looked like a cluster of islands. As he wandered in imagination through the vanished city, he described it thus:

> We walk along the street toward the sluice, or *sjlies* as the older Jews usually call it rather than the standard Dutch *sluis*. Toward evening the old Jewish Quarter lies in terrifyingly desolate melancholy. Through the ruins of Jodenbree Street, high in the sky, we can just make out the treetops in front of the *Snoge* [Portuguese Synagogue]. To the left is the Montelbaan, where the almost vanished Jewish life had a beginning. . . . Under the bridge, a slow, flat boat glides by through filthy water.[15]

He walked farther, going from house to house, recalling all that he knew on the basis of what no longer existed, for "if all that we saw had any meaning, then it was this. All the generations of Jews have lived in vain unless we recover their path—which in times of joy and of sorrow they never forgot. Following their tracks will indeed be difficult. Because we will never, never be able to forget this Amsterdam."[16]

Jaap Meijer's postwar nostalgia left out one important aspect—life had been hard in those times. In the middle of the old neighborhood was Waterloo Square, with its market for second-hand goods. Let us return to Meijer de Hond, the contemporary eyewitness, for his observations:

> *Waterloo Square*. A battlefield. Struggle for existence. Never an armistice. There is nothing more cruel. From early morning to late in the evening, eternally. Furious vendetta against worry, cursing hatred against want. Everyone fights for himself. Need dictates the onslaught. No one is spared, for no one sees anyone but himself. Hear those cries—one continuous sound all day long. The stench of garbage and the reek of decomposition; moldy

dregs and the color of decay. Deceased splendor, to be reborn in hovel and shack! On the battlefield of Waterloo one learns the value of the worthless. Shoes you would not even hurl at a mangy cat are fought over. Rags you wouldn't dare give a beggar cause quarrels. Laughter, laughter! The struggle for existence does, after all, have its own humor![17]

Waterloo Square had its own laws and customs, no doubt stemming from the hard struggle for survival. De Hond showed that clearly. Contrasts with non-Jewish markets primarily concerned language. Jewish Dutch (for Yiddish was not in fact spoken) was hard to understand. It had an unfamiliar intonation and was riddled with Yiddish and Jewish expressions. The differences between the Jewish culture of the poor and that of the non-Jewish poor arose from the closed life of an immigrant minority that for centuries had managed to maintain its religious identity in spite of a hostile environment. Whatever description one reads, whatever story one requests, Jewish culture was noisy and descended from a kind of merchant mentality that had little in common with that of the Dutch Calvinist merchant.

We wander further in our thoughts. Behind Waterloo Square was the poor Vlooienburg, which ended at the Blauwburger Wall and the Zwanenburger Wall. Nothing is left here. On the corner, however, J. D. Meijer Square still exists with its stately Nieuwe and Grote Synagogues (now the Jewish Historical Museum) and the Portuguese Synagogue on the other side. We walk with Meijer down Rapenburger Street, the street of many synagogues, behind which lay the broad Nieuwe Heerengracht. But as van den Eewal already noted, the Jewish Quarter was also composed of small lanes and alleys that empty into the broad thoroughfares.

Over the bridge behind Jodenbree Street one found Uilenburg and Marken, islands like Vlooienburg and Rapenburg, where the poor lived in warehouses that served as a kind of civilian barracks. This was the real Jewish Quarter, where the market was held on Sundays, attracting folk from all over the country who came just to gape. Thousands came to stare at the countless screaming stall-holders. Uilenburg, epicenter of the hubbub and misery, consisted of two streets plus innumerable passageways and side alleys where the sun never shone. The Jewish Quarter was one enormous human warehouse; no one could say where the crush was worst.

It was not, of course, just an ugly neighborhood, as such stories of misery might lead us to think. There exists a nostalgic literature that denies the ugliness, and remembers, in various ways after the war, the vanished culture. Each author sought the right form to give verbal expression to his own grief. In the previous chapter I mentioned Sluyser; van Praag and Sal Santen[18] also deserve inclusion. What these authors have in common is that, through their sensitive language, we hear again what they heard, and see again what they saw in childhood. We catch the odor of second-hand goods and through the mists glimpse the contours of a cityscape that is now gone forever, replaced by modern architecture. The area was demolished during the war by people scavenging for wood in the abandoned houses. If the old inhabitants ever came back, they would have to see about restoring the Quarter. If . . .

At first, Sluyser and van Praag do not seem to describe the neighborhood in very different ways. For both, it serves as a backdrop for a theatrical performance, yet also has a life of its own. By calling up familiar images, they make individuals come alive in this theater. The scenes are familiar, the descriptions at times sentimental and full of clichés; yet their work is not pedestrian. These books are better and more meaningful than might appear from this description.

There are differences of degree, however, in emphasis and in the relationship between fantasy and narrative. In Sluyser's work, for example, it is the atmosphere that is most central; he directs a flickering, magic lantern at the mass of the Jewish proletariat. The journalist Osnowicz, on the other hand, allows the smells and the noise to drift into the room along with the sights, and the Friday evening meal around a white cloth-draped table takes on a festive air. Van Praag excels in remembering his old surroundings, and the people he found striking and whom he cherished. He deals with the Jews of the Spinoza Quay and Sarphati Street—hence not the proletariat. Finally, in Sal Santen's book, creatively reworked personal memories form the central theme; his neighborhood and the Jewish Quarter are the stage on which his autobiography is acted out.

For these writers, Amsterdam was "a body with a great hollow within its loins," as van Praag put it. In *Jeruzalem van het westen* [Jerusalem of the West], his great book about Jewish Amsterdam, the principle character was writing a book about the city. In the following passage van Praag explores his own motives through the thoughts of Ruben, his character:

> Why are you writing this book, Ruben? Do you want to rid yourself of the homesickness that you have for the lost world and give an exhaustive description of Jewish Amsterdam? He shook his head. Those times are over. . . . I believe my book is going to be one of sad wonder and of concern, always concern, for the future. For is it not true that every Jew who deeply loves his people is himself Israel's mother?
>
> People surge into my memory. Are they all naturally connected with one another, or must I artificially weave their fate into a novel? By what, then, are they united? [19]

The genocide that overtook the Amsterdam proletariat is so stamped on later works of literature that they can never convey the true atmosphere. The Israeli psychoanalyst Friedländer, in his *Reflections on Nazism*, maintained that no story about the war can ever capture its ghastly reality. Language is powerless in the face of so much inhumanity. In this, he was in part relying on the work of the literary scholar George Steiner, who discussed this claim at length in *Language and Silence*. The point specifically concerns the inability of the literary narrative when the horror is too dreadful for words to describe. Then the image, Friedländer felt, can more effectively convey the truth.[20] Therein lies the strength of *Shoah*, a nine-hour-long film made on the basis of interviews with victims and eyewitnesses of the Holocaust. The film's strength lies not in its realism but in the fact that literary conceit is replaced by visual images of what cannot be expressed in words.

I would go a step further than Friedländer. It is my impression that an eyewitness deals more effectively not only with murder but also in describing what has been murdered.

Aside from the stories, the streets that remain speak for themselves, and perhaps there is, after all, reason to long nostalgically for the past. Even now one can see existing houses that hint at their past beauty (for example on Uilenburg and Marken) and how the islands were oriented toward their links with the Zuider Zee. The barges left the city through the canals. Transportation was by water. Warehouses full of rags were not placed out there on the islands simply because rag dealing was a Jewish occupation. Quite the reverse: the warehouses were located close to the open water and the local people—Jewish people—worked there. In addition, of course, many Jews in Amsterdam and elsewhere traditionally traded in rags and other used goods.

Yet, despite the great numbers of people who must have been found there, the proximity of the harbor gave the streets a kind of beauty. In those days they lay near the sea, and even now that the sea has been replaced by fresh water through the building of a dam, the wind blows along the streets from that side, creating a special atmosphere. In those days it must have been a real sea breeze. Strangely, no one called attention to this; they wrote only of the loveliness of the place.

The ghetto, if one does away in imagination with the stench and the over-crowding, was beautiful. At the same time (and not without justification), it was reviled for its poverty and filth. This contrast was noted in an investigation of the Jewish working class in a number of European countries, written in 1898 by the still largely unknown author L. Soloweitschik. That work, a lengthy report in which the author notes the relatively favorable position of the Jewish working class in the Netherlands, describes the Amsterdam ghetto as follows:

> It is one of the oldest parts of the city, and the Jews there live packed one upon another in old houses. During the week, and above all on Friday morning, this is one of the filthiest parts of Amsterdam. Yet on Saturday this all changes. The streets are clean, the houses and sidewalks look newly washed, the old houses acquire a kind of dignity, and all this makes a great impression if one wanders the streets on a Saturday. Through a window one sees an old Jew wearing a velvet skull cap on his head, who after a week of work is now relaxing by studying the great books of the Middle Ages.[21]

Yet all descriptions have their limitations; overshadowed by the war, they can be written only in terms of mourning and nostalgia. Many of those I interviewed (whose turn comes later in this book) wished to contribute their own impressions, and I do not flatter myself by imagining that I have managed to free myself entirely from nostalgia. The only thing that I can do as a historian is to map out the forms and then ask myself why people employed the particular language they chose.

During the first half of the twentieth century the Jewish Quarter spread beyond the old ghetto and its neighboring streets. There was a large strip of the city on the Amstel River and along Weesper Street that was predominantly populated by Jews. Areas of Jewish concentration could be found in Lepel Street, Nieuwe Kerk Street, Vrolik Street, and Blasius Street. For those who were better off, there were the new streets in South Amsterdam. In chapter 4, the migration from the ghetto to these neighborhoods will be covered in a more systematic manner.[22]

DEMOGRAPHIC BACKGROUND (QUALITATIVE AND QUANTITATIVE) AND SOME PROBLEMS WITH NUMBERS

Statistics can give only a rough indication of the numbers of Jews in the country, and even direct census counts are always skewed by implicit decisions about who is Jewish, who must be regarded as Jewish, and who is to be included among the Jewish population. Thus the statistical data from the 1930 census were based on what people themselves gave in answer to the question concerning religion. It seems that many failed to count themselves as followers of the Jewish religion. The figures were therefore based on each individual's definition of Jewishness—a definition for which the critical factor was religion. Yet from such a definition, the most that can be extracted is an impression of the individual's attitude toward religion. Precisely at a time when assimilation was on the increase, and in a society in which socialism, free thinking, and modernity encouraged people to abandon religion, such figures must be treated with the greatest caution. The "fuzziness" inherent in the data becomes even greater through the increase in the number of mixed marriages and conversions during this period.[23]

Whole bookcases have been filled with writings on the question of who is a Jew. Halachic law states that only those born of Jewish mothers are to be regarded as Jews.[24] This law (which does not lend itself to concepts such as "half Jewish") has withstood centuries of Christian tradition based on patrilineal inheritance. There are others who regard the Jews as a people or nation, or what Anderson described as an "imagined community."[25] They are a group of people who, although they do not live in one country and perhaps are not even a single people, nevertheless regard themselves as belonging to a single community that persists in myths, legends, and stories. Others define Jewishness on the basis of a Zionistic ideal and declare every Jew to be a potential citizen of Israel. That was true even before the existence of Israel provided a basis for such a definition, but the disputes over the Law of Return show just how unclear descriptions like that can be.

Definitions of Jewishness based on limits on inheritance or other restrictive mechanisms do not seem satisfactory to me. It is crystal clear that many who scarcely thought of themselves as Jewish nevertheless continued to call themselves Jews, and that despite their ambivalence they did indeed feel themselves to be Jews. People did not think either that they were or that they were not. Being Jewish was an experience, a strategy for survival that could weigh heavily on one, but that one could either leave behind or cultivate. And, indeed, many of these attitudes could exist at the same time.

My position is to regard the Jews as a people and thus exclude those who were not members of the group. And, like Anderson, I am interested in precisely those people who in the 1920s and 1930s no longer regarded themselves as belonging statistically to the Jewish people, yet sometimes behaved and experienced their daily lives as Jewish and sometimes did not. For example, the archives of the Nederlands Israelitische Hoofdsynagoge [Principal Dutch Israelite Synagogue] contain a large number of letters from people who could not or would not pay their tithes because they no longer believed in the Jewish religion. Had they ceased to be Jews?

My interviews clearly show this ambivalence toward what is implied by being Jewish. J., whose father held a high position in the Algemene Nederlandsche Diamantbewerkers Bond or ANDB [General Union of Dutch Diamond Workers], the social-democratic diamond workers' labor union, was sent to a Jewish school. His family lived in the Transvaal, a neighborhood that was home to many members of the SDAP or Sociaal Democratische Arbeiders Partij [Social Democratic Workers' Party], who "thought individuals should not be judged according to their race or religion and that all people were equal. There was one single human race. There were no significant ties to a country, just the earth. Well, of course, there was Holland, . . . but there was the whole world." [26] My surprised questions in reaction to the contradictions implicit in the Jewish school, the fact that his father chose the Jewish "working hours," with Saturday free, and the breaking of all ties with tradition, elicited this response:

"Look, the average Jewish diamond worker didn't deny his Jewishness. He was simply part of the assimilated proletariat. That meant that they were absorbed in the broader mass as a group. Yet that didn't mean they denied their specific cultural characteristics. . . . Ties with the Jewish people were not broken; in fact, the opposite was often true. But it was a question of wanting to be absorbed by the whole. . . . It was a different kind of assimilation from what was found in the middle classes. Look, the truly assimilated person, the one who never mentioned or covered up—okay, was embarrassed by his

Jewishness—that wasn't it at all. Of course you were Jewish, but after all that meant nothing. You were a part of the international bond of human beings. You didn't have much to do with religion, though your speech was saturated with Jewish words. Your friends were all Jewish, and on Friday nights you ate well. You had a kind of respect for Jewish customs, even if you didn't keep them any more. That was no rejection of Judaism!"[27]

What answer should such people give to the question concerning their ideological bent? Some would undoubtedly classify themselves as Jewish, others would not. The distortion of the official Dutch figures arose through a kind of egalitarianism that refused to recognize in the statistics minorities that were nevertheless Dutch. Yet also those who no longer counted as Jews, simply because of the nature of the statistics, are part of twentieth-century Jewish history with its hope for emancipation and integration.

One of the reasons for identifying oneself as Jewish, one that has nothing to do with belief, can be to avoid offending the prejudices of others. But it can equally well be something that, like the preference for a particular funeral service, is a matter of identifying oneself with a tradition. Rationality, atheism, and adopting a modern and assimilated lifestyle can often find themselves in conflict with what the French historian Braudel called "the dungeons of time immemorial." Michel Vovelle, a French historian of ideas, wrote about the matter in these terms: "States of mind are thus above all a matter of remembrances, memory, forms of resistance, in other words what we can call ...'the inertia of mental structures.'"[28] Traditions, superstition, ways of life, and customs maintain themselves, albeit sometimes in new forms. Such things can be invoked because they are known to everyone.

The hidden persistence of cultural differences and traditions sometimes showed itself in "mixed marriages." This was graphically portrayed by the Jewish socialist writer Herman Heijermans in his 1904 novel 'n Jodenstreek [A Jewish Trick], in which the traditions of a Jewish man and his Christian wife clash again and again despite their intentions as enlightened people to pay no attention to such outdated differences. The wife turns out to be more Christian and (above all) the Jewish man far more Jewish than either had expected.

In 1904 mixed marriages were still rare, and ideas about them were determined by the expectation that such marriages could not turn out well. At the very least (certainly in Heijermans's view), the persons involved would first have to become socialists. Heijermans shows us, quite subtly, how substantial the cultural barriers are. Misunderstandings grow, the parents undermine and never accept the son- or daughter-in-law of the other faith. Eventually the old society, which needs to be done away with, succeeds in overpowering the new humanity.

Jews might believe that they were no longer Jewish. Yet however modern they might be and whatever their attitudes toward tradition, they are repeatedly victims of racism. They might wish it were otherwise, but their ideology, the realities of their lives, and their judgments regarding future opportunities for Jews in Holland are not necessarily based on a historically accurate picture. This criticism of the way in which the Dutch authorities collected and processed the statistical data must not be equated with the criticism of those same figures expressed by the occupying forces with their racist laws. The Germans also felt that too many Jews had been missed by the census. However, they included people in the Jewish population on the basis of racist politics and their fear of mixing the blood of racial groups. To maintain the racial purity of non-Jews, their goal was to define Jewishness as broadly as possible, and in this way to maximize the number of potential victims.

ECONOMIC BACKGROUND

AMSTERDAM'S SOCIOECONOMIC SITUATION

Amsterdam was a city with numerous mid-sized and small businesses,[29] and the harbor that employed virtually no Jews was the most important business of them all. It was in industry that the Jewish poor found employment.[30] Research shows clearly that industry was closely dependent on the transport of goods through the harbor and on the kinds of merchandise traditionally stored there.[31] When the harbor found itself in difficulties, industry also had a hard time. The foundation of that industry was the semi-finished goods that were exported through the harbor, and the raw materials such as diamonds and tobacco that were brought in through the same channels.

There was virtually no heavy industry in Amsterdam. This, combined with the way the harbor functioned, created an unstable economic situation in the city that was unusually sensitive to international trends. Economic recessions led almost immediately to massive layoffs, especially in the finishing trades such as those dealing with diamonds and tobacco. These two areas were closely interwoven. If even a diamond worker could no longer afford a cigar, then the bottom fell out of the market for the countless tobacco workers who made cigars at home.[32] On the other hand, both sectors of the economy enjoyed periods of rapid growth.

A number of writers have argued that the particular form of capitalism found in Holland induced a special kind of labor movement.[33] When trading capital dominates an economy, the labor situation differs substantially from the form it takes when dominated by fully developed industry-based capitalism. Life is more a matter of living from hand to mouth, and the solid foundation needed for an effective labor organization is not present. The close ties between trade and industry in Amsterdam created a situation and organization for workers in the city that was totally different from those found in cities with heavy industry.

A sharp distinction existed in the Amsterdam working class between those who worked in industry and other workers. Industry workers lived in a cultural climate that was totally different, and their political organization was also quite distinct from that of other workers. Harbor workers, for example, were often radically left-wing in outlook and anarchistically organized; they often lost in the struggle for better living conditions. On the other hand, workers in the growing industrial sector tended to enjoy successes.

Those achievements, however, were often diminished by threats to relocate industries to areas exhibiting less labor unrest or where the pay was lower.[34] The diamond industry, for example, was moved largely to Antwerp at the end of World War I (though the move had begun earlier). The practice in Antwerp of having much of the work done at home kept the wages low.[35] There were also threats to move the textile industry to the province of Twente in the east,[36] and clothing could be made more cheaply in the province of Zuid Holland. Further to the south in Brabant and Limburg, there were opportunities for exploiting workers in the cigar industry, and cigarette manufacture was also more lucrative there.[37] In the reports of the Amsterdam Chamber of Commerce and in the annual addresses of the chairman of that body, there are occasional references to progress and gains made by the harbor workers and those in industry, but words like "expansion" and "growth" rarely appear.

The SDAP recruited its members from the industrial working class and also organized the municipal officials and workers, who were traditionally organized on left-wing principles. On average they were paid more than similar workers elsewhere in the city. Since it was assumed that higher pay for these workers would tend to have a favorable influence on other pay scales in the city, support for their higher pay became part of the leftist platform in municipal politics. In his memoirs celebrating the 150th anniversary of the Chamber of Commerce in Amsterdam, the historian de Vries claimed that the higher pay enjoyed by municipal workers irritated other workers since it was one of the causes of Amsterdam's shaky economy.[38] In this way, he implicitly blamed the failing economy on the great influence of social democracy on municipal government.

To the extent that any industry existed at the end of World War I, it was not concentrated in one area. There were small industries in the Jordaan, the Pijp, and the Jewish Quarter. This, together with the middlemen (also operating on a small scale), determined the complexion of the city. Around 1900 a certain concentration occurred, especially in connection with the diamond industry, but the precise relationships that developed between the larger and the smaller concerns have not yet been investigated—and this is also true for the relationships between the various small concerns. Because of this, it is impossible to generalize about the way of life resulting from these circumstances.

For example, a tiny business that consists of the owner and his wife, perhaps helped by their children, produces a totally different set of labor relations and living conditions than those resulting when a business has even as few as five employees. I show in chapter 5 how often Jews worked in such kinds of small businesses—as peddlers, salespersons, cigarmakers, or carpenters. Often they were helped by family members. But without further research, it remains an open question as to how far the numbers of Jews engaged in such work differed proportionately from those found in other population sectors.

During the years between World War I and World War II, things did not go well for the harbor, nor for the local economy. Industrial activity continued to decline, and there was considerable unemployment and poverty. A sketch of economic trends during a given period is generally based on data drawn from major industries and the harbor. Production figures, national income, the turnover of merchandise, and quantities of goods produced are what count. These figures are derived from data concerning firms large and profitable enough to be counted.

Trends can also be determined or corrected on the basis of unemployment figures. This gives a more human picture of suffering and poverty. Another possibility is determining the number of positions available that provided reasonable wages—or investigating variations in requests for unemployment benefits made to municipalities and philanthropic organizations. These last two instruments suggest that throughout the interwar years, even during the 1920s, the economy of Amsterdam was depressed.[39]

Amsterdam's economy followed national trends: a brief recovery that lasted until about 1920, followed by a depression that started before the end of that year. The postwar boom was so marginal that it was scarcely noticed in the cigar and cigarette industry, liquor distilleries, and eau de cologne manufacturers. Printing, paper, and diamond industries began to decline in 1920. The trend rapidly extended to other sectors, and there was a drastic increase in unemployment, which was most serious in the luxury trade (cigars, tobacco, clothing, cocoa, printing, and diamonds). In the construction industry, unemployment was particularly high among painters.[40]

A slow, gradual economic recovery took place between 1923 and 1929. The first sign was an increase in traffic through the harbor. By 1926, industrial development was regarded as stable. The cigar industry, where a relatively high proportion of Jews worked, continued to experience problems despite government support. How many people were involved cannot be determined, due to large numbers who worked at home or independently. In 1926 there were only two cigar factories in existence, and one of those went under. The transfer of factories to areas with lower wages (or their conversion to cottage industries) had begun even earlier, but after the workers lost a five-month-long strike in 1913, it became an increasing trend. Cigarette manufacturers moved to areas where the owners were able to get away with paying lower wages. According to statistics in 1925, 44.5 percent of workers in that industry were unemployed, but the hidden unemployment among those who worked at home was much higher. In 1927, official unemployment decreased to 28.1 percent, but in the long run the improving economy was unable to rescue the industry. A similar pattern occurred in those sectors of the economy concerned with mirrors, clothing, baking, and diamonds; aside from very brief periods of recovery, things did not go well with them.

In other economic sectors, the Great Depression did not begin until the middle of 1930. The devaluation of the British pound in 1931 further worsened the situation. Among other things, a number of contracts (especially in the diamond industry) that had been drawn up in British pounds led to direct losses. The Scandinavian countries quickly devalued their currencies as well, making competition even harder for the Dutch.

An increase in electricity usage in 1933 makes it likely that some kind of improvement occurred in that year, but by then industry in general had already been weakened. The diamond industry was especially hard hit in 1929 when the Depression, which had been lurking in the wings since the end of World War I, assumed catastrophic proportions. By the end of that year 60 percent of the diamond workers were out of work. The following year, this grew to 67.9 percent, and by 1932 it was 84.3 percent. Government subsidies on the cutting and polishing of smaller stones helped little, and the competition from Antwerp meant that the situation in the 1930s was as bad as it had ever been. Diamond workers remained poor and unemployed. Excluding the diamond workers, there was a slight improvement in the city's economy beginning in 1937.

The depressed state of the wholesale sector between 1929 and 1936 hit the retail trade especially hard. It led to a worsening of the problems that had originally resulted from the reduced purchasing power of the local population. Statistics dealing with small industries help little in attempting to measure prosperity and in determining how far economic fluctuations affected it. This is even truer for firms operating in distribution. In that area, statistical analysis seems to have failed entirely, even in regard to the number of firms involved, until 1934, when a number of regulations were introduced that reduced the chaos.

There were many little shops that were not registered and many peddlers who were prepared to sell from their homes. A market stall-holder often had a little store in addition to his stall—and the same was often true for a peddler. There was great social mobility among storekeepers, market traders, and peddlers. This is obvious from applications to the municipality for permits related to peddling, market stall-holding, and retail storekeeping of foodstuffs. The same names crop up again and again in many different roles. A number of the people starting businesses had obviously been employed earlier as manual workers, even diamond workers.

How unclear this situation was can also be seen from the way figures were juggled during the Depression in Municipal Council debates when attempts were made to bring the distribution sector under control. For example, some communists and radical left-wing members of the Council contended that a proposal to reduce the number of licenses needed to set up a small store would ruin a lot of people and branded the proposal a mere extension of capitalistic interests. The SDAP, on the other hand, attacked this and found the proposed regulations *social*–democratic—a healthy kind of reform.[41] (Both parties were correct, for even good reforms can have victims!)

In fact, there had been a continual depression for many of Amsterdam's poor since the end of World War I. The difference between the 1920s and 1930s was, at most, a matter of temporary work occasionally being available during the earlier years. Yet even then people repeatedly had to rely on government welfare—which certainly was reduced in the 1930s but was not enough to live on even in the 1920s. All in all, throughout most of the 1918–1939 period, Amsterdam was characterized by unemployment, poverty, and an army of workers who depended for money on a variety of welfare sources and on scratching around for petty work. There were certainly short periods during which things improved, but for the most part few Jews worked in the sectors that were affected. In order to demonstrate this, we will first show where Jews worked—and whether this changed during the 1930s, the years of malaise and the Depression.

OFFICIAL EQUALITY AND UNOFFICIAL INEQUALITY: THE JEWISH ECONOMY

A report on the situation regarding refugees written in 1935 attempts to determine whether the refugees arriving from Germany posed any economic threat to the Jews of Amsterdam. This report points out that since 1815 there had been two government ministers of Jewish descent and not a single Jewish provincial governor or mayor. Of the 4,000 *wethouders* or municipal aldermen[42] in the country since that year, only 10 to 15 were Jewish, and there were only 7 Jews among the 590 members of the Provincial Council between 1815 and 1935. Moreover, the number of Jewish teachers was proportionately much lower than in the rest of the population.[43] Although the Jews had been officially emancipated more than a century earlier (in 1796) and officially enjoyed equal rights, they were nevertheless excluded from a number of professions. They concentrated their attention on certain areas in which, for the most part, the pay was lower, and for the rest they worked in various trades and in a few independent professions.

The structure of the labor market was quite different for Jews and non-Jews. This can be seen from two reports dating from 1926 and 1936. The tables contained in those reports (though not precisely comparable) show clearly that there was a "Jewish economy"—in other words, Jews were unevenly distributed through the various industrial sectors. Their distribution deviated significantly from the norms, both locally and nationally. Jews worked in a number

TABLE 1

PERCENTAGE OF JEWS IN VARIOUS OCCUPATIONS (1906 AND 1909)

	percentage of Jewish population in 1906		percentage of entire population in 1909	
occupation	male	female	male	female
Diamonds	29.2	9.8	5.4	1.5
Construction	1.3	—	11.3	0.2
Clothing and cleaning	2.9	17.1	3.5	21.2
Food	8.3	0.1	9.4	1.6
Other	4.5	1.1	19.0	2.9
Total in industry	46.2	28.1	48.6	27.4
Commerce	38.7	11.7	20.4	11.1
Transport	2.5	0.7	16.0	5.3
Agriculture and fishing	0.3	—	0.8	0.1
Independent professions	3.8	1.8	2.0	1.0
Domestic service	0.4	52.0	4.4	46.5
Civil servants	5.8	—	2.5	—
Unemployed	0.4	0.3	4.2	2.4
Other	1.9	5.4	5.1	6.2

The total for clothing workers is not correct, since those in cottage industry are not included. The high number of Jews in the retail sector results from the fact that storekeepers and peddlers are included. The number of women is high due to the fact that saleswomen are included. Tobacco is included in the food industry because it is a stimulant. According to van Zanten, young Jewish women worked mostly in the diamond and clothing industries. However, their proportion in commerce and domestic service increased as a result of the changing economy.

Source: J. H. van Zanten, "Eenige demografische gegevens over de joden te Amsterdam," *Mensch en Maatschappij*, vol. 1 (January 1926), pp. 8–9.

of specific sectors, while other sectors remained closed; only a distinct, limited labor market was open to them.

In his demographic research of 1926, van Zanten determined that the Jews were virtually limited to the diamond industry. Only a small number of Amsterdam Jews worked in other branches of industry. Table 1 gives some of the results from that study. The figures give the percentage of the population in question employed in each branch.

The differing distributions of Jews and non-Jews over the various sectors of the economy during the 1930s is confirmed by a report written for the Jewish support organization, American Jewish Joint Distribution Committee of New York. Table 2 gives the relevant figures. The table shows the percent-

TABLE 2

PERCENTAGE OF JEWS IN VARIOUS OCCUPATIONS (1936)

occupation	percentage of Jewish population	percentage of entire population of Amsterdam
Diamonds	8.0	2.0
Clothing	12.7	7.8
Food	7.7	6.0
Construction	1.0	7.2
Metal*	2.0	8.3
Textiles	0.6	0.2
Other industries	5.0	7.4
Total industry	37.0	38.9
Agriculture	0.1	0.8
Retail	45.0	20.9
Transport	4.5	14.4

* including bicycle sales and plumbing.

Source: Report on the Conditions of Jewish Social Work in Holland (Amsterdam, June 1936).

age of the Jewish population and of the entire population working in particular occupations. In addition to the areas shown in this table, Jews worked in banking, insurance, religious organizations, and teaching.

It is not meaningful to compare these two tables since the bases on which the statistics were obtained differ too much.

The different distribution of Jews as compared to non-Jews over the various sectors, and within sectors between the various occupations, derived originally from the refusal of many businesses to employ Jews. Or, rather, when there was a choice among applicants (which in periods of unemployment was generally quite considerable), non-Jews tended to be chosen. An example of this from the banking sector in given in chapter 5. The formal reason for not accepting Jews was often the different calendar. However, where there were large numbers of people who wished to be free on Saturdays (as in the diamond industry), "Jewish time" prevailed. On Thursday evening they worked extra late, on Friday they left early, Saturday was free, and Sunday was a workday.

Work was found by going along with someone—a brother, a sister, some other member of the family, or a friend. In this way, the Jewish labor market developed its own social stratification.

Certain occupations were more respectable, and this culturally-based judgment had its own effect on the labor market. In the diamond industry, for example, workers passed the trade on to their children and those of their closest colleagues. It was extremely difficult to enter the diamond industry from outside. Next to diamonds, working in the Bijenkorf [Beehive], a major department store, was respectable. For the better-educated children of people in the diamond industry or small shopkeepers, the Bijenkorf was the most sought-after place to work. In St. Antoniebree Street little drapery stores were established, mostly staffed by Jews, where each worker was properly ranked within the internal hierarchy of the store. Older sisters took younger ones along to the workplace, where they helped them slowly tread the long path that led from snipping little pieces of thread to cutting and sewing entire dresses. In trade, too, people helped each other, and peddling was almost exclusively open to Jews—something about which I will have more to say later.

I show in chapter 5 how the Depression throughout the 1930s made unemployment even worse in those sectors where many Jews worked—sectors that were already suffering far more than most. The Jewish economy was hardest hit, and hence the Jews suffered the greatest poverty. They had been poor for ages, and the brief blossoming of the diamond industry was not enough to free them from their economic inferiority. Their vulnerability is evidenced by their total lack of prospects for the future. Even when the economy as a whole improved at the end of the 1930s, their prospects did not.

THE SOCIAL AND POLITICAL LIFE
OF THE PROLETARIAN JEWS

PROLETARIAN CULTURE: THE RISE OF THE ANDB
AND ITS INFLUENCE

In this book I deliberately call the culture of the Jewish poor "proletarian" because the proud proletariat of the diamond workers with its aggressive socialism had a strong influence (both positive and negative) on them. I have not adopted a strictly class-based analysis in which those diamond and clothing workers who depended entirely on wages for their income are distinguished from the peddlers, the small storekeepers, and a proletariat clothed in rags; all fall under the concept "Jewish proletariat." As a matter of fact, this entire group was a *Lumpenproletariat*, not a middle class at all, since it barely held its head above water. Neither was it a working class, since these people did not work in large numbers in manufacturing.

It cannot be emphasized too strongly how vital the influence of the diamond workers' trade union—the ANDB—was, both on the development of the modern trade union movement in Holland and on the factors that raised the Jewish poor out of their misery. The principles of organization underlying the ANDB provided the foundation for modern unionism. These principles influenced the SDAP via the Amsterdamsche Bestuurders Bond (ABB), the coordinating body of the Dutch trade unions, in which the leaders met for discussions and mutual consultation. This influence led to the development of union strategy—concentration on achieving small victories that did not necessarily involve pay raises.

Over and above the struggle for better pay, the ANDB concentrated its attention on improving the quality of life for its members. The union fought for the eight-hour workday and was the first to see this introduced in those areas for which it was responsible. As a result, its members could begin to enjoy some free time—time in which to organize—and (the ANDB hoped) to develop some degree of culture. Its members were to develop from a rude mass into a group of civilized workers.

The formation of the ANDB took place during a strike in 1894. Henri Polak and Jan van Zutphen managed to neutralize the opposition between the Jewish and non-Jewish diamond workers, thus bringing together in a single union everyone—both male and female—who worked in the production process,. By overcoming the differences between the Jews and the others, the centralized ANDB was formed, providing a model for the workers' movement in other sectors.[44]

The power of the diamond workers depended in part on the fact that many of them were simultaneously both workers and traders, which made their bosses more dependent on them than was the case in other sectors. They were able to assemble sizable reserves of money to support strikers for long periods.

The union not only concentrated on organizational matters, it also paid much attention to raising the standards of its members. Originally, diamond workers were thought of as a rather crude and uncivilized group who spent most of their wages in cafés. Scarcely ten years after the formation of the ANDB, its members formed a cultural elite within the working class. Week after week they read Polak's advice in their paper, the *Weekblad*, on how a modern worker ought to think and live. His editorials ranged over all kinds of topics: from the fact that the world is a single unity within which all people are equal and in which it is old-fashioned and counter to the goal of emancipation to maintain traditions, through to advice on how to furnish a home appropriately—no longer full of little flounces, but more sparsely, with simple, good, easily maintained furniture.

To be a diamond worker, and therefore inevitably also to belong to the ANDB, had become a way of life. In the *Kaapse Tijd* [Cape Period], from 1876 through 1879, when money was plentiful, this found expression in the purchase of nothing but the very best—French furniture and luxuries, big houses in the Plantage neighborhood—and the rejection of the typical Dutch custom of saving money. After all, you could pick up a grindstone in the morning and use it to earn as much as you wished anywhere you wished. So why save money? No one knew what tomorrow would bring!

The ANDB had a library, and arranged cultural events for its members and their children. In short, it was a cultural organization. Because it was so closely tied to the rise of Jewish workers, it left its mark on many other activities in the Jewish Quarter. The emancipation of the Jewish working class influenced the way in which the poor thought about how they could improve their lot. In his study of the Jewish workers' movement in central and western Europe, *Le pain de la Misère* [The Bread of Misery], the Belgian writer Nathan Weinstock correctly pointed out how exceptional the position of the Jewish working class in Amsterdam was compared with that of their counterparts elsewhere.[45] They would not hear of an organization based solely on their Jewishness.

Weinstock regarded as unique the Jew's solidarity with the rest of the working class, and the way in which their interests were so closely inter-woven with those of the larger group. He quoted Sam de Wolff, the leftist Zionist activist, to illustrate his surprise that the Jewish influence on the SDAP had been so strong that its leaders sometimes even made use of Talmudic expressions.[46] He asked himself why this was so; what had given rise to this network of interrelatedness between the Jews and the national workers' movement? The fact that the two groups lived in separate neighborhoods and, to some degree, worked in distinct economic sectors would lead one to expect that they would organize into separate movements. Among the reasons he suggested for the development that occurred was that no one was conscious of any real difference between Jews and non-Jews, and that there was little anti-Semitism among the lower classes in general. To the contrary, Jewish and non-Jewish workers seemed to experience a powerful kind of solidarity with each other in their daily lives.[47]

Weinstock's view is one-sided. He takes too much for granted the idea that Jews and non-Jews generally live apart, organize apart, hate each other, and that the stronger inevitably persecute the weaker. He lays too much emphasis on central and eastern Europe, where the anti-Semitism of the masses was quite virulent. Yet despite the fact that the Jews in Holland were in a more favorable position, we cannot ignore the fact that there was a division within the ANDB (and later within the SDAP) between Jews and non-Jews. Despite the fact that the SDAP was a party full of Jews, some anti-Semitism could be found even within its ranks, or (and this is something quite different) the Jews were regarded as "strange."

Amsterdam was the only city in western Europe where the leading group of the Jewish proletariat worked in industry. As a consequence, Jewish social-ism developed as a distinctly *industrial* tradition in cultural and ideological bias and was the expression of a consciously organized working class. This differed sharply from socialism in cities such as Paris and London, where Jewish interests were generally those of the small shopkeeper. There, the specifically Jewish socialism of the sweatshops and peddlers' pushcarts had little to do with the development of trade unionism; it was a far less practical struggle. In both instances, of course, there was a dream of better times to come. In Amsterdam, however, that dream had a more practical foundation and was more closely bound to the non-Jewish trade union movement.[48]

But it would be wrong to compare the ANDB (as so often happens in nostalgic tales) with the workers' movement of the Russian Jews—the Bund—which was so powerful and around which so many myths grew up. A comparison between that movement and the workers' movement in the United States also suggests itself quite readily. Those are the two other countries where a tradition of industrial struggle existed among the Jews. Yet it is hard to compare the Dutch movement with the Bund since the latter was a specifically Jewish organization that was the expression of a Jewish *national* movement. It was also a political party.

The Bund's Jewish nationalism was a reaction to the double oppression of Jewish workers under the czars—they were oppressed as *workers* and also as *Jews*.[49] The Jews in Russia had to organize in an extremely repressive society where it was impossible to form a powerful trade union movement that could really help its members. Every organization was ruthlessly suppressed. The Bund was far larger than any workers' organization in Holland, but it found itself within a society in which anti-Semitism was rampant. There was not the slightest chance of a socialist future in which all would be equal irrespective of nationality—which was the philosophy of the ANDB. Equality between the various ethnic and cultural groups was unthinkable in czarist Russia.[50]

The other comparison already suggested was with the Jewish workers' movement in the United States. There, too, the movement developed within the context of industrial relationships. However, in America, the Jews were immigrants. They were employed as scabs. They arrived from Europe so exhausted and persecuted that they were willing to take on any sort of work imaginable—even work as strike-breakers. The immigrants joined the Bund and the anarchistic movement, which was dominated by Jews. Beyond that, all comparison ends. The specific nature of American society, in which the Jews were simply one of many minorities and in which it was normal for each minority to organize as a separate unit, makes it impossible to pursue any other analogies.[51]

Because of the dominance of the ANDB in Holland, ideas for a separate *Jewish* workers' movement never took root. Indeed, the ANDB never had to mount any explicit opposition to them. Henri Polak was perfectly aware of the problem of Jewish nationalism.[52] (Here we are dealing with non-Zionistic nationalism. Zionism will be dealt with separately below.) But feelings of Jewish nationality did not belong so much in the workers' movement as in the religious populism of Rabbi de Hond, in tradition, and in the outdated ideas expressed by a little group of east European immigrants in the Yiddish cultural society AnSki.[53] There was an attempt to found a Jewish workers' union (Betsalel, the Union of Jewish Workers and Clerks) in 1895, a year after the founding of the ANDB, but it never really succeeded. The union remained very small.

The socialism of the ANDB and the related SDAP must be distinguished not only from populism but also from three other movements: left-wing liberalism, communism, and Zionism.[54] Only the first of these enjoyed a significant following among the Jews of Amsterdam. At the end of the nineteenth century, those among the Jewish working class who were able to vote because of the size of their incomes supported mostly the Radikale Bond [Radical Alliance]. At the time, the radicals were the most modern in their thinking; they created the Handwerkers Vriendenkring [Friends of the Manual Worker], a fund for workers that was to play an important role in the construction of housing. Although the modernizing influence of the progressive liberals was already organized from 1901 in the Vrijzinnig Demokratische Bond [Democratic Alliance of Free Thinkers], some support for the non-socialist progresive ideas remained among the better-off Jewish working class. There were also many members of the Jewish proletariat who voted liberal democrat between the wars out of opposition to socialism.

There was little support for communism. To vote for communism represented a radical break with the Jewish past. Although there were some who regarded membership in the SDAP of Amsterdam as a break with Jewishness, there were so many Jews in the organization that membership in no way resulted in a real loss of Jewish culture. With few exceptions, the communist party hardly ever used the Yiddish expressions that were common among non-Jewish social democrats.[55] As a result of their cultural isolation, Jews in the communist party constantly sought contact with each other.

Finally, Zionism was marginal and primarily something that concerned the well-to-do. Until somewhere between 1933 and 1935 it did not concern the proletariat.[56] As a result of German politics after 1933, the Zionist movement grew rapidly, especially socialist Zionism.

As has been pointed out already, the ANDB was originally an elite that set its mark on the Jewish proletariat through its influence. From the turn of the century this elitism was no longer true due to the decline of the diamond industry. The social mobility between the diamond workers and the others increased so radically that it becomes meaningless to describe them separately from the poor or the peddlers. They were unemployed far too often. Although they maintained some pride in their occupation and although they felt themselves to be more cultured, an unemployed diamond worker was nevertheless often forced to set up a little store or stand behind a stall in the market. The cultural differences between organized workers and others began to disappear. Unemployment was rife. What was once the proud culture of the diamond workers steadily degenerated into the lost glory of an increasingly rough group of hard-core unemployed.

Former diamond workers provided me with countless examples of this.

The "modernity" of those who lived in the new socialist neighborhoods that had sprouted in the eastern part of the city was nothing more than poverty shared by the employed and unemployed alike. At the most, there were differences in attitudes toward the education of the children and in the attempts to ensure that the children would get on in life. It was a matter of uncertainty for practically all of them as to whether they would be able to continue living there, whether they would keep their jobs, and whether they would continue to earn any money at all.

The elite group of relatively well-off workers had disappeared forever, absorbed into the mass of the poor. Their culture and ideals persisted a little longer than their money, but in time even those diminished.

Those who went through the experience bear witness to the decline and to the increasingly coarse atmosphere in the workplace. In the following interview, B. tells about the poverty and emptiness that lay behind the façade of socialist culture. During the 1930s he was unemployed, and his tale shows just how little remained of the hope that a shining new dawn would bring with it a totally changed life:

"The dwellings weren't actually tenements—they just had nothing inside them. . . . It was like this: people who had a place to live just couldn't keep up with the rent. There were plenty of vacancies, so they just moved from neighborhood to neighborhood. Because they couldn't pay the rent. And then the landlord would offer to paper the walls a bit—if they would just come and live there. But there were a whole lot of people who couldn't keep going in an apartment. Because of the rent. And then they just got poorer and poorer. Let me put it this way. From a sort of respectable neighborhood, they would drop down and down to poorer and poorer neighborhoods. And so they would end up on Zand Street or on Rapenburg—the people from East Amsterdam. . . . Those who had nothing to live on just got worse and worse." [57]

Proud ANDB members, who had talked for hours on end about music, Henri Polak, and the cultural richness of the Amsterdam diamond workers, told how little of this was left once the holes in their shoes could not be mended any more, clothes fell off their backs, and unemployment was more normal than work. Sometimes, through the shame that followed the economic crash, they fell into rough ways. Their culture seemed little more than a thin layer of varnish. Those were painful memories; they conflicted sharply with the nostalgia felt for the ANDB.

R. told me about the climate during this time in the factories, where ANDB members worked—men who had been the prototypes of better culture among the workers. The cruelty, presented as little jokes, was sometimes terrible. There were rough sexual jokes, such as men smearing a salesgirl they had undressed with the paste left over from the grinding operations. And there was the man who thought he had lost all his trading goods:

"The man began to bawl like a little kid. He must have been about 60 at the time. All his little disks (which were what he sold) had disappeared. They had hidden them in a closet. He said, 'I've nothing to eat today; what am I to do?' 'Well, go and look somewhere else for some disks, because we don't have them here.' They were that crude. Well, he went back home but an apprentice followed him with some money in an envelope. For four weeks we didn't see a sign of him; he just went off boozing with the money he had gotten from the diamond workers. . . . They were pretty crude but then they tried to make it up with money. . . . They didn't really understand what they were doing, and they thought everything could be fixed with money. But that isn't always so. That girl (the one they smeared with grinding paste), it seems to me, she got a real psychological shock."[58]

For years the ANDB had been trying to raise the Jewish working class to new levels and to carry them toward the rosy dawn—or at least to give them a glimpse of that dawn. Building on the premise that there was unity between Jewish and non-Jewish workers, they created a climate in which it was possible to turn from the ghetto without losing touch with Jewish culture. The SDAP, the party in which so many Jews were active, took over that culture.

As the elite of the social democratic movement, the diamond workers continued to leave their mark on the party and on its life for many years. The way in which they organized is reminiscent of the organization principles associated with eastern Europe, even though the conditions in Holland did not lead to the establishment of separate institutions. Little remained of their proud culture. It was in the "Jewish economy" that the Depression became worst. From an elite they were transformed into a prime example of the misery produced by the Depression. Yet, despite all that, they often remained in the SDAP, firmly rooted in the industrial tradition. That was true even when only a tiny fraction of the Jewish population continued to work in industry. Because of this fact, I have chosen to continue to write about them as the *proletariat*. Beside being descriptive, it also reflects a matter of choice.

SOCIAL-DEMOCRATIC MUNICIPAL POLICY:
ORGANIZATION AND CIVILIZATION

Since the social democrats were first voted into the Amsterdam Municipal Council in 1902, they attempted to carry out the municipal program devised by P. L. Tak.[59] This program provided guidelines for municipal organizations that were designed to improve the quality of life for people living in large cities. At the same time, the results of municipal policy are intended to serve as propaganda. The people had to see for themselves that the socialists really could make changes in their lives. This became possible in 1913 when, for the first time, the SDAP was able to put forward one of the elected aldermen— Frank Wibaut.[60] From that time on, the SDAP increasingly influenced municipal policy—even in those years when the SDAP had no aldermen on the Municipal Council. Amsterdam provided a particularly good example of social democratic municipal government and served as a model for other cities where socialists had a say in local administration.[61]

The paper *De Gemeente* [The Municipality], the publication of the Vereniging van Sociaal–Democratische Gemeenteraadsleden [Association of Social–Democratic Municipal Council Members], provided information between 1918 and 1940 about what had been achieved. In addition, there were more theoretical discussions in *De Socialistische Gids* [The Socialist Guide] concerning the possibility of controlling the free market and, through relatively minor regulations, bringing an end to the chaos of capitalism. The municipal politicians and theoreticians[62] formed a counterweight to the more radical wing in the SDAP, which felt there would be no real improvements until the party was able to join the government or, even later, until the beginning of a socialist society.

The pragmatic approach was strengthened in 1918 when the chairman of the radical wing of the SDAP expressed his revolutionary ideas in such an extreme form that many conservatives, democrats, and members of Christian denominational parties became increasingly alarmed at the thought of the rise of socialism.[63] After his failed attempt at something that looked like a revolution, a committee was set up to put together a platform in which economic reforms would gradually be introduced in such a way as to make socialism possible over time. Along with the municipal program already mentioned, which dealt far more with areas such as health care, housing, and the provision of a minimum basic standard of living, the *Socialisatierapport* [Socialization Report] they produced provided guidelines for socialist economic policy in the years to come.[64] On the one hand, the report recommended gradual changes in those sectors crucial to the economy as a whole; on the other hand, it dealt with ways of regulating mid-sized and small businesses.

Especially the unregulated growth of small businesses was an irritant to the municipalities. It was impossible to plan in the face of such development, since it could not be properly organized. There was also murderous competition, which in turn led to reduced wages and made it impossible to regulate working time. Attempts had already been made during World War I to gain some control over those firms operating as middlemen. Hunger made it important for the authorities to maintain control over the quantities of foodstuffs distributed, and this laid the foundation for municipal regulations governing the sale of foodstuffs. After the war, attempts were made to broaden the area under control so as to ensure that everyone had access to affordable food. This was expressed in the struggle concerning public testing of milk quality and in connection with the importation of inexpensive meat.

The foundations of this policy can be found in the brochure *De weg van producent tot consument* [The Path from Producer to Consumer], written in

1931 by the social-democratic alderman Rodriguez de Miranda. This was
consciously aimed at the middle classes, who would be negatively affected by
such an effort by the authorities to control the situation.[65] Any attempt to
control the distribution sector would involve regulations dealing with retail
stores, open-air markets, and peddlers. At the same time, this development
would have to be integrated into the national policy regarding the middle
classes.[66] The high point of the program that began with the Socialization
Report was, in fact, the social democrats' *Plan van de Arbeid* [Plan for Socialist Employment Policy] introduced in 1934, which proposed a semi-Keynes-
ian policy to deal with the Depression by means of generous government
spending.[67]

At the municipal level, de Miranda gave form to this through a plan of his
own. In effect, that policy was a matter both of reform and of regulation,
which in practice meant strengthening the ordinances governing the permits
needed to open a business. The fact that not every diamond worker ended up
behind a peddler's pushcart was in large measure due to this policy; no matter
how much they might have wished it, the new regulations made obtaining a
permit almost impossible. Attempts to increase the spending power of the
population during the 1930s were not successful, and any increase in purchasing power resulted from the fact that the Depression itself was easing.

To make the economic reforms effective at the local level, a degree of
independence from the national government in The Hague was needed. It was
also necessary if the municipal programs were to be carried out. The Municipal Council, dominated as it was by social democrats, had to do battle on two
fronts. The first was against The Hague, which was intent on carrying out a
blinkered social policy based solely on economizing, and the second against
the Chamber of Commerce, which tried to exploit every opportunity provided
by a power vacuum in national policy to turn this to the advantage of big
business.[68] The municipality emphasized its independence in 1924 when
Wibaut, in his executive capacity, succeeded in obtaining a loan of 22 million
guilders from some English banks after the Amsterdam banks had refused to
provide one. Even though the local banks formed only a part of the Chamber
of Commerce, this represented a victory for the municipality.

Yet their independence was very limited. This was clear from the number of
times the national government in The Hague refused to approve the municipal
budgets and many social ordinances passed by the council. There were even
cases where municipal decisions failed to win approval at the provincial level.
Examples of this are the provision for extra bathhouses in working-class neighborhoods, which was not approved, and problems with rendering welfare.[69]
Moreover, a new law controlling municipalities was passed in 1929 that abolished the existing system of municipal taxation. Collection was centralized and
a portion of the taxes was returned to the municipalities. Amsterdam thus lost
its independent source of income, making it impossible for it to carry out an

autonomous social policy. To be unemployed now meant the same in Amsterdam as in other places, and most of the social ordinances introduced by the socialists fell away as a result of the national policy of economizing.

In addition to its economic program, the municipality wished to carry out its original reform plan. In the first place, housing had to be constructed. The *Woningwet* [Housing Act] of 1901 provided possibilities for this. The question was who would construct the housing and how much profit should they make. The SDAP (above all because of Wibaut) managed to initiate the building of public housing in Amsterdam on a major scale. Other results of their initiative were the building of bathhouses and laundries, the spread of public utilities (in this they adopted the liberal program), and the improvement of teaching, infant care, and health care. These improvements would very possibly have been made even in the absence of socialism, but it was a political struggle to determine how much the public had to pay for them. In this struggle, the SDAP came down on the side of government subsidy and of affordability.

The socialists played the same role in the modernization process elsewhere in Europe, and even on an international level there was an exchange of ideas on such issues. The public housing of Amsterdam attracted international attention even before the SDAP came into power in municipal government. Amsterdam served as a model for Hamburg and Bremen, as can be seen from the archives of the relevant municipal officials. Vienna was a shining example of how good housing could be provided for the working class and how the finances of their families could be kept in order. But the radicalism that lay at the heart of Viennese politics was not popular. Austro-Marxism, which blossomed after the socialists' election successes after World War I, made free use of terms such as "revolution" and appeared to be far more radical than the Amsterdam socialists both in economic policy and in the struggle for municipal autonomy.

Yet the difference was smaller than one might expect on the basis of the underlying ideas. Although the work of someone like the Austrian Marxist Adler to elevate the working class is certainly much more radical in spirit than the achievements of an alderman like the Jewish social-democrat de Miranda who held the portfolio for foodstuffs in Amsterdam, the strategies behind them were much the same.

In Vienna, as in Amsterdam, there was an immense poverty-stricken Jewish and non-Jewish working class, which had to be led toward the rosy dawn. In addition, in both places, it was necessary to show not only that the socialists could institute a revolution but that once in power they really would do something for the people. The effects of government housing construction served as propaganda in both cases. Various statistical studies argued for supervision and control of the city budgets for this construction in Austria,[70] and the Bureau of Statistics played precisely the same role in Amsterdam. Furthermore, there were many unfinished and unpublished studies as notes and memoranda in the archives of the Amsterdam aldermen. People trusted the power of figures—they would provide the foundation for a socialist municipal policy that would banish poverty and misery.

The SDAP was also the party that led the struggle to turn the members of the Amsterdam working class into "modern" (i.e. respectable) people. The model was the educated working man, a vision that received its clearest expression in the association for youth, the Arbeiders Jeugd Centrale [Central Workers' Youth Organization].[71]

The Amsterdam sociologist A. de Regt shows how, starting in 1870, the working class was approached first by the radicals with all kinds of strategies intended to make the masses more easily handled, more civilized, and better educated. In Amsterdam, the leadership in this offensive was taken from the outset by the SDAP.[72] I show in chapter 4 that this amounted to a kind of disciplining for some of the Jewish proletariat. Those who failed to comply were excluded.

In relation to this, de Regt writes:

> When their behavior fell far below the norms of respectability and decency, their very proximity became unbearable. Private homeowners, building cooperatives, and municipalities made use of these attitudes to evict unacceptable families from their lodgings—to protect their own possessions, of course, but also "following the wishes of good tenants." In this way, what had been a fluid difference between respectable and less respectable families became sharper and was formalized into the distinction between "respectable" and "unacceptable" families.[73]

In the case of the Jewish proletariat of Amsterdam, the process of disciplining also involved bringing them into line with non-Jewish culture, so that they turned away from old customs before they were able to replace them with new ones. They were expected to adopt a new, socialist morality as their way of life, and these changes naturally led to ambivalence and uncertainty. Jewish culture was so devalued that only what was modern, social, and new was regarded as respectable. Ghetto life was not respectable almost by definition. A whole system of social supervision was based on the disciplinary process, the best-known example being the housing inspections. These were carried out by female inspectors who determined whether one's house was being kept in a respectable fashion.

The Jewish workers were also expected to be "modern"—socialist not merely in conviction but also in behavior.[74] The ideal family, as conceived of in the upper working class, served as the socialist model. It consisted of a small family, the father in a permanent job, the mother tidy and focused on the immediate family, and not too tied to relatives. The policies were designed to increase the number of families that met such norms.

Alongside this picture of what for them was worth striving for, the interviews made it clear that it had become important to deny what was specifically theirs, what was Jewish. Were Jewish customs worthy of approval or should they be discouraged? Were they really obsolete, or were the social reformers mistaken? Sometimes the process received approval; sometimes the interviews were filled with harsh words concerning the extent of the disciplining. Mostly, the dilemma was expressed through confusion. An active process of acculturation, of passing on a new civilization, if successful, is not simply something that outsiders do to "unhappy" victims. What distinguishes it is that the new norms become internalized and everyone becomes part of the process. At least in hindsight, looking back on the process, one is often happy to have become more civilized.

CONCLUSION

Despite formal integration into the broader society and the fact that this succeeded more in Amsterdam than in many other places, a Jewish proletarian group lived in the city between 1918 and 1940. Their economic situation was clearly different from that of the rest of the population. Their geographic distribution, as well as their traditions and history, were not the same as those of the rest of the people in the city. At the same time, their concern for international socialism distinguished the Jewish poor of Amsterdam from their counterparts in other west European cities.

The kind of socialism that was popular in Amsterdam was linked to a climate of municipal politics, which, within Holland, was unique to that city. Municipal policy, which was strongly influenced by Jewish aldermen such as Rodriguez de Miranda, Eduard Polak, Boekman, and the progressive democrat Abrahams, exerted a great deal of influence on the way of life of the Jewish proletariat before World War II. This resulted primarily from the fact that the policies in question encompassed an active process of civilizing or acculturation that denied and indeed attacked that which was unique about Jewish identity. At the same time, the Jews were so deeply integrated into the social structure of the city that the advantages of the civilizing process did not pass them by. The interviews show above all how successful it was, for the norms that were instilled forty years earlier were now internalized.

Can interviews show us more than a reflection of internalized norms? Is there a layer of stories and memories beneath that can give us more insight into it? In the chapters that follow, such questions are central to the discussion of the changes in the Jewish proletariat.

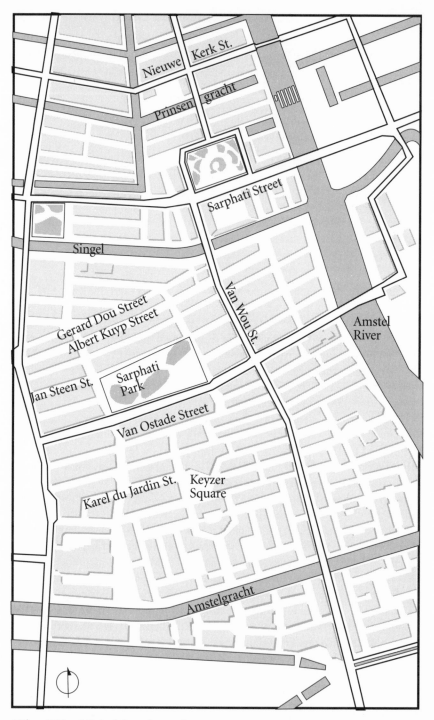

The Pijp Neighborhood

CHAPTER THREE

THE OLD NEIGHBORHOOD

THE LITERARY TESTIMONY

Those who lived in the old Jewish Quarter dwelt in misery and filth, surrounded by poverty. Between the Prins Hendrik Quay and the Amstel River, a huge garbage dump developed where those who could afford nothing better made their homes. It is true that some of the worst buildings were demolished and replaced between 1918 and 1929 in the expectation that this would improve the neighborhood as a whole. Yet the ghetto culture of poverty and (as many believed) backwardness survived these changes. Some of the local people found this perfectly acceptable; for them, it was dependable and safe, it was their way of life.

The loss of this closed society, and with it the social norms that guided the behavior of the people, was equated by some with the fall of the Jewish religion, and indeed of Jewishness itself. Perhaps the most notable among them was the rabbi of the poor, Meijer de Hond. A Hasidic figure who had been denied the formal title of rabbi, he was nevertheless honored as one, and it was he who provided the driving force behind the endeavor to maintain strict adherence to tradition even among the poor.

The threat of assimilation into non-Jewish culture led him to glorify conditions in the busy neighborhood. How could it have been otherwise? Precisely in that area, where it seemed everyone said the ghetto made life impossible, his followers not only managed to live but maintained the old traditions and continued as they always had done, experiencing both happiness and sorrow. So there was no reason to turn suddenly against the ghetto. He believed that the aversion people felt toward the old neighborhood resulted more from socialist propaganda, which he considered a threat, than from the situation itself. In his 1926 book *Kiekjes* [Snapshots] and in many less-well-known writings, he tried to characterize the everyday joy in eternity that he saw around him.

The nostalgia of this eyewitness is diametrically opposed to the attitude of

the social realist, Herman Heijermans, whose well-known novel *Diamantstad*
[Diamond City] sketches the activities and sufferings of the inhabitants of the
Jewish Quarter. His writing was shaped not only by his desire to present a
picture of the world as he saw it but also by contemporary socialist literature.
In the Netherlands, Heijermans is best known for his realistic plays; aside
from those, his contributions on literature to the socialist movement under the
pseudonym Sperber brought him some notoriety.[1] He maintained that any
attempt to portray reality, as in realistic theater, never yielded a truly accurate
picture of the real world, and therefore he chose to adopt an overt political
stance.

The literature based on the Jewish Quarter was either black or white. One
defended the old ways, and the other the new. This was a choice between
extremes; no one attempted a compromise. In that sense, the literature of the
old Jewish neighborhood was always inescapably polemical—an expression
of one author's attitude toward what the future should hold for Jewish traditions and culture.

Heijermans, brought up in a milieu in Rotterdam that took assimilation for
granted, was horrified by the ghetto; as a socialist, he wanted nothing whatever to do with it. The world, viewed with such distaste from within the home
where he grew up, had to disappear, to be replaced. He saw the slum dwellers
as dirty, rough, and coarse. The caricature in *Diamantstad* of the Jew who
fretted his way through life was an expression of his contempt for and horror
of that way of life.

He pitied those who lived in a slum in the year 1906. This finds expression
in the following passage, where he is describing the water rising in a basement dwelling:

> "Bloody hell, just look at that! . . . Just come and take a look at it! . . .
> You'll all drown! . . . What a bloody shame! . . . And that's what it's like all
> the time, every time the water rises a bit, that's what we get. Come and get
> an eyeful of that!" . . .
> Together they stood, shoulder to shoulder—the door was really small—
> looking into the cellar with its flooded floor. On the white wooden table
> stood a small lamp that gave a flickering glow to the water, filthy water that
> rose above the red tiles and the deep, dark joints between them, which for
> all the world looked like a checkered spider's web. The plastered white
> walls rose abruptly, sharply pale against the darkness of the beams above.
> In a bed niche with wide open doors sat three children, frightened into
> wakefulness. The youngest, a little girl with an ashen face, sobbed as if in
> pain, and as the tears fell she rubbed her little fists so hard into the hollows
> of her eyes that her cheeks were soaked with tears.
> "Shut your mouths!" the woman raged. She had taken off her shoes and
> socks, wound her black dress high around her hips, knotted the cords on her
> bloomers well above the knees, and was trying to mop the water into a pail.
> . . . The stench of filth that has been brewing in warmth for ages and the

disgusting smell of sewers and cesspools, released by the flood, rose above the mirror-smooth surface of the water the woman was attempting to bail out.[2]

His horror shows clearly not only through such accounts but also in his descriptions of the people themselves:

In the still air hung the stench of the islands Marken and Uilenburg, oozing from ancient, creaking houses that were propped up tightly against each other. There, creeping up in his memory, was the venerable, gray, gloomy life within the houses, where the shadows shrank away from the walls, where light scarcely penetrated, and where eternal darkness sapped the strength of the women and received from their heavy bellies the wailing newborns—where everything was fruitful yet never shone the sun. There he knew the drowsiness of innumerable courtyards and blind alleys, gray cement and drab, dying brickwork—the coming and going of Jewesses, withered and pasty in their kerchiefs and beribboned caps—the grubby little games of the red-eyed urchins—the shadowy night surrounding these tiny, glowing, overheated rooms where the lamps hung and lips sighed.[3]

He told how the main character, the "faithful Jewish people," degenerated in this way, "dying without ever having lived their own lives, dying in the shells of old, sad, dreaming houses—poor shadows of an erstwhile lovely dream—how they would now forever have no choice but to hate."[4] And of course he included himself in this.

In his earlier novel, *Sabbath*, he was more sympathetic. Although even there, in vivid, realistic sketches, he expressed his outrage, at the same time he displayed some positive feelings toward the atmosphere of rest enjoyed by the eternally toiling proletariat on Friday evenings. Of course, this attitude was compatible with that found in the rising wave of socialism, which from the start sought to bring about the six-day week. *Sabbath* shows how necessary one day of rest was for the exhausted outcasts, and how well they knew how to employ such free time.

This earlier novel was less deeply marked by Heijermans's own desire to distance himself from the life of the ghetto. Indeed, the pictures he painted of Friday evenings in the narrow streets, where it grew dark so early and the candles were lit behind the windows, are full of love. Behind that love lay a kind of poverty that, despite all the sorrow, valued itself and was keenly aware that things were better somewhere in the world. The description avoids nostalgia and is shot through with a vision of hope: a better world was sure to come—even to the people of the Jewish neighborhood. Heijermans's work can justly be called "antinostalgic."

But there are other writings, unlike these, that identify with poverty, confusing it with the preservation of tradition. The world of the ghetto, along with its poverty, is seen as the old world, and thus poverty is viewed as romantic, something we can look back on with longing. This literary tradition continued well into the twentieth century, the principle representative being the Jewish woman writer, Sani van Bussum. In her novel *Een bewogen vrijdag op de Bree Straat* [A Gentle Friday in Bree Street], she continued to romanticize the Jewish ghetto even in 1930, when it no longer existed except in her pages, where indeed it seemed to live on. Even in her later work, *Het Joodsche Bruidje* [The Jewish Bride], she gave the impression that nothing had changed. As an orthodox Jewish woman in a time of change, she longed for the old atmosphere, which she valued, perceiving it as loyal, sympathetic, caring, and comforting. In that way, she ended up confusing poverty with Jewish proletarian culture. In her love for tradition, she was unable to see that such a narrowly closed life with its social pressure to conform could be oppressive.[5]

In fact, all the literary descriptions of the Jewish neighborhood are somewhat romanticized eyewitness accounts. The reader catches a brief glimpse of everything. The abundance of the literature raises the question as to what was it about the old neighborhood that attracted the attention of so many writers? And often they treated it nostalgically rather than as a perfect example of what could not be tolerated and had to be eradicated, or as so old-fashioned that it did not fit into the modern world. Why? Were they attracted by the exotic, by danger and disease, or simply by poverty?

In my interviews it was commonplace for memories of the old ghetto around the time of World War I to be phrased nostalgically, in a form that clearly had its origin in literature. Sometimes I was treated to the backward-looking nostalgia of Meyer Sluyser; at other times the source was literature that the subject had read long ago—Heijermans, for example. Literary images played a considerable role in the interviews with people who had backgrounds of socialism and were relatively well-educated. The norms and values of their newly acquired, cultured world were internalized, and again and again the speakers expressed themselves in terms that seemed to have sprung directly out of the works of Herman Heijermans. For them, the ghetto was old and filthy, and it had been essential that it change. And yet—this, of course, was where the contradiction arose—although change had been unavoidable, they nevertheless found themselves thinking fondly of something or other that had persisted through all the years. The grief they felt for all that has vanished quickly replaced any confusion, and the conversation continued—about a world that no longer existed. This grief dominated the interviews with the "socialists." There was grief in other interviews as well over the loss of Jewish identity, and a little-understood feeling of somehow being "different."

Along with the nostalgia there was also the remembered misery; the ghetto had been so poor and dirty that the marks of deprivation were clearly visible in the interviews. For example, there was the story of C., a woman from East Amsterdam who had known perhaps better than anyone else I interviewed what it was to be poor. She told about the ghetto a couple of years after World War I. Among all my subjects, she alone had been one of the poorest of the poor—from the Rooie Leeuwengang [Red Lions' Alley] in the old Jewish neighborhood. C. was brought up in her grandparents' house. Her parents had been unable to find living quarters for themselves and thus lived there. There were just some mattresses lying around:

"It was filth beyond filth! We did everything in a bucket. There was an entrance that was smaller than a door. . . . There were tiny little rooms, a sitting room, and then just little alcoves really. An alcove—I mean just a hole in the wall, where the people slept."

She moved to Valkenburger Street when she was four. There they were just as poor and lived in a tenement. Yet it was just a little better than the Rooie Leeuwen Alley:

"We didn't sleep on blankets. We didn't have any; we slept on old news-papers. So when my father woke up in the morning we could sometimes read on his cheek: 'Tidy maid needed.' . . . His ears were sometimes bitten by the rats. . . . No toilet; there was a bucket, and once a week the poopwagon came by. That was a refuse wagon that came to empty the bucket. In the summer-time it stank something awful after a week! That was poverty. As for the men, they sat in front of the doors on orange crates playing cards. There was nothing else to do. It was their only pastime."

She had this to say about the Rooie Leeuwen Alley:

"I think there were two floors above us. Well, I'm not really sure whether it was one, two, or three. But the little room where my grandmother lived was to about here from the lamp [about 12 feet], and what I can remember of my years there seems to have been spent behind the little bed niche and in a tiny little kitchen where we washed ourselves, too—washed our hair."

They moved in about 1925:

"Then we went to live above a wagon shed; . . . next door was a place where they plucked chickens. Under us lived a real character, a woman who knew the whole of the city, who walked around selling fruit, and she had a really crooked mouth so we called her 'Sarie Scheefs' [Sarie Scheefsnoet, lit. Sarie Crooked Snout] and we lived above her."[6]

There is a level of experience here that we do not find in literature. It concerns the trivia of a never-ending everyday struggle to stay alive. Against the background of poverty a picture emerges that above all concerns attempts to distance oneself from the poverty. Even de Hond, who gave the impression of setting nothing between himself and poverty, maintained his distance. The reader is shown specific situations, but real life is never merely the sum of such specific, special experiences. It is a combination of the unique with the ongoing, everyday humdrum. The authenticity of the interviews gives greater insight into how people fought to maintain their existence on a daily basis than does any combination of "heroic" deeds. In the stories I heard, it was true that the neighborhood was filthy, yet the family of the storyteller was always, by contrast, clean. Again and again I heard how they alone, amid the dirt, were an exception. Above all, their mother was especially neat and tidy.

In the miserable slums, among the ruins, there was a never-ending battle against bedbugs. There were families that still had the stamina to keep up the fight, but there were others in which the women had given up. When there were many children, it was impossible to keep their clothes clean—especially if a couple of them still wet the bed. Two-roomed apartments, where parents and children alike slept in stuffy bed niches, were sometimes so overcrowded that lice brought in from outside thrived prolifically. In such families, it mattered little; it was normal. On the other hand, in those families where the housewife battled against the dirt and vermin, the plague was seen as a failing, a shame, and a punishment.

One of the former slum dwellers, Jacob, provided a good example of such a combination of the special and the commonplace that made up such a life in his story about the fight against lice. Batavier Street was being fumigated:

"There were bedbugs throughout the neighborhood. Every area was full of them, and the first step was that the fumigator—as they called him—came by. And he went and looked the whole place over, and then, well, you can say that almost everywhere had to be fumigated. . . . We didn't have them; my mother was a dreadfully clean woman. But the neighbors did."

"But didn't you sometimes have just one or two?" I asked.

"Oh, sure, you could put it that way. And my father, well, he was always stopping up holes, and every now and then something would fall out. Then a day or so before the fumigator came, there'd be another. Mother was in a panic, of course. So she borrowed ten guilders from—someone, oh, I don't know who—to bribe the fumigator if he found one. He didn't find any."

"Was it really that bad?"

"We had guys in my class who had forty vermin picked off them every day. Honest. But my mother combed me and combed me. In the evening before I went to bed and in the morning before I went to school. . . . Look here, to say I never had them, ever, isn't true. Of course I had them. But my mother made darned sure I never went out of the house until I was rid of them. . . . So my first answer was wrong. Of course I had them; it couldn't be otherwise."[7]

Simon, who came from a much poorer family than Jacob's, was less embarrassed by problems with hygiene. His large family lived on Uilenburger Street; thirteen of them slept in a attic. At first, they had slept in the living room—the front room kept for special occasions. In the midst of poverty and with so little space, they nevertheless kept one room apart as their showpiece.

(This was not the only interview in which such a practice was mentioned as being perfectly normal.) Simon had this to say:

"They [the lice] were perfectly normal in those parts of the city—in the real working-class neighborhoods, where you had fleas and rats and mice, and lice. It was like that. . . . The people lived on top of each other, stuck together like burrs on a dog's tail. What kind of space was there? The kids peed all over the beds. Those thirteen big pallets, they were all stuffed with straw, and in the morning we got up, and, heck, it was so small . . . we had a heater, and we stood like this [holds a hand out in front of him] drying our shirts, and when they were dry, we put the rest of our clothes on. So you didn't get a clean shirt—well, who could wash all that stuff every day for all those children?"[8]

Tales like this, told live, add subtlety and balance to the literary images. The stark, rather absolute contrasts in written accounts were a natural expression of political polarity—the black and white ways of thinking. The opposites of modern–old, Jewish–non-Jewish, socialist–religious were too strong to allow for nuances. Although each subject's attitude regarding such contradictions colored the interview, the results as a whole nevertheless offer some insight into the truth, for the interviews themselves were the product of the conflict between a political viewpoint and nostalgia for what has vanished. Moreover, the attempts to raise the cultural level of the masses did succeed insofar as no one wanted to continue living under the old circumstances.

In the rest of this chapter, I examine the political forces existing at that time. How did those who dealt primarily with the Jewish neighborhoods and Jewish culture view their concerns, and what influenced their thinking? The political climate was created by experts, those who sought change, and those who resisted it.

REFLECTIONS ON DIRT AND FEARS OF CONTAGION

In his classic treatment of the origins of the Paris working class during the early years of the nineteenth century, Louis Chevalier showed how, as a result of social change, a city can experience what he called a pathological state of affairs.[9] He was above all concerned with the fixation on crime, that dominated every contemporary description of Paris at that time. He compared this fixation on criminality with the attitude toward cholera during the period around the epidemic of 1832. Cholera itself became a crime, for it raged primarily in those areas most feared by the bourgeoisie as sources of revolution. There was thus every reason to deal as harshly with cholera as with crime itself.

Analysis of how the bourgeoisie and the authorities feared cholera can provide a basis for research into the biological and physical origins of social antagonisms—antagonisms of which only the ideological aspects are dealt with in traditional history. Chevalier argued for research into what he called the biological causes of events—death, sickness, and sex.[10] Such research is most easily carried out in periods of crisis, major disasters, or when every-thing seems to be in flux. The hidden vortices determining biological survival begin to appear beneath the traditional categories of historical description during such times. They create a window through which to observe social practices. Such observation is generally regarded as the domain of contempo-rary intellectual eyewitnesses, sociologists and novelists, about whom Cheva-lier wrote:

> There is an enormous difference between the way sociologists and novelists view our city. It is as if there were two cities, each equally excessive, incomplete, and oversimplified.[11]

I want to apply Chevalier's methodology—an examination of aspects of human biological rhythms—to investigate the fear of contagion found among those dealing with the Jewish proletariat of Amsterdam during the period we are examining. It was felt that the Jewish Quarter represented a potential source of contamination from which disease would spread throughout the city. Contamination could, in principle, arise from any source, and for a good number of people one of the prime candidates was socialism itself. Yet along-side such politically engendered fear of the unfamiliar and radical Jewish proletariat, there was fear and anxiety about the significance of having such a large mass of the poor huddled together so close to the rest of the city and yet, given their isolation, so out of reach.

Amsterdam was politically polarized. Physicians, writers, demographers, and other authorities were concerned about the high mortality in various neigh-borhoods. The emphasis was on the old Jewish Quarter, which was regarded as the principle source of contagion. Whenever an epidemic broke out, that area, because of its overpopulation, infestation with lice, and lack of modern sanita-tion, was feared as one of the most likely foci from which contagion would spread throughout the city. In fact, contagion and dirt represented more than just possible sources of disease. They were also an indictment of the inhabi-tants in those areas, an outgrowth of ignorance concerning the people and their "strange" culture, and perhaps also a mild form of anti-Semitism.

Just before the turn of the century, the cleaner and better sections of the working class became increasingly important to the city planners. No longer was it a matter of pretty plans for the future and design competitions. What mattered now was something that would actually benefit workers' families—something they could lay their hands on. The expectation was that the work-ing class would now follow the models set up by the bourgeoisie, albeit on a modest scale.[12]

At the end of the century, new construction consisted mainly of narrow workers' houses, many of which still exist in the Ooster Park and Dapper neighborhoods.[13] Within the area known as the Wallen (the old boundaries of the city), the appearance of the city changed as a result of the departure of Jews who were better off from the stinking streets of the poor Jewish neighborhood. During the prosperous *Kaapse Tijd* between 1870 and 1876, the increasingly well-off diamond workers more or less took over the respectable area around Weesper Street, and the middle-class families who had formerly lived there moved away, taking up residence in Sarphati Street and later in the Plantage, the area around the botanical gardens.

In the newer areas, beyond the old city walls, new Jewish neighborhoods arose. People sought each other out as they moved south and east.[14] In his monumental historical work, *Amsterdam die groote stad* [Amsterdam, That Great City], written in 1936, after years of union activity and service in the Municipal Council, Henri Polak, leader of the Amsterdam diamond workers, described how practically all the Jews lived together in the Jewish Quarter until late in the nineteenth century. (There were a couple of exceptions: some of the very rich, who lived on the broad canals, and a few of the poor, who ran canteens and eating places near the markets for the benefit of the peddlers and stall-holders.)[15] But when the better-off left the old neighborhoods, the poor remained—those who could not manage to scrape together enough to rent a better place or who were unable to find one. The impoverished neighborhood that resulted became an object of great concern to the city authorities.

THE NEIGHBORHOOD AS A CAUSE OF MEDICAL CONCERN

The Municipal Board of Health repeatedly indicated that the miserable conditions existing in the basement dwellings and heavily populated areas of the city were a cause for concern. However, the mortality figures for the old Jewish Quarter actually compared favorably with those for other areas. This was in part accounted for by Stephan (a contemporary physician) as the result of a lower incidence of alcoholism and "(perhaps as a result of this) less syphilis among the Jews." The fact that there was less abuse of alcohol would in turn have had a favorable effect on the ability of the women to breastfeed their infants, and this, together with the generally greater level of care provided for children, would explain the relatively low infant mortality among the Jews.[16]

In the course of his work on nineteenth-century medical care, the sociologist Verdoorn suggested that there was a similar discrepancy between Jews and non-Jews elsewhere in Europe.[17] Verdoorn also cited the German physician Theilhaber, who sought to account for this not only by reference to differences in lifestyle but also through what he termed "racial disposition" and unusual socioeconomic relationships among the Jews.[18] According to

Verdoorn, the phenomenon received attention from a number of Dutch medical practitioners.

In his book published in 1864 concerning differences between Jews and Christians, Coronel, a doctor from Middelburg, established that the Jews of the lower classes in Amsterdam had a longer life expectancy than the rest of the population. Among the contributing factors suggested were breastfeeding, the fact that Jews tended to work in less dangerous jobs, the frequently cited tendency of Jews to drink less than their counterparts, and finally the fact that family life involved stronger bonds among the Jews than in other sectors of the population.[19]

Saltet, a physician who conducted a comparative study of infant mortality in Northern Ireland and the Netherlands, also concluded that the poverty of the parents did not determine the incidence of death among children, and that the greater the tendency to breastfeed, the higher the infant's chances of survival.[20] Another doctor, Pinkhof, in research conducted in Amsterdam in 1907 on "medical paupers" (those who received medical assistance from the municipality) came to the same conclusion.[21] Despite the fact that the Jews lived in miserable circumstances, infant mortality among them was not as high as among the rest of the population.[22] According to Pinkhof, if a Jewish mother was forced to resort to bottle feeding, the difference in the survival rate disappeared. It seemed that the influence of the dark streets and cramped housing was then more powerful than the "vitality of the Jewish people."

Many other diseases also occurred less frequently among the Jews. According to Sanders, another physician, this resulted from the strength of the "Jewish race," which had managed to survive "despite centuries of persecution" as a result of the "survival of the fittest."[23] An exception was tuberculosis, much feared among the diamond workers. The high incidence of this disease among the Jews was attributed not to bad hygiene but to their involvement in the diamond trade.[24]

Because Jews provided better care for their sick than others did, they were thought to die less often from diseases caused by poor hygiene, in particular tuberculosis. It was certainly true that the Jewish Quarter suffered more than its share of diphtheria.[25] It was generally assumed that the Jewish neighborhood was where diphtheria "raged most virulently and remained the longest." The Jews, however, were not blamed for this, since "only rebuilding the Jewish neighborhood will get rid of this source of all kinds of infection, which originates in overpopulation, in countless filthy little nursery schools, and the dirt and trash in the streets."[26]

Sanders (cited above) observed that Jewish mothers followed medical advice more faithfully and called in medical help sooner than others did. It was his opinion that this was necessary because Jews suffered more from stomach and intestinal ailments. These reports were summarized by Verdoorn who concluded that the overall lifestyle of the group, including their attention to foodstuffs (which resulted both from religion and from tradition), constituted a strong, invisible barrier against all kinds of danger.[27] There was therefore no reason to reject the traditions out of hand as outdated and old-fashioned.

Demographic research confirmed the difference in life expectancy between Jews and non-Jews. Jewish children indeed had a greater chance of surviving their first year. Moreover, around 1905 the life expectancy of Jewish men and women far exceeded that of non-Jews.[28] These were the first indications of a demographic pattern that spread through the entire working class in the course of the twentieth century. They enjoyed a greater longevity, and hence had more older people among them. In the remaining population of Amsterdam, the mortality rate began to fall around 1910, and once that trend started, the Jews quickly lost their advantage. After 1928 the survival rate among Jewish males dropped far lower than that of their non-Jewish counterparts, and their lead was definitely gone.[29]

This change occurred during the period in which Jewish traditions—religious laws and customs that ensured a high degree of cleanliness, embedded in a pattern of strictly regulated social relationships—steadily lost their hold on people. Until that time, fatal diseases followed a distinct pattern among the Jews. Heart problems were a relatively common cause of death, while tuberculosis and other contagious diseases were not. The loss of the traditions does not provide a complete explanation of these changes. As will be shown below, it was during this period that the Depression hit the Jewish population really hard, and there is no doubt that this economic decline contributed greatly to the fact that they lost ground to the rest of the population of Amsterdam, which was now conforming more to the contemporary demographic pattern. Be that as it may, there was certainly a decline in the life expectancy of the Jews.

The medical authorities argued that if the housing conditions were improved, life expectancy would improve. After all, poor housing was one of the main reasons why epidemics of infectious diseases such as the cholera epidemic of 1886 were able to take hold. The worst areas were what were called the "Islands" in Amsterdam.[30] These were not traditionally limited to the Jewish neighborhoods but included the poor working-class areas that were built practically in the sea during the expansion of the northern part of the city. The fact that so many people died in those areas was attributed to lack of hygiene. The Jewish Quarter, where the conditions of life were just as bad (if not worse), came off relatively well, since fewer people died.

THE INFLUENCE OF SCHOLARLY AND POLITICAL ACHIEVEMENTS ON INNOVATION AND TRADITION

Did the Jews really live in such a different manner from the rest of the population, or was it a matter of image alone? The Jews, who were among the avant-garde of the modern industrial working class, were influenced by neo-

Malthusianism as a way of countering poverty and instability. As a result, the number of large families generally declined among Jews.[31]

But were there other differences? Comparisons of Jewish and non-Jewish culture formed part of a more general debate around the turn of the century and cannot be separated from a *political* anti-Semitism that was rising throughout Europe at the end of the nineteenth century. This made judgmental use of what was found to be specific to Jewish culture. The emphasis on what set the Jews apart was also a consequence of the desire for emancipation among the Jews themselves. Integration into the surrounding society as a whole would inevitably lead to the disappearance of certain specific aspects of Jewish culture. Obviously the Jewish way of life had protected the people against infection. The changes were therefore received with mixed feelings; this can be seen from the activities and ideas found in the Jewish trade union Betsalel.

In this debate, there existed the enlightened viewpoint, held by many academics, that all people should be regarded as equal. Most of the doctors referred to above adopted this attitude. They were liberal in outlook, many being themselves Jewish, and they considered emancipation desirable. Yet alongside this consideration it appeared that from a medical persective the loss of the special properties of the Jewish population would lead to the disappearance of certain things that had actually given them an advantage over other sectors of the population in the past.

A totally different argument emerged in the Jewish community itself, which saw its identity disappearing—especially when religion provided the measure of that identity. My great-uncle, J. Leydesdorff, who obtained his doctorate from the University of Groningen in 1919, contributed to this debate in his dissertation, which was then the standard work in social psychology on Jewish customs in the Netherlands.[32] He asked whether:

> Dutch Jews, who through their continual assimilation into their surroundings had been provided with an environment so much more favorable than in most other countries, had, in effect, become no more than Jewish Dutchmen.[33]

This is really a matter of the persistence of Jewish customs and traditions and the conscious and unconscious maintenance of those customs and traditions. He was of the opinion that Jews were busy assimilating as fast as possible, and he regretted this.

Unfortunately he did not differentiate between the various social classes and income levels in his book. From our viewpoint, his conclusions have only limited validity for the proletariat. It is also advisable to use caution when interpreting his findings, as they were reached in the earliest phase of the development of social psychology. It does not take much training in contemporary social psychology to discover problems in the way his research questions were phrased and in the development of his material.

Like the medical researchers, this social psychologist emphasized that Jews drank little and rarely contracted syphilis. As far as alcohol went, Leydesdorff bemoaned the fact that its use was increasing, and that "in the course of time they will succeed . . . in becoming assimilated."[34] Leydesdorff argued strongly against the notion—put forward by Sombart,[35] among others—that the Jews were capitalists.[36] He suggested that the scale of their charities and the importance in Jewish tradition of the commandment to give alms to the poor were sufficient proof to the contrary. Above all, his book is an attempt to counter the many prejudices that existed in his time against the Jews. He wrote:

> I believe that in the preceding pages I have demonstrated that the unusual situation of these people causes both their diseases and their distress. Slowly but surely they are going under: virtues of which they have always been rightly proud, such as their close family ties, their chastity, and their temperance, are all disappearing, while vices such as alcoholism and dissolution are increasing to a disquieting degree. Crime is growing, suicide is becoming ever more common.[37]

How right he was, and how wrong, when he wrote this. At the end of his book, he suggested that the only way to save the Jews was for them to have a state of their own. Even he could not have known what would happen twenty years later. He survived World War II, but never took this idea up again in his writing.

Did the Jewish proletariat of Amsterdam really drink much less than others? And was it part of the culture of those who turned away from the ghettos to drink less? Before the formation of the ANDB, it was repeatedly emphasized that the Jewish diamond workers drank heavily, and this is confirmed again and again in stories of the time.[38] Even later, it was often necessary to take measures against drunkenness. This emphasis strongly suggests that the problem had not been eradicated in the section of the working class that fell under the ANDB, despite a measure of success.

Similarly, the fact that syphilis was less common among the Jews cannot be explained on the basis of their close family ties. The notion that Jews did not visit prostitutes seems more myth than reality. There were enough Jewish men who were paid their wages in a café (Polak himself tried to fight this), and, so the story goes, paid a brief visit to the brothel on their way home on Friday afternoons. My interviews confirmed that any other view is fantasy. On countless occasions I was sworn to secrecy and told how my subject knew perfectly well about his or her father. True, these stories are from the 1920s, rather later than the medical opinions cited above. But it is clear that Jewish prostitutes operated alongside the others at that time, and there were pimps of every creed.

THE POLITICAL FIGHT FOR BETTER HOUSING, AND ATTEMPTS
TO RAISE THE CULTURAL LEVEL OF THE PEOPLE

After passage of the *Woningwet* or Housing Act of 1901, it became the task of the municipalities to improve the living conditions of the poor. Dirty conditions and lack of sanitation were reasons to give priority to certain areas. The Amsterdam Board of Health decided to undertake an investigation, the results of which were published in 1903 under the authority of a later housing inspector, Johanna ter Meulen.[39] This study shows that the Jewish Quarter was the most heavily populated area. It had 1,444 dwellings and a population of 7,701. In the 774 one-room dwellings alone, lived 3,522 people.[40] Above all, many large families lived in the smallest of these, and 64.47 percent of all dwellings in the Jewish neighborhood had no toilet.[41]

Aside from the reports of the health authorities, Dr. ter Meulen made use of thousands of reports concerning the living conditions of the Amsterdam poor in individual housing units, which were compiled by organizations dealing with housing. There were the accounts of the Vereniging Liefdadigheid naar Vermogen [Association for Charity according to One's Means], which attempted to alleviate the worst of the conditions, working alongside the municipal authorities responsible for the relief of poverty.[42] In addition, she tapped the resources of those authorities themselves, using their reports drawn up in connection with the allocation of municipal poor relief.[43]

Among the Jewish poor, she came across serious overpopulation. Many families had more than nine members, mostly occupying the less expensive dwellings, and the cheapest housing was occupied by the larger families. About this she wrote:

> Although in general families larger than nine are relatively rare among paupers, such families are found shockingly often in these dwellings. These figures, which should awake in us the greatest alarm, show that such families are found even in dwellings of [which the weekly rent is only] 0.51– 0.75 [guilders]. Mostly they are found in the range of 1.76–2.00 [guilders], and, interestingly enough, only rarely in housing [costing] above 2.25 [guilders].

Typically, families living with others gave their occupation as "peddler" (male and female), and next in frequency came those without occupation, porters, rag merchants, dealers in waste food, and female domestic servants. Concerning the peddlers, ter Meulen wrote:

> Those who have come across these petty merchants as they go about their business, above all, those who have had occasion to visit them in their homes, will be deeply convinced of the desirability—indeed the necessity—of providing most, if not all, with some larger or smaller area that is set apart from the rest of the dwelling and connected with the outdoors. A place where they can store their wares, mostly foodstuffs, in a manner that

provides some protection both for themselves and their customers. Those who, like me, have come across red and green cabbage under the table, apples beneath the bed niche, trays full of candy open and uncovered in an often smoky, dirty place, are deeply convinced of this. Where a large number of the Jewish poor are occupied in this business, I believe it is essential to keep this problem well in mind and to see whether it would be possible in new housing to provide separate storage areas in various parts of the neighborhood that could be divided up and rented out very cheaply. [44]

It would then be obligatory to make use of these storage areas, so that unsightly sheds would not spring up in the little gardens between the new houses.

Above all, Dr. ter Meulen recommended that in all new construction, the houses be small and that firm measures be taken to limit the numbers and types of families permitted in them:

Let the building be substantial, yet thrifty and severely simple, obedient only to the threefold need for light, air, and space. . . . Let the people be taught the ways of better living, that they recognize the necessity to live well. There is no better way of achieving this than to offer them housing and to destroy the slums. While slums exists people will live in them; let there be no illusions about this. The slums will not simply gradually disappear on their own. [45]

Strict reeducation of those who had lived in the old uninhabitable houses implied something that was not explicitly mentioned—the need to adapt. Only by meeting whatever demands were made could would-be tenants find new housing.

Living conditions in the middle of Amsterdam were not merely a thorn in the side of the health and housing departments, they also worried the emerging trade union movement. After the Tweede Kamer or Second Chamber of Parliament passed the Housing Act in 1901, the Amsterdamsche Bestuurders Bond (ABB) [Amsterdam Administrators' Union], which consisted of representatives of the trade unions, cooperatives, and branches of the SDAP, met for consultation and to take joint initiatives. The ABB requested the social democrat Louis Hermans to carry out a study of the slums of Amsterdam. Hermans, who received the commission in January, immediately set out to cover the poor areas of the city—the Jordaan, the city center, the Jewish Quarter, and the Islands.[46] He was assisted by the young artist Albert Hahn, who supplemented the grim account forcefully with his work. A good example of Hermans's writing is his description of the Wijde Passage, which he had already written about in the *Jonge Gids* [New Guide]. He cited, as it were, his own work:

Here the people wage war against vermin, often suffering the indignity of defeat. In summertime, when the nights are mild, father and mother go to sleep lying along the window sill, for the biting of the bedbugs is then so formidable, and their numbers so vast in that dark hole they call a bed niche that sleep is impossible there. Only the children can sleep there, for they are so tired, so totally exhausted from peddling or begging that sleep comes to them even though they scratch till the flesh bleeds while they dream.

It is not only the bedbugs that come to torment them, but rats, too, great ugly beasts that they are. What I saw there surpassed all else, for I found houses that had obviously been used at some earlier time as warehouses to store goods of some sort and now they store people. They were warehouses once, and warehouses they remain. I was warmly received there, and some-one invited me to step inside.

I found myself in a small room, the ceiling so low that I almost had to walk stooped over. It was so dark that when I stood in the middle of the room I was unable to see well enough to make my notes and was forced to make my way to the window. Everything was pinched and cramped, a hovel for the poor, exhausted race. Right by the children's bed niche stood a commode. In the bed niche itself, it was impossible to distinguish a single object although it was broad daylight outside. Next to it, a chest of drawers and then the parents' bed niche. Oh, how miserable it must be to lie there ill, in such a dark, dreary cave.[47]

Yet he had this to tell as well:

An old Jewish woman, who said she was 82 years old, spoke to me. She had been born right above where we stood, loved the building, and had no wish to move away. She had nothing but praise for the building: it was perfectly fine to live there, wonderful, healthy, and peaceful.[48]

This attitude can be explained by fear of the Board of Health, which was responsible for condemning houses. And thus, according to Hermans, one grew accustomed to one's chains.

I return to the house I visited in 1887. The same overwhelming darkness holds sway. How can anyone be permitted to rent out such a cave? Not a glimmer of light within, and so damp that the wallpaper hangs down in tatters. The family of a scissors grinder lives there. The woman tells me she has to set planks against the wall in the bed niche, since otherwise the bedding becomes so damp it is impossible to sleep there at night. The family has been there only one night so far. They will not stay long; she feels sure she will become ill if they do.[49]

Again:

The man and woman who stand talking with me have not been married long. He is a salesman, a peddler, but has no money to purchase goods for sale, and while still on their *wittebroodsweken* [honeymoon, lit. white bread weeks] they are hungry. The weather is raw, yet there is no fire in the room; in fact, there is no stove at all, just a few unmatched scraps of cloth on the floor, a couple of chairs, and a table. So much for furnishings.

They have no support whatever from their religion because they married recently, and are apparently "forbidden" to be hungry, perhaps above all because he belongs to the Portuguese congregation (Sephardi), she to the high German (Ashkenazi). When it comes to finding excuses for withholding relief money, religious boards sometimes seem quite ingenious! [50]

Hermans complained most bitterly about the refuse that was dumped in the street. The women of the neighborhood were blamed, since the wagons of the municipal sanitation department passed by quite regularly. However, it is too much to expect high standards of hygiene and cleanliness from a group of people who never had a bit of help from the municipality. On Monday, 4 March 1901 at 11:00 in the morning, Hermans counted twenty heaps of garbage on Uilenburger Street. One of the alleys off Valkenburger Street had in fact been turned into an illegal garbage dump.

He ferociously attacked the municipality for permitting the condemned houses, those declared uninhabitable, to degenerate into breeding grounds for vermin:

> I have already pointed out above that the municipality has not lifted a finger to help the people of the area maintain standards of decency.[51]

He cited with approval the well-known speech made in 1898 by the physician and health inspector H. G. Ringeling:

> The population density in the Jewish neighborhood is about seven times what it is in the city as a whole. The percentage of houses in the area in which an infectious disease occurred during 1896 was greater than that in the entire city by the following factors:
>
> | | |
> |---|---|
> | Measles | 14.0 |
> | Scarlet fever | 13.5 |
> | Diphtheria | 2.5 |
> | Typhus | ± 2.5 |
>
> Likewise, the incidence of death from certain infectious diseases was markedly higher there than in the rest of the city.[52]

When a population lives seven times closer together, sicknesses like measles and scarlet fever occur twice as often. The difference between contagious diseases and those like typhus and cholera, which can be fought by careful hygiene, is significant.

Who was correct? The physicians, who determined that in 1886 cholera had attacked fewer households in the Jewish Quarter than on the Islands? Or was Ringeling correct—were hygiene and overpopulation a problem in the Jewish Quarter as well as on the Islands? Packing together masses of people could well lead to the spread of infection and to epidemics, and thus threaten the entire population of the city. Was the resultant fear of epidemics exaggerated?

The doctors and health authorities were unanimous in regarding the Jewish poor as less likely to contract all kinds of sickness, thus implying that the behavior of the inhabitants of that neighborhood constituted no special danger. However, from about the turn of the century, the trade union movement argued for an improvement in the living conditions in the area, along with the reeducation of the inhabitants.

According to the doctors, the Jews' unfamiliar way of life had been confused with conditions that produce danger of infection. The fear that disease would spread from there had originated because Uilenburg was indeed a warehouse packed with people. Yet there was little reason to fear infection from the inhabitants themselves, provided they were permitted to run their lives as they chose. It was precisely their customs regarding hygiene, which struck others as so strange, that stood them in good stead and protected them from infection. Only the fact that they suffered from overpopulation could lead to explosive situations regarding diseases against which hygienic measures had little effect.

The judgments made by people in the labor movement regarding the inhabitants of the Jewish areas (including both Hermans and ter Meulen) were far harsher. Ignoring the question of whether Jewish culture could lead to alternative ways of living in society and other hygienic norms, they argued for reeducation of the inhabitants. The conditions of life would first have to be drastically improved. After that, people would be brought up properly, and all could live in the same way.

From the viewpoint of the workers' movement shortly after the turn of the century, nothing was to be gained from encouraging alternative lifestyles. Modern life was to be lived in just one fashion. This fundamentally moralistic attitude within the movement, and the emphasis on the role of the workers' movement itself as a source of education for the working class, drove the movement to speak out about antisocial behavior for the first time. Those who could not or would not live according to the ideals of a modern, enlightened working class were regarded as antisocial.

STORIES ABOUT HOUSING CONDITIONS

Were the dwellings regarded by the inhabitants themselves as uninhabitable? Their tales confirm what outsiders say. I asked B. about Uilenburger Street in the 1920s:

"How big was the place you lived in?"

"Oh, well, not much to tell. There was the kitchen. You know, I see it right before me—over there, for example, was the sink [he indicates a point about five feet away] and here . . . next to it was a window, and you could see outside. That was the only light that came in. Next, a sort of chimney and then a bed niche. And then sort of a wall, really another bed niche. Oh, then, right there, you had the door to the outside. The toilet was in the hallway. So, that was the room we lived in. The front room had to be kept clean and tidy. That was generally how it was."

"The front room clean and tidy? Yet you all slept in that one room?"

"In the bed niches, we slept in the bed niches. Now, how many children were we? Father and mother slept on one side in the bed niche, and we slept in ours."

"All nine children?"

"No, one of us slept at the butcher's; there were seven of us." [The baby slept with the mother.]

"You managed?"

"Well, sure. We had to! Then my father—this was on Uilenburg, and we lived on the fourth floor, and there was an attic with all those thin laths dividing it up for the people on each floor—it was shared—and he broke out all the dividers, the dividers between the spaces for the people from each floor. So there was just a single space in the attic. Repaired the flooring, and when that was done, made a bed frame, a bed just exactly the size of the attic, and pallets were piled in there, three, six, nine. Three next to each other. So we all slept there—we children." [53]

They were all hard up, there was seldom any financial reserve to take care of unexpected events like sickness or births. Burial they saved for with the *chevra* or Funeral Brotherhood—the messenger came each week to collect the dues. In return, they received a box of matzos at Passover, when Jews eat only unleavened bread.

Mrs. K.: "My mother always said how when I was born there was nothing to eat in the house. Then we had, oh yes, I was the thirteenth—don't forget that—four already dead. Well, when I was born, so my mother said, she had a couple of *stuivers* [nickels]. You used them at that time to feed the gas meter. And she'd saved them in case something happened, when I was on the way, so that then . . . well, if the light went out, then she'd have a couple of *stuivers*. . . .

"When I was about eight, I think, there was talk of the whole neighborhood coming down, at least the middle bit. Batavier Street had two sides, and there was Uilenburger Street with two . . . then we rented a place for *f* 4.50 a week, and that was on Blasius Street. It was three rooms, one behind another, and a closed-in porch. Well, that was a real change . . . because in the two on Batavier Street the boys slept on the floor, the girls in the bed niche. But my mother and father, that was usual, they had a separate bedroom." [54]

Everything was better, living there; for the most part, change meant improvement.

The people wanted to survive; they wanted just enough to eat to get through to the next day, just enough money to pay for their little hovel. Good luck was temporary. Hunger was the norm, yet in such miserable circumstances they nevertheless wanted to live as happily as they could. To manage that, there was a whole fabric of social practices, including their own definition of propriety, the use of the children to acquire necessities, social contacts in their houses, and when everything seemed unbearable, ways to bend the rules so as to survive.

Hunger figured prominently in the interviews. In the following conversation with a woman, this was brought into relation with poverty and with a quite distinct view of what was proper. The latter was so important that pride won out against embarrassment in regard to what was really important.

"Have you ever been hungry?" I asked.

"Really hungry? Well, now, I would be fibbing if I said that. I wasn't ever truly hungry. But I'll tell you, I never had a pastry and I didn't even know what whipped cream was—or pineapple."

"So you never had to go to bed without eating?"

"No, though we were often right on the edge; and then I would have to go to the grocer, and my mother would say, 'Just try it one more time,' and I would run along to ask the grocer if I couldn't maybe have a loaf with a quarter pound or so of hard cheese—otherwise we would have to go to bed with no supper. And that was no exaggeration, that's the real truth."

She was fully aware that her story was incompatible with any feeling of nostalgia and indeed emphasized this:

"You must have heard them say, 'We had it real good back then at home.' But I can't say that, because it isn't true. And you know those people who say that, well, it just isn't true. I know that all too well. . . . People don't want to admit it wasn't good in those days. Me, I want to remember it, because what I've now been able to become is so fine. My mother always used to say, 'We are real poor, but we are not like all the others. . . . ' By that she meant that though we were poor we were properly brought up. Because my father brought home clothes from his pushcart, and mother would wash them and iron them carefully, and she did that beautifully. . . . "

"Did you usually eat potatoes?"

"Potatoes and rendered suet."

"In other words, it wasn't lard."

"No, suet. Beef suet."

"And what did you have as a treat?"

"What we called a *jongetje*, a 'little guy,' a dry cookie. Or a sourball, a boiled candy. Once my father came home and saw a little bag like that with sourballs in it, and he was so angry with my mother for bringing that home. They cost five or six cents a hundred grams, and we just couldn't afford that. Well, he was so angry that he threw the bag out the window. And we rushed down and picked them all up. . . .

"And I had to get the table ready on Friday evenings; you'd expect, of course, that there'd be a cloth, but my mother would say, 'Hey, hey, its Friday evening. We'll put *Het Volk* [The People; a social-democratic paper] on the table.' That was a newspaper. During the week we had the *Tribune*, the communist paper."

"Were your parents communists?"

"No, they weren't communists, but my father certainly brought papers home, sometimes from his pushcart, and they went on the table at night, and when I had washed and needed something to dry myself with, she would say, 'Use your father's shirt from yesterday.' . . .

"I was a girl about 13 when I said, 'Ma, I don't have any shoes.' 'Well, then,' she said, 'we'll go to the corner on Sunday.' She meant the Jews' Corner but she just called it 'the corner.' So we went to the corner and there, in front of the Batavier School, there was always a man with second-hand shoes, and my mother asked, 'What do these cost?' The man answered, 'Guilder and ten cents,' and she said, 'I'll give you a guilder.' Then, when I complained, 'But they don't fit,' she said, 'That's not possible—everything fits a poor child.' "

That same woman sometimes slept at her grandmother's.

"In the bed niche with her?" I asked.

"Oh, yes, in there; it was full of fleas. And I would go looking for fleas on her. I searched for fleas in her blankets. It was so filthy, but that didn't really worry me. My grandmother wore a *toor* [*sheitl*, a wig worn by orthodox women], something to cover her head. It was made of hair, and it was packed full of lice, and I would try to clean it. At that time I was about nine or so, and she lived in Folie Street, and she wore stockings, not panties, and the toes got holes in them so we cut them off and sewed them up again and so she had stockings again. . . . We had no blankets, we covered up with a jacket. Like you just took off, that's what covered me at night, not a blanket." [55]

She is proud, and rightly so, of her success at the grocer's, of the second-hand clothes, of eating little, of picking up the candy from the street, the substitute tablecloth, the shoes that were too small, and the battle against lice at her grandmother's. The fact that she managed to do so well is, as she herself seemed to remark, part of the explanation. No doubt she was proud at that time of many things she doesn't even remember now. Everyone lived in similar circumstances. In the world they lived in, such things were accepted.

I asked another of the people I interviewed, L., about his childhood. How did they manage to live together with so many others in one space? When were they at home? His answer gives a picture of overcrowding that is shocking. Nevertheless he has memories of a happy childhood, partly because his memory is clouded by nostalgia, partly because he knew no better at that time. Everyone slept in overcrowded lodgings, girls and boys all together—and not just at his home. He, like everyone else, adapted.

"Did you play outside after school?"

"Yep. What they called 'inside,' that palace of ours, well, you've just got to imagine it for yourself! There was a room and a tiny kitchen. And everything took place in that room, even the bed niches that we slept in were in there. We were four in one bed niche, two at one end of it, two at the other, with our feet in the middle. That's how we slept. My sisters slept on a couple of folding chairs that were pushed together under the table during the day; they were pulled out in the evening. Papa and Mama also slept in a bed niche. So that's why I say, 'You mustn't imagine much was there.' When I see my home now, I can't think how I managed to live back then with eight other people."[56]

Images of childhood are determined by how they now view poverty. Pride about having managed to get through it is often mixed with horror at what things were really like. On the one hand, that life of poverty was grim because through our eyes today the poverty itself seems unbearable. On the other hand, the intervening war strengthened the positive aspects of a life in which a sourball was heavenly and, despite everything, you somehow managed to get along with each other. Interestingly, poverty itself is not viewed as pure misery. On the contrary, the struggle to survive was conducted in a world of codes and strategies, with some contestants coming out on top. Those who did so were simply better than the others, and felt it.

AN EVALUATION OF WHAT WE KNOW ABOUT THE OLD NEIGHBORHOOD: THE DEMOLITION

The environment of those who remained in the old neighborhood differed materially from that of the people who left. That much is certain. Those who departed were often younger, and many worked in the diamond industry. Although the workers in that industry had gradually become a part of the proletariat due to one crisis after another, they remained an elite (at least culturally).

Nevertheless, it is unclear how far the lives of those who stayed on differed from the lives of those who gradually left the area. The people who could afford to do so were certainly inclined to mold their lives to the image of the modern worker and thus opened themselves to the possibility of moving into the culture that surrounded them. They moved to new neighborhoods. Yet new ghettos were quickly formed as a result of the widespread demolition that occurred during the 1920s, forcing large groups of the inhabitants to leave the old ghetto.

It is also wrong to say that only large families stayed behind in the ghetto while the new neighborhoods contained nothing but smaller, more "modern" families. That was true only of the more expensive housing that was built in the Transvaal area during the 1920s. In the case of devout families, there was a far greater chance that they would stay behind, living near the Jewish institutions around Waterloo Square. The fact that such a family was unlikely to use contraceptives on religious grounds meant that it would probably be large. Yet the divisions were by no means absolute. Political considerations, with the social-democratic Municipal Council of Amsterdam as protagonist, tended to favor all attempts to combat poverty among large families in stuffy little one-room apartments by demolishing the bad housing, at the same time pointing out the advantages of conscious family planning.

Who precisely stayed on in the old neighborhood we will never know. We can only say for certain that by the end of World War I, not all the modern workers' families had departed. Many diamond workers still lived there, even though that is the group one would most expect to have departed. In 1906, 27 percent of the Ashkenazi Jews continued to live in the older areas of Uilenburg, Marken, Jodenbree Street, and Vlooienburg in the ghetto.[57] Vijgen estimated that by 1920 this had been reduced to 17 percent because of the demolition of Uilenburg. Moreover, the percentage of the neighborhood population that was Jewish fell from 95 to 80 percent. A similar trend is to be found in the areas directly adjoining the four mentioned above.[58] The sociologist Heertje used the address list of the ANDB to investigate how many Jews still lived in the Jewish Quarter. According to a list dating from 1896 or 1897, 539 of the 909 ANDB members still lived in the old Jewish Quarter, 150 on neighboring Weesper Street and Lepel Street, and 111 on Utrechtse Dwars Street, an area where initially diamond workers could begin to better their lives. In 1936 Heertje wrote, "The Jewish neighborhood is now seldom considered by young diamond workers."[59] He was himself a product of those modern times and revolted against Jewish traditions.

Was it the misery itself that forced a showdown, or was it a matter of poverty being attacked in the old Jewish neighborhood as part of a greater plan to take widespread measures? There was absolutely no guarantee that the great mass of Jews, even when uprooted from their old and trusted environment, would be able to meet the standards set for obtaining new housing. Clearly they were different, and this remained true wherever they went to live. Unless the differences could be eliminated through a concerted effort, and unless the Jews themselves wanted this to happen, there was every chance that the same miserable conditions would rapidly return to the new neighborhoods. Or was it a matter of poverty—was it that the fight against poverty had had unexpected consequences?

DEPARTURE

In 1911 the Municipal Council decided to demolish the houses on the island of Uilenburg. This was a logical consequence of the Housing Act of 1901, which gave the municipalities the power to provide affordable housing.[60] One measure taken in order to house those who would be displaced by the demolition was the founding in 1912 of the Stichting Bouwfonds Handwerkers

Vriendenkring [Building Cooperative of the Friends of Manual Workers].[61] This cooperative was founded as one of the activities of the Handwerkers Vriedenkring, a social organization that was originally progressively liberal and later strongly allied with the ANDB.

In that same year, 1912, the cooperative commissioned a study of the living conditions and housing requirements on Uilenburg. The results (which were never published) are still available in typescript. According to results from this questionnaire, there were 393 families living on Uilenburg, or 2,053 persons in all. Of these, 390 families were questioned; 160 expressed the desire not to leave the neighborhood, giving as reasons old age (19), habit (40), and the fact that their income came from the neighborhood (69, of whom 20 had a store there). There were 32 families who had religious objections to leaving, did not wish to leave part of the family behind, or had other reasons.

Of the families that did not wish to leave, most belonged to those who paid the least rent, and thus were among the poorest of the poor. However, among the 218 families who in principle were prepared to move to another part of the city, more than half paid less than 3 guilders a week in rent and thus should also be included among those who enjoyed relatively inexpensive housing.[62] These families consisted for the most part of four to nine people, "who would like to leave as quickly as possible just as soon as they can find a suitable dwelling they can afford."[63] Many families were on welfare or were among the poor who could just barely support themselves without assistance.

The report concludes:

> We feel that we cannot end this report without clearly indicating that our own research has fully supported the conclusion, which accords with the opinions commonly expressed that the living conditions in this neighborhood are in general appalling. Here and there it is possible to find entire dwellings where adequate light and air enter the structures; nevertheless, by far the greater part of the houses that we visited fully deserve to be called slums. Anyone who, like us, has climbed the staircases of some of the tenements, and has found on five floors, one after another, back and front, an apartment for a family, must have asked himself that disquieting question: what would happen if fire broke out in one of these places? Each time, one feels anew the urgent need to ensure, with help from the government, that situations like these are brought to an end as swiftly as possible.[64]

In 1913 it was still true that of 861 dwellings scheduled for demolition, only one that had been declared uninhabitable had been vacated. The major work was yet to begin. Where could those hundreds of people go, now that there was such a shortage of affordable housing? "The question here is yet again whether, even if affordable housing were available elsewhere, the people would not be bound to this neighborhood by their occupations."[65] Above all, it was unclear whether the people wished to remain by choice or out of necessity. There was continual movement away from the area to other neighborhoods, such as nearby Ooster Park. Because of this, and because many claimed that it was better there, the municipal administration assumed that necessity was what kept the others in the neighborhood. In correspondence with the municipality, the Handwerkers Vriendenkring repeatedly emphasized that many of the inhabitants of Uilenburg did not want to leave. This opinion carried weight with the municipal authorities since the old houses were not being vacated, even though new dwellings were available.

NEW CONSTRUCTION AND THE CONSEQUENCES OF WORLD WAR I

In order to provide places for the inhabitants of the old Jewish Quarter to move to, it was decided to build a new neighborhood in what was to become known as the Transvaal district. There had already been a certain amount of new construction there. When the first of the new dwellings was ready in 1916, it was possible to start with the demolition of Uilenburg. In 1911 a new portfolio was created in the municipal administration—that of director of housing—and the position was occupied by the social democrat Frank Wibaut. He provided the great stimulus that resulted in an ambitious program of building inexpensive dwellings, and he is known in Dutch history as the great builder of housing.

Those who lived in the buildings to be demolished were either moved to a new place or provided with temporary housing until something in their price range became available. To regulate the new housing, and to see that the inhabitants treated it appropriately, a housing service was set up in 1915.[66] The dirtiest and most antisocial families (who were suspected of being contagious) were whisked off to quarantine in Zeeburg.[67] In the course of 1916 the actual demolition of Uilenburg began.[68] Little was done on Marken until 1926.

With the disappearance of the worst slums, the area looked quite different. Filth gave way to empty lots. Entire streets were boarded off. It seemed as if new buildings would rise very rapidly. With the departure of the people, the bustle and crush of the streets disappeared, along with a part of the social climate. People who had lived near each other for decades suddenly saw each other no more. Attendance dropped at the regular meeting place, the *sjoel*, since those who had moved found other synagogues near their new residences. The women no longer had their families living on the same street— the children lived elsewhere in the city. Something had disappeared and would never return.

In this way, a climate that encouraged nostalgia was created. This was evident for the first time in the exhibit arranged in 1916 in the Stedelijk or Municipal Museum (called the Suasso Museum at that time). The show was originally Zionistic in intention, but it became caught up in the need to honor everything that was good, safe, and closed, and to set up barricades to dam the flow toward emancipation and assimilation of the Jewish working class. It was assumed that when they were dispersed throughout the city, their unity would be weakened. Clearly something would be lost; thus the good qualities of the ghetto—its quaintness and its closeness—should be honored. The Jewish elite and working class labored together to ensure this.[69] Rössing wrote that the goal was:

> to strengthen the unity of the Jews and to recognize the power of family, church, and social life even in a district such as Uilenburg, where the houses are like a slum, and all the conditions for a good life are lacking.[70]

There was a nostalgic yearning for the misery on Uilenburg:

> This neighborhood is being demolished primarily for the good of the people and for health reasons, and everyone has to go elsewhere. All the inhabitants fight their way out, or simply leave. Yet something is being left behind that unified all of them through the good and the evil—the synagogue, that lovely eloquent building. [He meant the Portuguese Synagogue.][71]
> Uilenburg!
> The very day I write this, 20 November 1916, the blows of the sledge hammer are raining on Uilenburg as the demolition of the houses throughout that neighborhood gets underway. Bricks fall to the street with dull thuds, while planks, beams, and window frames are snapped apart and hurled to the ground. Tar paper is ripped off the roofs. The razing of Uilenburg has begun. From Batavier Street, Batavierdwars Street, and Uilenburger Street, the flat barrows laden with bricks, timber, and roof tiles trundle off to the quay at Oude Schans, loading up barges with the remains of house number whatever-it-was. Those old places with the familiar little signs "Declared Uninhabitable" give no resistance to the sledge hammers and crowbars. This morning they began—and already this afternoon a little building that in former years was the center of lively activity lies in ruins, little more than a heap of crumbling walls. "Let them go ahead, as long as they don't try to demolish my place," says one of the few remaining inhabitants of Batavierdwars Street as she watches old mortar and bricks crash to the sidewalk right next to her home.[72]

The "necessity" to demolish the old neighborhood was made clearer by what happened after World War I. Even for those who—up till then—had been able to manage, the future now became uncertain. The diminished purchasing power of the diamond workers meant that the tobacco industry was dragged down as well. By 1910, exports had already begun to stagnate, and there was an avalanche of layoffs. The increasing poverty during the war affected not only the Jewish Quarter. In the eastern Islands, the Jordaan, and in other working-class areas there was hunger, caused by scarcities and a poorly balanced diet.[73] The threatened food shortages led to rationing and regulations governing access to the inadequate supplies of food, which in practice meant that housewives in the poorer districts had to spend hours waiting in long lines in front of the stores.

Mrs. F. gave an account of this, and her story is similar to that of many others.

"Was it a difficult time—the war years?" I asked.

"Oh, terrible! We lived on Blasius Street, and that was handy because there were stores there. Sometimes we would sit for hours in front of our window just looking to see if they had delivered any butter to the store on the other side of the street. Or whether one of the boys had come with a barrow full of fish . . . or whatever it was. Then we would all run downstairs, each of us letting the others know, 'Meat's arrived,' or 'This or that has come in.' " [74]

Sometimes the relief that came in the form of food was unacceptable to the people of the Jewish Quarter. Even for those who were no longer following the religious dietary laws, eating pork was unthinkable. In the Municipal Council in 1915, A. B. Kleerekoper, a social democrat and a Jew, showed how the Jews had been worst hit by the war; he referred in particular to the miserable state of the diamond industry. And, he said, pork did not help the Jews. Reacting to an interruption that, "But those aren't religious Jews," he said, "I heard Mr. Jitta saying, 'Those are *spekjoden* [Jews who eat pork, lit. 'bacon Jews']' but these are seldom found among the people we are talking about. They do not eat pork." He did not regard this as a matter of conscience, just tradition.[75]

In 1918 the famished population of Amsterdam suffered terribly from Spanish influenza. This was spread by contagion and the lack of hygiene was not responsible. In the council debates that were held to consider how the problem could be dealt with, there were repeated referrences to the continued persistent overcrowding in the Jewish Quarter. Alderman de Miranda, who always defended the interests of the poor Jews, admitted that there was little that could be done to fight the disease, especially in areas where children had to play together in narrow stairwells and could not be isolated from one another.[76]

The typhoid epidemic of 1919 focused the attention of the municipal authorities and of the general public alike on the unhygienic conditions in certain neighborhoods. By 12 October 1919, about 300 cases had been reported, and it seemed likely that the number would increase. In the newspaper *Het Volk*, the medical column, signed with the initials "L. H." (probably Louis Heijermans) was devoted to the topic. In questions asked by E. Polak (SDAP) during the council debates on the subject, he emphasized that in addition to the dirt and bad sewer system in certain neighborhoods, the quality of the milk was a source of infection.[77] This initiated an attempt by the social democrats for many years to bring milk distribution under municipal supervision.[78] Still, the greatest problem lay in the living conditions. Even though the old district was already being demolished, there was still a danger of infection there, like a smoldering fire that threatened the rest of the city.

As far as living conditions went, Johanna ter Meulen, the housing supervisor, was correct: where there are slums, there are people. Yet the situation gradually changed. Those who were better off moved elsewhere, and it was primarily the very poor who remained. The neighborhood, of course, became even poorer. Sajet, a member of the Municipal Council, a doctor, and a social democrat, wrote about the situation in 1923: "When you walk through the ghettos of Amsterdam, through the little lanes and blind alleys of the Jordaan, you see children with crooked little legs, children who just can't grow properly."[79] Sajet abhorred the poverty and clearly saw the need for profound political change that would forever end the circumstances that led to it. But at the time he was writing, there was—with the disappearance of part of the old neighborhood—the first romanticizing of the old-fashioned, the antique, the picturesque. In a much cited (and therefore presumably much read) book, G. J. Gimpel reacted to the demolition in this way:

> The secrets of her little streets, the picturesque ruins and tiny rundown houses, the charming lanes and blind alleys, and the sudden sight of a diminutive harbor or the little curve of an old canal—for thousands, those have been a revelation, and as a "vanishing ghetto" the despised neighborhood has enjoyed its own art exhibit—more crowded, indeed, than the old neighborhood itself ever was.[80]

A CHILDHOOD IN THE NEIGHBORHOOD: RECONSTRUCTION
AS A KEY TO SOCIAL STRATIFICATION

Uilenburg, and later Marken, really did disappear. When that happened, there were grounds for rejoicing—though for some also mourning. How would the old inhabitants manage when they no longer knew everyone living in their street? Would new also mean better, or had everything simply changed, becoming less Jewish? Wouldn't people miss their old streets, despite everything? According to what I heard, people were happy with the changes at first, and believed that the worst poverty was behind them.

In order to answer my questions about the changes, the people I interviewed had to dredge up some of their earliest memories. Often they were no more than the vaguest images, but in this way a start was made on reconstructing what it was like to be a child in the old Jewish Quarter.

What did the children do? Did someone watch them? Who did they spend their time with? And since the homes were so crowded, where did they play? The only written record I have been able to find is an unpublished memoir by a woman who described how much better it was on Rapenburger Street, where she came to live, than on Valkenburger Street, where her family had formerly lived. She wrote: "Great improvement! We were proud to live there."[81]

In the interviews, too, there were sharp images of material progress when they moved out of the houses declared uninhabitable. The stories of childhood offered more than just memories; they provided pictures of the many kinds of poverty they suffered. The extent of the poverty they experienced as children and the point in their lives at which they left their old apartment often yielded a key to the interpretation of the rest of an interview.

For those who moved only a short distance from their old environment (which was often the case in the early stages), it was possible to maintain close contact with the former neighborhood. This story, which makes my point, is from C., whom we met earlier living in the Rooie Leeuwen Alley. Her family moved to Valkenburger Street on the other side of the canal. The family was clearly less well off than that of the writer just quoted, but quite satisfied.

"Yes, that was a bit better. My mother was expecting her second child and couldn't stay in the Rooie Leeuwen Alley any longer. As for me, I sometimes just had to have some raisins late at night! You know, I was horribly spoiled by my grandmother, and I just went off at one in the morning to get some raisins from an old-fashioned store in the old alley—filthy, but they'd let me have a penny's worth of raisins. They all knew me there." Her father was a rag merchant and did not work regularly, and as for controlling the children— there was little of that.[82]

Jacob, another of the persons I interviewed, was born on Batavier Street, the son of a man who was unable to make it in the diamond industry. The family later moved to East Amsterdam, where the father kept a little cigar store, as he had before.

"We lived below, in the cigar store. The store itself was about eleven feet square, and behind it was a room about 11 by 15 feet with a little alcove, and behind the room was a kitchen that had been built on and an old-fashioned privy.

"There were lots of rats in the area, and we put traps down and sometimes there would be five, six, seven rats in a trap. Often those big traps with flaps, and the rats went inside . . . they came after the food but couldn't get to it, and more and more rats came in. Then in the morning we drowned the rats in the canal, in the Oude Schans, for example. 'Course I found it a grisly sight— when we pulled them up. Then we all stood around, and they were half dead, or still alive. There was always a stone inside and I found that pretty cruel . . . but at one time there was a basement in the place over the road, and when it rained hard the cellars would fill up . . ."

"Did people live there?"

"Above. . . . Not in the basement. I remember as a kid, when I wanted something to do . . . a long stick with a bit of string on the end and a chunk of bread, and I went fishing there in the cellar. Hoping a rat would come, which never happened."

"Was everyone on the street equally poor?"

"There were a lot of poor people. Mainly old ones who had no children."

"Children who could have earned a little extra?"

"Yes, who could have brought in a bit of money. Or their children didn't live nearby or had emigrated somehow if they had had the chance. . . .

"A lot of people in the neighborhood sold oranges, plums, pears—fruit in general and vegetables. . . . I ate a lot of fruit because those people—they had higher standards than people of that sort today—and they picked out the stuff that was getting overripe and dumped it in boxes. Of course I would see them do that and found it and ate quite a lot of fruit. All just a bit too ripe but still good to eat. But they threw it out because they wanted to sell only good fruit at the market.

"The real entertainment was the fights with sticks, barge poles, and belts on the bridge between the Oude Schans and Koning Street. The bridge is still there. . . . No one was ever killed, hardly anyone really hurt. But there was excitement when one gang came rushing up on another, right in the middle of the bridge. And, yeah, the ones who were there, they'd rush off, and. . . well, then there was a sort of status quo. Those weren't Jewish boys. From Koning Street."

His tale of how they spent their free time made continual reference to poverty:

"I still remember the First World War really well, we . . . I certainly went to bed at times without eating. My grandmother would ask me not to eat, and there wasn't any bread. Miserable, but, oh, whether it was ten times or twenty, I don't know . . . obviously not every day, but . . . it happened."

"It happened, and you understood when there was nothing to eat?"

"I understood. It just had to be so. It really had to be. And that was a pretty dismal feeling, it just had to be. . . . But I don't believe I was mad at my parents. No, I wasn't mad."

"It had to be so?"

"Yes, because you heard about it from others." [83]

Did children like this come in contact with non-Jewish children, aside from getting involved in fights with them—or did they live in a world that was sealed off? The dominant picture is one of Jewish exclusiveness. Yet in practically every interview I was told about non-Jewish children in the neighborhood. The Jews were in the majority, and you spent most of your time with them, of course, and the overall picture of what was remembered had no place for non-Jews. Yet the fact that there were indeed non-Jewish children with whom one came in contact runs counter to the nostalgic image of the past in which things were good because people belonged together and *everyone* was Jewish. In the following excerpt, the same man contradicts an earlier picture he sketched of an environment that was exclusively Jewish.

"Were there non-Jewish children in the class, too?"
"At first I sat next to a non-Jewish boy."
"Was he different?"
"Dikkie? No way!"[84]

It seems that the gray masses about which the municipality wrote actually had many colors. There were ranks and positions. The poor were divided into paupers, vagrants, and proletarians. Among these there were countless small groups, separated from each other by their expectations for the future, yet inseparable since they differed so little from each other. Those who managed to climb out were proud of this and did not belong any more. Their children went to schools with better facilities or to ones where attempts were made to give the children more culture through the existing facilities. Intervention by the government, when it involved basic needs or hygiene, was generally seen as positive.

In what follows, Herman tells how his parents tried to rise above the greatest misery. They sent him to the public school, but that school was a bit better than many others in the neighborhood and thus was considered to be "modern."

"I was born in Amsterdam on Hooge Kadijk . . . a street that was in part Jewish—the part that runs into Kadijk Square. The others, none of them were Jews. . . . My mother, that's simple, she was a woman from the Amsterdam Jewish proletariat—my grandparents had a little store where they sold bread.

"My mother used to tell how—as soon as she was big enough—she went to help clean the van Praag butcher shop on the other side of Rapenburger Street on Friday afternoons. She earned a few quarters or dimes this way. Then, every morning before school, she took the bread to different customers. . . . My mother said she was always sleepy in school, and I never saw her read. . . .

"There was a bedroom and there was a living room, a little kitchen and behind it a kids' room. Or another room anyway . . . and there was a big plank on which my father sat cross-legged, tailor-style. The machines were kept there, too. . . . My parents slept in the front, and I slept with them in the bedroom—certainly till I was 3 or 4, till my little brother came along. After that, in the living room."

He came from a family that was slightly better off, but along with children from the poorest sector of the population, he went to the Talmud Torah school (in Boerhaave Street) for a Jewish education.

"You have no idea at all what the poverty was like among those kids. I regularly came home with lice in my hair. I can often still see my mother combing my hair with a lice comb. But that was normal. And the children went around in tatters, while my mother sewed all my clothes. . . .

"There was the schoolmaster and once or twice a year the school doctor came by. Then you were weighed. Your height was measured. Then you had to look up—so!—and they wanted to see if you were anemic. Again and again I was sent to the vacation camps as a "paleface." (Those were the vacation camps of train 8.28 . . . a group sent "palefaces" to the beaches at Wijk aan Zee or Egmond.) Of course, Jewish kids never saw the sea [i.e., never went to the beaches with their families]."[85]

His story resembled Sara's for she, too, gave the impression that her family was just a bit better off.

"The school was so modern that it had twelve shower stalls behind the gym."

"So you could shower regularly?"

"Oh yes, and on Friday evenings we were given a bath."

"In the tub?"

"Yes, of course, where else? My oldest sisters, they always washed us. My mother had stood in the kitchen all day—for eleven people. And the others who dropped in, friends, or an uncle or an aunt, an uncle with a niece, or whatever. . . . If you weren't working, you didn't get a penny; you had to go and eat with someone else. For a while there was an uncle and a niece who sometimes came round in the evening to eat. We had a table, of course, that went from here to way over there. . . . Not enough chairs for everyone, but there were bed niches . . . and along the edges were planks, so you wouldn't fall out at night, and we called that a 'horse.' Well, we put that on two chairs, and the table was really long, so then we set as many chairs as we had and the horse on top. A couple of people then sat down and then everyone, sitting on the horse and the chairs.

"Well, to come back to that school, I was six in 1908, and there were twelve showers. They didn't have that in any other school. All the others had to go out to a street that used to be there called Stadstimmertuinen where there was a bathhouse. . . . Then the teacher said to a couple of kids, 'All right, in you go to the back; I don't need to watch you.' The others had to stay near the front so the teacher could check that they soaped and washed them-selves properly.

"They all came from large families—in small apartments; some lived in cellars, others in the alleys of Marken. Some were clean; others not."

"Did you do laundry once a week?"

"Of course. Now that I come to think of it, my mother had several wash-tubs. And she spent the whole day like that, behind the washtub."

"When did she start?"

"Saturday evening. If the weather was nice while my father was still alive and felt well, they went for a walk. And then they came back, and if my sisters were home, they warmed the meal. Of course, we didn't cook much on the Sabbath; they'd just warm it up for when my parents returned. And we could just eat it; the cloth was on the table. Then my mother took off her good clothes and put on her everyday stuff; straight after the meal she started hauling buckets of hot water from the firehouse round the corner on Uilenburger Street. Everything was put on the gas, along with soap and soda, and it boiled away. That was on Saturday evening; then we'd put a blanket or something over it to keep it warm and next morning, whoosh, over it went into a tub, and everything would be washed."

"Did they rinse in cold water?"

"Oh, Lord, no! It was washed twice like that. Everything was washed twice. My sisters helped."

"All that hot water was hauled from around the corner?"

"Well, no, not by that time. We took water from the faucet and boiled it on the gas."

"You said that on Friday you cooked enough for two days, so that was also for the Sabbath. You didn't cook on the Sabbath?"

"We just warmed the stuff up . . ."

"On your own stove?"

"No, we never had a stove. We had kerosene rings and gas; no, we never had a stove."

"The oven was at the baker's?"

"If only you could have seen that! On Friday afternoon all the Jewish women would walk, they would all walk with . . . my mother, for example, she would make the batter for a cake, so she'd have . . . it was a kind of enamel dish, and she made the cake in it. When it was done, she wrapped it in a teacloth and took it to the baker. It was baked there. And they put a number on it, because you got a little ticket with a number. . . . Marvelous, I can see them now, all golden-yellow." [86]

C.'s much poorer family used those very numbers to get something to eat. Here you see how seventy years later someone can be proud of a little thievery that enabled the family to survive: "I got home, and I asked, 'Mama, what are we going to eat?' and she said, 'Well, that depends on you, because if you run along to the baker's shop and say: I lost my number. . . .' So it's off to the corner and I say, 'I came to get a cake.' And she says, 'Don't you have a ticket?' 'No, my mother lost it.' 'Well, do you know what it is?' 'Yup, . . . there it is, that big one.' She says, 'Thirty-four?' . . . So I'm off and away home with a cake. . . . Mama says, 'Boy, someone's going to quarrel tonight!' So there we were, eating someone else's cake." [87]

Memories of childhood thus provide a key to the social stratification of the people I interviewed. There were those who carefully fetched their own cakes; and there were others who could not afford to be honest. There were children who washed if they cared to, and no one noticed because it was assumed in their family that they would do it, and there were others who were carefully looked after. One's social position determined how one would react in further confrontations in the battle to raise the cultural level of the workers.

For some it was no battle but a way of confirming certain modern norms they had already internalized. For others it remained a lifelong source of worry and strife.

There were many kinds of poverty, so the tales tell us about many kinds of childhood. Since the Jewish proletariat stood on the threshold of great change, it is impossible to give one unambiguous picture of how childhood was experienced at that time. Clearly the experience was different from how it was sketched in literature or in the writings of those who brought the children up. Memory yields more detailed information, no matter how vague and untrustworthy it may be. At the beginning of an interview, through long discussions, it was sometimes possible to make out what a particular environment had been like, and my subject would know once more where he or she had come from. Along with the often strongly romanticized surroundings there also emerged houses, furniture, and streets—in short, entire worlds of experience.

In particular, the extent to which children were used is noteworthy—and this issue has never been mentioned by other sources. They had to work on the sympathies of the increasingly poor shopkeepers in order to bring in a little food when there was none in the house. That was normal practice. Helping in the struggle for survival made up a good part of childhood. Children were hard to resent and hence could be sent out on such errands.

Learning was an important part of life in some households. Even when the parents had had few (if any) opportunities, the learning of some occupation—or just learning in an intellectual sense—was greatly prized. It was seen as a chance to escape from misery. However, in the dark little houses of Uilenburg, learning was impossible—there was no table, there was simply no room. The same was true in the nearby streets in the Ooster Park neighborhood. There, too, the houses were overcrowded. If these children were to be brought up as respectable, educated citizens, they would need more opportunities. Over the next two decades, government policy was directed to this end.

Conclusion

The demolition and redevelopment of the Jewish neighborhood created the preconditions for nostalgia. Something special had disappeared from the city, something about which feelings ran high. Contamination and dirt had been the overt issues, but in fact they represented much more. Repugnance toward the unfamiliar was a factor. Yet it was the special character of the Jewish culture that helped them survive in circumstances which, if their customs had been different, could have caused epidemics to break out. Their way of life protected them from that. The municipality's struggle to raise their cultural level was directed toward the abolition of the miserable conditions in which they had been forced to live, and at the same time involved an attempt to educate the people to adopt a way of life in which there was little place for cultural differences. This was experienced as both good and bad.

In the interviews, it was necessary to delve back into childhood in order to reconstruct this experience; as a result, the picture that emerged was never entirely sharp. Conflicting information inevitably leads to the conclusion that what was experienced during this time of change can only be properly assessed when it becomes possible to determine precisely what such a childhood was like.

Jewish society was no longer a homogeneous group of the poor. Some of them, even some who still lived in the old neighborhood, had nevertheless (at least partially) made the change to a modern way of life. Praise of the modern is, as such, in conflict with nostalgia for the old ways. The interviews show how people felt about such things at the time of the interview, not at the time of the experiences themselves. There are multiple layers in the processing of old experiences, and the present picture is founded upon layers of memory. This was evident in the confusion that sometimes arose during the interviews, when praise for the rising cultural level of their society was in conflict with complaints about the way they were forced to change, and the impossibility of living up to the new standards. It is also to be found in the fact that—despite the judgment that life in the ghetto was impossible—people lived there, and that—despite the filth—people were happy there. The filth was not always experienced as bad but simply as normal. And, although it was now considered shameful to live there and do nothing about it, in the past this had not been at all shameful.

A picture of the old Jewish neighborhood as it disappeared will never be more than a reconstruction. It can be built up from material available from government sources. In that case, the neighborhood appears to be poor and the people in need of proper education. The picture can also be constructed from literary sources. The interviews yielded a picture that is richer than both of the others and in part escapes the limitations imposed by the attitudes of that time. In contrast, they are colored by the attitudes of today and postwar nostalgia. The picture they give confronts us with these questions. Why these particular distortions? Why do people look back positively on what must have been misery? Why are they proud of the petty thievery of that time, of the poverty that could not be hidden, of the courage with which they faced life then?

The nostalgia was not simply caused by the intrusion of the war. The demolition of the old neighborhood also affected the way the past is now perceived. It was influenced by the various political strategies, some of which supported change while others opposed it. Nostalgia existed in the 1920s—and possibly even before the demolition began.

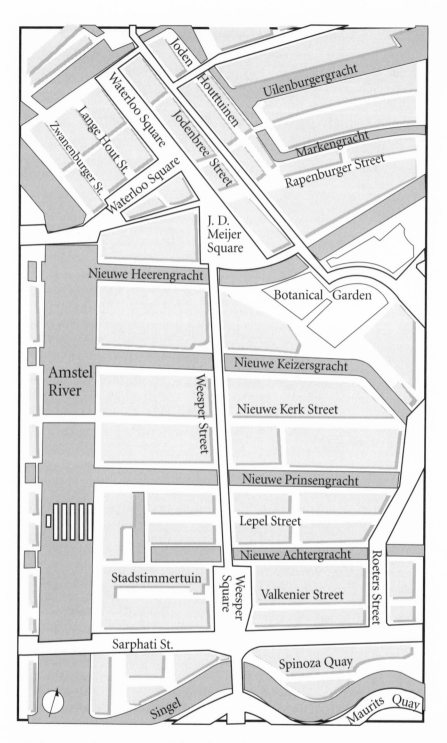

Weesper Street Neighborhood

CHAPTER FOUR

LIFE IN VARIOUS NEIGHBORHOODS

STAYING BEHIND, LEAVING, AND MOVING ON

The borders of the old Jewish neighborhood gradually expanded and became looser, and those who lived in the "Jewish" Quarter no longer needed to be Jewish, or to feel that they were living in a Jewish neighborhood. In fact, it became unclear precisely where the Jewish neighborhood was, as more and more non-Jews came to live in Uilenburg and an increasing proportion of the population living on streets farther away was Jewish. Indeed, in the years after World War I, the term "Jewish Quarter" had been so expanded that it also referred to Nieuwe Kerk Street, which was well outside the original ghetto. Waterloo Square was not far away, and many of the remarkable figures associated with the streets of the Jewish neighborhood also frequented that area. Many from the ghetto moved to the Weesper neighborhood where the Portuguese Jews had originally lived. When that area was full, people fanned out to the streets around Ooster Park and the similar Muider Gate quarter.

In the new districts, according to the Jewish social-democratic alderman Boekman, Jewish neighborhoods arose, and within them there were Jewish "quarters"—areas with a high proportion of Jews who lived a ghetto-like existence. People continued to move steadily away from the old ghetto, yet the physical distance did not necessarily mean a total break with the old way of life.

The busy appearance of the streets in the new areas was also heavily influenced by the presence of the Jews. When the distance from the old neighborhood was not too great to hamper close contact with those who continued to live there, Jewish social and cultural life continued to flourish, oriented toward the institutions of the old quarter. Living conditions were better in these new neighborhoods, the lodgings more modern, and the people often had more money.

A number of myths were generated by the assumption that the Jews who moved away enjoyed greater affluence and better living conditions. It might seem that life outside the old Jewish Quarter represented a step in the direction of emancipation—freedom from the stifling customs of orthodoxy and the possibility of more intimate contact with non-Jews. Closer examination of the situation, however, raises doubts about this. Those who continued to live close to the ghetto, in the shadow of the big diamond works, often continued to live the old life of poverty. They were hardly examples of a successful attempt to raise the cultural level of the people. To be sure, once the worst areas of the old ghetto on Uilenburg were demolished, there remained little difference between the old ghetto and the newer neighboring areas. Admittedly there were no tenements on Lepel Street; the buildings there did not lend themselves to such developments. Yet they were clearly overpopulated, poor, and dirty—certainly once the depression in the diamond industry set in and the majority of the diamond workers were unemployed.

In 1927, 37,815 people lived in what Alderman Boekman regarded as the Jewish Quarter. Of these, 22,044 (or 60 percent) were Jewish. They constituted only about one-third of the total Jewish population of Amsterdam. The others had left for areas in which they made up less than 20 percent of the total population. There was a greater concentration of Jews within the belt of canals—20 percent, or 11,730 in number. In the city center and in the polder (formerly known as Watergraafs Lake) they made up 13 percent of the total.[1]

Boekman correctly raised the question whether it was appropriate to speak of a "Jewish Quarter," since so many non-Jews had moved into the old Jewish neighborhood. At the same time, he showed how any overview misrepresented the situation, because concentrations of Jews had once again developed in the new areas. There were Jewish streets: "Within the new neighborhoods the same phenomena are to be found as in the city as a whole: a nucleus forms, and around this the other streets—and then neighborhoods—are so arranged that the percentage of Jews decreases steadily as the distance from the nucleus increases."[2] Some streets were almost exclusively Jewish. Yet even Boekman's facts are in a sense a misrepresentation, for within the areas to which he refers there were variations in the percentages of Jews living in different areas and even in *parts* of the same street. There was a Jewish section of Blasius Street, and a more heavily Jewish section of Andreas Bonn Street. There people lived below, above, and next to Jewish neighbors. (These two streets are both outside the old Jewish Quarter.) The new districts appeared to offer an alternative for those who could afford it.

In the old Jewish Quarter (the area formerly occupied exclusively by Jews), the slums were mostly in private hands, and they were rented out for next to nothing. Yet even the low rent was often too high for the people to pay. In 1928, 358 of the 581 dwellings—61 percent—were unoccupied on Ouwe Vlooienburg, the name of several streets in the old neighborhood. In the remaining 39 percent, life went on as before.

However, the slum demolition did not go any further. The surrounding areas (for example, Folie Street, where the slum conditions and worsening poverty had moved) were not cleaned up at all. The city had run out of money. There were still 120 dwellings on Uilenburg in what was regarded as reasonable condition.[3] The improvement ceased, and in 1926 one could see that for ten years nothing had been done. Above all, the Jodenhouttuinen (another Jewish area) was in bad shape. In 1929 there was a plan to expropriate the housing there; it described the situation as follows:

> Many of these premises have businesses on the ground floor while the upper floors are used as dwellings, each divided into separate front and back apartments; these are among the worst found in Amsterdam today. . . . Folie Street is just as bad.[4]

The fact that many people did not want public housing, but chose to seek housing in the private sector where the apartments were "often just as bad," constituted a problem.[5] An increasing number of businesses came into the half-boarded-up neighborhood where people still lived, filling the gaps. The area suited families on the move who, for example, had been turned out onto the street because they were unable to pay the rent and now could live temporarily in a damp hovel for a pittance. The growing number of small businesses there made it increasingly difficult to attain the goal of the municipal government—to separate housing from commercial property. "From generation to generation, the Jewish slum-dwellers are devoured by poverty," lamented Alderman Rodriguez de Miranda at the celebration of the twenty-fifth anniversary of the Handwerkers Vriendenkring. It was the socialists' task to end this situation and to bring the Jewish working class into the modern world.[6]

Assimilation and a greater measure of separation from the old way of life were not automatically guaranteed by living farther away from the old ghetto, for example, in the Weesper or Ooster Park neighborhoods. Even where there were no tenements, where the neighborhood was not regarded as a breeding ground for infection due to overpopulation, where there was no need to rebuild the entire neighborhood, and while the attention of the municipal authorities was directed elsewhere—even in such parts of the city the poverty was comparable to what was found in the old Jewish Quarter. In the tiny alcove apartments—scarcely more than holes in the wall—large families lived. Still, the sanitation was better and the streets were wider. There was air to breathe and room enough to keep things clean—yet the cozy atmosphere of the old Jewish Quarter was not entirely lost. To live in the Ooster Park neighborhood bordering the ghetto was to take the first step outside, the first step toward a non-Jewish lifestyle, and the first step toward assimilation.

The area around the Ooster Park and the Muider Gate quarter (around Muider Gate, one of the old city gates) had been planned as a middle-class neighborhood. But workers' dwellings were built there right from the start, and the original design of the buildings beside the Amstel had to be changed. Streets were made narrower, and the plans for little gardens were discarded. For the most part, the apartments that were built were small alcove dwellings instead of the palatial houses that had first been built in the area. The center from which the Jews spread out was Vrolik Street and in later years Blasius Street. Other centers were Swammerdam Street and the 's Gravensande neighborhood.[7]

Migration to mixed neighborhoods was common at that time. Some settled in the Pijp where that neighborhood bordered on the Amstel River and in sections of Old West. A few even ventured toward the Spaarndammer neighborhood and to the north. It was a new experience to be a stranger, a member of a minority, to others recognizably Jewish, visible, and therefore potentially the object of feelings of hostility. Obviously I asked about that in the interviews: *How were people received in those streets where up until then no Jews had lived, and what were their experiences?* In the interviews reported in this chapter, I also asked about the degree of contact maintained with the old Jewish neighborhood and about life in the widening circle around it. I also inquired how far people had broken with the atmosphere of their parental homes.

The interviews in this chapter are arranged according to the distance the subject lived from the old ghetto, beginning with those who lived closest. Significantly, the distance from the old neighborhood is correlated with another kind of distance—cultural.

I was interested in how the poor from all areas of the city reacted in their new, assigned housing. Whole streets were often displaced and rehoused simultaneously when the original dwellings were demolished. In such circumstances, the people had to adjust far less than when they moved into existing areas with an established neighborhood life. The newcomers could create for themselves a new lifestyle, and the atmosphere in the new districts of East Amsterdam therefore differed significantly from that in the areas where the Jews were in the minority and had to fit into existing ways of doing things.

Among so many non-Jewish neighbors it was often difficult to maintain the old Jewish values, even when one wanted to do so. The wish of the Jewish proletariat for emancipation assumed a form in which assimilation and integration into the non-Jewish world were equated with progress. People often consciously desired this, even when they ended up living among Jews in the new areas—as was the case in many parts of East Amsterdam. Nevertheless the drive toward the more "civilized" and "modern" often took shape in such a way that tradition and custom played a role, albeit perhaps unconsciously. People did not break with their history, no matter what they said. They remained Jews, and symbolized this through their actions, for example, the white tablecloth on Friday evenings, or the way in which family life was given form. Another link with tradition was the manner of eating and the way in which food was prepared. The questions I asked during the interviews often explicitly sought to bring to light those ties, no matter how symbolic they were.

There was considerable movement through Amsterdam, especially once the municipality decided to speed up the construction of public housing in the 1920s. In the boom years between 1922 and 1925, 27,000 new dwellings were constructed. In 1914, when he first became the alderman responsible for housing, the social democrat Wibaut submitted a plan to build 3,500 dwellings, but this was delayed by World War I. At the end of the war, de Miranda (one of his successors) proposed building 30,000 new housing units for workers—12,000 to be constructed by the municipality and 18,000 by private building cooperatives. This plan took advantage of the fact that starting in 1918 the national government made financial support available for low-income housing.[8]

However, these ambitious plans were only partially completed.[9] During the entire period there was a housing shortage in Amsterdam, and many people lived in deplorable conditions. The plans for expansion proposed in 1934 were intended to bring an end to this situation. Ideas that were gradually developed over a period of years finally led to a blueprint for workers' neighborhoods, where living and working areas were kept totally distinct.[10]

In 1930, a civil servant in the city housing department kept records on 97 families, noting where they moved from and where they went to. During that time especially families that moved from the Jewish Quarter were large. On the basis of independent evidence (e.g., names and official records), it was possible to determine with certainty that nine of the families in question were Jewish. Seven of the nine moved to East Amsterdam and the Transvaal neighborhoods, one to the Indische neighborhood, and one to West Amsterdam. All but one were extremely poor—so poor that the tiny amount, whatever it was, that they paid each week as rent must have been very important to them. In one case, they paid *f* 2.40 less than in the previous apartment—but this lower rent still amounted to *f* 5.10 out of a total income of *f* 10.75 a week. Given such an imbalance between rent and income, it is a mystery how they managed to live off their income.[11] Moving to East Amsterdam was by no means always a sign of affluence; it was often a way of escaping the usurious rents charged for the dilapidated ghetto housing.

Many moved from one neighborhood to another, and it is impossible to generalize about which ones were better off. The socialist position was that the further away from the ghetto, the better, but this flies in the face of the facts. People moved back and forth throughout the area between East Amsterdam and the old Jewish Quarter. Their experiences were determined less by the extent to which they had managed to internalize (to some degree) the drive

toward culture embraced by the socialists and more by the material circumstances in which they found themselves. Those who were out of work moved
to a new area; those who were working sought the best possible place to live.
If that proved to be too expensive, there was always another, cheaper to be
had. And if there was no work, then moving to a new area could always turn
up something new.

One of the subjects I interviewed told a typical story of moving through
the city. Esther's father was a shoemaker in Reguliersbree Street, but was
turned out of his home and business by the owner who had other plans for the
premises. They came to live on Nieuwe Kerk Street.

"I still remember when we went to live there. My mother ended up living
on the fourth floor. Apparently she found that fine to begin with. It was
spotless, and she was so fastidious, so she found it all lovely. My father went
to work in a factory for 12 or 13 guilders. But my mother was used to
luxuries, because in those days when you owned your own business you
naturally had things better than when you had to work in a factory. So he
went off each morning early to the factory and came home about five or six in
the evening. And, of course, he got his salary once a week."

Everything revolved around poverty; her sharpest memory is how, despite
what her father earned, it was impossible to celebrate the holy days appropriately. Although the Jewish holy days were already less important for the
family, traditions were nevertheless maintained on those days.

"But after he had worked there for a year or so, my mother couldn't
manage as far as food went, and so. . . . Take Purim or Passover, you ate
goose at that time. [She is confused and must mean Hanukkah, the Feast of
Lights, which celebrates the resistance of the Maccabees and when by tradition goose is eaten.] But, well, my mother had no more money and on Friday
she said, 'Now it's Yom Tov [an expression referring to Jewish holy days in
general] . . . and there's no goose.' On Fridays we always had a white cloth
on the table and we had a Menorah and candles. No Jewish prayers or anything like that, but we had those sorts of things. But my father came home,
and I can still see him walking in with a goose under his arm.

"We lived there for four or five years. A rag merchant came to live below
us, for there was such a housing shortage. And he stored his rags there, and at
one point it seemed that vermin had gotten in, you know, bedbugs. . . . We
didn't have them at first, but one year at Passover my mother was busy
cleaning. The picture frames came off just once a year, and she took them off,
and there they were, crawling around. She nearly died of fright. You can
imagine—she was such a clean person. I saw my mother cry for the first time
then. 'Oh,' my father said, 'those are bedbugs. They're coming in from the
rags downstairs. Guess it's time to go.' And he said, 'Anyway, I can't stand it
in the factory; I'll look around and see if I can't find another apartment.' He
did. An apartment on Lepel Street, and after a while on Derde Oosterpark

Street. A place was vacant and we landed up there, and my father opened a little store, a notions shop, not a shoemaker's business. After that he set up a shoemaker's shop again on (Nieuwe) Prinsengracht. And after that, well I sort of grew up on Tugela Road [in modern East Amsterdam]."[12]

Esther ended her youth on Rapenburger Street. During her time in East Amsterdam she came into contact with socialism, but she was not yet involved in politics. The move to East Amsterdam changed virtually nothing for her family, and when the business on Tugela Road failed, they looked for another apartment. The bedbugs had driven them away, and poverty drove them back.

IN THE SHADOW OF THE LARGE DIAMOND CUTTING WORKS NEAR THE JEWISH NEIGHBORHOOD

Since the demolition of the slums, Weesper Street and the new canals where the wealthy lived came to be included in what was thought of as the Jewish neighborhood. In the side streets, the diamond workers and their families lived together with numerous small merchants, artisans such as shoemakers, and shopkeepers. The fall of the diamond industry after World War I brought increasing numbers of people with other occupations to the narrow side streets that intersected Weesper Street. Others went in the opposite direction and, crossing the Oude Schans, went to live in the Koning and Jonker neighborhoods. These were tobacco workers and people in the garment industry, also the unemployed and poverty-stricken—those in need.[13]

The Jewish neighborhood in fact extended beyond the boundaries of Marken, Waterloo Square, and Uilenburg and occupied a larger portion of the city. It was easier to define the area that was *outside* the Jewish neighborhood, for no one knew precisely where the neighborhood began. Vague descriptions were in order; everyone knew what was not the Jewish neighborhood. You could equally well live *in* the neighborhood or *near* it, near Waterloo Square or behind Weesper Street. The important thing was that many Jews lived there.

On the broad canals that crossed Weesper Street, the rich lived in spacious dwellings where there was light and air enough to breathe, but in the streets behind, the buildings filled the whole space and the inhabitants endured a dingy existence that differed little in substance from the misery of Uilenburg. On Weesper Street, the cellars and the shops above ground housed big families. Some who lived on that street were comfortably off, but others were miserably housed in basements behind and under shops or in side streets. The living conditions were not as bad as in the ghetto, but the overcrowding and dirt remained. Life offered few prospects, and it was improbable that better times would ever come.

Much of the old community life from the ghetto continued, finding expres-

Chapter Four

sion above all around Purim and other Jewish holy days. Purim celebrates the story of Esther, and at the same time it is the Jewish carnival. On the evening of Purim the neighborhood was in turmoil. The Book of Esther was read aloud in the synagogues and in many homes. At each mention of the name of the enemy, Haman, who wanted to kill the Jews, the children were allowed to scream and (depending on the circumstances) to make a great din with rattles as a commentary on the behavior of Haman and to drive away his evil spirit.

Costume balls were held at Purim, and little masked groups wandered through the neighborhood. Partygoers would go into the houses, demanding food for themselves and to take away and to share with the poor. Others, masked and in costume, would themselves carry round food to share. Everything was so noisy and exaggerated that many told me how frightened the children would get. The way in which so many people were prepared to barge into each other's homes says something about how close-knit the neighborhood must have been, everyone knowing everyone else.

There were only a couple of other events that rivaled Purim as an expression of the street culture of the area. One was the burning (around J. D. Meijer Square and Weesper Street) of those things that could not remain inside the home during Passover, or Pesach, when the exodus from Egypt is remembered. Leavened bread, for example, was burned in remembrance of the fact that during the exodus the bread had no time to rise. Teenage boys lit the fires in the late morning before the feast. However, these activities occupied only the younger men, while Purim was mainly a children's festival, celebrated within the home.

Children also played a central role in the feast of Simhat Torah [Rejoicing of the Torah], in which wedding candies were handed out; sometimes this was the only candy the children ever saw. Groups of little boys would run from one synagogue to another, trying for more than one handout. Large-scale participation in these festivities continued principally in the Weesper neighborhood; I was never told of any significant number of fires or Purim partying in other areas. Of course, Purim was celebrated elsewhere, and little groups would wander around, but it was no longer a real part of the street culture, even in predominantly Jewish streets. In fact it was associated with a way of life from which people were specifically trying to escape.

On the other hand, there was the Seder, celebrated quietly around the table, which has been the subject of numerous literary works. There, in a dedicated and joyful manner, the exodus from Egypt was celebrated, not with the exuberance of Purim, Simhat Torah, or the burning of leavened bread, but with an emphasis on togetherness.

E., a very old lady who came to Amsterdam around 1910 from the more middle-class city of Rotterdam, told me how she never put down roots in Nieuwe Kerk Street (one of the side streets off Weesper Street near Waterloo Square). She described the street as an archetypal Jewish ghetto, where she amused herself as an onlooker—but from which she also held herself aloof. She was married to a diamond worker and had found an apartment there. In the following brief extract she describes how ghetto-like the street was:

"When I came here from Rotterdam, it really was an eye-opener for me. All those street characters, all those characters—well, we didn't have them in Rotterdam. I lived on Nieuwe Kerk Street, but only temporarily. I didn't want to live there because I found it a horrible street. But you get used to all those Amsterdam things. It was just very different at our place."

She moved to lodgings farther from the ghetto, behind Weesper Square. I asked her, "Was that better? Was it a nicer apartment?"

"I'd say a nicer place and better company. Totally different environment. It was also completely Jewish; just not typically Jewish." Clearly "typically Jewish" meant ghetto-like—picturesque, old-fashioned, low, dirty, and backward.

"Did you find Kerk Street very, very Jewish then?"

"Yes, very. All those women sitting in their doorways cleaning vegetables! I just wasn't used to that. . . . On Sundays I went to Jodenbree Street. That was such fun. There were all the Christians, all the people who came from other cities, wholesale merchants who were buying for trade—and what I always found so lovely on Bree Street were those cellars with the geese. . . . That was such a treat for the Jews!"

The story is well known in Amsterdam. Extra trains had to be brought in to handle the people drawn to the market. On Sundays the Jewish Corner was chock full of people who came to gape at the antics of the stall-holders. You could buy anything there. Virtually every interviewee had something to say about it, and the literary record contains countless nostalgic references like this to the market. What complicates the story of Mrs. E. (who despite her age remembered so much) is the fact that she did not see the character of the Amsterdam Jewish market as negative. She was attracted to the picturesque, and as soon as she arrived she began to seek out the striking figures of the neighborhood. They fascinated her, as did the Jewish market on Sundays.

However, she could not get used to living amid the din and dirt. And she had learned in her middle-class Rotterdam upbringing that certain lifestyles did not fit in the modern world. If one wanted to escape from the life of the ghetto (which for her was synonymous with making progress), it was necessary to break with what was regarded as Jewish.

In the following section of that interview, surprise mingles with her positive reaction to the picturesque:

"Bree Street (on Sunday) was full of handcarts with New Year's cards and fruit. There was a man with dried dab [a sort of flounder] and salted salmon, and you could get sourballs for six cents. And at Hoofiën—that was a cellar—you could get fresh cheese for six cents per 100 grams. I had never before seen people buying 50 grams of coffee. The diamond workers were having a really hard time then, and they got 12 guilders welfare. So on Mondays all their stuff was hauled off to the pawnbroker's and on Fridays they got it out again. . . .

"You know what really got to me? There was that old Schapedief who was always quarreling with his wife out in the street. But they sang in their own special way and went round with a little can to collect money afterward. When I heard them for the first time, I really wanted to get a closer look, and I followed them—and I burned my dinner. . . . I found them so quaint!

"And that Japie Schapedief. He hadn't a clue as to what was going on . . . and in the middle of summer he walked around in a winter coat with a rope. I asked, 'Why are you walking around in a frayed winter coat?' And he answered, 'Why do you have hair on your head?' "

In the interview with Mrs. E., her fascination with the Jewish Corner compensated for the horror she felt at the misery and the strangeness. She wanted to tell me about more than just her abhorrence since she was all too aware that those images of the streets had disappeared for good. (She herself was a survivor from a concentration camp.)

How bad was it, really? And how much better was it elsewhere? I wanted to get back to the difference between her two apartments in order to grasp better what was nostalgic and what was truly ghetto-like. So I asked her to tell me about the advantages of the new apartment.

"The one we went to, now that was a bigger apartment. We had a pretty front room there, a pretty back room, too, two little bedrooms, and a small recessed balcony." According to her, it was less Jewish. I wanted to know more about what she meant by that, because after all she moved to a street on which at least as many Jews lived as on Nieuwe Kerk Street. I wanted to know why those things she called less Jewish were better:

"Could you explain to me what you mean by 'too Jewish'?"

"Well, Nieuwe Kerk Street was a messy street. There were a lot of families living in cellars. And they dumped the tables and chairs outside, and then they sat there cleaning vegetables. I found that a pretty odd sight! And in the evening playing cards outdoors. They sat in cellars. I never went in, and I had no intention whatsoever of living in one, for I came from a lovely home in Rotterdam."

So "Jewish" meant ghetto culture, poverty, and perhaps also dirt.

"Was it very dirty there?"

"Well, you know, the poor certainly were not squeaky clean, not clean at all. And all those vegetables out on the street . . . "

Mrs. E. did not maintain a traditional or kosher household, but she did keep Friday evenings. That was her bond with Jewishness—a different sort, certainly, from the Jewishness referred to so far in her interview. The two notions were maintained side by side and interwoven. I was interested in this other meaning of Jewishness—tradition. When I asked about the way Friday evening was kept, she answered:

"I got that from my mother's example, and I continued with it. But it's true, as time passes, it grows weaker—the longer you're married. Occasionally we even went away on Friday evening. But in the early years I certainly kept Friday evenings, and on Yom Kippur I fasted. . . . That gradually fell away."

Did the loss of tradition also mean a change in her social environment? "Were your friends all Jewish?"

"Jews, all of them were Jewish." [14]

Clearly, being Jewish could be experienced and lived out in many different ways.

Lepel Street, another side street off Weesper Street, was probably no longer referred to as part of the Jewish Quarter. Yet if you lived there, you certainly lived in that quarter. With the demolition of Uilenburg, many poor people came to live in those narrow houses, and the people who already lived there grew poorer. Nevertheless, the socialist atmosphere created by the SDAP continued to dominate the street. In contrast to Nieuwe Kerk Street, right next door, this was a street where you preferred not to live unless you were a socialist.

I asked Ab about the Jewish character of the area and about the "others" who had always lived there. Ab came from a family of diamond workers. His family was also no longer religious, yet they were still somewhat affected by religion. Ab received an education, turned orthodox, and moved to Palestine. Despite his late conversion to religious Zionism, he was proud of his political origins in the SDAP and ANDB, which he was fed along with his first spoons of porridge.

"Uncle Henri is my cousin," he said during the interview, referring to Henri Polak, the leader of the diamond workers. Reacting to my surprise, he assured me that this was a common way of talking and symbolized the closeness of ties with socialism—everyone claimed to be Uncle Henri's cousin. He continued:

"I was born in 1923 on Lepel Street, the part that is still standing, number 83—between Weesper and Roeters Street. My father was a diamond worker. My mother didn't work. I don't remember any polishing being done in the apartment, though I remember them being cut and split. My father worked in the factory on Nieuwe Achtergracht. I went to the Jewish school, though there was no specifically Jewish atmosphere at home, certainly not consciously orthodox. My parents lived in a ghetto, a sort of ghetto, a voluntary ghetto. Let's take a look at Lepel Street, that little bit where we lived; I could count the number of non-Jews living there on two hands. There was a greengrocer who wasn't Jewish, and a grocer. . . . The [public] school was closed on *shabbes*. For years there were two non-Jews in my class of thirty or thirty-five kids, and a few more in my brother's class."

"Did you ever notice any differences or discrimination when you were little?"

"Oh yes, certainly, out on the streets. Not only on the part of the non-Jews."

Ab meant that discrimination went both ways—his own group excluded the non-Jews.

"At school you found it, too. I didn't suffer because of it, but I remember how they'd say, 'dirty, rotten Jew.' And as time went by, it grew worse . . . there are memories from Lepel Street . . . " He said no more. Was he thinking of the anti-Semitism of his childhood, or was he reacting to the knowledge of how Lepel Street was later emptied? Memories overlap each other, and it was Lepel Street that figured so prominently in later literature—one raid emptied the whole street. The suddenness of the raid was described after the war by Marga Minco in her book *Bitter Herbs*:

> The following morning I walked along Lepel Street again. It was strewn with paper. Doors hung wide open everywhere. A gray cat sat on the steps of one dark porch. . . . A few buildings away, a door hung off its hinges, the panels split open, and the mailbox crookedly suspended from a nail. Some pieces of paper were sticking out of it. I could not make out whether they were letters or printed material. Curtains billowed out from a number of windows. A flowerpot lay overturned on the edge of a window sill. Through another window I could see a table, ready-laid—a bread roll on a plate, a knife stuck in the butter.
>
> The butcher's shop where I had bought some meat the day before stood empty. A plank had been hammered across the door so no one could enter. Someone must have done that very early. . . . (p. 80)

Ab was obviously dealing with a combination of memories from the Holocaust and other unpleasant events. Throughout my contact with him he made it clear that one of the reasons he had moved to Israel was to escape anti-Semitism—an experience that had started when he was very young.

The family moved from the narrow Lepel Street and followed the same pattern as many other members of the SDAP, moving farther east:

"We later moved to East Amsterdam because the apartment was too much for my mother. Through the social services, the welfare department—I don't know what it was called—helped us find another place."

"Larger than the one on Lepel Street?"

"Yes, four rooms in comparison. A bedroom, a front room, an alcove, and a little side room. It was an old building [the one on Lepel Street], at least 60 or 70 years old when we lived there. I remember how a toilet was installed later. When I was little, there was an old-fashioned, well, what you'd call a privy. So it had to be really old. There were new buildings as well; for example, just a couple of doors down from us lived Professor Groen. He lived in a new apartment, twenty years newer than ours."

Ab moved to Retief Street and when we deal with the Transvaal area, we will take up his story again. He told how even on Lepel Street they were better off than his sister who lived on Rapenburger Street:

"Some of the people who moved out of the Jewish neighborhood had to do so because the houses were torn down. . . . Because it had been partly demolished, the living conditions for those who remained were extremely poor. But I can still remember how there were people living on Marken and Uilenburg with a single faucet for the whole building. At first my sister lived on Rapenburger Street till she left for the Indische neighborhood. She was the oldest of the children, already married. I remember water being brought into the buildings—they worked to install running water in every apartment. I remember that." [15]

Going to live in the Indische neighborhood was exceptional; this was one of the few times that the district was mentioned at all. A very limited number of Jews lived there. They formed 3.6 percent of the population and were often well assimilated. [16] Living in such a neighborhood, like living in Oosterburg, was a sign of assimilation.

Ab's parents, on the other hand, remained in the sheltered environment. To get a clear picture of how great an influence the socialism of his parents had on their way of life, I continued to ask him about his upbringing and about the extent of his contact with non-Jews. I wanted to know what values he had received from his parents. Being a socialist family meant, according to most of the literature, that there had been at least a partial severing of religious ties. Religion was not a central part of his upbringing, though most of the people with whom he dealt were Jewish.

"My parents' acquaintances were mainly diamond workers, and then just a few of the neighbors. Ninety percent, perhaps more, were Jews. The children at the Jewish school all had a more or less Jewish character—even if this was only, as you'd say today, a matter of reciting the Kaddish [prayers for the dead]. I am a religious Jew, but my parents were certainly not desperately eager to make their children religious. According to them, that only brought trouble. But if someone didn't know *aleph* and *beth* [the first letters of the Hebrew alphabet], he was in pretty poor shape. My parents went along with the socialists in general, but they weren't all that outspoken. As an ideology, they had no quarrel with it. Moreover, my mother came from a background that was quite orthodox by Dutch standards." [17]

The poverty and miserable conditions described in the Municipal Archives of Amsterdam include countless examples of the allegedly antisocial attitude of the inhabitants of the buildings around Nieuwe Kerk Street. These people had to be educated, since the conditions in which they now lived seemed comparable to those previously found in the ghetto. That was intolerable. Jewish culture was clearly confused with antisocial behavior. It cannot be denied that in addition to the popular culture—the celebration of Purim, sitting out in the street, etc.—there were indeed some things that were antisocial. If we pay careful attention to the following account of a family written by an official of the municipal welfare department, we get a tragic picture of poverty, degradation, and misery. The passage, written in 1929 about one of the families that had been stigmatized as antisocial, makes a pitiful impression.

The family lived with three children in one of the basement apartments that had been declared uninhabitable. The man was a cigar maker. The woman was dreadfully high-strung and found it impossible to concentrate. The five of them lived in a back room containing two bed niches, a sink, and a privy. In the front room there was a bed "which was never made because there was a dog on it who wouldn't get off." The bed niches stank. [18]

One woman, Mrs. S. (because of the nature of the story, she wanted to remain anonymous), also lived on Lepel Street. Her mother died when she was very young. Her father was a diamond worker. There were eight children, and the household included a grandmother and an aunt. The aunt did the housekeeping, and the mother, while she was alive, was a diamond cutter. The story differs very little from accounts of life in the old ghetto. There was paid work done in the home, a family that was too large in lodgings that were too small, a very busy family life, and in this case drunkenness. S. was the only person I interviewed who was prepared to talk openly about the way the wages were paid out in cafés. The family had known good times—something that was evident from the way the front room was seldom used, despite the lack of space:

"My mother sat working all day. At home. It was like that then—a diamond cutter would work at home. My mother would sit at a little table, working. . . . Now, how can I describe it for you? She sat at that little table with a tray in front of her. She called it a tray, and in it were the stones to be cut. Like this, with both hands moving."

"One diamond against the other?"

"Yes, apparently. . . .

"We had a front room, an alcove or bed recess (as they called it then), a back room, and a side room. The boys slept in the side room, the girls in the alcove, and my father and mother in the living room in a bed niche. . . . My aunt slept with the girls in the alcove. . . . At both ends, two at the head and two at the foot. That used to be called a crib. We had a front room, but were only allowed to go into it on Saturdays; it was the best room. In the living room there was a huge table with a lot of chairs. In the front room there was a smaller table and chairs and a little cabinet, a really beautiful cabinet. There had to be one best room because on Saturdays we had to go and sit in there."

"People came to visit?"

"Of course."

"Family or friends?"

"Family, for in those times you had so many relatives that you hardly had any friends."

"Were your parents religious?"

"They observed Saturday. That was because . . . my father was in the diamond industry. On Friday work finished, and my father came home. I can see it all in front of me. At one o'clock he came home. Then there was always a piece of steak for him. That was a Jewish custom. Two people were earning in our family because my mother worked, so we did well. In other families there was sometimes a piece of beef heart waiting for the father when he came home if they hadn't enough money to buy a real piece of steak. Then my father would have to go along to the café to reckon up with the boss. The fellows had to do that, you know what I mean, don't you."

"Did he come home drunk—or didn't he drink? You know how they say that the diamond workers didn't drink."

"At that time they did! The workers who had Friday afternoon free would begin drinking because they were sitting in the café with all the others. We had a settee in the room, and when he came home he'd just flop down onto it."

"But he had been working hard all week!"

"Yes, but my mother had been working hard, too; she and my aunt had been working hard at housekeeping. As a child I found it awful. How he behaved and that he was drunk. I've always resented that. I knew that it made my mother unhappy. You notice such things as a child. He only drank on Friday, which was a feast day, yet it was the worst day of the week."

Despite her nonreligious upbringing, Friday evening was not without meaning for her. All along the street the people were at home, sitting around the table:

"Because you know how it was with us on Fridays. We worked ourselves to death. The table was set more carefully, always with a little more, a little better. Much more sociable, and then my father got in the way of that. Of course he was at home, but there were very few Fridays when he sat happily at the table with us. . . .

"We didn't really have anything to do with religion, but on Fridays not one of the children was allowed out the door. There were always candles and a white tablecloth on Friday. That was the custom. And when we were ready to eat, we got the candle holder and the candles and lit them. But there were no prayers said, or anything like that."

"I can imagine how, at that time, if you walked down Lepel Street on a Friday evening, there'd be all those families behind the windows, sitting down to eat."

"Yes, that was it on Friday evening, and not only on Lepel Street. You could say that out of a hundred Jewish people, ninety-nine were Jewish [in origin and way of life].[19]

"The children older than me all went to the Jewish school for religious education. There were teachers there who hit the children. When it was my turn to go, my father said, 'You don't need to go there to get beaten.'"

The diamond worker was clearly modern in outlook when it came to upbringing and whether to beat a child or not. But that did not mean that his own behavior was civilized. The custom of going to the cafés together to drink was consistently condemned by Henri Polak (the leader of the diamond workers), yet it persisted. The mother and children knew that it was not good, and were ashamed of his behavior. They not only felt themselves let down by his drinking, but separated from their surroundings by it in two ways. First, traditional Jewish life did not countenance excessive drinking. Second, socialism regarded alcoholism and decency as irreconcilable opposites.

When her mother died, S. was taken in by a family living on Blasius Street near Campert Street. It was a different environment: "Rougher, yes, it's odd to say that, for I grew up there."[20] Despite the alcoholism and the bad housing, her early upbringing was actually a bit better than some. Perhaps that came about because of the background of the diamond workers. Blasius Street was farther from the old ghetto, but that was not enough to make it any better.

The idea that only the *crème de la crème* lived in the neighborhood of the Ooster Park was already well out of date. True, the houses built around one part of the park and those put up in the 1870s beside the Amstel River were larger and the streets there were wider. Real poverty generally did not penetrate this area. Wealthy people and those who had never known scarcity lived there. But behind the richer sections there were narrower, poorer streets. The people who lived in the wealthier area were often assimilated and lived there for longer periods. In the poorer parts there was more movement. Some streets were really messy. Handcarts stood everywhere along the streets, the people lived on the stoops, and the apartments were overcrowded. What little prosperity they had enjoyed disappeared with the Depression.

This variation in prosperity within one neighborhood was connected with the different phases of emigration from the ghetto to the area around the park. The first generation that came from the ghetto consisted of parents with small families. But the families that came later were no longer small.

The center of Jewish life in this area was Blasius Street, where both the richer and the poorer lived. For some, this area was just a halfway house on the way from the ghetto to somewhere else. Despite the ghetto-like character of the place, people felt better off here than in the ghetto itself.

Suze, a diamond worker who had never known hunger, came to live in the Jewish part of Blasius Street. Her father was a diamond worker, and she also chose that trade. For her the break with the Jewish neighborhood was not great; she enjoyed returning to visit her family. This is her story:

"I lived on Blasius Street. . . . My father was a polisher, and we, too, had been through hard times—but not bitter poverty. My father had ten brothers and sisters, my mother also. My mother had a religious background. I had a very respectable family. Still, we did have some real troubles, I realize that; for diamonds just went up and down. Then my grandmother would take us in. There'd sometimes be as many as ten or twelve people with her. My grandfather had a cigar stand at the market, and everyone . . . could eat at their lodgings on Weesper Square. I can still see the cigar boxes; my grandfather wearing his cap, I can see him right there in the living room; because, of course, you never had big apartments. A bed niche, with four or five to a bed. Yes, and a quilt."

"Did your relatives live close to them in their neighborhood?"

"Weesper Street. Everyone, actually, lived in the old Jewish neighborhood. Oh yes, and on Weesper Square." [21]

The ghetto-like character of Blasius Street, which was not part of the true Jewish neighborhood, was made clear in many of the stories I heard. Sara, a contemporary of Suze whose background was similar, said, "It was so nice on Blasius Street—you could buy everything. And, you know, on Thursday evening—that was a real Jewish custom—you could get fish. And then in winter there were *kuitjes* [fried fish roe]." [22] It was an untidy street, especially the Jewish part. The children played among the handcarts, and the atmosphere gave no indication that the once-proud Ooster Park neighborhood had originally been built for the respectable middle class.

The separation between richer and poorer began in that neighborhood. Up to this point all the interviews were with people who either themselves or through their parents consciously or unconsciously chose to maintain ties with the life of the ghetto. That is not to say that people living elsewhere ignored tradition. In the other areas, however, it was not Jewish proletarian culture that set the tone, but socialist culture—and seldom anything else.

THE SYMBOLIC SIGNIFICANCE OF EAST AMSTERDAM: SOCIALIST CULTURE REPLACING THE JEWISH PROLETARIAN CULTURE

In the Ooster Park area, there were some streets where life was governed more by contemporary socialist ideas about the modern worker's family rather than by traditional values. The movement to civilize the workers was apparently a great success in these streets—the myth had become reality. These modern workers were conscious of being better than everyone they believed they had left behind. East was a metaphor; it meant a new way of life and a new future.

Marcus, in his story of a childhood spent on Beuken Road, treated the Ooster Park district as part of East Amsterdam, scarcely distinct from the Transvaal area. He did not see it as an extension of the ghetto. He deliberately opted for a different way of life. Since the families were smaller, the children would have greater opportunities. Marcus himself came from such a small family whose apartment was adequate in size. "In that neighborhood limits on family size began. Yes, in contrast to the places they came from, they had learned their lesson. And if I think back carefully, . . . my friends were all in about the same situation. . . . Families with lots of kids were less common in East Amsterdam. Those who left the ghetto for the East had a different point of view. They wanted to be different from what they'd left behind."

Nevertheless, he was sent to a Jewish school, which did not suit him. Then he was sent to an ordinary public school, and in the first year was top of his class. In addition, after school, he still took classes in Judaism. His parents moved to the new districts in East Amsterdam and then back to the old Jewish neighborhood where the dilapidated lodgings were cheap. "It was dirtier there, although the Ooster Park neighborhood was hardly what you'd call really comfortable—there were no bathrooms in those apartments. Still, the places in the old ghetto were even less satisfactory—often teeming with vermin, too." [23]

However, this case was an exception. Those who had grown away from the Jewish proletariat in the Ooster Park district and had created a "modern" existence for themselves could generally deal much better with this change than others who had moved to East Amsterdam. The people who lived near Ooster Park had not been moved there by the authorities. As a result of being in somewhat better circumstances, they had chosen to move to an area that had nice gardens and spacious squares. They regarded themselves as modern and assimilated, the latter being in fact a necessary part of being modern.

The following interview gives us a picture of that modern proletariat of highly-qualified diamond workers, some of whom retained their jobs even during the Depression. Despite the collapse of those sectors of the economy in which large numbers of Jews worked, there were also highly-skilled workers who were never out of work, such as the cutters who worked on the finest quality diamonds. They were always needed, and though their wages fell, they never had to rely on charity. Even during World War II, a number of these top diamond cutters were exempted from deportation. The German occupying forces saw the value of letting the rich Amsterdam diamond industry continue operating for as long as possible. When the processing of smaller stones moved to Antwerp during the 1930s, the cutting and polishing of expensive stones and large pieces remained in Amsterdam.

Louis was an example of one of these highly-qualified workers. His story shows that he was far more assimilated than the people whose stories we have read so far.

"I lived on Iepen Square; that was a really mixed neighborhood. But I think there were more Christians than Jews living on the square itself. We lived on the third floor, and below us were Christians, and below them Jews."

"What were relations like among those people?"

"First rate. . . . I always hung around near the Ooster Park; we had a small open space at Iepen Square with a nice playground . . . we played soccer, and we held cycling contests."

His father came from Zaandam, which had a small Jewish community. These little communities outside Amsterdam were called *medinas*. People from such places did not have the experience of living continuously in a ghetto. The *medina* in Zaandam, with its shabby, lower-middle-class life was described by Carrie van Bruggen in *Het huisje aan de sloot* [The Little House by the Ditch]. Behind the drab, patched curtains, a kind of Jewish life flourished that regarded the Jewish proletariat of Amsterdam as, above all, frightening. The ghetto—that was filth, a corruption of Jewish life. There, narrow-minded village Jews maintained tradition in the strictest form. The non-Jews around them were the enemy. People hid themselves from the non-Jewish community.

Louis's parents had adapted to life in the city. They chose the respectable part of the Ooster Park neighborhood with its high standards of decency, which gave new form to Jewish life outside the ghetto. Thus Louis learned to live in a mixed neighborhood, one where it was no longer the case that almost everyone was Jewish. Louis had grown up in such an environment, had gone to school with non-Jews, and had scarcely been brought up as Jewish. I wondered whether he had later become integrated into that community as a whole or had limited his circle to his Jewish neighbors. Was he assimilated? His ambivalent attitude became clear through the story he told of his "Christian" friends who adopted Jewish customs. Since Louis is younger than the other people I interviewed, this account deals with the early 1930s.

"I don't know if you are familiar with the Ooster Park area, with Vrolik Street. Many diamond workers lived there. Your friends were mostly drawn from that area. We didn't have anything against religion, we weren't against it. It was just that we couldn't allow ourselves to be religious, and we had to work on Saturdays. . . . It's odd, I had Christian friends, and I found that they adapted to us rather than us moving in their direction. In expressions, Jewish expressions and so on. Honestly, I saw no difference between Jew and Christian. And if anyone yelled at you for being a Jew, then it was mostly because he was drunk. And then the Christians defended us." [24]

Past the area of Ooster Park lay the Muider Gate Quarter and the Dapper and Indische neighborhoods, which were very similar to each other as far as the structure of Jewish life goes. But the Indische neighborhood was a little more Jewish since it adjoined some Jewish streets farther up in East Amsterdam. There was a little *sjoel* there, and you could buy kosher goods. This whole area was somewhat more isolated from the centers of Jewish life than others like Ooster Park, since a railroad had been built across it. As I wrote earlier, to live there was a sign of assimilation. In the shabby nineteenth-century buildings, many people had traditionally lived who were more leftist than the social democrats. It was a typical example of a middle-class area that had become a workers' neighborhood through neglect and expansion.

Herman lived with his family for a while in the Transvaal area, farther out in East Amsterdam, where a large number of Jews lived. There, he felt, life was better. But in time the family came to live in the Indische neighborhood, which was clearly less satisfactory. Yet despite everything he romanticizes it:

"As for real poverty, I see Molukken Street; having no supper before bed—I see Molukken Street. There was always a *boterham* [bread with jam, cheese, or thinly sliced meat] in the morning. But, you know, the funny thing is—and that was how it was then—you were actually a bit proud that you had been able to get to sleep without any food. You didn't suffer terribly because of it, or whine for food. No. My father managed, my mother managed, and so did I! I suppose it had to do with a kind of solidarity with the proletariat, I don't quite know how to put it . . . . From Molukken Street we moved to an area where there were more Jews."

I asked Herman what it was like to observe Jewish traditions in a mixed neighborhood.

"I had my Bar Mitzvah on Molukken Street. And I went with my father to a little *sjoel*. Actually, it was a living room, just an apartment on the ground floor, with a little *sjoel* above it . . . a few wooden benches, it was really very shabby . . . the Bimah [a platform in a synagogue] and the Aaron Hakodesh [the Holy Ark where the Torah scrolls are stored]—perhaps they had a couple of scrolls. But the man who read aloud from the Torah came from Rapenburger Street. He, too, had moved to the East. No, there was no rabbi, and we all took turns at being the *chazzan* [cantor]. And there were no *drosjes* [sermons]. If a rabbi from elsewhere came to see how we were doing, we treated him like a demigod."

How little the neighborhood there understood Jewish traditions is clear from the following account. At his Bar Mitzvah, Herman was given new shoes, which hurt his feet. After the service, the people went back to his parent's home. "The Monday after that she went over to the neighbor's at the store, the greengrocer's. My mother told them proudly, 'Well, we had a real good party! Herman came of age in the synagogue.' 'Yes,' said the woman, 'we saw you pass by on your way home, and when I saw Herman limping I said to my husband: You see there, it's a big party, little Herman has been circumcised today.' . . . They didn't have a clue." [25]

Although the neighbors understood very little of Jewish tradition and scarcely anything of Jewish religion (as is shown by Herman's story), it was clear that all of the people interviewed lived close to or among so many Jews that in their own way they were able to shape a new way of life together. You could say that it was a Jewish–socialist life, in which integration into the surrounding society was so minimal that people still essentially lived with and among Jews. The character of the socialism there was in part determined by Jewish tradition, despite—and at the same time because of—the fact that the image of a new socialist world was specifically contrasted with that tradition. Quite a number of the people I interviewed in East Amsterdam denied that

Jewish culture played a dominant role in the creation of this socialist culture. The people really thought they were dealing with something quite different—that they were breaking away from Jewish tradition. Yet even if their goal was to break with the past, nothing guaranteed their success.

UNCERTAINTY AND CERTAINTY ABOUT ASSIMILATION AND INTEGRATION

The farther one lived from the old Jewish neighborhood, the more assimilated one was thought to be. Thus the upwardly mobile diamond workers, proto-typical products of the attempt to raise the cultural level of the proletariat, lived in the Pijp to the south. Parts of that area could be regarded as a Jewish neighborhood were it not for the fact that those who moved there adapted to existing neighborhood customs, which were not Jewish. In West Amsterdam, there were similar districts with their own customs, where a few Jewish workers or members of the middle class had gone to find work among the non-Jews. Mostly this resulted from the socialist belief that differences would disappear. Sometimes people moved without such a conviction and were merely trying to earn more.

More than any other district, the Pijp was the place to which the better-educated workers moved. They saw in the dignified streets around Sarphati Park and the houses with their wide verandas an environment in which they could live in the style they felt was appropriate. They employed household help, and their children attended the more expensive schools. Many of them were self-employed diamond workers who bought stones to cut and polish. The migration to the Pijp originally dated from the diamond boom at the end of the nineteenth century. For these diamond workers, living there meant assimilation—often so much so that it was unclear just what remained of Jewishness in the Jewish families in the Pijp. Had assimilation really proceeded so far that the Jewish character had been entirely swept away? Or was this just a myth about living in the Pijp? There were poor streets there as well, and a *sjoel* on Gerard Dou Street that had attracted market stall-holders, among others, for years.

Many of the interviews confirmed that assimilation had proceeded a long way in the Pijp. Bloeme, daughter of a communist worker, talked about it and, in her own fashion, threw light on the tension that existed between the Jews and assimilation.

"We lived on Van Ostade Street, a side street off Van Wou Street; I remember it being a building with little alcove apartments. The second floor was so low that the newspaper man could hand the paper to my mother by stretching upward while she stretched down toward him.When I was seven, we moved to Lutma Street. I think that was a bit better, but not much."

Bloeme came from a small family with only two children. Her mother had moved in from the *medina*, her father from the ghetto.

"My father grew up in indescribable living conditions. There was a single room for the whole family, and the toilet was a bucket. It stood in the hallway for general use. . . . It was unimaginable poverty, and I can see how proud my father must have been of his five-room apartment. He had set religion aside quite radically in deference to the ideas of communism and socialism—the rabbis had failed us while this new way of life was very promising. . . . Early on he joined the workers' movement, the ANDB, and played a role there."

I asked her what that implied regarding his attitude to his background—the ghetto from which he had come.

"He had broken away from religion but he remained a Jew, heart and soul. It is remarkable, but it is not just religion, it's also . . . er . . . a national awareness before its time. I well remember how we were out for a walk once and we met someone and he used a Yiddish expression. I stiffened, small as I was, for I knew with certainty what it was about. And after the meeting was over, I asked, 'Why did you say that?' He said, 'Well, he's also Jewish!' I said, 'How did you know that, how could you tell?' And he said, 'You learn.' "

Did she know non-Jews as well? To what extent did people mix with them? Was her family completely integrated?

"Although we lived very much within a Jewish environment, we certainly had non-Jewish friends. But I always felt some distance between us without it ever being made explicit. More important, I was seven years old before anyone yelled at me for being a rotten Jew, and I ran home crying for I felt it was nasty but I didn't really understand it. On Yom Kippur I was given a note to take to school asking that I be given the day off. But I never knew what I had to do with it: I wanted to express my commitment to Jewish traditions, and I wanted to find out which of the children I had thought were Jewish attended school on Yom Kippur. But I didn't really know what I should do. I felt very ambivalent."

Life had long since ceased to be ruled by the Jewish calendar alone. In Bloeme's circle, new holidays and customs existed. Hanukkah, the Feast of Lights, had been replaced by St. Nicholas, a new evening to exchange little packages:

"St. Nicholas was enthusiastically celebrated at our home. That was one of the high points of the year, and my mother saved up for it for months. But you mustn't imagine that the presents were all that fancy—underpants, for example, which we needed anyway. But also little luxuries like toys, those too."

Did they go so far as to celebrate Christmas, a truly Christian holiday? "What did you do at Christmas?"

"Well, that was a rather low-key occasion. My father definitely didn't want a Christmas tree and so on in the house, and I think my mother agreed. But we did light candles when my mother—who had a natural talent on the piano—played Silent Night as well as truly Jewish songs. And I sang along and felt no ambivalence at all—I only saw that later."

"Did you keep Friday evenings, Yom Kippur, and Rosh Hashanah [the Jewish New Year]?"

"Well, we didn't keep Fridays, though way back in the past I have some memories. There was a white tablecloth, way back. Nothing was done that was really Jewish except . . . the tablecloth, good things to eat, and no one went out on Friday evenings. That was *gar nicht im Frage* [German, out of the question]."

"You said that your earliest memory of anti-Semitism was being yelled at?"

"Yes, to be precise, by the little girl who sat next to me in school. It shocked me, for I still feel it and that happened fifty years ago. It would have been better to forget it but I didn't. I think I vaguely knew we were Jewish, but it had no name, no clear name. . . . In retrospect, I see how Jewish my parents were. They had nothing to do with the religion, yet we never saw pork on the table."

"What do you mean?"

"The world as they saw it had no place for Jewishness, as a religion, aside from these one or two little things. I believe my mother had let Jewishness fall away under my father's influence. At least the religious part. . . . She only taught me things unconsciously.

"For example, when she was baking a cake she'd put the egg in a glass and look at it before throwing it into the batter. When I began to follow kosher practices in my home, I learned that you had to look at the egg to check if there was blood in it. I thought my mother was looking to see if the egg was bad, but she did it because, watching her mother, she had seen that she had to look for blood. . . .

"They had certain educational goals, and I don't believe the ghetto was compatible with them. Teaching about sex, for example—my mother had a lot of trouble getting that past her lips, but she managed. At first she prattled on about the birds and the bees, and as a child you didn't know how to make the connection. She said that I came from the baby tree, that they had seen me hanging there and immediately found me a sweet, attractive little baby and said: 'We want that one.' Well, I took all that in and pretty much forgot it. At least it assured me that they had really wanted me. But when I was six, the truth dawned; I came home from school and told my mother: 'It's not true about the baby tree—babies come from the bellies of their mothers.' At which my mother took me onto her knee rather solemnly and told me the truth."[26]

The people who lived near Sarphati Park had a more or less middle-class way of life. This area was also full of Jews, but daily life was no longer Jewish. Annie, whose story follows, went to a school that had hardly any other Jewish children. Even in childhood she longed for the past, and nothing gave her greater pleasure than to tell me about her visits to the old Jewish neighborhood. She clearly suffered from the fact that her parents had left the familiar surroundings behind. That was expressed in her longing for the rest of the family, which had been left behind in the ghetto. Annie was born in the Pijp, on Jan Steen Street where there were few Jews and which was relatively far away from the old neighborhood. Her feelings about being uprooted centered around her experiences at school:

"You never went to school in the Jewish neighborhood?"

"Never. I remember speaking to friends later who had been to school somewhere on Hoog Street or Bree Street. It was a really well-known school, and these children always said how much fun it had been. It was a nice school with all those Jewish children. They were in their own environment; we weren't any more. I went to school with rather irritating, vulgar kids. Round about Passover there were a couple of *shiksahs* [a mildly contemptuous word for non-Jewish females] in our neighborhood who were pretty nice and we gave them matzos. There were Jewish children in the area, too, and I played with them. At school it was mixed."

Yet her story was all about her feeling of being isolated. Was that because of the school?

"It was partly because of the school, yes absolutely because of the school. You didn't feel you were Jewish. I felt myself isolated, and that came about in other ways. We were simply misplaced, that whole generation. You no longer belonged in the ghetto, and yet you still didn't belong anywhere else. Very difficult. Then there was that difference between what actually happened and what you imagined in your head should happen. My parents were displaced, socially misplaced. Everyone wanted a bit more. Yet you remained a Jew. I believe we were among the first families that moved away from the Jewish district."

"Can you remember anything of the differences?" (This question was an attempt to penetrate the nostalgia for the old neighborhood. Perhaps it would clarify the advantages of the Pijp if we talked explicitly about the differences. The summary of the differences in fact led to yet more nostalgia for a world in which roles and customs were clearer than they were at home.)

"Yes, I had an aunt, one of the poor members of the family. She worked at the market. The Nieuw Market. She lived on Koe Street, and I found that great."

"Did she sleep in an 'alcove'?"

"No, in a bed niche. She had ten or so children. And I thought it was just lovely—she served great big hunks of *boterkoek* [butter cake] baked to perfection, so rich and dry that you could sit on it in a white dress, and it was wonderful to go there. And those people just loved me. On Saturday afternoons I always went to my grandmother. And then we would go visit her sister who lived on Weesper Street where she had a shop. And she would say, 'Here, little lady, have a piece of *boterkoek*—lovely!' "

"Was it still considered respectable in your family to live in the ghetto?"
"Not any more. I remember a fine family who continued to lived there. We found that a bit odd, you know. For if you actually came to think in a rather more modern, civilized way, then you left. I never lived there. You turned your nose up at it a bit. It was nothing—just the Jewish neighborhood."[27]

Freddie (a woman) was one of the few people I interviewed who lived in the Staatslieden area on the western boundary of the city, and this alone marked her as belonging among those families who had resolutely turned their backs on the ghetto in order to lead a "modern" life. Catholic and Protestant workers made up most of the population. Many were radical leftists. Scarcely any were Jewish. Most, like Freddie's parents, lived in buildings belonging to the Amsterdam Woningbouwvereniging [Municipal Building Cooperative]; they were built according to the formula: small but nice—and above all inexpensive—to live in. This was an area where the real working class lived—longshoremen, carpenters, and industrial workers. It was a typical Amsterdam workers' district, but far poorer than the Pijp, far less social democratic, and less Jewish than the Transvaal area.

Freddie's father was a taxi driver, a decidedly non-Jewish occupation. In that way he managed to scratch together a living. Her story is marked throughout by the regret she felt for the fact that, at the time, she had been ashamed of her parents' way of life. They were too poor and above all, despite everything, too traditionally Jewish, too distinct from the rest of the neighborhood. Out of embarrassment caused by the lack of assimilation, Freddie herself thoroughly embraced the wish to assimilate. She belonged to the generation that consciously wanted to assimilate and to leave behind entirely the attitudes of the ghetto. Her parents, of course, also wanted this, which is why they had gone to live in a non-Jewish neighborhood. But they had not succeeded.

"When they were first married, my parents had their first apartment on Schaepman Street in the Staatslieden district. Those buildings had just been put up by the Amsterdam Building Cooperative. They were the first modern workers' dwellings. And there were already quite a few Jewish people living there because, oh . . . they were all socialists. On 1 May, it was all red from the red flags. . . . It was a four-room apartment, a comfy apartment.

"My father was a diamond courier, and during the Depression that became very difficult. He was among those on welfare who were assigned work, and at the last moment got his driver's license. He became a taxi driver. I believe he was the first Jewish taxi driver in Amsterdam. Our family became much poorer. The furnishings and the floor covering were damaged, and when I had girlfriends round, I found it awful. I was ashamed of how things were."

"Was the neighborhood a little better off than you were?"

"No, it was pretty general, but there were people whose income was secure."

"Were your parents orthodox?"

"They had abandoned it all."

"They were the first generation to abandon it?"

"Yeah. . . . My mother was the youngest of a big family, and she had a sister who was, . . . oh, at least 13 years older than her who looked after . . . she wasn't married, she looked after my brother's family. They lived in the Transvaal area. They were a poor but intellectual family. On my father's side they were more commercially oriented, not so socialist."

"But of course those who went to the Transvaal district were socialists?"

"Yes, but they were also what you might call religious. The aunt had a suitor, but they were never married, in part because the aunt looked after the whole family, all those people. And her friend, he was a religious man, orthodox. When he came to visit, everything had to be done according to the rules."

"So you didn't have any Jewish education?"

"No, but to my way of thinking that was unfortunate. They wavered between two worlds. As a result of the neighborhood, I think, they abandoned more of the religion than would have been the case if they had lived in a Jewish neighborhood. And they more or less chose socialism. Quite freely . . . we went to public schools, my father actively defended the public schools. But it was also true, at least I had that feeling, that it was nicer if you brought a Jewish boy home so you could have a blessing on the marriage."

"Did you keep Friday evenings?"

"Oh, just a little bit, and it was true that the social aspect of . . . but actually Saturday evening, too. . . . My aunt, that aunt, she was called Eef, she was a bit like a grandmother to us all. And when we ate with her, it was all much more Jewish than at home. . . . My mother baked butter cake for the whole of West Amsterdam. And that went to the baker's oven; of course, you didn't have your own oven then. She could bake really well. She baked butter cake for everyone all the time."

"Were you the only Jewish child at your school or in the class?"

"Pretty much so, as far as I could tell. It was a real working-class neighborhood."

"Did your parents try to hide the fact that you were Jewish in your neighborhood?"

"Oh, no, not at all. So you wonder where you got it from [she had spoken about her feeling of inferiority]. We were a family that was sort of caught between two worlds."[28]

New apartment buildings were constructed to the north of the IJ Harbor, across the water that divided the city in two, and the Jews there lived in even greater isolation than in the Staatslieden area. The isolation was somewhat lessened by attempts on the part of the Jewish community to form some kind of organization. However, precisely because of the isolation and the wish to assimilate (on the one hand) and the fact that this was not succeeding (on the other) this plan led to new kinds of ambivalence.

Recha told about her childhood north of the IJ. There was considerable pressure to move among the non-Jewish majority. And Jewish life was far away. There was no Jewish butcher or poulterer, so it was hard to continue eating kosher. Every Friday Recha's mother crossed on the ferry and walked to the poulterer on Oosterpark Street, which must have taken her more than an hour. There were a number of reasons for doing this. In the interview, Recha told how the isolation led to problems of identity and changeable behavior regarding being Jewish. Her father was a consciously socialist worker, a typesetter, and a trade union member.

Recha said, in regard to this: "He wasn't active, but he did go to every meeting. He never held any administrative function, yet he went to the meetings. He was socialist, and he really didn't want to go on living in the Jewish neighborhood. He wanted to get out. He didn't want anything to do with the atmosphere of the ghetto. I was perhaps two years old when we moved to the other side of the IJ, and there I went to grade school. There were other Jews; my father stood out from most of the other workers who lived there. He was musical and was always going to concerts."

"At home, was it traditionally Jewish or . . . ?"

"Oh no, actually it was up and down, really only Friday evenings. You know, all that with the white cloth and the chicken soup. . . . That is strongly associated with my childhood. . . . The yellower the chicken the better. I still shudder at it. She would go completely . . . my mother would go right over to the other side of the IJ, to where friends of ours lived near Iepen Square, because the chickens there were so yellow . . . that's the fat. Yes, they were yellow, those chickens. Their skin, everything . . . you don't get them like that any more."

And they had to be yellow inside as well, from the fat. Birds like that from the old neighborhood were the only ones you could eat. The food they ate symbolized the relationship between the people and the old way of life. This observation agrees with research done among Jewish immigrants in France where, again, the food symbolized solidarity.[29] Moreover, the journey to the family near Ooster Park allowed them to keep abreast of the latest news. There was a good excuse—if they did not go, they could not eat. The mother said it was principally a matter of getting the chicken; at the very most she would pop in briefly to see the family. On Fridays, the pickle seller came to the three Jewish families on the street—a large number for North Amsterdam.

"The Komkommers lived next to us for a short while, and then the Schuitenvoerder family, who were very assimilated. They lived there all those years, till the very last [she is referring to the deportation]. For a while my father was . . . took the responsibility for Jewish life north of the IJ. So, suddenly I was not permitted to go to school on the Sabbath. And I found that awful, really awful—as I experienced it at the time—all at once to have to go to the Jewish school. And I didn't like that, didn't like it at all. Because it was so unusual at my school. I was the only child who didn't go to school on the Sabbath. I found it awful."

She was the only Jewish child in her class, and there were very few in the whole school.

"Did they ever look at you strangely because you were a Jew at that school? Did anyone ever say anything about it?"

"No, not at school. I can't remember it happening. . . . My youngest brother had it happen to him—he was yelled at once as a "Sammy," that kind of thing, but still, I think we stood out as being Jewish. There were always ties with the family [on Vrolik Street, across the water], and I really liked to go there, and I liked to go to the Jewish neighborhood on Sundays. My father would take me to the Jewish Quarter on Sunday mornings. . . . I believe he had really found his niche in North Amsterdam till, for whatever reason—I don't know—he decided to try to stimulate Jewish life.

"Then a Jewish association was set up, which he helped to found, and it consisted of assimilated Jews. With Mr. K., a civil servant who lived on Van der Pek Street, and he really liked that . . . he really did, but then he fell out with someone, and all of a sudden, of course, I had to go to school on the Sabbath again. I was a bit, well, really a bit frustrated!

"That time when he really felt Jewish, that was a good time for him. He went to the *sjoel*, and he liked being called to the Torah. It was in a café . . . the Tollhouse café. There was an upper floor, and that was furnished as a *sjoel*."

She started to work, and her parents insisted that she find a job that did not require her to work on the Sabbath.

"I believe it would have embarrassed them if, with the background of the Jewish association and its leadership, I had gone to work on the Sabbath. It was unacceptable. I don't think they *really* cared, but it simply wasn't proper, in that environment you just didn't do it."

As a consequence, she earned very little. People who did not work on Saturday were more vulnerable and could be exploited. She ended up working at the Bijenkorf, the largest department store in the center of the city. For a long time this store had been in Jewish hands and preferred to employ people from the better sector of the Jewish proletariat. As far as observing Jewish traditions went, there had been separate rules for Jews there for years.

"I think that that was also because there were so many Jews there. I don't think they liked the idea of my going to work as a clerk in a Simon de Wit grocery store on the other side of the IJ. But there [at the Bijenkorf] I was protected by the presence of a large number of Jews who were not in the minority. They were in the majority. In retrospect, I think that was true. At the time, I didn't think about such things and little was said."[30]

In Recha's tale the father's ambivalence is a clear example. Eventually she came to work among Jews, yet she spent her free time in a rather un-Jewish way. Since she earned money, she went out dancing on Friday evenings. This was in dance halls where the girls followed strict codes of behavior. For example, they never accepted anything to eat or drink from a man and never danced with the same man for consecutive dances. While dancing, the man and woman maintained their distance. Those who broke the rules were courting.

In time, she met a politically active man who was not Jewish but from Surinam. Bringing him home was not easy, and her father wondered what he had brought his daughter up for. For her, however, this was the logical conclusion of the socialist premise that every person is equal. From that viewpoint, tradition came to seem less important.

The northern parts of the city were the most distant from the ghetto, and there, as in this example, the ambivalences were strongest. Despite the conscious decision to leave old traditions behind, apparently some traditions and values could not be wiped out simply by a decision. Recha's father had noticed that and had vacillated in his reactions. Even this man from a very assimilated background had let himself get snared into furthering the cause of Jewish life north of the IJ. Yet his heart was not fully in it; if any problem arose, he came down, as it were, in favor of the other side of himself. He spent his life wondering whether to grasp the opportunity of embracing socialism and a new humanity, and this conflicted with the question whether to further the old religion—Judaism. His doubts affected the lives of the children. They were confronted with a father whose opinion could change from one day to the next. This changeability clearly affected the whole family's way of life.

Such ambivalence came to light in almost all the interviews and clearly undermined the idea that socialist convictions did away with Jewishness. The same was true for any generalizations about breaking ties with the old way of life. This was the first generation that had escaped the distress of the ghetto, and they had to suffer all the doubts and uncertainty that went with it.

In general, the farther away they went, the smaller the percentage of Jews who lived in the new neighborhood. Yet their attempts to lose themselves in the mass of non-Jews failed for the most part. Their children often went a step further. The first generation both looked down on their background and held fast to it. Every neighborhood yields different stories, and the choice of people to interview might seem rather arbitrary. The self-image of people who were present at the time and now look back can conflict with their memories. Yet what remains constant through all of the interviews is the great variety of experiences, all balancing the old with the new—and all the ambivalence that this entailed. That it should be so seems logical; a group that has persisted for centuries in a closed society cannot, within a brief period, cease to exist.[31]

Socialist expressions filled the void created when religion became less

important—life without an ideal is not possible. Socialism was modern and
not Jewish, but it was itself not a breaking away from Judaism. It was the
outcome of a newly adopted morality and was confused with being modern
and respectable. Jews themselves excluded non-Jews. L., from a highly assimilated family, spoke explicitly about this:

"When I was young, I used to be really annoyed by the negative way in
which even the speech of liberal socialist Jews, like the family in which I
grew up, described non-Jews. . . . This arose from a feeling of superiority
among the Jews that, to my way of thinking, had no basis. Somehow or other
from the notion of a chosen people." In his family, anti-Semitism was regarded as "purely the result of the class struggle; once classes were abolished,
anti-Semitism would disappear of itself. Precisely how that would happen
was not clear, but those were ideas they clung to. The mother of one of my
best friends, Mrs. . . . , literally said to me, 'We don't need religion; socialism
is our religion.' It was clear that people felt great pride in what the socialist
aldermen of Amsterdam had managed to achieve; it foreshadowed what a
completely socialist society would be. Then you went into the Jewish Quarter
and you saw how distressed the life of the people there was and how much
poverty there was." [32] Thus you became convinced that the socialist attitude
was the right one.

LEARNING TO LIVE IN A NEW ENVIRONMENT

The showpiece of social democratic municipal politics was the Transvaal
neighborhood, and most accounts deal with the standards that had been realized in that area. There, the idea of creating modern living conditions for the
Amsterdam working class would be realized. More than other places where
new dwellings were being built, the social democrats set their stamp on the
cultural environment of the Transvaal housing, and hence on the expectations
of the new inhabitants.

Yet despite the goal of equality, the district was divided into poor and rich
streets. In order to join a private building cooperative one had to pay 25
guilders, quite a sum in those days. [33] Consequently, public housing was the
least expensive. Moreover, the private building cooperatives had the right to
choose their members. The Catholic and Protestant building cooperatives
naturally gave preference to their own church members. The municipality, on
the other hand, had to accept anyone who needed a place to live, including the
"poorly adjusted" and "antisocial" families. [34]

The apartments in the new buildings were assigned according to rigid rules
aimed at maintaining peace and order. There were female building supervisors whose job it was to ensure that slovenly housekeeping practices would
disappear and that the poor who had escaped the ghetto would live as modern
workers. In filling the 1,500 apartments, the working class was therefore

divided into the poor, the very poor, those with large families, and the malad-justed or antisocial. It was the job of the municipality to provide for these people and to see to it that they lived in suitable conditions.[35]

A mechanism for social supervision was therefore set up, and those who broke the rules were sanctioned. In other words, they underwent a period of strict reeducation in the public institutions Aster Village and Zeeburg.[36] The adjustment was painful and upsetting, far from easy for everyone. Slovenli-ness and the habit of continually moving from apartment to apartment had to cease, and the rent had to be paid on time. This last was a real problem, especially once the Depression was in full swing. In general, places to live in the Transvaal area were not cheap, and people had landed there simply be-cause their previous dwelling had become uninhabitable. They were given little choice.[37] Most of them came from the streets in the center of the old ghetto where there had been a large Jewish population.[38]

In the Transvaal area, there were apartments with higher and lower rents, and there were wealthy and poor streets. The average rent was ƒ 6.65 a week in the old part of the area. In the newer, simpler areas, the rent varied but the average was between ƒ 4.70 and ƒ 4.76. In most instances, the people moving in had to pay more rent—202 families as compared to 62 who had no rent increase. Many people protested against this. According to the housing de-partment's tax records, a large percentage of the families spent more than 25 percent of their meager income on rent.[39] Starting in 1931, there were tenants' committees in the Transvaal area that argued for a reduction in the rents.

Those living along the Transvaal Quay had seen how their once rural neighborhood, set among meadows, had been caught up in a new expansion of the city. Moreover, the influx of people from the slums and ghetto changed its appearance. "The Quay has degenerated. The rustic peace and the lovely view are gone. Because it is now overpopulated with children, it has become a dumping ground for stakes, stones, and sand. In addition, peddlers clean all kinds of handcarts on the Quay and throw fish and other refuse into the canal."[40] The apartments on the Quay were more expensive than those built later by the Handwerkers Vriendenkring, and they were more spacious. The rent often had to be paid from a miserable income. One has to realize that support for the unemployed diamond workers was often less than ƒ 10.75 a week. Under such circumstances, a rent of ƒ 5.50 is extremely high. In 1931, of the 24 families who moved into the neighborhood who were certainly Jewish, 18 paid more in rent than before they moved.[41] There was therefore every justification for demanding that whatever progress had been made should not disappear.

As the Depression worsened, the number of evictions increased. The dwellings of the poor who had remained on Jodenhouttuinen were demolished so they, too, moved to East Amsterdam. But the remaining dwellings in the Jodenhouttuinen slowly degenerated to the point where the rents dropped.

The peddlers who remained in the Jewish Quarter, many of whom lived on that one street and as a result were engaged in cutthroat competition, could not pay even the new, lower rents. The money needed for rent was unavailable since food had to be bought as well. At the end of December and the beginning of January, things were especially bad for the peddlers. It was cold, spring was a long way off, the days were short, leaving little time for selling, and fresh fruit and vegetables were in short supply. The peddlers' association wrote to the aldermen, pointing out that in some city blocks people were having to pay 50 percent of their income as rent.[42]

During this period the Transvaal district was also a source of real worry for the municipality. Prosperity had not materialized, poverty was rampant, the rents were high, and the people had not learned how to avoid dirtying the neighborhood as they had done in Uilenburg. At first, it was the female building supervisors who were supposed to maintain standards. With the development of tenants' associations and the adoption of a civilized lifestyle by more and more of the working class, these supervisors increasingly confined their attention to a small number of blocks that were not in the hands of building cooperatives. These were the buildings owned by the municipality where the former ghetto dwellers lived. These buildings housed people who had no other place to go. In the worst cases, they first had to spend some time in the halfway houses of Aster Village and Zeeburg. The private building cooperatives had their own standards and would not permit these people in their buildings.

In the reports on families housed in Aster Village or Zeeburg, countless former ghetto dwellers are mentioned. Some were most likely criminals and maladjusted people, sick or degenerate, as described by the social psychologist and psychiatrist Querido in his 1933 study of Zeeburg.[43] But even he mentioned the fact that there was a surprisingly large number of peddlers in Zeeburg—which suggests that this perhaps had something to do with their occupation. A careful study of the reports on the people on Zeeburg and in Aster Village drawn up by the municipality makes it likely that poverty and hopelessness were important factors in considering people to be "inadmissible."[44]

There were poignant examples: people who slept on the floor at their parents' home in Rapenburg. They were desperately poor yet perfectly respectable. Once they landed in Zeeburg, they could not stand living there.[45] They received guidance on how to run a respectable household, but found the rigid supervision unbearable. What, other than poverty, could have caused the misery and filth experienced by a Jewish family in 1933, in which the man was a peddler who could not earn anything? They ended in Zeeburg because of arrears in rent, but they were in fact too respectable for the place.[46]

Reading through the reports, one quickly comes to doubt the validity of the psychiatric stigmatizing labels used in observations on the inmates made by

Querido. He divided them into categories in such a way that only a tiny fraction of those suffering from the disorder "antisocial" were regarded as curable. He set the place up as an institution for the antisocial. Even in the institution the people were threatened with eviction if they could not come up with the rent.[47] "The fact that I ran up debts was caused as follows: I lived in Zeeburg village, where there was no way I could earn a cent . . . " wrote a peddler. He found some kind of job that paid f 5 a day, for which he had to slave so hard that he spoke of "blood money, but that is better than nothing."[48] From the perspective of the end of the twentieth century, hopeless poverty is something quite different from antisocial behavior, and the cause of such poverty is no longer blamed (solely) on the poor themselves. It is also quite clear how poverty can cause people to neglect their environment and social contacts.

Querido's contribution was the research that he undertook in this institution, which was founded by Louis Heijermans, the brother of the socialist writer Herman Heijermans (pp. 70–71 above). He investigated the question of how far guidance and education could help people who had been generally abandoned as hopeless. He had his own doubts, but in the course of his work provided a good deal of information regarding the people there and it is in part through such research that we know the limits of what can be done through reeducation camps like this. His accounts were not totally objective, yet they could not hide the fact that people came to Zeeburg and Aster Village on account of poverty, that they wanted to get away, and that some were kept there unjustifiably long, for they were not antisocial at all.

The blame for failing to live in a respectable fashion was placed on the women, not on poverty. That is the clearest message that emerges from these reports on families. The Jewish family A. had twelve children when they came to Aster Village for the second time. During the time they stayed, they had three more. The parents wanted to leave, since it was no place for children. The family was regarded as dirty and untrustworthy. Although there were no problems with the family's morality, nevertheless, "the woman simply could not do her job with all those children."[49] The building supervisors and the other women responsible for supervising the families assumed a set of norms and values in which the task of the woman was rigidly defined. She was responsible for the housekeeping, and any suggestion that a man and woman might switch roles to cope with a woman's illness was disparagingly characterized by calling the man a "housewife."[50]

An application for public housing in East Amsterdam, or a request to continue living there, was judged by the same criteria.[51] It was irrelevant that assigning such a fixed role to the woman was totally at odds with a culture in which the woman was reared to have her own occupation—as was the case within the Jewish proletariat (see chapter 5). This was one of the ways in which the disciplining of the Jewish working class in East Amsterdam contributed to a form of assimilation: they were forced to adopt the norms of the dominant culture in which the role of the housewife differed from that in their own.

The family reports were evaluative and not objective—a part of the attempt to civilize the workers and modernize their way of life. In this instance, it took the form of an invasive attack that repelled people and was considered to be threatening, regardless of how much the culture being offered was seen as beneficial at the time of the interviews. In this sense, the research for the present study corrects the tendency to underestimate the effects of the attempts to raise the cultural level of the working class. The people were afraid of being inspected and time and again failed to understand what was expected of them. In a study of the origins of Aster Village and Zeeburg, Reijs wrote:

> There was no word [on the part of the housing officials] regarding the high costs of staying there, the continuous supervision that kept them down, loneliness, especially if all their old neighbors had landed on one street in a new district; all reasons why they might prefer to hide away in a slum in their old neighborhood.[52]

Efforts to raise the cultural level of a group of people are seldom without some ethical problems, though when those concerned are truly in great difficulties the issues may seem clear-cut. But what can we say about the remark of the woman supervisor who claims that a particular family is doing well because the man made a window box, and because "He is no longer following any particular political persuasion"! (He had been a communist.) Or, a couple of months later, "His communist tendencies have disappeared once more. Presumably he has learned about the less ideal aspects of the party."[53]

A disciplinary assignment or "cultural task," or whatever one calls it, means something that encourages adjustment to the dominant culture—a move toward living life as it is supposed to be lived. The content of the judgment as to what that is supposed to be is, of course, not neutral, and neutrality or even-handedness was never a characteristic of Aster Village or Zeeburg. The ongoing quarrel between the director from the housing department, Keppler, and Alderman de Miranda, under whose jurisdiction he worked, presumably had to do with this. The desire to raise the cultural level of the people was so strong in Keppler, who was driven by this goal, that de Miranda refused to support the housing act proposed in 1925.[54] He considered the rules to be too strict and, coming as he did from the Jewish proletariat, he understood that they would be extremely difficult—if not impossible—to follow.

The stream of new inhabitants from the old Jewish Quarter and Ooster Park to the new buildings that had been constructed in the Transvaal area caused the district to degenerate in a number of areas. Some streets were more "respectable," and those who could pay the rent tried to escape the ghetto by moving to those places within the neighborhood.

In one interview, Mr. B. told me the story of his family's progress. The family came from Uilenburg, and they were ecstatically happy with their new place. His mother had tuberculosis, so it was extremely important that they obtain a new, clean apartment.

"Look, when we lived on Uilenburg, my mother was in the hospital more than she was at home. When we moved to Magers Fontein Street, she had her own bedroom; it was a really modern building at that time. A big apartment, though on the fourth floor. And my father just said, 'Now why the fourth floor? How could someone with a wife in such poor health that she could never manage to go outdoors again wind up on the fourth floor. . . . Why are perfectly healthy people assigned to ground-floor apartments?' They had little gardens, too. But, OK, it was a leap from hell into heaven. There was a bedroom, doors, a little balcony; the doors could be opened, and that was pretty good for that time." [55]

His mother was ill, but a ground-floor apartment would have required not only that the apartment itself be well cared for but also that the little garden be kept up. The family was already in difficulties because of the mother's sickness, and it was thus assumed that the garden would be too much for them.

The story of Sara, who also came from Uilenburg from a family of educated workers, makes it clear how a move to the Transvaal area could be a step in the wrong direction: "Then we got a place from the building cooperative on Transvaal Street. We found it marvelous. Oh, no, first we went to some other street and that was a really nice place, too. We had a really good place there. But suddenly the area went downhill—all kinds of people came, people that you couldn't get along with."

"From the old ghetto?"

"Yes, a lesser sort. We said, 'Oh what have we down there now—we had one entrance for two apartments—horrible!' "

"What was horrible then?"

"A different kind of person, one with whom you really couldn't get along."

"Dirty?"

"Yes, and—everything."

"I'd really like you to explain it for me; I don't understand yet."

"Well, I can honestly say, a lower sort,"

"Were they dirty or antisocial?"

"Yes, antisocial, I guess they were antisocial. And so we said, 'We've got to find a way to get out of here.' And that was when my mother died, in 1938 . . . May 1939. There was an advertisement in the paper that an apartment was going to be vacant. Two of my sisters went to look, and it was beautiful. And then one of my sisters said, 'I'm not going there. It's totally messed up. It's badly run down. And that's horrible.' But it had a lot of possibilities. It was a beautiful place, four rooms and a lovely big kitchen and also a balcony. But we did have to clean it up."

"Was it in bad condition?"

"Filthy, absolutely filthy. It was on Transvaal Street. We looked out onto that little square. That was nice. When the children went off to athletics or came back from the AJC [the socialist young people's organization] they'd always meet there. We didn't have much time to enjoy it. We got there in May, no, August. . . . In May we arrived and in August there was the mobilization. That was that—in a very short time. The first thing we said was, 'Thank goodness that mother didn't have to go through this.' To think that she might have been deported!"[56] (The Netherlands was occupied by the Germans in May 1940.)

We were silent for a long time after this, for we both remembered that the Transvaal district was the assembly point for Jews from outside the city.[57] The Jews were driven together onto the square before being taken away in groups. Anxious groups of people packed together on the square is an image familiar to many. The story is often still told. The family, which had moved there to escape the overcrowding of Batavier Street, was once again faced with overcrowding. For Sara, that neighborhood was associated with the war.

Probably Sara was trying to give verbal expression to the fact that the Transvaal neighborhood was indeed made up of both rich and poor areas. The higher rent of the better areas itself imposed a selection on the inhabitants. The rent in the part known as the Afrikaner district lay between f 6.59 and f 6.65 a week, and a family on welfare could never pay that much.[58] Many who could not pay were evicted.[59] According to the statistics maintained by the municipal officials, a large number of families earned less than f 20 a week while they nevertheless had to pay between f 4 and f 5 a week in rent. Five families with an income of less than f 10 a week paid the minimum rent of f 4.25, which meant that more than 40 percent of their income went for rent.[60]

Mrs. A. talked about the new apartment and how pretty it was: "We didn't go there directly when our neighborhood was pulled down. First we went to Magers Fontein Street—that's near Tugela Road. And I found it so funny! My mother had been to see the apartment beforehand. There were eight apartments altogether off one staircase—left and right. And my mother had gone up and down looking, and she had found the number 8 next to a ground floor apartment. Then, during the move itself . . . everyone was helping . . . my mother said, 'That is not my apartment.' It was an apartment with a living room and a tiny little kitchen and it was on the fourth floor. There was a side room, and a back room, and then a staircase up and two little attic rooms. And in those rooms there were still two wooden bed niches. And my mother was beside herself . . . "

"Why?"

"When she had come to look at the place, she had seen the number 8 to the right of the outside door, and 6 was on the left, but she had not noticed that. She should have told them she wanted 6, for the apartments were not all the same. Number 6 had a big kitchen and one little room less. And now she had a tiny kitchen instead of a big one, and one little room more. That little room was a scullery—you couldn't really fit two people in there, standing. And a tiny little recessed balcony, just big enough for the trash can. Everything was small, but there were all those little rooms and a toilet, which we were not used to. But otherwise just a faucet in the kitchen and nothing more. Anyway, it was light, a window in every room. And, of course, we didn't have that in the old Jewish neighborhood, you didn't have any windows . . . there were windows, of course, though not in the bed niches or alcoves."

She was from a respectable family and was very aware of the attempts being made in the area to raise the level of the people: "I told you already about that Mr. Zodij—he was kind of a god, there, the supervisor [the chairman of the Handwerkers Vriendenkring]. In the Jewish neighborhoods the bedding was hung out of the windows—blankets or whatever they had. There weren't any recessed balconies there, and if you wanted to air a bed . . . they were used to it. And that was not allowed. And Mr. Zodij came to tell you it was not allowed. The same happened if you left a door open. That, too, was not permitted."

"You had to lock your door?"

"You had to shut it, and the people just weren't used to that. Of course there were doorbells in the Transvaal area, but not in the old neighborhood. We had no doorbells, we would stand at the door and call. When someone came, they would immediately call your name . . . and as soon as the weather was pleasant, people would sit out on the street."

"Was that also prohibited in the new neighborhood?"

"Yes, because the people downstairs had gardens and often the others had recessed balconies. So they expected you to stay inside, and you did. If there were complaints or anything, people went to Mr. Zodij. And if the bedding was hung out, he would come by to say that it was not permitted. The people really had to learn how to behave."

"And if you didn't do it the right way?"

"You weren't punished, but people did talk about it. And, after all, it's not a pretty sight—all that bedding hanging out. . . . "

"It was much quieter and more respectable on the streets there?"

"Well, of course there were people out on the street with handcarts selling things, and they walked around; that certainly still happened. But really sitting out on the street—I didn't see that much there."[61]

C.'s story was as follows: "There was a woman who supervised the apartments who had a place on Kruger Street. My mother went there each week to pay the rent."

Their family was known to be respectable, so they were not supervised and they obtained extra clothes. During the Depression they could have obtained extra cans of meat, but her mother did not want them.

"Was it pork?"

"She couldn't be sure. . . . "

"What about the Jewish holy days?"

"Oh, then you could go out on the street naked."

" . . . ?"

"At Passover my father would take something extra from the pushcart, or my mother had ƒ 25 in stamps and she'd go with us to Oosterpark Street or Vroom and Dreesmann [one of the large chain of department stores], which also accepted stamps, or we had a little Peper store [another chain of stores] on Kruger Square, and my mother bought us clothes for Passover. A little dress for about 2 or 3 guilders and ankle socks, and then we were respectable again. And no matter how foul the weather, my mother would say, 'At Passover you can go naked,' which is to say without an overcoat."

"Tell me something about your uncles and aunts," I asked a little later.

"My father had two sisters and one brother . . . who had children, and the family ties were very good."

"Did they all get together in one home?"

"With bare bottoms and no stockings on."

[Clearly this had to do with the youngest.] "Didn't they have any underwear?"

"Sometimes they didn't, or sometimes one was being nursed, which was obviously the cheapest way to feed them."

This sounded very free—bare bottoms and nursing in public—but she said that as far as her own upbringing went, sexual norms were rigid, and her parents complained about her vanity. They made a clear distinction between sexuality and physical awareness. The body in general was treated much more freely than the strictness of her upbringing regarding sex would suggest. Her parents had been taught that they needed to be strict about that, and that morality needed to be firmly enforced in a modern family. In actual fact this educational plan did not match what was done in practice, for embarrassment about open physicality had not yet properly been internalized.

This is shown in the following story about her visit to the house of a boy who was a little older than her:

"We rang the bell and asked his mother if Ischi was upstairs. But Ischi was in the bathtub. We couldn't believe our ears . . . and we went upstairs, and there he sat in a bathtub in front of the heater. You can imagine how we burst out laughing to see a boy of sixteen in the bathtub. Then he said, 'Mom, give me my bathrobe please,' and his mother came in wearing an old shirt. Those are things you never forget. But we found it perfectly natural. Ischi had it better than we did—he sat in a bathtub in front of the fire." [62]

The Influence of Change on the Relationships between Men and Women

There were other changes in the lives of the Jewish proletariat in Amsterdam. However, their very nature makes it impossible to go beyond a few remarks about them, and one cannot say precisely when they occurred. They have to do with purity (or cleanliness), sexuality, and the separation of the worlds of men and women.

In Jewish tradition, cleanliness and sexuality are closely linked. This is symbolized by the visit to the ritual bath. At the same time, sexuality is linked with the idea of increasing the numbers of the Jewish people and cannot be separated from reproduction. The provisions in the marriage law regarding sexuality and cleanliness are a cornerstone of Jewish tradition. As is the case with most religions, neo-Malthusian ideas have no place in Jewish tradition. It was a sign of assimilation when a family was deliberately kept small, and it is interesting that it was among Jewish people that such ideas were first widely adopted.

Even with the help of oral history, it is hard to determine the extent to which the old ways were adhered to. It concerns the most intimate part of life; and for that very reason could serve as a measure of the relationship of the people to their traditions. I asked many women about visits to the ritual bath, the *mikveh*, and they all said that their mothers did indeed go there. As for themselves, they had often failed to adhere to all the complicated requirements. Whether their mothers eventually became less observant, they did not know.

I have always been impressed by the way in which the novel *De een zijn dood* [One Man's Death] by the *medina* writer Sam Goudsmit shows the ambivalence of a woman who is in the process of assimilation. She no longer attends the *mikveh*, yet does not wish to deny her orthodox background. Goudsmit describes this beautifully in a street quarrel between two Jewish women, an elderly aunt and her niece. I include the quarrel to provide some impression of the kind of intimacy that is involved, even though it takes place outside Amsterdam. More than any other writer, Goudsmit has managed to express in words the problems that resulted from the stuffiness of the traditional Jewish milieu.

> "Pious! Pious! Take care, *frotterin*! [Yiddish for a bad woman] " she [the elderly aunt] threatened, her old hand shaking. . . .
> "Now I'll ask you something, and you, you respectable woman, you respectable Jewish woman, you gotta tell me; now you listen, eh!" And she asked, turning toward the other woman as if to get her attention, "Now you gotta tell me when you last went to the *mikveh* and how often . . . eh? That you gotta tell me right now, you pretty Jewish woman!"
> Naatje stood there, defeated and speechless, as if her aunt had torn every stitch of clothing from her body and she stood naked among the grinning men.[63]

Goudsmit goes on to describe the shame of the woman who had been thus accosted, while he also explains that her behavior resulted from her lack of knowledge. Yet the attack on her, based on her failure to visit the *mikveh*, has something of the nature of a curse. She realizes that by failing to adhere to certain rules, she has broken with Jewish life—and broken with it far more radically than she can really see. To be attacked like that strikes at her in the most intimate way.

In the attempt to civilize the working classes, the term "cleanliness" was used more or less in the sense of modern bodily hygiene—with washing the body and the clothes and polishing the house. In Jewish tradition, the term "purity," or "cleanliness," is a different concept. It has to do both with hygiene and with tradition—with the ritual bath. A person who is pure or clean in this sense can be quite dirty by modern standards. The same word can thus have more than one meaning and be woven into a web of other meanings.[64] Such is the case not only for the concept "cleanliness, purity" but also for "housewife" and "mother figure." Their meaning can be assessed only from within a system of meanings possessed by other words and relationships. "Housewife" means something quite different in non-Jewish proletarian culture than in Jewish culture. In non-Jewish proletarian culture, the word stands, ideologically, for a fixed role in which the mother earns no wages, while in the Jewish tradition the economic role of a housewife determines whether her husband has enough time to devote to higher things—the study of religious treatises.[65] Thus words have cultural connotations that, in turn, reflect the division between the sexes.

In Jewish tradition, there was a separate women's culture, in which the women helped each other and celebrated women's events among themselves. This world was entirely distinct from that of the men. However, it was not discussed explicitly and menstruation was never mentioned. A brief extract from one interview shows the solidarity of the women: "I was fifteen-and-a-half when I became a big girl. I did not dare to tell my mother. I went to my granny's and my grandmother went with me. Then all the neighbors were invited for coffee."

"The men as well, or just the women?"

"Just the women. My mother said, 'So my Trientje has become a big girl,' and that was celebrated with coffee."[66]

The changed circumstances under which they now lived affected this separate women's world in important ways. In the standard work about families moving out of the East End of London to a garden city, the sociologists Young and Wilmott analyzed the consequences of such a move out of an old neighborhood in terms of how the world is experienced and the changes it brings in social networks.[67] They found that it loosened the family ties that tend to be so strong in a working-class neighborhood. A way of life to which people had been used fell away, and isolation, caused by the fact that people lived farther away from each other, increased steadily.

In this way, the relationships between men and women slowly changed. The men began to rely on the women for social contact and thus a situation arose in which they began to spend more time at home. This new state of affairs also led to greater social mobility. Living among new neighbors brought people in contact with others who sometimes had a better background or had a different view of life. In the new areas, the young people could respond more easily to the desire for a better life and a higher level of education. As a result, a closed culture that had been based primarily on family ties began to disappear.

Up to that time, the family had functioned as a safety net when times were hard. Many of the interviews told of how—during the person's childhood—the family had broken up in one way or another. One of the parents died, the children were dispersed among members of the wider family or went to live with another family. *These accounts did not originate with people who had grown up in the safety of a modern family.* The above findings agree with those of Young and Wilmott. The new way of life of the contemporary working class, on the other hand, created a new kind of safety and was in that sense one of the byproducts of the attempt to civilize the working class.[68]

In her article about women's networks in London before World War I, the American historian Ellen Ross emphasized the importance of ties among women who lived on the same street or in the same neighborhood.[69] Women's lives in London played themselves out in public, in the street. A private life, shut up in the home, was essential for the middle-class way of life as lived in other areas. Gossiping—the way in which women communicated their needs to each other and tried to help each other—changed in character. The disappearance of the peddler and the door-to-door salesman also interfered with the way the women had formerly communicated with one another on an informal basis.

The institution of an English version of female building inspectors could be viewed not merely as a form of regulation but also as a form of mutual help, whereby the state assumed part of the role of the family. The contributions of the inspectors were more or less accepted in this fashion. If there were no clothes, then they often saw to it that they became available, and if a housewife became ill for a long period, it was often the inspectors who gave advice about possibilities of obtaining assistance in managing the family.

In the new districts, there was more interaction among people in the homes, in part because—for the first time—they had a home to care for, something that could be looked after. The architecture of the buildings encouraged a somewhat isolated lifestyle within each apartment.[70] The style in which the houses were built was entirely directed toward the interior. The windows were small, so that people could not look into each other's homes. Moreover, the way the apartments were divided up was directed toward a central family life. The living room was the center of the house, ringed around by several smaller bedrooms so that the boys and girls would be separated from each other. Life was meant to be lived as a family—*en famille*—and in the later designs the height of the little windows ensured that everything not entirely respectable was hidden.

I have the impression that women originally came into contact with each other through the family, even when they moved to East Amsterdam. These contacts were originally also neighborhood networks, for everyone lived in such close proximity. In a great number of the interviews, people were asked whether anyone other than family came to visit in the old neighborhood. This was systematically denied. In the new neighborhood and at work, the younger generation found contacts outside the family circle for the first time.

Relatives now often lived too far away from each other to drop by, and the women sometimes became isolated. Many of those interviewed told about their mother's isolation. This was often intensified by the fact that women in the poorer classes tended to become ill in their old age—or perhaps worn out is a more accurate description.

This is true in the case of Ab, whom we came across in Lepel Street. His family was caught between a rock and a hard place since they had to pay the new rent out of welfare money. In all the time they lived there, his father worked for about three months. Managing to get by on the available household money was the task of the women. And all this came at a time of pressure to live in a respectable fashion, when the rest of the family no longer lived around the corner. They had a hard time of it.

The norm of respectability had to be combined with the old traditions of Jewish proletarian culture, which was often difficult. The extent to which the people were cut off from the world easily conflicted with the tradition of hospitality, which required that families gather together. In the old neighborhood, it was often hard to distinguish the separate families from one another. People came and went, and aunts were just as important as mothers.

In the new circumstances, men and women had much more contact, and it seems likely that such contact between the sexes was very different from that of the old Jewish tradition in which highly separate worlds of men and women existed. In that milieu, men had quite different and much more clearly defined tasks than women. People's parents had lived in that manner, as had generations before them. Jewish religion and culture are deeply imprinted with this difference, which in itself does not imply any hierarchical inequality. On the contrary, the total separation of women's and men's tasks gave women power over their material lives and their children.[71]

Dutch society in the period before World War II can be described as a denominationally segregated society. The people were divided into groups according to religious conviction, and this determined in great detail what could and what had to be done. Everyone went to a school run by his or her own faith, voted for the appropriate denominational party, and at the end was buried accordingly. This segregation also applied to the way in which housing was divided up.

In the Transvaal area, municipal policy sought to embody a socialist answer to the problem of civilizing the population—and this, too, assumed a kind of segregation, for it was based on the way the Protestant and Catholic authorities disciplined their own groups, persuading them to observe the rules.[72] Their blocks of buildings, which bordered on the Jewish areas, resulted from the denominationally segregated movement toward a civilized working class. These blocks were well cared for, and the apartment supervisors (who worked hand in hand with the church) saw to it that everyone was kept in order. In the same way, the Jewish proletariat had to become cultured and modern, and for this reason had to break with backward and outdated traditions from the ghetto—whether these involved the structure of the family, the orderliness of the home, or public behavior. Some took this break with the past to extremes and lost contact with their backgrounds.

Joop, one of the people I interviewed, described it as follows:

"When Uilenburg was demolished, there was quite a bit of resistance from the people there. They were provided with housing in the Tugela neighborhood, but they really wanted to stay on Uilenburg. My parents told me that the people who went there were not at all enthusiastic about it, even though their living conditions were better; they wanted to go on living in the old neighborhood.

"But that blew over rather quickly once they saw that the conditions were really better there, for example, and that although the character of Uilenburg had disappeared, the new district nevertheless was beginning to acquire a character of its own since the people there had all come from the old neighborhood. They began to feel at home. In the area around Tugela Road, Retief Street, and the streets in between, there were people who sold at the market, others from all kinds of occupations, and people whom you really couldn't tell exactly how they earned their living."[73]

Another man, also called Joop, told how the friends of his mother and father were all Jews, though the street on which they lived was not entirely Jewish. They also chose to remain with what they trusted, even though things might seem new at first glance. He lived on Pretorius Street, clearly the better section, and moved to the Amsteldijk once the neighborhood filled up. At about the same time, Jacob also moved to Laings Nek Street in the same area.

"We were not used to all that space. What struck me as very strange then was that the people all seemed to be more distinct and looked different. The grayish cast they had once had disappeared. It was suddenly a totally new life. The real Jewish atmosphere was gone—in a good sense. People seemed brighter as soon as they began to climb the social ladder.

"Next to us was a bakery and quite a different kind of Jewish people from what we were used to having around us. And above lived a childless married couple, and she was a real lady. So, suddenly all the people were just a little bit better. We lived more inside our homes because we had more there than before. The higher status enjoyed in the new neighborhood meant that unconsciously, or perhaps consciously, people avoided certain things."[74]

CONCLUSION

The first people to live in the Retief neighborhood saw newcomers arrive after they had become used to living in the new housing. Perhaps the newly arrived people struck them as strange slum dwellers. The newcomers had moved there in the early 1920s, when it was still possible to earn a living. Later that was not the case, and the new people had no time to catch their breath after moving in. In that sense, the political intentions of the municipality were not realized—not through any fault of the politicians, but because of the Depression. It was no doubt attractive to live in a new way, but people had to be able to pay for it.

There are many stories of how people moved out of the old Jewish neighborhood and began new lives. The most important myth concerns the way in which people in the new neighborhoods were said to have gained a "permanent" new apartment. However, the wandering back and forth between the new neighborhoods contradicts this.

In the new areas the official story was that people had created an assimilated way of life for themselves, distancing themselves from tradition and embracing socialism as the way to the future. This assessment, which dominates official history, is in conflict with what came out in the interviews and represents a vision that is colored by the disappearance of Jewish proletarian culture, which could correct such memories. The product of cultural change has become so one-sided as a result of genocide that ambivalence falls away. People seldom actually broke with their past, though they had various attitudes toward it. In the new neighborhoods they lived as strangers, as "immigrants," people absorbed in the new environment that they were helping to create themselves. Especially in the Transvaal area, this new environment also influenced their lives. Closer analysis of the interviews reveals the ambivalence once more, arising from the realization that one had been "much more Jewish" before the move, yet that the new assimilated world into which Jews were integrated looked very good—and people truly hoped that it would be wonderful.

The degree of this ambivalence does not really correlate with the distance between the new neighborhood and the old—though the nostalgic tales would have us believe this. The new environment certainly strengthened the ambivalent attitude toward old and new, and a choice for the new, stimulated and encouraged by the authorities, meant that lifestyles that had been accepted without question up till then had to be altered. The ambivalence itself was caused by the fact that no matter how much the changes were welcomed in daily life, this did not mean that they had become part of the inner make-up of the people.

That the non-Jews moved away as a result of the influx of Jews is not confirmed by anything in the archives. Thus Jews probably themselves chose to live near one another. What can be seen is that by the end of the 1930s, some of the streets in East Amsterdam were inhabited almost exclusively by Jews. What Boekman wrote in 1924 was correct: new nuclei were continually being formed. Catherina, one of the people I interviewed who came to live in that part of the city, confirmed this by what she said. It was 1943, and the Transvaal area was slowly being emptied after the Jews from the provinces had first been driven there. (Her family was not deported due to a variety of reasons.)

"We were the only ones left on President Brand Street, with one Christian family. We had the privilege of being witnesses. . . . "[75]

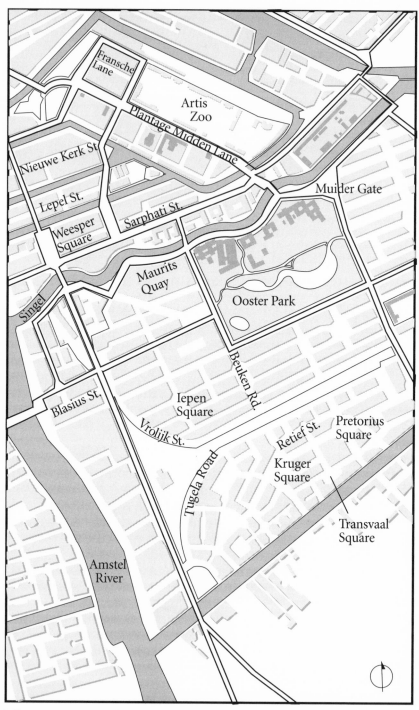

The Ooster Park and Transvaal Neighborhoods

CHAPTER FIVE

WORKING AND LIVING IN POVERTY

THE DECLINE OF THE JEWISH ECONOMY

Early in 1931 the social-democratic alderman Boekman (mentioned earlier) published an article, "The Prosperity of the Jews of Amsterdam" in *De Vrijdagavond* [The Friday Evening], a weekly paper read by a large number of Jews.[1] The title was somewhat misleading, since the article dealt with the decline of prosperity and hence principally with poverty. He based the publication on the *Statistische Mededeelingen* [Statistical Reports] of the Bureau of Statistics of the City of Amsterdam,[2] in which the income tax figures for 1929–1930 are analyzed according to neighborhood.

It was not possible to use these figures for a direct comparison of the income level of the Jews with that of the rest of the population. It was possible, however, to compare the incomes in neighborhoods where many Jews lived with those where few lived. According to Boekman, far more precise information could be obtained by analyzing the assessments for community funds made by members of the Jewish community, but no such analysis has ever been made.

The latest data available to Boekman concerning the spread of Jews throughout Amsterdam dealt with the situation in 1920, and these figures formed the basis of his articles for *De Vrijdagavond* written in 1924; Boekman only attempted to compare the "most Jewish neighborhood" with other neighborhoods. He meant, of course, the old Jewish Quarter. The picture that emerges is distorted, and Boekman did not adequately point this out. Those who were well off had left the old neighborhood first, followed by others who could afford a better and more expensive place to live. Moreover, the demolition of Uilenburg and Valkenburg had forced many of the poor to move, while others had returned because of the low rents. What Boekman did show was that the situation had greatly worsened for those who remained.

There were 7,076 income-tax assessments for the old Jewish neighborhood. Boekman admitted that it was impossible to determine what percentage

TABLE 3

PERCENTAGE OF INCOMES WITHIN STATED RANGES

	above 3,000 guilders (percent)	above 6,500 guilders (percent)
Jewish ghetto	8.9	2.3
Rest of the city	18.5	3.51

TABLE 4

PERCENTAGE OF JEWS RECEIVING WELFARE

	absolute figures		percentage of Jews among those receiving welfare	
	Dutch Jews	Portuguese Jews	Dutch Jews	Portuguese Jews
year				
1925	1,681	153	7.7	0.7
1926	1,980	163	8.3	0.7
1927	2,070	160	8.3	0.6
1928	2,034	141	8.9	0.6
1929	2,048	165	9.2	0.7

of these were Jewish and what percentage was not (Boekman actually wrote of "Christians" and "Jews"). Of the total, 91.1 percent of the people had an annual income below 3,000 guilders. However, 160 of the 632 assessments that concerned incomes higher than this were for incomes above 6,500 guilders. As for the incomes below 3,000 guilders, it seemed likely to Boekman that many lay far below this figure. His comparison of these figures with those for the whole city is given in Table 3.

From this table it is clear that assessments above 3,000 guilders were less than half as common (percentage-wise) in the old Jewish neighborhood than in the rest of the city. Only in the Jordaan and on the Islands were the percentages lower. Thus there were very few rich Jews.

Boekman also analyzed statistics provided by the Amsterdam Council for the Poor, the results of which are given in Table 4.[3]

According to Boekman, fewer Jews received welfare than was true of the rest of the population, about 13 percent of whom were on welfare. This could lead, he said, to the incorrect belief that Jews were less in need of welfare. That was not so. Many Jews did not request welfare on a long-term basis but made use of "business subsidies" to tide them over temporarily. These subsidies amounted to between ƒ 15 to ƒ 100 (occasionally more) to buy a few items, stock for a store, or a peddler's license.

One person requesting such aid wrote the following letter, confirming with concrete, vivid images Boekman's abstract figures:

> I come to you because I'm at my wit's end and can't go on any longer. I am a market seller. For seven years I have sold at different markets in Amsterdam with a stall full of stockings and socks. In recent years things have gone very badly, and I have slowly eaten away my financial reserves for buying merchandise. Bills arrived and I couldn't always pay them all, so I got into debt. So now the Company . . . has claims against me for *f* 250.00, two hundred and fifty guilders. This debt was much bigger, but I made and agreement with the Company. In the beginning I paid *f* 10.00 then *f* 5.00 then *f* 2.50, and now I just can't pay anything off. . . . I can't go on like this. I can't buy more merchandise because I have no money, so now I have almost nothing to sell, which means I keep selling less. Today I got a *kwartje* [quarter of a guilder] and to keep my stall I had to borrow a guilder from a relative. Truly I am not exaggerating. I have nothing more to eat. But I don't want to be added to the legions of people on the dole because first I would like to try a milk round or a kerosene round. Could I get a small business subsidy and a peddler's license from you? I have promises from relatives and friends that they would buy from me. I would rather earn my living and work hard for it than to ask for welfare money.

The letter is dated 17 December 1935. The writer was arrested immediately following the February Strike of 1941 and, as a result, the family was reduced to abject poverty. His wife waited a number of months for his return, and in the meantime applied for welfare. The records show that in December 1942 she "left" for Germany (in other words, she was deported). Thus this one document concerning a request for help, like every such document, throws light on the perfect bureaucratic apparatus that was in place and continued to function during the time of the deportations. This family is a typical example of despair, of how people somehow "managed," yet in the end failed to make it through the hard times. The account also shows the attitude of the bureaucrats who were "forced" to reduce their payments when the husband was arrested—since the family had shrunk in size—and eventually worried about the fact that no formal death notice had been received. We will meet the family again on p. 175, where I refer to them as the "family of a peddler."[4]

In the article mentioned above, Boekman also wrote about "business subsidies" (the kind of support requested by the trader in the story just told) and interest-free loans that were provided by welfare organizations in the hope of stimulating trade. Boekman felt that it was not good that relatively few Jews requested aid during this period. He pointed out that large numbers of them had requested aid during 1925–1929, a period relatively free of economic malaise, and thus a period when a decrease in requests for welfare was to be expected. He went on to express concern regarding a new depression that was sharply intensifying as he wrote. Given the weak economic position of the Jews even during times of relative prosperity, he feared the worst for them.

It is hard to determine whether the Depression alone was responsible for the shifts in the distribution of Jews across various occupations. It could also be interpreted as a sign of the assimilation of the Jewish working class. How the development continued can only be seen in retrospect on the basis of a "research report" undertaken in 1942 as a result of the registration of Jews by the German occupying forces in 1941. This report was based on racial characteristics, but nevertheless contains useful data.[5] Despite the fact that the author admitted that "this report makes no claims of a scholarly nature" and "is only intended to be used for a certain kind of research," he claimed that his study further developed the work of the well-known *Demografie van Joden in Nederland* [Demography of the Jews in the Netherlands] by Alderman Boekman.

The researcher wanted to show that the definition of Jewishness used in recent research distorted the number of Jews, making it too low. He also wanted to show that there were many more Jews in Amsterdam than appeared at first glance. He no longer inquired about the religious affiliations but defined Jewishness in racial terms. Thus Jews included not only those who were thoroughly assimilated and had consequently stopped paying any religious assessment or those who failed to pay throughout their lives for a Jewish burial. Jewishness extended further than this. Therefore the absolute numbers emerging from this "research" cannot be used, but the relative percentages give an indication of the composition of the Jewish working population.

Jews were heavily represented in a number of occupations. Table 5 compares the percentage of Jews in certain occupations with the percentage of the rest of the Amsterdam population working in the same occupations in 1941.

When this table is compared to Table 1 of chapter 2, the decline in the percentage of Jews working in the diamond industry is striking, for this is the sector in which there was the greatest assimilation as a result of socialism. A study that corrected earlier research using criteria based on race rather than religious conviction could be expected to have shown more rather than fewer Jews in this sector. Moreover, the researcher was interested in finding increased numbers of Jews and claimed that earlier research was inaccurate.

An explanation of why there were fewer Jews in the diamond industry can easily be found in the poor state of that industry at that time. There were fewer jobs available. A more challenging hypothesis is that the culture of the diamond workers—however assimilated, socialist, and nonreligious it might be—had remained a consciously *Jewish* culture, and moreover one that was proletarian. Given this premise, many diamond workers would have reported themselves as Jewish in the earlier census and occupational surveys, thus the newer figures could be accurate after all.

The idea that these workers no longer considered themselves to be Jews

TABLE 5

PERCENTAGE OF JEWS IN VARIOUS OCCUPATIONS (1941)

	percentage of Jewish population	*percentage of non-Jewish population*
Diamonds	5.8	2.0
Clothing and cleaning	20.0	4.8
Retail	32.4	20.9
Other occupations (including professions)	18.1	8.3

Source: A. Veffer, *Statistische gegevens van de Joden in Nederland*, p. 37.

would then be a part of a postwar distortion resulting from the diamond workers totally abandoning their Jewish past. During the 1930s the people in question (including the diamond workers) lived in utter poverty and were threatened by eviction from their homes. During that period they were inescapably Jewish. There was little point, then, in renouncing their religion: from the viewpoint of others they remained Jews. On the other hand, after the war it was less relevant to deny that they were Jewish; denial failed to improve their lot, and their faith in progress had diminished significantly.

The statistics also show a surprising increase in retail activity, including the Jewish share of it. This was the sector where the unemployed diamond workers and tobacco workers wound up. The garment industry was different, however; the amount of work done at home increased, according to contemporary reports, but there are no reliable figures for this. Women had always continued to work—at home—after they were married, and this work was never reflected in official statistics. Early in the 1930s the number of people working in home workshops declined, but the number increased again with the arrival of the immigrants from Germany. Due to an abundant supply of labor, the pay for this work went down. Many women told of extremely long workdays and low wages.

The figures agree with more global data provided in a work from 1935 by the Zionist Birnbaum, who claimed that there was a change in the occupational structure of the Jewish population.[6] He described a trend to drive Jews out of the industries in which they had been working. The remedy, he suggested, was to promote training for Jews in new professions by encouraging them to go to trade and horticultural schools. Jews needed to learn to work in agriculture and to learn trades. This idea matched the foundation of the Zionist efforts in Palestine, where it was also felt that Jews needed to move away from their traditional occupations, bound as these were to the cities, ghettos, and oppression. The solution lay not in assimilation but in new kinds of education.[7]

Below I describe a number of Jewish occupations. It is not my purpose to give a detailed description of a branch of industry but to provide a picture of a way of life. Sometimes this picture becomes clearer when the oral and written sources are compared with each other. For the tobacco industry there is no written account of the day-to-day experiences of workers, so one is forced to rely on oral sources, although these have been criticized. Nevertheless, the life history sketched in that account shows the connections between hired labor, retail, unemployment, and exclusion from other possibilities. It is told by someone who in the end rose above his environment.

THE GARMENT INDUSTRY

A seamstress from the garment industry would sooner work for less money than accept the lower status of working as a peddler. Often, too, working at home was a way of supplementing her husband's pay. In a brief study of such work done in 1934, the sociologist Heertje showed how the reorganization of the industry led to an increase in work by younger, unmarried girls and to lower wages. These young girls came from the countless families that were finding it impossible to make ends meet. Although Heertje was not dealing specifically with the Jewish character of the garment industry, but with the industry in general and with the work done within it by girls working at home, his account nevertheless gives a picture of their work.

Heertje's tone is moralizing (especially when he deals with the sex life of the girls).[8] Their lives had changed, he felt, through the reorganization of the industry, which made working in the *ateliers* or small sewing shops boring and spiritually deadening. "Yet the girls did not feel the spiritually deadening nature of their work during the early years; only later would they become conscious of its effects. The cause of this is clear: the young girl makes no demands of her work—she does not choose a career, but rather a source of income. Industrial work means income and freedom; in domestic service (for example as a maid) this could generally not be attained." Traditionally, domestic service had been regarded as more respectable.

Heertje's focus on the sewing shops ignored the miserable circumstances in the tiny businesses, sweatshops, and cottage industry. There the conditions were abysmal, often involving 14-hour workdays. It was impossible to supervise those working at home, since legislation effectively blocked control over their working hours.[9] The existence of a cottage industry made it easier for an employer to lower wages; the trade unions were weak in this area. In contrast to the popular image of the garment industry at that time, it was predominantly filled with married women. According to Heertje, the unemployment among the men, or the fact that their earnings were too low, was an important reason for the low wages: "They would accept *any* pay."

The popular misconception of the garment industry was probably also caused in part by the wearisome struggle waged year after year by the single women working in the sewing shops of that industry. They formed one of the pillars on which the Dutch trade union movement was built.[10] Their leaders were primarily young Jewish women brought up in the families of the diamond workers.

When educating their daughters, proletarian Jewish families assumed that the girls would have to earn a living. In many families, the father had tuberculosis—the typical illness of diamond workers—or the mother had died, often as the result of the large number of children she bore. When this happened, the mother's earnings as a diamond cutter or seamstress were lost. The eldest daughter had to take over the role of the mother and look after the younger children, while the other grown daughters helped to scratch together an income for the family. This willingness to seek work must not be regarded as showing disrespect for the role of housewife. On the contrary, following Jewish tradition, marriage and the family remained the most important goal. However, before marriage, the women needed to be independent and to learn a trade. The personal experiences of those who lived through this shed much light on the subject.

Sara, who formerly lived on Uilenburg and who worked for years in the garment industry, had this to say: "My mother really depended on us. Do you know what I earned? Well, now, let me just tell you! My oldest sister, she became a maid because my mother had no money for her to learn a trade—in those days, if you wanted a girl to learn a trade, you had to pay for it. That was ƒ 150. You could pay it off in weekly installments, but you still had to pay for it. And my mother didn't have it then, so my sister became a maid. That was one mouth less to feed but my mother found it awful. She had learned a trade herself, and she said, 'That's not going to happen to you, no matter what I have to do.'"

"She wasn't prepared to accept that?"

"No, . . . I guess she found it offered too little. We had to learn a trade."

There were so few people still able to pay for an apprenticeship that she answered negatively when I asked about paying for training. I asked, "Did they pay money?"

"No, not for me; they didn't pay for my sisters, either. Well, they did pay for one sister . . . I don't know exactly, but I do know they were always saying 'ƒ 150' and that had to be paid off in weekly installments."[11]

The desire for daughters to be able to earn money was confirmed in a number of the interviews. Domestic service was not enough; it offered no future. Like domestic service, being a seamstress was regarded in part as preparation for potential marriage, and was therefore a respectable occupation. This was confirmed in the following interview with a former seamstress.

"There were four of us children: three brothers—and I was the only daughter. That was in 1914 when war broke out between Belgium and Germany, and I had to learn to sew. I always wanted to become a maid in some household. And my mother said, 'That's not going to happen! You have three brothers and you'll become a drudge for them; no, you have to learn a trade.' So I went and learned a trade, I became a seamstress."

"In other words, your mother found it more important for you to learn a trade than just to keep house?"

"Oh yes! She said, 'You have to learn to sew so that if something needs to be mended you'll know how to do it. But if you go into service, you'll become your brothers' slave, polishing shoes and everything, and that's not going to happen." [12]

Wages in the sewing shops were poor. As the Depression and the competition increased, the paid vocational school was abandoned, and it became a matter of working hard for low wages. During the early years, the people were said to be "in training," apprentices—it had become impossible to pay for training. The work was organized more efficiently and the wages were reduced. The people involved had a lot to say about this.

I asked Sara, "What did you earn to begin with?"

"Well, they made out as if we were lucky not to have to pay any more, which was pretty crafty for such a large business. The first week I earned a guilder."

"For working the whole week?"

"Well now, what did that work consist of—pillow cases and sheets needed button holes, and you had to cut out the scalloping. As a child of 13 you were set this task—say you finished four the first day, you'd have to do five the next, then six, and so they brought you up. . . . I was there eight months before I sat behind a machine, and then I got f 1.50."

She continued the tale of very gradually rising wages: "It wasn't that you had to pay for learning the trade any more, but they got more than their money's worth out of all those children." [13] Later, she also taught children.

From the f 1.50 she earned, she was allowed to keep a guilder to buy clothes. She had 25 cents pocket money and had to pay the other 25 cents for her food. Early in the 1920s her job disappeared, and she found work in a sewing shop off Karel du Jardin Street, outside the ghetto but within walking distance. It was run on the most "cost-effective" principles—an awful place!

"There was a woman in charge. Was she bad news! . . . She'd come by and say, 'So, you're busy with that—but when's it gonna be done, eh? I want it today.' Then someone else would have to take some work over from you, and you'd have to pay her back. . . . If I had six dresses on the go and I didn't finish them, someone would have to help me so I got them finished that day. So let's say she did six hours work on them, I'd have to do six for her—that will make you go stark raving mad; in the end I couldn't take it any more." [14]

Heertje wrote of a process of maturation in which, as a result of her financial contributions, a young woman gradually "gained power" over her parents. He also noted that there was one area in which they did not control her. Through the material circumstances in which the girl found herself, she was inclined to give free rein to her "primitive erotic feelings":

> Disturbing situations were brought to my attention by reliable sources. Some girls had had sexual relations with members of their own families in the presence of their parents. I was told of countless cases of incest. The girl sees and hears too much, is seldom alone, keeps company with people who are under stress, and is faced time and again with the misery of poverty and the bad or coarse relationship between her parents. The street has its notorious evil effect on her—an effect that the rumors certainly do not exaggerate. The girls try to hide such things from everyone. However, in the course of this study (which lasted several months) I heard a great many times from the most trustworthy sources so much that I believe it can be safely concluded that this occurs with great frequency.[15]

The most shocking example that Heertje came up with was a case where two girls lived with their father and a housekeeper in one room. Since girls wanted to marry so that they could stop working, he believed the majority of them had had sexual experiences prior to their eighteenth year.

These "moralizing" observations did not fit the picture that emerged from my interviews. Those tell of absolute obedience to the parents and of considerable shyness in sexual matters. That was certainly true of those families where the sons and daughters slept in the same rooms or where the children slept near their parents. This was repeatedly referred to in the interviews. Many I interviewed told how they did not know where children came from or how they were made until quite late. Even in those cases where initial sexual experiences led to unwanted pregnancies, the happenings and the actions that accompanied them were viewed by those involved as prohibited explorations in unfamiliar territory. Sexuality and menstruation were absolute taboos, talked about only by women among themselves. Sexuality was a subject that could be discussed only the day before the wedding, and then only according to the codes prescribed in the Jewish ceremony. This is equally true of the accounts given by the women interviewed who were thoroughly assimilated.

Perhaps, as a result of internalizing these norms during their adult life, the sexual freedom these women enjoyed before marriage was suppressed or they were too embarrassed about giving a negative impression. Even so, this does not automatically support Heertje's allegations. His claims cannot be confirmed by the interviews.

It is also impossible to investigate questions about forced marriages and abortion using currently available sources. Interviews can scarcely be employed for such purposes, since people tend to present themselves either as very virtuous or thoroughly promiscuous when it comes to sex. That is the nature of the subject. However, even those who regarded themselves as "promiscuous" were generally not inclined to boast of having broken the rules of morality. This raises further doubts about Heertje's results.

Esther remembered her childhood as one great protest against her parents. She, too, had to be home by eight in the evening and thus barely had time to meet her boyfriend in the place behind Tugela Road where such flirtations ran their course. "You thought up a story and got your mother to believe it—you were going to your girlfriend's, but then, of course, you'd go off with the boys. . . ."

Probably all these accounts had an element of truth in them, but we must remember that Heertje had an axe to grind in the name of culture. The daughters' income was necessary and could give the family an important boost. If some members of the household were unemployed, their benefits were reduced or withheld if others were working, and this created great mutual dependence. Besides, the days were long, and one worked hard. Yet the fact that they had an independent income on which the family relied gave the girls a measure of freedom. This freedom was new and contrasted with the socially controlled family life their parents had experienced in the old neighborhood. Simply being in a position to keep a little pocket money and not having to slave away in the home the whole time—just the fact that they went out—was new. Their parents never had such an opportunity.

The young women were also more flirtatious and changed jobs more frequently than their parents had done. According to the women interviewed, their parents could not stand this and considered the frequent job changes to be scandalous, even a sign of loose living. In earlier times, anyone with a job in a sewing shop would stay there and gradually make progress, eventually earning a little more. But during the Depression this was virtually impossible.

Esther told of how she began working in a private sewing shop. She changed jobs frequently and landed in a sewing shop on Prinsengracht, where about fifty girls worked. "You started there for 50 cents a week, and you had to work a whole week for that, and you learned the trade. . . . You began with handwork; at first you had to snip off loose threads . . . from the dresses. And, boy, was that a boring job for someone as full of life as me! But I did it. I wanted to learn the trade of seamstress. . . . That was for about six or seven weeks, cutting off the loose threads; and you had to do that. If you didn't, you'd be out of there fast—and for good." [16]

Secretly, without telling her parents, Esther went to work in another factory when she discovered she would have to remain in training for another year. A couple of small pieces of cloth she had pulled out of a waste basket led to accusations of stealing, and within a week she found herself out of a job. She then tried to pass herself off as a dressmaker, but cut a dress in two during the first week. Then she found a job on Waterloo Square making cushions—and landed in trouble. She bought some fruit at noon one day and ran into her father, who asked what she was doing there. She was supposed to be somewhere else! She was earning much more money than before but had held it back.

This account shows a rebellious child who does not dare to be honest with her parents, a child well aware of the monotony of the sewing shop and driven by it into insubordination. The story is extreme, but it also clearly shows how far the parents had control of their daughter. Esther certainly had boyfriends, but more in order to make fun of them than to make love to them. She completely forgot about one of her first dates: "My father asked the boy when he came to fetch me, 'What have you come for?' He answered, 'I didn't come to bring shoes [her father was a shoemaker]; I've come for your daughter who's sitting over there. She made a date with me, and when she didn't show up . . . ' 'Well,' said my father, and he thought it was great that I was sitting there behind the counter [she was polishing shoes], . . . 'she must first finish polishing those shoes, and then when they're all done, she can go out for an hour.'"

Her suitor was soon allowed to come visiting, since her mother was glad to marry her off to a man who was employed. In her naiveté she became pregnant, not because she knew so much about sexuality, but rather because she knew absolutely nothing about it.[17] I heard such stories of naiveté on other occasions.

Heertje's view of the Jewish seamstresses of the sewing shops was distorted. His study dealt with seamstresses in general; he said nothing about possible differences between those who were Jewish and the others. According to him, the married women at the shops told the young girls certain stories that misinformed them. In those apartments where the girls slept in a single room with their parents, the young people certainly knew where children came from—but not how they were made.

The upbringing of a Jewish seamstress was strict. The brazen attitude that Heertje came across involved a totally different kind of relationship between men and women than was normal to him, and certainly not one that he regarded as desirable. On the one hand, there was more freedom and people were more brotherly and sisterly toward one another; on the other hand, this was only possible in a small community where everyone knew everyone and where there was so much social control. The codes regulating the limits of freedom were clear. The shrieking and screaming of the girls, which so annoyed him, were probably just one aspect of a different way of communicating.

Moreover, there was more than one kind of seamstress. The daughters of diamond workers and their cousins (even those who had not grown up in a diamond worker's family) felt they were more respectable than the children of workers in the garment trade. Yet they all worked together at the sewing shop. Even though the girls with a background in the diamond industry were in the minority, at many of the sewing shops they determined the attitude toward the work and the social status of those who worked there. Certainly, wherever their attitudes were dominant, unbecoming behavior was unthinkable. Such behavior was not "modern," according to the standards of the

ANDB, and thus belonged to the unorganized (and hence uneducated) working class. Thus the socialist movement influenced not only the trade union
organization but also the culture in the sewing shops.

THE DIAMOND INDUSTRY

In chapter 2, I described how the diamond workers were the elite of the
Amsterdam Jewish proletariat for many years. Their industry had flourished
during the *Kaapse Tijd* in the nineteenth century. Their powerful union, the
ANDB, had been the great stimulus behind the formation of modern trade
unionism in which workers from many industries cooperated, resulting in the
Nederlands Verbond van Vakverenigingen, or NVV [Dutch Alliance of Labor
Unions]. The wealthy union coffers and the development of a strong organization helped them win many strikes. The union leadership guaranteed deci-
siveness and clarity.[18]

The majority of diamond workers, and especially the cleavers of large
stones, were Jews, many of whom lived in the Ooster Park neighborhood and
in the newer areas of East Amsterdam. The Christian diamond workers lived
mainly in the Jordaan and West Amsterdam; they generally worked with
smaller stones. Diamond workers considered themselves craftsmen; in their
opinion, there was no other work. There is a well-known story of two male
diamond workers who happen to meet in the harbor. Each is carrying a heavy
load. One says to the other, "I see you're not working either."

The diamond industry was the pride of the Jewish neighborhood, and diamond workers were proud of their craft. They considered themselves better
and more civilized, and they belonged to an elite. Their training was lengthy,
their union organization was the best, and their political consciousness was the
most developed. Their union had demonstrated that good organization leads to
progress. Henri Polak had fought to ensure that the union would also raise their
cultural level. Polak's goal was not only to organize the diamond workers but
also to get them out of the cafés where they received their pay.

Education was to change their way of thinking, to enlighten them about the
higher values in life. And so the ANDB brought them culture, sobriety, and
smaller families—in short, what they understood to be emancipation. Now
that the wives were not totally exhausted from constant child-bearing, modern
morality could be introduced into the diamond workers' families, and after
work husbands were supposed to take an active part in family life. There is no
need to prove that, at the same time, there was a reduction in the amount of
work done by married women. The demise of the diamond industry ensured
this, for there was no longer enough work for them.

The morals of the diamond workers' daughters were considered to be high.
They were brought up in a cultured environment. Even when no money was
coming in and the diamond workers had to turn to some other occupation, as I

was told in an interview, "the conversations among the diamond workers at a factory like this were on a level that was so much higher—music, literature, . . . that was all at the time when the diamond workers' union was set up. Henri Polak and so on. The people who published those papers every week or every month, the ones you could learn so much from . . . and you always had meetings where you felt conscious of being a socialist, that . . . it was great."[19]

The sociologist Heertje, who has been mentioned several times, wrote a dissertation dealing with the craft in 1936. It contained a detailed account of the decline of the industry after 1919 on the one hand, and a clear picture of how the contemporaries of the diamond workers viewed them on the other.[20] He described the decline of the diamond after World War I, the transfer of activity to Antwerp, and the terrible poverty that resulted. He claimed that there were between 6,000 and 7,000 unemployed diamond workers in 1920. In 1921 they averaged 7,000, or between 80 and 90 percent of the total ANDB membership of 9,000. As a result, the union lost members. The years after that were somewhat more favorable, but the sharp competition with Antwerp (and to a lesser extent with the cottage industry in Germany) prevented the union from demanding any improvement in wages. There was no way to prevent it—time and again they agreed to wage reductions. The small businesses were continually being driven out, and the industry became more and more concentrated in the hands of a couple of large factories—which further increased the fragmentation of the tasks. The number of employers was drastically reduced.[21]

The 1929 Depression was catastrophic. The number of unemployed was distressing. For the first 13 weeks, those out of work drew on the unemployment fund to which employed diamond workers contributed a guilder per week. After that, they had to fall back on "Depression relief," but eligibility for this was limited to those whose names had been selected by drawing lots. The rest became entirely dependent on welfare—which meant a further deterioration of their situation. During the time just after the Depression started, the union was in part responsible for assigning Depression relief.

The government decided that unemployment in the diamond industry was so bad that workers from that industry were not to be directly dependent on support from the municipalities but were to be treated as a separate category. The files for the unemployed diamond workers during the 1920s were archived separately; these will be used in the section on unemployment (pp. 183ff.). But for those who were still working, conditions were getting worse. The economic distinction between the diamond workers and other workers was disappearing, and the cultural differences with it. Scarcely anyone had permanent employment. The once proud culture of the diamond workers became no more than the past glory of a group that was becoming coarser by the day.

In the ANDB the leaders were idolized. Everyone knew Henri Polak who, inspired by the British trade union movement, had organized the ANDB.[22] "There is only one Henri," sighed L. in one interview. There were, indeed, many "unique" heroes of popular culture on the level of Louis Davids, a well-known cabaret artist, but none was so exceptional, so special as Henri. The diamond workers had erected a palatial headquarters for their organization on Fransche Lane in the middle of the Plantage neighborhood where, during the *Kaapse Tijd*, the newly rich small jewelers and independent workers had established themselves. Outside the ghetto, they built for themselves ornate houses appropriate to their new status as an elite—elegant, French in style, and full of their new-found wealth. *De Burcht*, the Citadel, as the diamond workers called their palace, had been built by Berlage.[23] The majestic character of the building was described as follows in *Het Volk* [The People], the socialist newspaper:

> And high, high overhead, the citadel is crowned with crenelations, the moldings hidden behind graceful folds, symbol of unity, from which the tower rises, massively square above the entrance. In the tower is the shining diamond, the joyous light of unified labor, streaming over the narrow, crowded buildings of the city. For those who come as friends, the building of the ANDB is indeed hospitable.
> View the entrance as a funnel through which the multitudes are taken in. Broad steps lead to it, flanked on either side by tranquil stone watchmen.[24]

The building is indeed imposing, impressive, gigantic. At the present time, it contains the Museum of the Trade Union Movement.

Annie is one of the many people who met Henri in person. "I was—that was at the 25th anniversary of the union—I was allowed, since I was the youngest—16, I think—to give Henri and that other person flowers."

"Was that a great honor?"

"Yes."

The diamond workers had escaped from the ghetto and now lived a "better" life. The union offices, also located in the new Jewish neighborhoods, were splendid.

"You could find the best books there, a lovely library. You walked, I think, from Henri Polak Lane [as Fransche Lane was later called] up onto a high porch, and it was all paid for—the whole building. You yourself had partly paid for it. It was your very own building, with meetings . . . I experienced it all; but later on rather less happened there."[25]

It was not easy to join "the trade." The trade schools seldom allowed anyone other than the children of diamond workers to enroll. The training was expensive, and obtaining a position often depended on having connections in the industry. Here again is Annie, the diamond cutter. She tells of her own experiences as a trainee:

"I went from school, elementary school, to night school, and there I learned the diamond trade. First on Oosterpark Street for a couple of years, and then . . . I worked on Zwanenburger Street in one of the factories, and I rented a place there. . . . I never took work too seriously. My father said, 'Just don't work too hard,' for I thought I was in the wrong place—I really felt that. Don't work too hard—because he worked really hard so it wasn't all that necessary."

By day she learned the diamond trade at work and in the evenings she went to vocational school. I asked about the school.

"That was really interesting. You learned as a group. There were a lot of young people and that was fun. At the factory—this'll interest you—later, when I was at the factory, . . . I rough-cut the diamonds, which meant that you made the little stones round. But there were only a few jobs because there were always more facet-cutters than rough-cutters [so there was rivalry for the available jobs]. The facet-cutters cut the facets on the stones."

Then, regarding the school:

"There was this woman. She lived there and she had taken on a group of trainees. She was a cutter, and she asked the parents for ƒ 350, which was a whole lot of money; and she said 'Three years.' You had to train that long. But in fact you learned everything in a couple of months, and then for the rest of the time you just sat there working for her. Because she took the work in for money. She was called a teacher, and there was no other way to learn. . . . It took 'three years'—which was a swindle."

Eventually she managed to work her way up to handling a diamond saw at the factory.

"I came in and said to myself, 'I'll find work.' You had to find a sponsor who would give you work. So I came inside—I remember it well—and there were a lot of little rooms with tiny windows between them through which they could talk. So in I came, thinking I was really something. . . . 'Hey, look at what just walked in, we haven't ever seen the likes of that, the princess herself . . . can she cut diamonds?' I found a boss and when I didn't earn enough I went to him and said, 'Look, I did my work well, but I'm not paid enough.' And he said, 'Enough for the cafeteria.' I was terribly hurt." [26]

Annie really wanted to work but her boss thought it old-fashioned for women to work.

Suze also came from a diamond family. First she tried working for a paper company. But even when she was put in charge, she earned precious little. "So my father said, 'You have to learn the diamond trade. That'll be better for you.' And I got a really good boss to train me . . . I was lucky."

I asked about her first day.

"I had to watch, and then I had to sweep the floor and check whether there was a stone missing. If a stone got lost, I had to join the search. Everyone did. If you let a diamond fall. . . . I was in training there for three years; you learned, and half the money went to the boss." [27]

Jacob was the child of Jewish parents who had come from Poland. Their situation was a little better than some, and he came into the diamond trade from a background that was somewhat more secure. But what is security? As things became worse within the industry and the power of the ANDB declined, it became possible for him to work with diamonds even though his parents had not done so. A number of diamond workers opened their own training school, which enabled other unemployed people to enter the trade. In practice this meant that they took in a number of trainees and exploited them, just as Annie's teacher did. Jacob had this to say: "It became so bad that it was no more than an assembly line; I mean, everyone made just one tiny bit of each diamond."

He came to work in Soep's shed, where on Monday morning the men staggered up the steps soused with drink. To my explicit questioning about the use of alcohol, he replied (and this directly contradicted the findings of J. J. Leydesdorff in his *Sociale Psychologie van Joden* [Social Psychology of Jews], mentioned in chapter 2, and likewise the official view of the industry promulgated by the ANDB): "There was the time of Henri Polak. . . . Money was earned like water in the diamond industry." In Polak's time the diamond workers were an elite. But with the onset of poverty this changed. It was Jacob who told how the atmosphere in the factories became rougher, how the men became addicted to drink, and how the dignified culture of the diamond workers was forgotten.

We returned to the training process:

"At first—I don't know if you know about the diamond industry—when there was a pile of unfinished stones, once in a while one would fall on the ground. As kids, we'd hide it if we found it. We could go on looking all day. Didn't have to work. That's what was great about that time of life. But then you got a year or so older, and in the end you had to put food on the table—I mean you had to learn the trade, so you did your best. And you got a stone to train on. To do it yourself for once! And boy, you really ground away at it. I mean, you made a mess because you were still learning. You didn't really know how it had to be done yet. But in the end it came out right. The bosses watched what was happening, they paid attention. In those days you had to learn every aspect of the trade. Later this changed, just as I said—it became assembly-line work. One got the top to polish, another the underside. But in the past, you had to do the whole thing. Because I was among those who worked with the really large stones."

"Those who worked with very large stones?"

"Yes, the larger the stone, the more difficult the work, and the higher the pay."

"As a trainee they ribbed you, and of course you had to run errands. . . . But it was a terrific *gezellige* time. There was so much distraction. People would come into the room with all sorts of things to barter and sell."[28]

According to Jacob, poverty led to slovenliness; and during the Depression it seemed that all the apparent refinement was no more than a thin veneer. He felt that a good example of this was the way people failed to use clothes hangers; the clothes they had worn were simply dumped anywhere. When I pointed out that this happened in the wealthiest families, he said that it was regarded as a disgusting thing to do. He also indicated the lack of interest shown in courses offered by the ANDB and the fact that the young diamond workers no longer had much interest in social or political matters. He called this "counterselection," [29] since whoever was clever enough tried to earn a living in some other way, thus escaping from the continual threat of poverty.

In contrast with the drop in standards sketched above (which had also occurred in the home), the sociologist Heertje described the furnishings of the diamond workers' homes as still being those of a working class that nevertheless could pass for middle class:

> The dwelling is well furnished. Diamond workers who are engaged to be married save for this for years; a kitchen is often paid for by means of a collection of pennies and nickels. Whenever possible, the furniture is custom-made by a cabinetmaker from a pattern or a sketch. Household articles bought years ago by the diamond workers are often still well preserved and in use. Henri Polak's many lectures and articles from the beginning of the century on how to furnish a home and decorate the walls had a great deal of influence. His advice—avoid stuffing rooms with mahogany tables and chairs with elaborately curled feet; choose instead simple, solid furniture and a restful color scheme—were taken to heart by the then young diamond workers. Heavily upholstered easy chairs and settees were replaced by simple couches and armchairs and furnishings in the rustic style. Flowered wallpaper was replaced by simple monochromatic paper. [30]

According to Heertje, the heavy housework was generally done by maids until 1930. When times got bad, they were kept on as long as possible, but gradually became less common. The picture he paints is clearly much rosier than what emerged from the interviews and from materials I have read. Only very rarely did the interviews deal with anything but poverty.

Moreover, union campaigns aiming to stabilize wages had the effect of lowering them, since foreign diamond works provided formidable competition, as the wages they paid were so low. Even Heertje recognized that he was unable to gain a precise picture of the conditions among the diamond workers. His attempts to study their budgets failed. He admitted that wherever the scourge of unemployment had been present for years, "relatively large amounts are paid out on rent and food and little is spent on clothing. Many suffer from 'hidden poverty,' which is scarcely evident to friends and acquaintances." [31]

Heertje idealized Jewish family life, which he distinguished from that of the Christian diamond workers' families primarily by the extent to which family members regularly visited each others' homes. He wrote of the central position of the parents' home—even after the children married—of the generosity found in times of prosperity, the great affection between brothers and sisters, and the quarrels that such close contact brought with it. At the same time, he emphasized the importance of good friends.[32] That he did so is striking, in light of my own findings. In almost all interviews, I asked about the relative importance of family ties and friendships. The opinion that the family was most important was virtually unanimous. More significant was the fact that it was only in exceptional circumstances that friends really visited each other's homes. There were two sorts of contact. First was contact between women; in this case, family members came before women living on the same street. Second was contact among men outside the home, either in cafés or at work.

Finally, it should be mentioned that Heertje's account implies a surprising number of diamond workers who had no religious affiliation. It is generally assumed that Jews made up 70 percent of the diamond workers. Since 57.4 percent of the workers claimed to be Jewish, approximately 18 percent of the Jewish diamond workers must have been nonreligious. If this is correct, the percentage of Jews who were nonreligious must have been lower than the percentage of non-Jews who were.[33] This result also seems dubious.

Annie gave expression to the hopelessness resulting from the general decline. There was nothing more to idealize, just poverty:

"There was always unemployment. I remember how my husband started out on his own. It was a bad time in the diamond industry. Some years there was just no work at all, and the people didn't know what to do. This is also one reason why children had to learn two trades. They had to learn the diamond trade and another one. What was so interesting, was that most chose music! I realized that later; a whole bunch of them stayed in music. . . . I remember how, after he had been out of work for a couple of years, perhaps a year and a half or two years, my husband said, 'Well, I'm going to have another go at it.' So he bought rough diamonds and tried again. Apparently he had written to these people [diamond workers]—naturally they had no phone—and they were to come by one evening. I still had a maid at the time, who opened the door. And I said, 'May I take your coat?' (It was a rather cold evening.) The first said, 'No, no. I'll keep it on.' With the second and third I told the maid, 'Don't come out again to take coats.' They were embarrassed to take off their coats since their trousers had holes in them, or the trousers or whatever they had on under their overcoat was threadbare. They were embarrassed. They were that poor."

According to Annie, they looked down on you if you worked in diamonds—you were Jewish, poor, and worked in a factory. But such people were, in her words, the most respectable people. Once she saw what was happening in Germany, she wanted to go to America. She fled too late, with the traditional "diamond in the vest pocket." But the majority no longer had any diamonds.[34]

"There is little prospect that the Amsterdam diamond industry will revive quickly," wrote Heertje in 1936.[35] By then, Amsterdam was already unable to justify the title "Diamond City," and Heertje's prediction that the decline in the industry would be permanent ultimately proved correct. After World War II, almost no Jewish diamond workers were left, and Antwerp took pride of place in the industry.

RETAIL

A SALESWOMAN IN A SHOP

The daughters from the better educated workers' families often became saleswomen. Through contact with customers, they learned good taste and behavior that was socially acceptable in better circles. At the same time, the girls learned details of the specific trades in which they worked. These skills could sometimes be used after marriage, for example, when the husband had a business. The more modern and larger the store, the more fashionable the situation. The mecca of culture and refinement was Hirsch, an extremely large department store where the saleswomen knew a few words of French; however, workers' daughters were seldom employed there. The saleswomen there came from the middle class. The Bijenkorf [lit. beehive], the large department store in the center of the city (which, like Hirsch, was in Jewish hands), was regarded as a good place to work, as were the large fabric stores along St. Antoniesbree Street.

How did a girl from a poor Jewish family come to work in the Bijenkorf?

"My mother said I had to learn to sew, so that I could do the mending. And in housework, you're your brothers' drudge. You can polish their shoes and take care of their needs. . . . A woman, a neighbor, asked me if I would like to come to the store to learn how to be a salesgirl. Well, my mother was so proud!"

This story was told by the former saleswoman Mrs. P. She said it was very cold in the store because the door had to remain open, and she was also supposed to go out on the street to persuade people to come inside, though she did not want to do that.

"I earned a *kwartje*, 25 cents a week, and for that I had to mop out the kitchen and do household chores for them. I said to my mother, 'I'm not learning to sell; I'm just helping with the housework. And they want me to persuade people to come into the store, but I won't do that.' "

She moved to another store.

"I went there and was to earn 3 guilders a week. . . . The first 14 days were murder! You have no idea. On Sunday . . . the store was bigger than these two rooms and wider . . . ten of us were there on Sundays, carrying bales of fabric out to the customers. And the haggling! That was the custom in those days; but did we sell some fabric—unbelievable! When I'd been there 14 days, he [the manager] paid me 3 guilders. I said, 'That's not what we agreed. . . . You told me: You'll be here 14 days on probation, and you'll get 4 guilders for that.' " She got the 4 guilders.

During the Depression the store began to lose business and she looked for another job. She went to work for a store on Dam Street and stayed there for years. But because the owner was "no good" and refused to give her a raise, she applied for a job at the Bijenkorf.

"I had to go upstairs and tell them what I did at the other place. And I had to show myself off, so they could see how I walked and how I looked."

She was made a head saleswoman and left only because she got married. Her husband had his own business and could well use her help.

Only the very best could work at the Bijenkorf; the recruitment policy was highly selective and they only took girls from the better Jewish working-class families.[36]

Recha also went to work there: "I went with my mother to the Bijenkorf to try for a job, because you didn't do that—apply for a job—alone. A nice girl didn't do that, and I wanted to be a saleswoman."

She was tested and found unsuitable for the work but was given a job in the administrative side of the business; she was quite happy with it because it was a good job.

"If you got a permanent job, your family envied you. . . . It gave you security . . . and respectability, too—in an office!"

When the Depression worsened, the temporary workers were laid off. There were many in that situation. "In that case, they really didn't care about you, and they could take you on by the day. We felt the effects of the Depression in the diamond industry at the Bijenkorf, for they came in when the books had to be balanced and during the holidays in December. All of them by the day; they'd stand there in the street behind the store next to the Stock Exchange, waiting to see if they'd be taken on; and many of them were Jewish diamond workers and so on." Unemployed men especially were taken on by the day.[37]

There was a great difference between working in a small store—the world of the small independent business people—and working for a large company. The difference in status between the saleswomen in the big department stores and the mass of impoverished street peddlers was even greater. There seems to have been a fairly fluid gradation between the small business and pushing a handcart. The peddler generally kept his wares at home, and thus people would sometimes go there to buy as well. If he lived on the ground floor, his home in effect became a store. Yet the peddlers were generally accorded a lower status, since a real store brought with it a suggestion of being a real business.

TABLE 6

NUMBER OF JEWS AND TOTAL NUMBER OF PEDDLERS
BY MERCHANDISE

branch	Jews	Total
Fruit	382	604
Fish	251	878
Flowers	246	801
Vegetables	102	473
Ice	92	410

The number of street vendors dealing in rags is not known.

Source: I. Santcroos, "Het aandeel der Amsterdamsche joden in de straathandel," in *De Vijdagavond* (24 October 1930).

PEDDLERS

Selling in the street was a way of earning money, a form of small business plied by many Jews for centuries. Although there was a difference between someone who sold goods from a regular stall in a market and a street peddler who had to trudge around offering his wares, this difference became minimal when things got bad. Before the Depression, Jews formed a disproportionately high percentage of the peddlers.[38] The well-known socialist writer, I. Santcroos, wrote in 1930 that their numbers had increased in a disturbing way as a result of the Depression. Their standard of living was declining rapidly. Aside from the trade in rags, most street vendors dealt in food. The rag merchants were overwhelmingly Jewish. In 1921 a system of permits was introduced, which limited their numbers. Too often, unemployed Jews automatically became rag merchants, so that there were too many of them and not enough business to go around. Also, the rag trade is sensitive to competition; rag pickers are dependent on what a middleman will recognize as rags.

In Amsterdam, 31.6 percent of the peddlers were Jewish, but this did not include the rag pickers, so the percentage was in fact higher.[39] The next most common were the Jewish street vendors who dealt in in fruit, fish, and flowers. Table 6 shows the number of Jews and the total number of peddlers by merchandise, according to Santcroos.

Santcroos investigated the causes of this overrepresentation of Jews in peddling. In order to obtain information, he wrote to welfare organizations and institutions concerned with the lives of poor Jews. He came to the following conclusions, which are reproduced here at length:

> In former centuries, the Israelites were not admitted to guilds. They were thereby prevented from learning a trade or becoming proficient in one, or working in one, so that they were forced to occupy themselves with buying

and selling. Moreover, employers found it unacceptable—and indeed still do—to permit an observing Jew to take Saturdays and religious holy days off and to work on Sundays.

Orthodox parents know that if their children are trained to work with their hands, they will experience great difficulty in finding an employer, and will therefore be inclined to accept employment with a non-Jew, thus being compelled to work on the Sabbath and other holy days.

Santcroos also noted the reluctance of employers in the garment, iron, and construction industries to hire Jews. The total number of Jews working as civil servants for the municipality was 1 percent, so they could not expect employment there either. It was unusual to hire a Jew. As a result, street trade had become a tradition for many Jewish families. "The children grew up in the business they saw their fathers practicing, and sometimes they helped him—it was a tradition that was coupled with a certain degree of convenience."[40]

The great increase in the number of peddlers was also due to the number of unemployed diamond workers. This observation is supported by the welfare archives of the diamond industry during the Depression. Many unemployed diamond workers tried to help themselves by peddling. Relief was mainly given in the form of business subsidies to buy wares to sell, but it was not adequate. Of the 2,276 families that were helped in this manner during 1928, 1,484 of them requested business subsidies again in 1929.

Peddling was passed on from father to son, from one family member to another. They helped each other with trading and with the supply of good merchandise. Connections with wholesalers were used to help others. Peddling was a business that involved the entire family.

Catherina told me: "My father brought in clothes from his handcart for my mother to wash and iron."[41]

The history of the peddling profession in Amsterdam can be found in the authoritative work on Amsterdam peddlers by the sociologist Huberts.[42] Published in 1940, this study is also full of opinions about the Jewish race and racial characteristics, which clearly represent many prejudices regarding Jewish peddlers. For example, she describes the manner in which peddlers worked the streets, and from her description it becomes apparent that she is talking about Jewish peddlers. Her study of the character of peddlers is characterized by observations like:

> The way they sell things requires that the peddler possess certain special abilities. In the vernacular, they are called 'screamers.'
>
> Gesticulating grandly and with breathtaking, rapidly repeated shouts, the peddler announces the price, product, and quality, trying to occupy the busiest parts of the streets and squares and endeavoring to attract the attention of the public at large. *Het is te gèèf*—'I'm *giving* it away,' is one of his cries as he laughingly and admiringly squeezes the juiciest oranges and pears before the eyes of his public or pushes the scent of roses under the

nose of greedy buyers. . . . Full of emotion, he attends to the buyers, at the same time dealing out contemptuous little jokes to the hesitant.[43]

Huberts described the unexpected increase in the number of peddlers, which resulted in the introduction of regulations to control their numbers. In 1934 a system of permits was introduced that was supposed to end a situation in which too many peddlers were receiving aid to set up their businesses. It was felt that the number of peddlers should be limited so that those who remained would truly be able to support themselves. At the same time, it would bring to an end a practice that was regarded as pointless: money was constantly being poured into needy businesses.

The uncertainty of such an existence could lead people to become less sympathetic to each other. Catherina had this to say:

"I was about 12 years old. My father said, 'You know what I'm going to do? I'm going to apply for a "subsidy."' You could get a business subsidy of *f* 20, and that was a lot. But then you also had a municipal worker come to your home. He came to see if you really needed the money. So this man came, and my mother had a pot with a beef stomach cooking in it; it had cost about a *kwartje* [quarter of a guilder].

The man said, 'Your husband has asked for a subsidy, do you really need it?' My mother replied, 'Come along with me to the kitchen.' He went with her. She lifted the lid off the pan and he asked, 'What is that, ma'am?' 'Fresh cat food, which I'm going to feed to my children.' And he said, 'Your husband can come tomorrow to pick up the business subsidy.' But my mother had misled him. It was simply tripe.

"I obtained clothes from Reigersbergen Street [the municipal depot]. It was school clothing: black stockings, which itched something awful, and a wine-colored dress made of a woolen fabric so coarse you could hardly wear it, and underclothing. That was standard school clothing, so everyone could see you had on school clothing. It was well known. Shoes, too, the high kind with laces. My father had to fetch them from Reigersbergen Street."

Her father had to shovel snow as a condition of receiving unemployment. "He came home with soaking wet socks . . . his head fell on the table, and he was sound asleep, he was so tired."[44]

The Depression hit them very hard. Her mother refused the cans of meat that were made available; you never knew if they contained pork. So she waited till her husband came home in the hope that there would be money enough to buy a beef heart. Although that is now considered to be dog food, at that time it was a delicacy.

Catherina was used to poverty. "My father had always been a ragman. Well, first he dealt in subtropical fruit in an alley. But when my grandfather died, his boss wouldn't let him take time off to go to the funeral. If he went, he would lose his job. Which he did. So he started with a pushcart, collecting rags."

"Where did he drop them off?"

"At Sal de Jong on Waterloo Square—he had several places there, though he collected his wares elsewhere. His area was Marnix Street and the neighborhood around it; later, after the war, he had Oosterburg."[45]

The preparation for a system of permits had already started in 1930 with the establishment of a municipal advisory committee. The exceptionally harsh winter of 1929 had made things very difficult for the market stall-holders and peddlers. In the Municipal Council, the social-democratic alderman de Miranda argued that the special position of the peddlers, who were sometimes able to work a few days and then had to stop, required a welfare system designed especially for them. The permit policy certainly meant that most of the peddlers had to give up.

According to de Miranda, the regulations dealing with the street sellers were introduced because of concern for the youth, fear that large numbers of peddlers would interfere with traffic, and recognition of the needs of those dealing with peddlers, as well as the increasing numbers of street vendors. Moreover, during the debate in the Municipal Council in 1931 over de Miranda's proposal to introduce a permit system, the right-wing parties expressly referred to the lawlessness of the peddlers, the camouflaged begging that went on, and the typically Jewish nature of that occupation. De Miranda wanted to remove such stigmas by regulating the peddlers.

Eventually, the final version of the ordinance became law in 1934. By that time, de Miranda was no longer an alderman. The communists quickly used their organ, *De Tribune*, to accuse the Municipal Council of an "attack." The number of peddlers was to be reduced from 7,500 to 4,000.[46] These numbers were far higher than those discussed earlier because they include the rag merchants. The percentage of Jews among them was very high—about 90 percent. In order to obtain a permit, one had to be able to prove that one had a good moral character. The number of peddlers was indeed reduced.[47]

The inventory and statistics that were completed later were confirmed by Huberts, who was in part an eyewitness. Many people were reduced to accepting welfare and thus could not continue as peddlers. The communists tried to deal with the situation by introducing "extra welfare," which was to take the place of "business subsidies," making it possible for the peddlers to find temporary relief. This was in conflict in particular with the policy of the SDAP, which was set on supporting only those peddlers who, as a result, would genuinely be able to keep their heads above water. Other employment had to be found for those who could not be expected to survive on their own. Speculation over the numbers who were involved and the success of the policy continued to dominate every debate about street vendors until World War II. In particular, the liberals often asked whether the stringent regulations were not in fact making more peddlers unable to earn a living and costing the city extra, since the municipality was now forced to provide them with welfare.

The regulations governing peddlers were closely related to the SDAP policy concerning the economic future of the city. The efforts to maintain the more successful peddlers in their trade, if necessary at the cost of the less successful, is analogous to the socialist policy of reorganizing small businesses in such a way as to favor the healthy companies. The prime example from the *Socialisatierapport* [Socialization Report] of 1920, a blueprint produced by the SDAP for a gradual change to a socialist society, was the bakeries of Amsterdam. These bakeries were once again discussed in the debates in the council meetings of June and July 1935. At the time, there were still 16,000 bread suppliers and 1,500 people delivering bread in Amsterdam—far too many to assure all of them a reasonable living. In some streets there were as many as 50 or 60 suppliers—it has been said that in one case there were two of them delivering on a single stairway. The SDAP wished to distribute these firms geographically, at the same time introducing a system of permits. This was not carried out until the passage of the act regulating the establishment of small businesses (*Vestigingswet Kleinbedrijf*), which came into force in 1937 after a long delay. Small businesses and the retail trade fell under this law. For areas that were overserved, a minimum turnover was required for the issuance of a permit.

These regulations were all intended to limit the activities of the many people who were attempting to start their own businesses. Only the strongest would be allowed to do so, and they would be assisted by the disappearance of competition from small dealers who were not really serious. As far as street vending goes, global figures are available, but it is impossible to determine how many small Jewish shops and businesses disappeared. Peddlers were fair game, and Huberts wrote of guerrilla warfare between them and the police who repeatedly tried to issue summonses to the illegal vendors.

At the outset of this chapter, the family of one particular peddler was mentioned.[48] That story vividly illustrates the decline of the Jewish peddler. The husband, wife, and two children first became eligible for support in 1935 after the man lost a permit allowing him to stand at the Waterloo Square market twice a week. He then began scraping together a living, meanwhile regularly applying for welfare, since he could no longer earn enough. As he earned less money, his various permits were revoked. He took on all kinds of small jobs.

In time, his family became one of those that depended entirely on social welfare. When the husband was deported to Germany in February 1941, the amount was not reduced, at least not during the first week, but the wife, too, according to the record, "left" for Germany on 3 September 1941. In the archives dealing with applications for support, the tragic story can be found without a single word being written overtly. At a certain point, the researcher sets the file aside, thinking of the gas chambers that lie hidden beneath the bureaucratic phraseology.

Many who had recently become peddlers were not prepared for their new station. The best-known story concerns a former diamond worker who walked behind another peddler. He was so ashamed of hawking his wares out loud that he was only able to call out repeatedly, "Me, too; me, too." [49]

Others found it a shocking way of life: "He [the father] did walk behind a pushcart once. What was on it? Vegetables, or cauliflower—heck, I don't know what it was. But he couldn't call out his wares, so he just stayed out for half a day. And then? Well, he dumped the whole lot, cart and all, in the canal. . . . He came home, and my mother asked, 'What did you sell?' 'I sold everything, everything's gone.' So—happiness—but there it lay at the bottom of the Oude Schans. The place we'd rented the pushcart from over in the Jodenhouttuinen, well, he goes to them and he says, 'I left my cart for a moment, and I went to have a cup of coffee with some people, and the children—they dumped it all in the water. . . . How do I get it out?' They got it out, but the money spent on the wares to be sold—that was gone." [50]

MARKET VENDING

The various occupations were not really totally distinct. A diamond worker could turn peddler from one day to the next, while a peddler could become a market seller, or a market seller a peddler. Originally there was a great gulf between the market vendors and the street vendors,[51] but the differences became vague and the distinctions increasingly fluid.

As a first example, here is the story of Leendert. His father had had a little bookstore on the island of Marken and a stand on Waterloo Square. He combined the ownership of a little store with working as a street vendor and market seller, though he was never a real peddler.

"My father was a bookseller, had never done anything else. That was his trade. During the week he stood on Waterloo Square. On Saturdays he was at the Nieuw Market, and on Mondays at Amstel Field. On Sundays he was in the Jewish Quarter, so he worked seven days a week, only taking off Sunday afternoons. Then he did nothing—that was his free afternoon. But don't think that meant much, for then he had to take care of odds and ends. Everyone knew him with his red moustache. . . . "

His father kept his wares in a shed on Waterloo Square, but he also had a lot in the attic. Leendert told a good tale about that, which illustrates their way of life rather well.

One of the customers, a certain Mr. K. who lived in Utrecht, bought all kinds of items relating to the royal family, mostly buying from Leendert's father and paying well. So his father bought up whatever others had for sale, and kept everything in a folder for Mr. K. The family lived on Valkenburger Street; the folder was stored in the attic. Mr. K. came to the market unexpectedly, and Leendert's father told him that the items were still at home. And although the father really did not like the idea, they trudged off together to the attic. While they were up there, one of the prostitutes in the street, Memeljoek by name, began quarreling loudly. She swore, "Don't I have clean pants on?" and lifted her skirt. Leendert, to whom such behavior was perfectly normal, realized from Mr. K.'s embarrassment how different his world was from theirs.

Leendert's father worked hard for a living. Once a girl was murdered on Waterloo Square, and no one talked about anything else all day long. He bought up a batch of books with the title *Murderer of Women*; the book was about a notorious murderer named Landru. He decked out his stall as an oven from which protruded two women's legs, taken from a store mannequin. Above them was a pair of women's lace panties. The stall had been smeared with buckets of cow's blood. On a board by the stall was written:

> I will boil you, I will roast you.
> But Levie will sell you Landru's tale,
> for just a *kwartje*, it's on sale![52]

"We helped set up and take down the stall as much as we could—more often we helped take it down because we had no time when we had to go to school; but usually it was taken down after 5 o'clock. We were at home then, and we had to help whether we wanted to or not."

His father opened a bookstore in addition to the market stall, trying in that way to help his family improve their lot. He also worked for the Mercurius, the union of market sellers, but refused a paid job with them, and the family remained poor.

"We were sorry he did, because we thought he'd then be free of the market. . . . Imagine, the cold of winter and the days when you couldn't open the stall because of the weather."

"Was he often ill because of the weather?"

"He was ill just once in his life, when he was hauled off to Poland. Before that I never knew my father to be ill. He was a strong man who had a lot of trouble with his joints."

Leendert took an apprenticeship with a tailor in order to learn a trade. However, "There came a time when my old man said to me, 'No, that's not for you, you must go into trading.' And I said, 'I've no money, are you going to lend me some?' He said, 'Lend! What do you think I am? How much do you have?' I said, '*f* 3.75.' 'Well, why can't you make a start with that?' Off I go, and return after a couple of hours with a couple of packages of books— because obviously I was going to go into the book trade. So he says, 'Bought something?' 'I bought something,' 'What did it cost?' 'In the end I got them for *f* 3.75.' I didn't have any more. . . . He said, 'If your father gives you a *daalder* [*f* 1.50] as profit, what will you say to that?' 'I'll not sell them for that,' I said. He asked, 'Why not?' 'If you're willing to give me a *daalder* profit, I know I can make far more from someone else.' "

Later, Leendert became a kind of partner to his father, "I didn't want to become a tailor, so I didn't." First he set up in the market on Albert Cuyp Street so as not to compete with his father, but later they sold and bought together. However, when the Depression came along, his training as a tailor stood him in good stead. He became a presser, which gave him a steady job and good wages, and in this way Leendert escaped poverty.[53]

Market sellers had Mercurius, the Market Sellers' Union, founded in 1897, which celebrated its 35th anniversary in splendid fashion in 1932.[54] De Miranda was the great leader of this union; he was revered by all, for he had done much for them.

Market people and peddlers did not belong to the same union. Mercurius and the Algemene Ventersbond [General Union of Street Vendors] certainly worked together but they represented different classes of people. Market people mostly sold from a permanent position at the various markets of Amsterdam.[55] They joined with the shopkeepers to complain about the competition from peddlers who were far more mobile.

As we have already seen, the inadequate distribution of consumer goods—especially those necessary for the basics of daily living—was a thorn in the side of the Municipal Council. The desire to bring some order into this chaos provided strong motivation to try to regulate activities in the many markets of Amsterdam. With that in mind, a central market was built in West Amsterdam as a showpiece for the initiatives of the social democrats. It was completed in 1934. Among other things, the market was intended to reduce the pressure caused by the vegetable and fruit market on Marnix Street—which at that point blocked the street—but it was also supposed to bring order into the chaotic situation in the markets in general.

This had far-reaching consequences for the Jewish market sellers dealing in specific products. They could no longer buy their goods freely but were forced to operate through regulated middlemen, subject to price and quality control. The new central market was also a considerable distance from the Jewish neighborhood, which led to transport difficulties and made the work harder. This also made it more difficult to seek out trade at the market on a *temporary* basis. Jews sold principally at Waterloo Square, Nieuw Market, on Uilenburger Street and Jodenbree Street, and on Amstel Field. From time immemorial there had been a Sunday market in the Jewish Quarter, and the whole city turned out to enjoy the rudeness and antics of the stall-holders. The market spread to every street in the area. There were 890 sellers, and special market trains brought people from the province of Noord Holland.[56]

Thus an old occupation, which had its own organization within the Jewish economy, was reorganized at the initiative of the municipal government. It was no longer permissible to change the kind of goods that were offered for sale on a daily basis. And if things turned bad in the diamond or tobacco industries, it was no longer possible to work a market stall as a temporary solution.

JACOB'S STORY:
MAKING ENDS MEET IN THE TOBACCO INDUSTRY

The Depression also led the tobacco workers down a hopeless spiral toward poverty. Some became self-employed as a result, dealing in very tiny quantities. Others sought employment in totally different areas. In contrast to the diamond industry, there was never any real hope that the tobacco industry would improve.

To give some impression of how the workers had to struggle, living from one day to the next, I have chosen the story of Jacob, son of a tobacco worker who had opened his own little business. This "solution" had been chosen by a number of people when the industry disappeared from the city. His parents had a hard life, especially his mother who had had to look after a sick grandmother for years. Because of that, she had never enjoyed a normal childhood.

His father was from a "diamond" family that had a good income. But within that family he was one of the weaker children, small and unable to concentrate well. Diamonds demand that the worker stick to one task for a long time. According to Jacob, he was a likable man who was interested in everything and very willing to help. But because he had no head for business, the family remained poor.

During World War I, he had purchased the large ribs and stems of tobacco leaves, which were then flattened and cut to make tobacco. The process was called *tabakstelen* (a wordplay on tobacco stems and stealing tobacco) and was a rather dubious method of producing cigarette and smoking tobacco. Through hard work, he had managed to earn a little money and had bought a quantity of tobacco stems. That was in November 1918. He brought them home, intending to sell them the following day—which was the day the war ended. Having paid 3 guilders per kilo for them, he was now able to get 3 cents. "If Michel bought gold and tried to sell it, it would turn out to be copper," was what they said.

He had occasionally worked as a courier in the diamond industry but he disliked it, so he kept returning to tobacco. He was proud of making his own cigars and refused to sell other brands. They lived behind the shop on Batavier Street. In order to get extra food, Jacob would often eat the worm-eaten fruit that had been thrown away by the peddlers in the street. His mother disliked cooking, so they ate a great deal of bread and cheese. Sometimes there was bread with chocolate. Occasionally he went and ate at his grandmother's. During World War I, he sometimes ended up having to go to bed without eating—if his grandmother had not invited him to eat there and there was no bread in the house. Therefore, just like his parents, Jacob did not have a really happy childhood.

His father, as stated above, made cigars at home. "A good cigarmaker made cigars that were practically identical to one another, but when my father made them, each was totally different."

"Really artistic cigars, then?"

"Despite his valiant attempts to make them identical. On Saturdays he would then go off to the Nieuw Market to sell them at 10 for a *kwartje*—but they really did have funny shapes."

Later he employed a cigarmaker. When the family moved to East Amsterdam, they had few possessions, for "what can you store in just one room?" His father rented a workroom on the other side of the street where the cigars were made. His father could not work any more since he had begun to have heart trouble after a bout of flu. It bothered him a lot. Moreover, he fidgeted constantly, and his frequent arm movements caused him a great deal of discomfort.

Jacob tried to escape from his background and did the rounds with books of multiplication tables—rather like printed adding machines—which he tried to sell to accountants and lawyers.

"I sold seven or eight a day and brought home some money. I didn't really like the work at all. It was kind of fun at first, but in the winter it wasn't fun at all. . . . Then, one morning, the key disappeared. All kinds of maids came there each morning, but I was the one who got blamed. I hadn't seen the key at all, I hadn't even been there. Obviously one of the maids must have made off with it." He nevertheless had to pay the boss 7.5 guilders, and he only earned 10 guilders a month. Eventually his father paid. It was a heavy blow to the family's finances. "It was really bad at home. The business was barely ticking over, not good at all."

The cigarmaking business was not going well, either. Everyone smoked brand-name cigars, for people just didn't buy handmade goods. "The price was about the same," and if people bought his father's cigars, it was in order to be friendly or simply out of habit. However, because of the reconstruction of the neighborhood, fewer people were around, especially after the construction of an elevated walkway over the railroad tracks—people no longer had to pass by his shop.

Jacob went to work in the office of a cigar manufacturer, but the latter went bankrupt. He was unemployed during 1923 and 1924. Then he found work in a shoeshop on Weesper Street, and after that moved to another shop selling shoes and related articles. His job was to deliver the goods that were sold, and he did this with a handcart. He refused an offer of a job from an accountant because he did not want to leave almost as soon as he had joined this firm. He paid for his loyalty, for the shop did not attract enough customers and went bankrupt.

"Then I was unemployed again, and did all sorts of different things for a long time. I was a milk deliveryman. I worked for a baker, delivering bread. We needed money to eat."

"You were the only one who earned anything at this time?"

"I was the only one who earned anything. My father was often ill . . . he was often in the hospital. At home I would put the little bands around the cigars—which showed that the tax had been paid."

"But when you were unemployed, how did you bring in any money?"

"Well, we had the little shop . . . something always came along, but . . . *ach*, it's a long story, but I'll tell you. My father was really dreadfully poor. Cigars were certainly being made. But they didn't sell well, so there was always a pretty good stock of them. That's what my father was like with money. So there was no more money, and my father needed money. We could tell that my father had a plan.

One day we were sitting at home, and my father went out. Suddenly we heard people crying, 'Fire! Fire! Fire!' Yes, my father had . . . it's sad but true. My father had bought all that tobacco on an installment plan, and it was dampened, made wet, and then dried to prepare it before it was made into cigars. It was always lying around the heating stove. In a pretty desperate situation, my father had set it on fire—and then immediately put the blaze out. He was no arsonist. Just forced into that by the circumstances. . . . "

"He didn't really want to send the whole lot up in flames?"

"Oh, no. So, all the cigars were on the ground during the panic when they got water from the faucet and tried to quench the flames, and so on. The firemen came. I can see it before my eyes right now. They got down on the ground, smelling to see if anyone had poured gasoline around. Apparently a fire had been deliberately set more than once, but there was no gas. My father just wanted to set a very little fire, or perhaps he had been clever enough. I had no idea how he'd done it. So we got money from the insurance. You get the wholesale price, not the retail price, but he got back what he had paid in wages as well as the cost of the tobacco. So he could have more cigars made—now that he had gotten rid of his inventory. It happened a number of times. . . . "

"A number of times, that little fire?"

"A number of times. We never spoke about it. You're the only outsider who knows about it. . . . But you can write it down. It happened fifty years ago.

"And then, during a thaw one winter, he made a little cut in the lead pipe, so the cigarettes got wet. Spoiled, too, of course; and to camouflage it—I saw this—to stop the water streaming down, as if trying to prevent it, he flattened the pipe out. But the damage was already done. He did it, and that was the last

time, for we kicked up a fuss at home and said that it was just too much. . . .
He had to do it, had to. Had to, yes, he honestly did. So I have to say that in
his own way, with his illness and all, he nevertheless looked after his family.
He couldn't do it any other way."

Later there was the issue of the little cigar bands. Every cigar had to have
an official band around it, a device that regulated the payment of taxes, which
in fact made much of the unofficial sale of cigars impossible. In this way,
small businesses lost ground to the larger companies. Jacob told the story
thus:

"And things happened just as we might have expected. They had to pick
on Michel [his father]. They just had to get him. That was the day . . . when
he said, 'Can you get me a box of cigars?' I asked, 'Banded?' 'No, they're
just going out the door.' So off I went across the street to get a box of cigars.
For a regular customer who worked in an office, a friend of my father's. And
as I came back with the box, I hadn't yet left the store on the other side, when
I was suddenly grabbed by the collar. Two officials from the inspection
department. He was fined, had to pay. Otherwise he'd have gotten no more
bands. . . . So we said, 'That mustn't happen again!' . . . It was too dangerous.
And it didn't happen again."

On a certain day, an official came to check that they did not have too many
unbanded cigars at home.

"The man searched and counted, and we had too many. Unbanded. But it
could be that there was some other problem. And the man said 'I'm taking
these with me.' He bent down, and I . . . a hatchet was lying there. My father
used tinder to light the fire for the drying. The hatchet was lying there, and I
came in, and I saw the man bending down. I saw my father grab the hatchet
and raise it, and I jumped between them and wrestled the hatchet out of his
hands. He'd have killed him. Honest. . . . But the man hadn't noticed a thing.

"A while later, the store window was built. Neat, all those cigars in there.
Well, you could either band each cigar . . . or you could put a seal on a closed
box. So the window was built. 'Nice window,' we said to my father. It had
been up a week when my father went away for a while. In came an official.
'May I have a box of cigars?' 'Fine,' said my mother, 'which would you like,
or would you prefer to wait till my husband returns?' 'No,' he said, 'just give
me that box in the window.' There was no seal on them. At that moment, in
comes my father and sees the box from the window."

Notations were made, there was a fine to pay, and they stood around
talking.

"My mother put the box under her apron and calmly walked out the back.
Standing in the garden, she tapped on the neighbor's window. . . . Her neighbor came outside and my mother said, 'Would you please keep this?' The box
of cigars was never found. The case was thrown out of court."

Jacob tried to improve himself by attending evening school. He became an electrician, managed to help his family, and again worked for a company that went bankrupt. Wherever he worked, the business went bankrupt. Finally, he wound up in Soest, but he was fired again. A company that did business with Germany refused to hire him because he was Jewish. The circle closed.

When his father had no money to buy cigarettes, Jacob went to talk to a firm. He managed to get a supply of cigarettes for his father to sell.

"My father sold the cigarettes at the market. Some of it was his own fault, but the debt kept growing; payments were made regularly, but the debt grew. Then my father couldn't get any more cigarettes." His father borrowed money from a brother, and after that things went a little better. After his father's death, his mother wanted Jacob to take over the business.

"I told her I wouldn't, I had lowered my standards so often that I wouldn't."

At the beginning of World War II the pressure on him to continue his father's business grew until he did so, getting an advance from the firm where his father still owed money. Tragically, things started to get somewhat better for the family at the beginning of the war.[57]

THE PLIGHT OF THE UNEMPLOYED

Unemployed diamond workers, more so than other unemployed, landed in a way of life that required coping with the invisible rules of financial welfare. They had lived under the delusion of safety and had felt superior to those who supported themselves by begging. Now there was no longer any reason to feel superior. For the first few weeks, welfare was granted by a committee that included union members (thus seemingly confirming their belief that the union would always take care of them). Nevertheless, the unemployed diamond workers were dealing with social control, with a committee that admittedly contained union representatives, but that decided in secret on the assignment of benefits. They also had to deal with poverty, which they had not known before.

Discussions in which the decisions over the allocation of support were made were kept secret from the applicants. It was important for the committee making the decisions to make good use of the available money and thus to create the impression that anyone misusing the right to receive support would always be caught. Those who tried to get around the rules were punished by having their welfare money withheld.

In the reports dealing with care of the poor (*armenzorg*) and the Municipal Social Welfare Department, as well as those of the Depression Committee, countless personal remarks are to be found. These often contain notes like "This is an untrustworthy family," "They lie," or "My advice is to stop their benefits." In a number of cases, relief money was held back as a result of suspicion that money was coming in from other sources—and the fact that the family did not die of hunger was taken as proof that this suspicion was correct.

"The family lives too well and should be refused support on account of their deception," was written in one instance. An entry made in the file ten days later, however, admits that "Inquiries show that the picture is not as rosy as the environment suggested earlier. It has been learned from various sources that the family is suffering from deprivation."[58] They were put on welfare. But less than a year later, the same family again fell under suspicion, and a new application for welfare was turned down. The reason was the following anonymous letter. (The poor spelling and bad grammar accurately reflect the content and flavor of the original Dutch.)

> dear Mr.
> Herewith I wish to give you enformation about Mr. P of Weesper Street, No. . . . His gentlemanliness has no need of a cent because he deals in gambling and in wool cloth. You must only ask about the attic room and you will see this yourself. Surely you know that these man could not buy a new coat just from the support money. same goes for new curtains if it is nasty weather he sits every day in the palace cafe playing cards. so too every Satday and Sunday morning. Also his daughter and son-in-law eats with them and so they have income from that too. so theres got to be others who need it much more than these people who eat chicken every Friday also big fish. This very Friday they was standing by the door with 4 big halibutt steaks which they bought by the door and if they could do that then they do not need support. She bakes a cake every week no one can do that from welfare money if nothing is earned others have to pay for this. Hoping you take notice of this and excuse me for sending it.

In the margin is written:

> And he has another woman on the side who he goes to 2x a week.

Betrayal and making true or false accusations were common. They generally had an effect. It is interesting that many of the letters were quite similar. Another example:

> because I must Tell you that you have been doing so thurough research in the Wrong places there are men who get support who apsolutely does not need it an another gets turned down who havnt got a cent but those gents are sitting pretty dealers they sell diamonds in tons and haff tons. they are diamond workers.[59]

Here there are clear signs of envy of the previously wealthy diamond workers' families who did not immediately abandon their former way of life and had difficulty in descending to the level of the workers' families who had managed on next to nothing for generations. Occasionally there was a hint of anti-Semitism, in addition to that envy, in the letters of denunciation, but more often there was a Christian moralizing that had apparently induced the writer to send the letter.

The system encouraged such behavior. The inspectors did the rounds of the neighborhoods looking for signs of hidden income. They gossiped with the neighbors and made use of every bit of discontent they found. Many of the unemployed diamond workers' families had wealthier relatives who brought a chicken from time to time. That was clear from the notes in the files as well as from my interviews. There were thus plenty of reasons for jealousy. Moreover, in the context of unemployment, the cultural differences between the diamond workers and the others and the "elitism" and self-conscious attitude of the former worked to their disadvantage. In their eyes, their trade was the only real work. They still had a few bits and pieces to pawn, and there was no clear boundary between still having something and having nothing at all. One man writes:

> While I was away from home, a decision was made by the gentlemen who made a house visit. I would very much like to talk to these gentlemen. Because I can prove that I have gone downhill during the time I have been unemployed by showing them several pawn tickets. I believe that it is bad enough when you have nothing more to pawn. And I believe that when you apply for welfare, you do not do so from a position of luxury. I am married and have one child of three years. You understand that the child does not earn anything.[60]

Another writes:

> I have heard about your notice that my request for support has been denied with great disappointment. . . . Had I and many others known how miser-able the plight of workers of diamonds, the Most Noble of all Minerals would become, we would have preferred to eat our own nails. But circum-stances forced us to apply for welfare money. . . . There was a diamond in the sand. But it was and remained a diamond.[61]

The errors and lack of clarity exist in the original letter.

As a result of unemployment, the various members of the family became dependent on each other. If any one person in the household had an income, however small, it inexorably led to the reduction in the amount of welfare. Any lack of clarity as to who could support whom, or sometimes the existence of a wealthier member of the family who was thought to be able to support them, always led to a reduction or withdrawal of the already miserly welfare. People struggled to show that they earned nothing extra. An example:

> To tell you something quite briefly, my father do live on . . . Street since the house is in his name. if that was not so then i'd be supported by the council much less than he cd support me. since that man is already 67 years old and completely supported by my sister and her husband whos there at his place and everything there depends on it. He needing help himself and is helped

which is a feet because they live at his house and I swear to you that if I do
not get help from a Friend who lends me money weakly that God knows
where i'd be but he earns only 30 guilders and he needs clothes for himself.
You cn asks him that and he is a Diamond worker and he works tempory as
a night watchman.[62]

Many people were suspected of working on the side and indeed many
probably did just that. The support was too low. After paying the rent, many
families had no more than 5 guilders a week for daily expenses, including
electricity. That was too little, and not just because the people had formerly
been used to much more. The markets, where people tried to scrape up a little
extra by dint of hard work, were becoming steadily emptier as a result of the
falling purchasing power of the working class. Less income led to the threat
of unpaid rent, a declining standard of living, deteriorating housing, and the
threat of removal to Aster Village or Zeeburg, which brought with it the
danger of falling through the cracks in the fledgling welfare state.

In these circumstances, reference was often made to untrustworthiness, as
if it were some innate, morbid characteristic. This method of analysis is
consistent with the way in which Querido approached the problem in the book
previously mentioned (on page 136) about Zeeburg. That there might be
reasons for the behavior in question, other than an innate tendency toward
deceit and untrustworthiness, that it was impossible to live month after month
solely on the welfare that was provided (especially if one was paying *f* 4.75
or more a week for one of the newer apartments in East Amsterdam), such
considerations did not fit into the picture. That picture was totally different—
it attributed all the difficulties to the "unsuitables," blaming them for the fact
that they were unable to fit into the pattern that had been created.

Mr. B., an old inhabitant of the Transvaal area, spoke of this in his account
of the misery there:

"It was like this in the old days—when people had somewhere to live, they
couldn't pay the rent. There were plenty of places, so they just moved from
one neighborhood to the next . . . and the landlord would offer them new
wallpaper—of they'd just come and live there. But there were a lot of people
who couldn't keep an apartment. Because of the rent. So they got poorer, and
they went from a sort of reasonably respectable neighborhood to worse and
worse areas. And they'd end up on Zand Street or Rapenburg in the old
ghetto, the people from East Amsterdam. Those who had no income. They'd
just go from bad to worse."

"How did they manage to eat, then?"

"That was through a kind of social worker who went to the people who
were better off and got food from them to bring to the poor. There was a lot
given away."

"Who saw to that—who paid for it?"

"It wasn't paid for; no one got anything for it. . . . There was practically nothing left any more. I mean, that's where the expression 'furniture from orange crates' comes from. It was a fact. If someone was a bit handy, he'd make furniture from orange crates. It was true poverty, nothing more. And it wasn't a matter of one or two families; it was true of many families."[63]

I have already pointed out that if the children who had returned to their parents' home to live as a result of poverty or lack of accommodation earned anything, it was deducted from the parents' welfare payments. But this did not only happen in such cases—it happened even if they lived elsewhere and had a good job that allowed them to contribute a little extra to their parents. This family involvement could reach out even to uncles, cousins, nieces, and nephews. The official policy was to encourage people to live in nuclear families in private dwellings. But when it came to welfare benefits, people found themselves being dragged back into an involvement they thought they had left behind—large families with relatives living together, things that belonged to the ghetto.

It is also noteworthy that the files show large numbers of adult children living with their parents, and I have the impression that their numbers were actually on the increase. Clearly it was advantageous to live in large units if the income of independent family members was to be included when calculating the amount of welfare. In one family I found five children aged 42, 40, 39, 37, and 33 living at home.[64] Such data confirm the impression gained in the interviews that children often continued living with the parents longer, and that more adults were living together in one apartment—whether they were married or not.

The solution often seemed to be setting up some kind of business or taking in work to be done secretly at home. One of the people on unemployment attempted to give a warning that he would be forced to engage in prohibited trading. In bad grammar he wrote to the committee:

> Since I am the father of 3 children I hereby makes the final appeal to your honored sirs If committee does not desire to meet my request set out in my repeated writing I see myself forced seeing as I cant wait longer in this way for an answer to my requests and my family at home canot escape physical undernourishment on an income of Dfl. 8.80 per week.[65]

What he would be forced to do he did not say.

CHILD LABOR

A clear picture emerged from the interviews regarding the way in which children entered the workforce, both in selling and in wage labor, thus helping to put bread on the table. It was standard practice for them to help look after the younger children, either in the place where the mother or father worked, or in the business or household of family members. Young girls were sent off to look after older people or the sick. This was a fairly normal occurrence in poor families.

"I had to help my father," said B. "If he had work to do at home, for example chairs to reseat, and the chairs had to be sanded, then he'd pick one out that I could handle, and then I sanded it using a bit of cork on which I put some sandpaper. . . . He certainly set us to work, and we couldn't say it was too hard. He just kept saying, 'Try! Try!'"[66]

Others told how they had to deliver clothes for their father who was a tailor. They took the clothes round wrapped in a black cloth. Tailors' boys were proud of the black cloth that they threw over their shoulders. It was a sign that they had important things to do. On the way, they would greet other boys with black cloths. There was a sort of primitive feeling of status; that cloth signified your father had work as an independent entrepreneur and did not work for the garment industry or for some wholesaler.

Esther told me how she had to fetch shoes for her father to repair. But it was a bit beyond her. One time she forgot to put a slip on them showing whose shoes they were. However, her father knew his clientele so well that he knew precisely from whom the shoes had come. He was not angry, either, for he knew she was not yet old enough to handle the work. Already as a very young child, she and her sister had had to stuff mailboxes with little notes advertising her father's workshop, and her daily task was to polish the shoes that had been repaired.

Another Esther had been given two *rijksdaalders* [each worth 2.5 guilders] to pay the butcher. When she reached Houtkopers Bridge she let one of the coins fall in the water. There she stood, crying sadly on the bridge, and soon a crowd gathered. Why was she crying? When she told them, they just stood by, worried, for it was a lot to lose. Her mother was sure that her child had drowned when she did not return and a crowd gathered on the bridge. She ran up to them, screaming, and everyone cursed her out for sending a little child out with so much money.

This Esther came from a poor diamond worker's family. Her father was often unemployed. She told how easy it was to get really small children to help find food: "My youngest sister was not yet born, so I was at most about five. And my mother told my brother, who was younger than me, 'Go and get two loaves of bread.' My brother came back, 'He won't give me any.' My mother said to me, 'You go, because you're small and a girl.' I went to the store—and I can see myself right now, standing in the store. . . . There were a lot of shelves in the store with bread on them, you don't see such loaves any more, the big, round ones (*vloerbrood* or floor loaves), two baked together. 'Two loaves, but I don't have any money. Mother had no money, but could you put it on account?' 'I have no bread,' said the baker. I looked, and I couldn't say a word, at least not then.

"I got home and I said to my mother, 'The shop is full of bread, but the baker says "I have no bread." ' My mother starts crying. A few moments later, there's a knock, and the woman from next door came up. 'What's wrong?' My mother said, 'I've got something in my eye.' Off she went. A bit later, there's the knocking again—people always knocked—and the baker's daughter was there with a big canvas bag and in it are two floor loaves. I guess I softened people's hearts as a little girl, and they thought the family really needed that bread." [67]

CONCLUSION

The interviews repeatedly illustrate the indescribable poverty of the Jewish proletariat. The situation was hopeless, and the misery forced people to resort to survival strategies that were not entirely acceptable, strategies that were rejected by the authorities as antisocial. It must have been extremely difficult for the authorities to maintain discipline among this unruly group of unemployed people.

One of the solutions seems to have been to regulate those parts of the economy that were more tractable, and especially the small businesses. Yet that was not really a solution, for it drove more people to rely on welfare and in turn more people were unable to pay the high rents. The only way out was to continue scraping a bit together in ways that were less than acceptable.

Those branches of the economy that were functioning reasonably well were still closed to Jews. The only true solution would have been to bring large numbers of Jews into new occupations. But that seldom worked, and at best it only affected the younger generations. Jews were not used to working in the harbors, and as for banking and most offices—financial work was too great a step up the social ladder. The people did not have the requisite training and, in most cases, the companies informally shut their doors to Jews.

Moreover, in every interview where this question came up, I was assured that it was impossible to work in certain occupations. When I asked for more details, I mostly received the answer, "They just wouldn't allow you in." Quite early in the research, a rather unpleasant picture emerged alongside the nostalgic stories about poverty. In part, that picture contradicted the nostalgia. Behind the "screen memories" (vivid memories that have no clear meaning but serve to cover other, more traumatic memories) were hidden stories about great poverty, hunger, and hopelessness.

It is also noteworthy that, in the case of poverty, nostalgia was never part of the memories of those who *had* known real poverty. Mostly they did not hesitate to talk about it. The extent of the poverty was clear from sources other than the oral interviews. In that sense, the interviews yielded no new information regarding poverty and work; they simply showed what it was like to work, to be unemployed, and to have to draw welfare. In this way, we glimpse the experiences.

The interviews make it clear how unthinkable it was to work outside the Jewish economy. Along with the closed character of the neighborhood and the culture, the economic structure functioned as a third circle of isolation that was crossed with great trepidation and only very occasionally. Breaking out of the economic circle would eventually lead to the integration of the Jews into Dutch society, or so it seemed. The irrationality of this segregation, which was totally at odds with the ideas of equality that were current at the time and were widely taken for granted even in Jewish circles, was yet another reason for the conservatives to feel afraid. The Jewish economy had neither money nor work to offer, and the departure of those who had no wish to remain poor all their lives was unavoidable. Would religion and tradition be lost, then? Municipal policies strengthened the trend to try to break out. Those parts of the economy where Jews worked were being restructured, and the old ways of doing business were being abandoned.

Had not the much-loved alderman Rodriguez de Miranda predicted that the humble trade of peddler would die out through reorganization? With the revival of the economy, not many people would want to follow that occupation. In this he differed with Huberts who believed that a certain kind of person is born with the urge to work in petty trading and peddling. She believed the Jews would only temporarily leave street vending. Once there was a reason again to go out selling on the streets, they would very likely abandon their education, see less reason to educate their children, and change their attitudes. They would probably once again revert to that ancient occupation for which no knowledge but a certain mindset and a voice were needed. To suggest such a thing, one had to be strongly influenced by a belief in innate properties and racial characteristics. De Miranda was right in believing that the Jewish peddlers would die out, but this happened far faster and more violently than he had expected.

CHAPTER SIX

CONCERN FOR THE POOR, OR
EFFORTS TO PRESERVE THE COMMUNITY

THE ABUNDANCE OF POOR RELIEF AND CHARITY VIEWED
AS A PROBLEM BY THOSE INTERVIEWED

Since 1901 the municipalities had had the right to take the initiative in providing housing for the people. The *Armenwet* or Poor Act of 1912 empowered them to develop their own policies for poor relief. While basic poor relief now became increasingly a municipal responsibility, individual gifts enabled the private sector to begin to specialize, thus perpetuating the private initiative.[1] Above all among the Jews, there was a network of institutions that attempted to relieve (at least in part) the most serious problems. Many of these organizations were founded during the first half of the nineteenth century, and originally functioned as religious charities. In this way, the government of that time wished to delegate responsibility for charity to the various religious organizations.

As far as Jewish religious organizations went, charity was handed out not merely as bread or money to pay the rent, but took the form of whatever was necessary to maintain the material aspects of the Jewish way of life with all the ritual that this entailed. There had to be enough money, for example, for kosher housekeeping, dowries—however small—for the marriageable daughters, a respectable suit of clothes for the Bar Mitzvah, and Jewish schooling. Strictly speaking, these went beyond "material" needs, since they included the maintenance of tradition in the spiritual sense.

The increase in alternative ideologies competing for attention within the Jewish community made the spiritual traditions increasingly important if the youth were to be held within the Jewish sphere and the homogeneity of the group maintained. Countless attempts were made to ensure this. In the case of the poor, these efforts were sometimes combined loosely with poor relief, sometimes in the form of neighborhood activities. The cornerstone of this effort was an expansion of work with the Jewish young people and of Jewish education.

As early as 1913, in a note entitled "A Serious Word to Members of the Community," the Jewish community was warned that more attention should be paid to the young people in order to increase their sense of self-respect. It was characteristic of Jewish social work that this pamphlet brought together attempts to counter Christian proselytizing, to support social work, and to maintain a sense of self-identity:

> The dignity and self-respect of our community demand that Jewish kinder-gartens be established in the various parts of our city in order to prevent the little children from being entrusted to Christian schools, which is currently happening, to the shame of our community. At present we have to tolerate this situation, since so many of our members are withholding the means to counter this evil, thus making a mockery of our religion. Such a situation does us great harm in the eyes of those of other faiths.[2]

The network of Jewish social services provided people with something extra beyond what they received from government welfare. These services contributed financially to the poor, and at the same time covered in some measure the extra cost of maintaining traditions. The various Jewish initiatives together fought for the allegiance of the mass of Jewish poor. This struggle was not simply left to the religious organizations. The Handwerkers Vriendenkring, which was instrumental in establishing the building cooperative later responsible for the construction and management of housing in the Transvaal area, started out as an organization devoted to the cultural development and entertainment of workers and their families. Next to cultural activities, social work constituted the most important task of this organization.

Strictly speaking, of course, the Handwerkers Vriendenkring was not Jewish but an organization with a more or less left-progressive character. Nevertheless, it possessed a sufficiently Jewish character to be disbanded in 1941 as a Jewish organization.[3] Also operating in this general area was the Arbeiders Jeugd Centrale [Central Organization of Workers' Youth], part of the "Red Family" (as the socialist organizations in general were called). The influence of such organizations was more or less limited to the "modern" sectors of the Amsterdam Jewish proletariat.[4]

The division of labor between the organizations dealing with a particular social class, age group, or neighborhood followed the lines of specialization within the private sector that resulted from the enactment of the Poor Act.[5] This trend was strengthened by structural changes within the Jewish community, which led to broadening the responsibilities of existing organizations and to the founding of new ones.

Assistance was needed. In previous chapters we saw how the "modern" nuclear family replaced the large family groups that formerly lived together;

as a result parents came to live farther from their grown children. Since marriages were no longer arranged by the parents, adult children began to live farther from their parents. Arranged marriages were the result of the economic needs experienced within the formerly closed society. The change away from arranged marriages occurred within the Amsterdam Jewish proletariat after the turn of the century, and the old and sick were no longer assured of assistance from their children and from members of their family. Families spanning several generations became less common.[6] Children no longer found it shameful to leave the care of their parents to others, since they had no choice.[7] Helping others had long been considered an expression of charity, but social welfare for one's own family had not been viewed as a right.

The institution that was most clearly in a position to provide both financial support and other forms of aid was the municipality of Amsterdam, which gained a preeminent position in this area after 1912. Starting in 1913, support for the needy was centrally administered in Amsterdam by the Armenraad or Council for the Poor, which coordinated both the information and the relief itself. There were 66 separate organizations involved, of which 41 were responsible for providing assistance in kind. It is striking how many of these were Jewish.[8]

The particular character of Jewish poor relief will now be examined through descriptions of several Jewish organizations that attempted to provide for the needs of their poor. To what extent were they trying to contact the Jewish poor in order to maintain Jewishness itself? Answering this question is easier than obtaining a clear picture of the experiences of those who had to deal with the organizations. How far did those who experienced it view the extensive meddling as an expression of caring?

The interviews certainly showed that it was not always seen as care—in fact the people who experienced it often felt themselves abandoned. Even those who received relief or assistance were humiliated by the resulting dependence and the paternalistic attitude they had to put up with. The better the reputation of the institution involved, the greater the confusion engendered in the recipients by their experiences. And when, after many years, people came to see how much they really owed the Jewish organizations, how many opportunities they had been given by them, the effect on them was similar. The most complex reactions were to be found among those whose childhood had been affected by Jewish social welfare.

Yet the people who were available for interview also distorted the picture. Those who had spent their final years happily as residents of the Joodsche Invalide [Jewish Invalid; a nursing home] could not, of course, be interviewed, for they are now dead. Those who remain alive include the offspring of broken homes who ended up in institutions and the orphans. In the case of the latter, the story was that of contemporary orphanages—stern, authoritarian, and characterized by a strict adherence to tradition.

In this chapter the stories will be told of two male orphans, one of whom lived in a Jewish orphanage, the other in a municipal orphanage in Amsterdam where as a Jew he was an exception. Both tell of the misery associated with orphanages and similar institutions of that period, but beyond the mingling of conventional thankfulness with horror, the story of the Jewish boys' orphanage is characterized by an awareness on the part of the storyteller of the fact that the orphanage permitted him to rise above his background. In all the interviews it is noteworthy that however authoritarian the Jewish poor relief organizations may have been, they were set up in such a way that those who were able to rise above their backgrounds were given an opportunity to do so. A similar picture is found in Lea Appel's book *Het brood der doden* [The Bread of the Dead], about a Jewish girls' orphanage to which the author looked back lovingly.[9]

Jewish poor relief possessed its own character and was interwoven with a whole series of welfare provisions that followed the individual from the cradle to the grave. Many of these activities were set up specifically to keep the youth within the Jewish community or to develop a loyalty to one specific interest or another, such as Zionism. But this is not the only reason to deal with the Jewish organizations separately. There was a general assumption that these institutions provided relatively more support than did their counterparts affiliated with other religions.[10] According to the Centraal Bureau voor Maatschappelijk Hulpbetoon [Central Bureau of Social Assistance],[11] Jewish institutions received more from private benefactors, and it was generally thought that the Jews were much more concerned with the care of the elderly. That was a matter of tradition in Jewish society.

Complaints that charitable contributions from individuals had declined, found in other communities at that time, were generally not heard in Jewish circles.[12] Reports on the attempts to raise money for the Jewish home for the disabled (which will be described shortly) make reference to the generosity of the Jews, suggesting that it could serve as an example to the rest of the Dutch people. There are no precise figures, and the subject deserves further study since the generally accepted picture could turn out to be no more than a myth. I have assumed that when there are contemporary references to generosity, a measure of truth underlies them, in part because the giving of alms is a cornerstone of Jewish tradition that continues to be honored even in the most assimilated families.

TSEDAKA AND LOVE FOR ONE'S NEIGHBOR:
THEIR EFFECTS ON VARIOUS CHARITABLE INSTITUTIONS

What is the origin of the differences referred to above between the Jewish charities and the others? No answer can be given without reference to *tsedaka*, a Talmudic concept that concerns the obligation of every Jew to help when needed. The word means "justice" and "righteousness," implying a view of charity according to which giving is not simply a favor to the poor but a matter in which the poor have rights and the giver duties. The giver does no more for the poor than the poor do for the giver. All a person's possessions ultimately belong to God, and both riches and poverty are in His hands. *Tsedaka* is as important as all the Jewish commandments taken together; it forms the heart of Jewishness itself.

Everyone is obligated to give. Even those who themselves are dependent on charity have an obligation to give to those who are less well off. Every Jew has a right to *tsedaka*, including the stranger from far away who lacks food. However, it is not merely a matter of giving money and food; *tsedaka* is relevant to a great number of laws that concern assistance—with death, for example, and burial, and practical matters like the dowries of poor girls who cannot be married without money. The rules have been worked out in great detail since time immemorial, spelling out just how there must always be food for the poor, even in a small community.

It is from this tradition that *tamhui*, the doling out of soup, emanates. In bad winters, soup was passed out in the old Jewish neighborhood to ensure that no one would starve. The soup kitchen of the winter of 1800 had long been a legend,[13] and it was repeated in 1928 when, in a school building on Uilenburger Street (the main street of the ghetto), gallons of kosher soup were once again handed out to ensure that no one needed to fetch soup from the nonkosher soup kitchen.

There is no question here of giving alms, nor is it a matter of becoming a well-known philanthropist. *Tsedaka* requires that people assist one another in such a way that those who receive the help are enabled to survive independently without having to express gratitude to anyone. In fact, it is best if the giver does not even know who receives the help. In the Jewish view of the world, poverty is simply a part of the misery of daily life—something that cannot be eradicated. It is the duty of every Jew, something explicitly required of each one, to do away with some part of that misery, even if only very little can be accomplished. And the gift must never be so great that it in turn brings poverty to the giver.

The Old Testament idea of *tsedaka* originally had an ethical and theological significance close to that of righteousness. The web of instructions that emanated from this notion differed from those implied by the Christian notion of brotherly love and of charity as based on it. The Christian concept was derived from a different view of the world, even though both the Christian and Jewish concepts appeal to the same Old Testament passages.[14]

In his work on the sociology of religion, Max Weber suggested that the Jewish concept of righteousness goes back to an old Egyptian tradition. It was the Pharaoh's task to ensure that everyone under his rule had enough to eat and to maintain life. That was his religious duty.[15]

The Canadian historian Michael R. Marrus, in his book about the assimilation of French Jews during the period of the Dreyfus affair, referred to the crucial role of *tsedaka* as a form of righteousness.[16] In this he appealed to the nineteenth-century French journalist and essayist, Maxime du Camp, who determined in 1888 that charity in the form of *tsedaka* played a major role in the cohesiveness of the Jewish community, which was otherwise severely divided by class differences and other issues.[17] He claimed that "Jews, no matter where they came from or how far they were conscious of their Jewish identity, remembered all too well the time of persecution, so that they had compassion for those who suffered." According to him, "the Hebrew word for charity, *tsedaka*, is also the word for righteousness."

In order to understand the concept of *tsedaka*, it is essential to see how *patriarchal* responsibility carries obligations with it. In Jewish tradition, this responsibility has come to rest on every Jew. It originated in a society based principally on *barter*. In the New Testament, the concept is rendered by the Greek word *dikaiosuné*,[18] a word that originally meant righteousness in a society in which barter had been replaced by a money-based economy. The exchange of goods to the glory of the Highest One has been replaced by a more ethical, societal concept—the giving of alms (*almoes* in Dutch), which represents an expression of compassion.[19] *Tsedaka*, in the form of alms-giving, developed in post-Biblical Judaism into a form of poor relief that is comparable to one of the five pillars of Islamic law—the extension of charity as a form of religious taxation (*zakat*).

In the eyes of both givers and receivers, the Jewish notion of charity differed from the related non-Jewish notions. No shame was attached to receiving. This difference, which placed *tsedaka* more centrally in the Jewish tradition than brotherly love was in the Christian tradition, might explain the generosity with which people gave to Jewish institutions. The persistence of this basic principle through the ages meant that it was possible for the Jewish people to maintain themselves, and to build up their institutions on the basis of abundant giving. By the end of the seventeenth century, the Portuguese Jewish community in Amsterdam had already established scores of charitable institutions;[20] these continued to grow in number as the numbers of Ashkenazim increased. In 1941 they were listed by the occupying forces so that they could be abolished.[21]

Nevertheless, it would be too simple to attribute the high level of charity established by the Amsterdam Jews to *tsedaka* alone. There were other reasons why the number of institutions maintained by a relatively poor community was so strikingly high. The struggle to maintain the integrity and homogeneity of the community was equally important.

It is clear from the scattered data concerning Jewish charity and charitable institutions (the processing of which would involve a separate project) that it is extremely difficult to disentangle Jewish charity from a concern for the maintenance of a distinct Jewish identity. Thus the establishment of the Joodsche Invalide was intended (among other things) to enable the elderly poor to enjoy their twilight years, while at the same time assisting the disabled and the blind. However, it was not limited to this goal. This institution formed part of an entire social system that was intended to make it possible for people to live within traditional Judaism and to bring yet more folk into that tradition. In this way, Jewish charity was not so very different from other forms of religious charity, becoming in essence a kind of Jewish proselytizing organ directed toward potential members of the group.

The establishment of Jewish charities was not only a result of *tsedaka* or of the desire to maintain Judaism; it was also encouraged by the external environment. While the Dutch government continued to accept little responsibility for the welfare of the less fortunate, the Dutch Jews had little alternative but to join other nongovernmental groups in building up a network of assistance. After all, anyone who ended up in a public poorhouse had no opportunity there to maintain Jewish tradition, an affront to the Holy One, an attack on *tsedaka* itself. At the same time, the obligation to give—even if only tiny amounts— made it possible to finance charities within the confines of the closed community. As a result, although poverty was the condition of the community as a whole, there nevertheless existed not only a Jewish economy but also Jewish charity and Jewish social welfare. It was the Jewishness of these that distinguished them from other institutions. Both charity and social welfare gave expression to a characteristic strategy and policy with respect to the Jewish poor and working class.

CHARITY, CHILD CARE, AND A JEWISH UPBRINGING

The Jewish child-care institutions were legendary, the best known being Beis Yisroeil (the Jewish equivalent of 'Our House'), which had hundreds of visitors every week. I interviewed Clara Asscher–Pinkof, a well-known Dutch author of children's books who survived the Holocaust and later wrote about her experiences. The wife of a rabbi, she was also the driving force behind this home for poor children. I asked her about her activities:

"We started in 1918. The Catholic mission had set out with candies to work among the children of the Jewish poor, and we felt the time had come to prevent them from going astray. We held 'evenings' and played games. . . .

Once we took them out on a walk. Have you ever heard of Dr. de Hond? He
was the idol of the proletariat. He was revered. He came from a frightfully
poor family and it was for that reason that he later founded the *Joodse Jeugd-
krant* [Jewish Youth Paper]. As soon as I heard of that idea, I wrote saying
that I wanted to help, and since then we have been friends. We went for a
walk with the children, and all the mothers came along to wave their children
off. That is so long ago. . . . "[22]

The children who went there were not reached by socialism; it was this
Jewish mission alone that gave them help and candy. At the same time, Beis
Yisroeil represented a way of reaching their mothers and discussing education
with them.

What did the children really need? What about the disadvantaged children
from the worst neighborhoods—what were they entitled to? Mrs. Asscher–
Pinkof could answer this question only in religious terms. She worked together with Meijer de Hond, who was so beloved by the poor for precisely
this kind of social activism. For him, every Jewish person was equal, and each
ought to be brought up within the Jewish tradition.

"Did other people help, too?"

"As time went by, people came and joined us. When I began, I got a young
girl to play the piano, and gradually various people joined us."[23]

When I asked, it became clear that these were ordinary people who had
become interested. As for Mrs. Asscher–Pinkof, the work was all voluntary.
In 1946 she expressed her grief over what had become of these children in the
dedication of her book *Star Children*:

> To you I dedicate this book
> Little star boy,
> You who played the harmonica
> In Hell.[24]

In that book, her great epitaph for those she loved, she described how the
star children formed a circle and, just after a roundup of Jews for deportation
had ended, sang a little dancing song: "The star children are singing, dancing,
choosing, recruiting. They neither see nor hear the sorrow that is rebounding
from upstairs to downstairs, from downstairs to upstairs" (p. 27).

This woman, who wrote about the children from the Jewish neighborhood
so lovingly, was well aware of the misery of their lives. She describes their
poverty in her book, which also deals with the time following the start of the
roundups when the Jewish neighborhood was already cut off. Yet it paints an
impressive picture of love that goes far beyond mourning:

> The patched, or sometimes no longer patched trousers are hanging around
> their thin legs. Their trousers are baggy and too long as well. But when the
> boys squat in the midst of their enthusiasm, the trousers suddenly stretch

and mercilessly reveal the patches or holes. But the boys are not aware of the appearance of their trousers and of the rest of their clothing. They have other things on their minds!

Evening is falling. . . . In the twilight their clothes seem less shabby, their hands, legs, and faces less thin.[25]

She remembered little more than this, she said, while with a sad expression she repeatedly tried to turn the conversation to other matters. Yet she wished to tell their story and to help in the production of this book, though she felt that in *Star Children* she had said all there was for her to say. Slowly the images returned, and she went on:

"The fathers walked the streets with their pushcarts, shouting themselves hoarse as they tried to sell their wares; and, well, I really don't know what the mothers did. I did hold evening get-together for the mothers, to which they came readily. We'd talk and sing songs, and so on, anything to entertain them."[26]

She described the black water that lay behind Valkenburger Street, and I asked her if it smelled.

"It stank. But they were used to that."

She could not tell me how she contacted the children or how she managed financially. Nor did she know just how many children were involved: "Don't ask me too much. Don't ask for numbers—they're really not that important." For her, it had been a kind of social work. When I asked whether she had done the work as a religious duty, her answer was strongly negative—it was to rescue them, and to keep them from the Christian mission.

In that respect, the AJC or Arbeiders Jeugd Centrale [Workers' Youth Organization], which was associated with the SDAP, was not in competition since that organization reached none of these children. The children that Clara Asscher–Pinkhof was talking about had no contact with socialism, even through their parents. Although their parents might well have voted for the SDAP, they certainly would not have taken part in any of the socialist cultural activities it sponsored. They were not yet ready to go that far. She spoke about the end of World War I, a time when only the elite of the ghetto were able to move away from it.

The most surprising thing about this story is the explicit denial of religious motivation. She emphasized that it had been perfectly normal social work. Another interesting aspect is the way she felt the Christian mission had to be kept at bay, as it were.

In 1935–1936, Gompers and Cohen described Beis Yisroeil in a series of articles about their wanderings through Amsterdam, which they called *Klein Jeruzalem* [Little Jerusalem]. It was, they said, a place where "relaxation in the true Jewish spirit" was possible. Clara Asscher's husband, Rabbi A. Asscher, founded Beis Yisroeil. The most important reason for its foundation,

Gompers and Cohen claimed, was the mission of the Protestant Reformed Church, which was attempting to make converts.[27] The well-known history teacher, Caroline Eitje, wrote:

> Ghetto Jews also felt powerless when faced with the question: How do I raise my children to be responsible adults? . . . We know them, those loud, rough girls, the rude boys, who think of nothing but dressing up and pleasure, stuffing themselves with candy, often lazy, self-centered, and sly when they are thinking about how to turn things to their own advantage.[28]

She felt that it was high time to protect the working-class Jewish children. According to her, Jewish families were no longer able to carry out this task themselves. In earlier times, immorality had been less common among Jewish women, but with the decline in religious belief it had become a serious problem. Tradition was thus regarded by Eitje as a protection against immorality.

At the same time, maintaining the traditions would provide an answer to the Protestant missions, which could be fought only by providing a place within the community for the children, somewhere where they could take courses and at the same time celebrate Jewish events as a group. Synagogue services were organized at Beis Yisroeil, as were Seders.[29]

According to Gompers and Cohen, mothers and fathers became directly involved in the activities at Beis Yisroel by participating in the evenings at which tips "for daily life" were offered. There, the young people could take part in a Seder with others, "one of the most important Jewish ceremonies that takes place outside the synagogue." During the year in which they wrote, the activities were extended to the new Jewish neighborhoods, branches being opened in East Amsterdam (the Transvaal), and in the Indische neighborhood. This last fact may seem to contradict what was written in an earlier chapter, namely that relatively few Jews lived there. Yet it is important to remember that there was a small synagogue,[30] and that sections of the Indische neighborhood bordered on the Transvaal area.

The historian of the *Memorboek*, Gans, recalled how the organization Magan David (he was a member of its governing board) entered discussions with Beis Yisroeil because both had organized a synagogue service in order to bring the young people closer to Judaism.[31] Magan David was not directed toward poor children, but toward the somewhat more mature youth from more affluent homes. To my question whether Magan David was seen as a counterpart of the socialist AJC, he answered that the organization was principally a reaction to the Zionist youth organization in that its purpose was to preserve Jewish traditions among the youth in its own way. The association also served a social function.

I have dealt with this example so thoroughly because it shows how hard it is for people who have worked in an institution to be interviewed in connection with the work they did there. This is even more true when those activities had religious or ideological connotations, and it applies not only to those who worked in such institutions but also to those who attended them. I was told about drama clubs, sewing circles, teen clubs, and dances that had "no religious overtones at all and served no ideological goals." Yet further questioning often showed that the truth was a little different. The members of the drama club, for example, primarily all Jewish children. (Clara Asscher had the children of Beis Yisroeil act in plays in a real theater.) The dances were organized by Bakhourai, an association that will be dealt with shortly. And the youth club, where they had such a good time, was part of the Jewish community. Thus reports about social work can be misleading, since the institution itself often tries to hide its true intentions.

PRESERVATION OF JEWISH TRADITIONS IN THE FACE OF TRENDS TOWARD ASSIMILATION AND OF MISSIONARY WORK

The Protestant mission was considered to be a problem in the Jewish community. The Christian churches had become more active in trying to win over the Jewish proletariat.[32] In fact, this was more a matter of anxiety than a result of the mission actually having acquired influence. For some time, the work of the Protestant missions was really no more than a factor complicating the attempts to preserve Jewish traditions. Only a few dozen individuals had been baptized.

Traditional Judaism was threatened both from within (assimilation), and from without (Christianity and socialism). The missionary work of the Christians—both Catholic and Protestant—was characterized by the emphasis laid on philanthropy and poor relief. The Jewish people were literally tempted into the churches. The Nederlandse Vereniging voor Israel [Dutch Society for Israel] operated within the old Jewish neighborhood. The theologian Hoogewoud–Verschoor, in her work on the mission to the Jews, referred to the shocked reaction in the *Nieuw Israëlitisch Weekblad* [New Jewish Weekly], where it was said that there was an attempt to "eradicate the Jewish religion." [33]

In order to fight back against this proselytizing, an "association to combat missionary activities, a Jewish association for the area around Nieuw Market" was set up. The Yiddish name for this was Bakhourai Mevakshai Yousher. The fact that quite a number of children had begun to take part in Christian activities for young people led to the founding of this organization. Moreover, according to Hoogewoud–Verschoor, Jewish children attended the Christian nursery school on Korte Keizer Street. These were children from extremely poor families.[34]

Hoogewoud–Verschoor gave the text of the club song:

> Come, sing in Bakhourai, . . .
> another way
> we must eschew

or pay
with sorrow there!
Long live Bakhourai
we'll stay, and stay,
to the joy of Him who has us
in his care.[35]

It is remarkable that it was not until the end of the 1920s that an organization was set up explicitly to deal with the Protestant missions and that no conscious strategy was adopted until that time (at least not in the old ghetto). In 1929 a Jewish kindergarten was founded, Het Trenshuis [The Bridle House], so that the Christian school on Korte Keizer Street no longer attracted enough children and had to close. At first, the antimission activities were limited mainly to club work and the founding of the kindergarten. Around the mid-1930s, however, it was extended to include work with individual families who seemed likely to convert. Still, the focal point remained the Bakhourai clubhouse with its Friday evenings for poor children and the attempts to do something for those children.

Bakhourai was thus explicitly directed against Protestant missionary zeal but in practice differed relatively little from other organizations that were set up in order to keep the young people within Judaism. The archives of the Nederlands–Israëlitische Synagogue mention Bakhourai in the same breath as Rekhouvous, the Jewish organization set up in the Indische neighborhood to "keep the young as much as possible in a Jewish environment." Among the activities of that organization was a children's theater club. Rekhouvous worked in cooperation with the Vereniging Kennis en Godsvrucht [Association for Knowledge and Piety], which ran the Herman Elte and Palache schools for Jewish education. Also concerned with Jewish education was the association Betsalel, which was responsible for teaching 157 children in the Retief neighborhood of East Amsterdam and 131 in the center of the city.[36]

In contrast with the poor relief carried out by Beis Yisroeil, the concern of all these organizations was the upbringing of the young and ways to keep them within Judaism, while, as already pointed out, Beis Yisroeil was originally concerned principally with social work. In 1936 that organization was still described as a children's organization, founded originally to counter Protestant missionary activity but not overtly dealing with religious matters in any way.[37]

In Gompers and Cohen's walking tour of Amsterdam, *Klein Jeruzalem* (mentioned earlier), this was described as follows:

Dayan Asscher, sensitive as he was to the needs of the young Jewish souls from the poor neighborhoods, understood well that if the attempts by the missionaries to lure the Jewish children with sweetmeats and companionship were to be rendered powerless, priority would have to be given to the establishment of a locale within their own neighborhood where the young could find entertainment within a Jewish environment.[38]

It is said that 1,145 people visited Beis Yisroeil every week, the activities having been expanded to include instruction for the parents. The classes were not limited to topics related to Judaism but were far more broadly conceived and included such subjects as sewing and singing.

One of those who took lessons at the center wrote a moving account, which was passed on to me by her daughter. In the following she tells of the sewing lessons:

> I was in beisjisroeil [Beis Yisroeil], a handicrafts club. I was once called to task by management for working too fast, because that cost the association too much. I paid three cents per evening, and I used thirty cents worth of materials. That couldn't go on, so I had to do one evening of handicrafts and two of singing. Everyone loved tear-jerkers! My singing moved the others to tears.[39]

In the better working-class neighborhoods, where socialism was dominant and offered much to the Jewish youth, the Jewish club and neighborhood activities were explicitly directed against socialism. In West Amsterdam there was Ahavo Ve'achavo, across the IJ Harbor was Sholoum Veraikhous, in South Amsterdam Bnai Taimon, and in the Vinken neighborhood there was a separate organization. In East Amsterdam there was Nakhalil, originally set up to keep the young within Judaism but eventually directed specifically against socialism.[40] This club was aimed principally at young adults. The minutes of the club, which have been preserved, report on the course of the bitter struggle. The following account of its foundation was signed on 20 November 1923, after the club had been in existence for one year:

> It was on [Jewish date] of the year 5682 that I was walking home from *sjoel* with Mr. Levenson, talking as we walked. The conversation soon turned to the *kille*, or subjects pertaining to the Jewish community; whereupon I said to my companion that a sizable Jewish neighborhood like ours was sorely lacking if, in the first place, it offered no opportunities for the study of the Torah, and, second, no meeting place where Jews from our neighborhood could come together at certain times for education and culture.[41]

According to the chairman, it took ten years to make all the necessary preparations. As part of the activities, every Jewish person living in the neighborhood was invited to speak about matters of interest to Jews. In October 1923 there were 204 members, though the payment of dues was not entirely satisfactory—something that the leadership attributed to the high level of unemployment in the area.

Originally there was optimism over the possibility of setting up a Jewish neighborhood society in East Amsterdam, but a year later, on 2 December 1924, this gave way to disappointment. The number of members had not increased, contrary to expectations in this Jewish neighborhood. Cooperation with the Jewish religious educators of the Talmud Torah School led to the establishment of some serious classes, but these were not well attended. On 25 November 1925 the annual report noted that there had been a decrease in the membership, "despite the fact that the neighborhood expanded." Although the association was in financial difficulties, the ideas it stood for were very popular.

It was decided to try to attract members from Beton Village farther away from the old ghetto, where many Jewish families had settled. But neither there nor in the older neighborhoods of East Amsterdam was it possible to revive the traditional Jewish way of life. The shops stayed open on Saturdays, to the consternation of the society, which tried unsuccessfully to have them shut on the Sabbath. The chairman lamented, "It is a deeply unsettling fact that in a Jewish neighborhood like ours—and we made special visits to the blocks of the HWV [Handwerkers Vriendenkring] and the shopkeepers in that area— such extensive breaking of the Sabbath occurs."

Eventually the society was consolidated into an association for conserva- tive Judaism and was never as powerful as the SDAP or the AJC in that area. They were operating within sectors of the working class that had moved to East Amsterdam in order to give expression to their progressive spirit, and so the association represented the only traditional voice in neighborhood affairs.

Those who participated in activities both at the club and at the neighbor- hood meeting place often had difficulties in separating the two. Boys passed back and forth between them, depending on what they found most interesting. Catherina told of her wanderings among the various organizations. Just how they differed she could not say, but she went to whatever she found most enjoyable.

"From five to seven [in the evening] I went to the Jewish school run by Rabbi de Hond. There I was told I could go to Nakhalil on Friday evenings. No one now knows what it was like back then. . . . It was a crows' nest and only for poor children. You could go there from seven to nine and then there was a plate, a dish with candy, some fruit and peanuts. They played games. I think that was with Miss Eitje. At nine we went home. The games were over.

"First I was in Beis Yisroeil in Plantage Park Lane and then you had Betsalel, and Miss Eitje and I had to go there, too, to a handicrafts and sewing class. . . . I was all thumbs, so that didn't work too well. Then I went to Bakhourai, for poor children on Kloveniers City Wall. There you learned a little dancing, Israeli dancing, and a bit of singing, everything together, and not much of anything!" [42]

In this summary, Catherina confused the various Jewish youth centers, and the sewing class was in fact a "swallow's nest." Swallow's nests organized meetings for young girls. The initiative for these came from the Jewish Women's Council, and their purpose was to counteract the demoralization of the Jewish girls and to support them in the workshops and factories. The organization followed the principle of "freedom through commitment," which meant that before any game was played the rules were carefully explained.[43]

The most important association of the Orthodox movement, active in education, was Betsalel, which grew out of the educational association Touroh Our. Betsalel published the paper *De Libanon* and was involved in the foundation of the Joodsche Invalide. Meijer de Hond and I. Gans (later the director of Joodsche Invalide) coordinated these various organizations. The history of this network clearly illustrates the fusion of elements of social work, preservation of Jewish traditions, separation from the outside world, struggle against socialism, dissemination of knowledge, and relief for the poor. The next section will be devoted to this.

Meijer de Hond, *De Libanon*, Betsalel, and the Joodsche Invalide

The Jewish association Betsalel was founded on 4 October 1908; it grew out of the working-class society of the same name, which had instituted classes in Jewish history for its youngest members.[44] As a working-class association, Betsalel tried to provide a counterbalance to the progressive character of the ANDB, and was originally aimed only at the diamond workers. It was not an entirely successful undertaking, since the majority of Jewish diamond workers opted for the ANDB and its successful struggle to improve their material existence. They did not view membership in the ANDB as a break with their Jewish past. Consequently they saw no need to organize themselves separately, as Jewish diamond workers. In the course of time, therefore, Betsalel found itself forced to work together with the ANDB in connection with labor concerns. Moreover, I have the impression that those diamond workers who were religious enough to join Betsalel had left for Antwerp after World War I, presumably because the diamond workers there were more religious. In 1924 Betsalel, still a working-class organization, had only 81 members, while the ANDB had 5,232 members, over 60 times as many.[45]

The educational program of Betsalel, since it was religious in nature, differed greatly from that of the ANDB. The history of Betsalel shows how the younger members of the organization began to press for a youth organization with a religious foundation:

> The religious Jew, and above all the young Jew, had a hard and difficult struggle dealing with his fellow union members at the factory. Happily the situation has now improved [as of 1927], thanks to the better organization and greater tolerance that have replaced the passion of former times, even in the diamond industry. But in those days the vast majority of union members not only failed to realize the value of religion but were vigorously opposed to it, wounding mightily the religious soul with the darts of sarcasm and irony.[46]

Yet Betsalel was not concerned so much with religion as with tradition. The association Toutseous Chaiim,[47] founded in 1905, was truly religious. Betsalel was meant to provide its members with good company and a sense of solidarity. Meijer de Hond was their leader, and the members all came from the study group Touroh Our, which published the popular periodical *De Libanon*, so dear to the heart of de Hond. His popularity continued to grow as time went by, not only as a result of his writings but also through his sensitive speeches. Touroh Our organized gatherings on Saturday afternoons at which he gave his famous *drosjes* or off-the-cuff sermons. The Jewish proletariat attended these meetings en masse, which made it clear that the time was ripe for a more general Jewish organization whose primary goal was not so much education as the maintenance of Jewish tradition.

Betsalel became that organization. The stated goal was to show the masses the "unassailable nature of Jewish lore," employing the theater to display Jewish life and practices. The idea was to use the educational potential of the theater. The play drew such great praise that "even a well-known dramatist and director [Herman Heijermans], whose drama group showed a completely different perspective of Jewish life than that of Betsalel, was apparently uncomfortable." The true character of the Jewish ghetto was represented not as a Jewish merchant ready to tip the scales in his favor with the tap of his finger, according to Betsalel, but rather as someone whose honesty and virtue have prevailed, enabling him to attain the ripe old age of 77 with an unsullied reputation and an unblemished name.[48]

The theater was a way in which youth work could be approached. Although the work was guided by respected leaders and the works performed were meant to be edifying, nevertheless a good number of women told me how they had had to struggle to persuade their parents to let them visit Betsalel. The right to attend such an organization was not automatically granted. It was a new kind of development, and above all the girls could not be controlled there. However, once their children had performed, the parents were proud of their achievements.

That pride is evident in the stories of those who took part in the plays. Unfortunately I was only allowed to record the account of Mrs. P., who in fact was involved in a different theatrical venture. She came from a typical proletarian family, and her story is taken up at this point in order to illustrate the parents' pride. She was in fact in a theater club for both Jews and non-Jews, but her story shows effectively how parents reacted. Given her background, she must have been a vain young girl, because she secretly made up her face before she would venture outside, and her worldly behavior led her to the theater.

"I joined the group when I was about sixteen. I couldn't tell my father, but my mother was a sweetheart. She found everything okay. Once I was walking along Bree Street with a couple of guys and some other girls when my brother came along. My oldest brother. He saw me, and I got a slap right across my face, and he said 'Going around with boys—aren't you ashamed of yourself?' Those boys didn't like that at all, and they walked me home. They came upstairs with me and told how Leendert had slapped me. My mother knew I was in a theater group, but my father didn't know a thing. So I said, 'We were rehearsing this evening and the show goes on in a couple of months.' Well, my father came along and they were all as pleased as Punch!" [49]

Of course, this tale shows the protective attitude of the brother within the family more clearly than it does the atmosphere of Jewish theater. Still, I have included it at this point to give a picture of the parents sitting with glowing faces in the hall while their daughter does something quite unthinkable—acts in a play. If she had done this within a purely Jewish context, it might well have given her fewer problems, but the picture of the parents would have been much the same.

Theatrical productions were not enough for Betsalel, and within a few years what began as a Jewish theater club became a Jewish association offering a wider range of activities. In 1912 the first Rashi class, commenting on religious texts, was organized. Then Jewish travel clubs were added. The activities were then extended to 12- and 13-year-olds who attended after school. Then the finishing touch was added—a choral group. All this was done with the goal of strengthening the solidarity of the Jews.

THE JEWISH HOME JOODSCHE INVALIDE

The most significant initiative taken by those associated with Betsalel was the founding of the Joodsche Invalide, or JI. As early as 1912, Meijer de Hond had complained about the circumstances under which elderly Jews had to live in the Amsterdam munipical poorhouse.[50] From the very beginning, he supported the initiative taken by the religious association Touroh Our in 1910 to do something for the Jewish disabled who had previously been placed in non-Jewish institutions.[51] If a Jewish institution could be set up, it would do away with the misery that followed placement in a home that was not Jewish. From that time on, *De Libanon* was continually campaigning for the cause.

From 1909 there had been a Jewish hall in the poorhouse, but that was not enough.[52] The people there were the responsibility of the Nederlandsch Is-raëlitisch Armbestuur [Dutch Jewish Poor Board], which had been set up in the first half of the nineteenth century.[53] The continual agitation had led to a decision by the Municipal Council in 1925, that every religious group should have its own facilities.[54] The first building of the Joodsche Invalide had opened in 1911 on Nieuwe Keizersgracht; in 1926 it was moved to a better building on Nieuwe Achtergracht, and after years of fund-raising the big building on Weesper Square was brought into use in 1938.

I was able to interview at length the son of Gans, the original director of the JI. I asked him about the kinds of people who were admitted, and he replied:

"First of all, the disabled. People often believe wrongly that it was a home for the elderly. In general they were old people, but that was not a matter of principle. In the first place, those who came were poor. The most disabled and financially most deserving were assisted first. Obviously, during the heyday of Dutch Jewry it was impossible to help enough. These were emergencies, people about whom the GGD [Gemeentelijke Gezondheidsdienst or Municipal Health Service] had called up and asked, 'Some people have been found. Can you take them in?'

"There was one emergency, I believe in 1935, when the municipality decided that the disabled—I mean those who were permanently disabled—could no longer stay in the hospitals but had to be moved to other institutions. The people were taken to Zeeburg, which was a disaster. So the conference room at the JI was cleared, just so those people could be taken in."

The central goal was to be able to place the sick, the disabled, the blind, and the elderly in a Jewish environment where they could live according to their own traditions and customs. This concern could extend, for example, to include a girl who was being given nursing care outside Amsterdam, at the expense of the (Dutch Jewish) Poor Board. In 1916 both the *Nieuw Israëlitisch Weekblad* and the *Centraal Blad voor Israelieten* (two Jewish newspapers) printed a story about a girl in Wagenborgen who was pining away among non-Jews. The worst of it was that she was forced to take part in their religious practices.

Not only those unable to care for themselves physically were helped. From the very beginning, JI established a tradition of caring temporarily for refugees in need. In 1914 refugees streamed in across the southern border after the German invasion of Belgium, and the daily paper *De Rotterdamer* gave an account of their reception at the JI:

> The call came Sunday evening at eleven. A man, a woman, four children—four years, three, one, and two months. The older ones in their parents' arms, the youngest in a baby carriage. All equally miserable, hungry, tired, and of course miserably dirty. . . . Because the nurses are busy no one can help them, but the director's daughter comes to the rescue and helps the little ones to a hastily-made bed.[55]

The JI became an institution, a symbol of social concern—not only for those who were Jewish. The requests for more support never ended. And there were countless tales told of people helped by the JI. Again and again it was pointed out that while there were many denominational establishments, too few of them were Jewish. It became a legend, a dream that had been realized. People who were in the greatest difficulties were taken in. In such circumstances it was essential to maintain order. The JI was a strictly orthodox establishment, a model institution with extremely stringent rules. No one, for example, could simply leave the building. Permission had to be obtained first. No doubt this was necessary in many cases, but in the words of one of those I interviewed, "It made one feel confined; really institutional."

In 1925 a lottery was first held to raise funds. The prize was a mansion with a garden. This new way of raising money caught on and became a trademark of the JI. The younger Gans, in the interview already mentioned, told it this way:

"Lotteries were organized by the JI, but because the number of lottery tickets that could be sold in Holland was limited, they came up with the idea of having a separate lottery ticket for each province. And then still another for Amsterdam."

For the first time, the radio was used for advertising, and it turned out that a good deal of radio time could be devoted to the JI. Even the Christian Prime Minister Colijn (and that was really something) and Oud, the minister of finance, spoke over the radio on behalf of the institution. During the broadcast, Jewish songs were sung.

Moreover, large-scale festive evenings were arranged to coincide with considerable publicity. On these evenings new campaigns would be launched or the winner of a lottery would be drawn.

"There were also the little collection boxes, which were really valuable. Every Jewish family in the country had one for the JI or for the Dutch Jewish Poor Board. These boxes meant a lot to a group of people who were quite poor, yet now had a way of contributing a penny or two from time to time. On occasion they played cards for a few cents, throwing their winnings into the box. Collections were also taken up at funerals, and there were JI matchbook holders. You saw those everywhere . . . and calendars, calendars where you tore the pages off and there was a picture of a collection box and a little poem each week. The newspaper ran a small advertisement every day, free of charge, in support of the JI. Mostly they were amusing. . . . When they drove the first piling into the ground for the new building, the advertisement read: 'Today a heavy blow struck us; help us bear it.' "[56]

Money was badly needed since the JI was ambitious and tried not to present itself as a charity. Old age and sickness had to be honored. In contrast, charitable foundations existed to deal with undesirable elements of the population. Moreover, since the JI was to set a trend for future Jewish projects, this gave an additional reason for having higher goals. Thus it was not only cabinet ministers who were called upon to help. Everything possible was also done to arrange a royal visit. When that took place, the entire Jewish neighborhood turned out—which of course created an enormous commotion—and that alone guaranteed yet further attention for the JI.

An institution like the JI was, in fact, badly needed. Many homes for the poor were miserable places where everything was done as cheaply as possible. Homes for the disabled and elderly formed part of the municipal system of poor relief. Most old people were dependent either on relief from the Poor Act or on their children. In either event, little money was available. Optional insurance for employees, which had been introduced in the Old Age Act of 1919, had changed little, certainly among the Jewish proletariat. They did not work year after year on a regular basis in the same branch of the economy, which was necessary to qualify for support under that act. In any case, even when they did have regular work, they could seldom spare any money for such insurance. The *Ziektewet* or National Health Insurance Act of 1930 did bring relief in a number of cases, but only a minority could claim benefits.

What was unique about the JI was that people were offered more than would have been available in a poorhouse for the elderly at that time. In this way, the JI served as a kind of model for modern homes for the elderly. Thanks to generous private donations, lotteries, and the aggressive manner in which fund-raising was handled, enough money was available to furnish the rooms in an attractive way. The building that was brought into service in 1938 was unusually modern and contained the latest equipment. The elderly were provided not only with a Jewish environment but with well-organized activities.

Originally the JI relied on the generosity of the Jewish community for money, but because of the modern lottery with its very attractive prizes, the entire country became involved. The Seder evenings were famous. Everyone was welcome at them—not only the disabled. The son of the first director, Gans, who has already been mentioned, told how a starving couple came to enjoy their first proper meal there:

"Anyone could come and eat. One Seder evening, there were many poor present, and one well-dressed couple, respectable people who lived on Nieuwe Prinsengracht with their daughter of about 14. They came to the Seder and after eating all three became ill. A doctor was called, and we were afraid they had been poisoned. It was hard to find another explanation. The doctor examined them and came up with the diagnosis—malnutrition."[57]

When the troubles began in Germany, the JI became a place where the refugees were always welcome:

"Immediately after Hitler's election, tables were set to await the refugees. I met them at Centraal Station wearing a white band—a little group of us stood there with white arm bands to receive them. A white arm band with a star. There were normally 60 to 100 refugees who sat down to eat."[58] (But there could be more when there was a large influx of refugees.)

Refugees were hidden from the police, who kept sending them back to Germany, and there was close cooperation with other organizations working to meet the most urgent needs of the German–Jewish refugees. The refugees entered the Netherlands illegally, because the Dutch government refused to recognize that their lives were in danger. Refugees who were caught were turned over to the Gestapo. This national policy changed only after *Kristallnacht*; then refugees from Germany were placed in an internment camp. That camp was Westerbork; later the Germans took it over and used it as a transit camp. Thus the groups of charitable organizations tried to throw up a dam of Jewish solidarity against the rising tide of fascism. But not everyone was in sympathy with this. Gans told me how difficult it was.

"During the time when the refugees were arriving, a meeting was held concerning ways in which existing organizations could help, and my father suggested that it might be necessary to make use of our financial reserves. Someone responded, 'That money must be saved for worse times.' My father became upset, and Abraham Asscher (later chairman of the infamous Jewish Council), who was chairing the meeting, asked, 'But what are regulations for in that case?' To this my father said, 'To be ignored.' When people are begging everywhere, and there is so much available. . . ."[59]

JI's new building had been in use only a couple of years when most of the residents were taken away on 28 February 1941.[60]

THE EXPANSION OF JEWISH CHARITY: EYEWITNESSES

Just as Jewish organizations were rendering more and more assistance to the poor and to charitable institutions, other religious groups were also increasing the amount of relief they were offering. However, the care given by the Jews had to do not only with preserving a Jewish identity but also with the duty they felt to ensure that people could live their lives in a familiar Jewish environment. The 1922 amendment to the *Kinderwet* or Children's Act, which regulated guardianship, led to the development of a network of Jewish foster homes.[61] These supplemented the care provided by existing orphanages and other forms of Jewish child care.[62] The Zadok Rosa Bonnist Foundation, for example, sent girls who were 13 years of age or older to live outside the city. In Wijk aan Zee there was a home maintained by the Joodsche Zee en Boschkolonie [Jewish Sea and Woods Settlement]. There was the Rudelsheim Foundation[63] for mentally retarded children and Misgav Leyeled for neglected and abandoned children. From 1920, the mentally ill were cared for in Apeldoornse Bos, an institution in Apeldoorn, while children from difficult homes were temporarily taken in by the Berg Foundation in Laren.[64] Children under institutional guardianship who required medical care were admitted to the Paedagogium Achisomog.[65]

In his 1926 article on the relationship between Jewish young people and government reform schools in *De Vrijdagavond*, J. S. Jessurum Cardozo pointed out that there were still very few Jewish institutions. The *Kinderwet* amendment of 1922, however, had in effect obligated the Jewish community to provide every child threatened with moral or physical ruin with a place in an institution.[66] A non-Jew could not understand the mind of Jewish children and could too easily reject the Jewish child as troublesome.

A few months earlier, Cardozo had worried about the fact that "train 8:28," on which quite a few children were still being sent out of the Jewish neighborhood on vacation (especially pretubercular children), was not being provided with kosher food.[67] In addition to these concerns, there were problems concerning prisoner rehabilitation. Prisoners in a cell lacking any means for draining water could not follow the ritual washing necessary before prayers.[68]

In addition to such concerns, there was normal poor relief. One foundation provided diapers to Portuguese–Jewish women who bore daughters; another—a separate foundation—provided them for those who had sons. Parallel to these there was a High German Foundation sponsored by Ashkenazim that distributed coal and winter coats. Girls were helped with dowries; boys were given respectable suits for their Bar Mitzvahs.

At the beginning of the chapter it was pointed out how hard it is to gain insight into the experiences of those who received help from the Jewish poor-relief system on the basis of the impressions of those who provided the assistance. Nevertheless, their testimony does help to complete the picture. It is also interesting to note how very difficult it was to interview the nurses and others responsible for giving out relief. I was generally able to talk to them, but they wanted to remain anonymous, and I was unable to take notes. In such cases, the conversations were dominated by grief for the many unfortunate people they had cared for who were ultimately murdered. One nurse remembered a whole hall full of people in Apeldoornse Bos, and talked with me for hours about all those people.

Only Mrs. M. wanted to tell me, despite everything, about the idealism with which she had worked in the Jewish orphanage. In addition, there is a wonderful report concerning the nursery in Plantage Midden Lane. In that report, former care-givers went into great detail about their work.[69] They were often highly idealistic.

Mrs. M. told how she looked after the little children. They began work at 10 in the morning and first made the sandwiches for lunch, which was at 12. She made sure that everyone had equal quantities.

Her biggest complaint was that the children all had their hair clipped off:

"Those who had first suffered the great loss of a father's death and poverty at home . . . so that it was decided to send them to an orphanage, entered a hostile world. They had just been torn from the home to which they might well have been deeply attached, and then, because there was once a case of headlice, off comes their hair and they get a *favus* cap instead. Treated with kerosene. It stayed on for three weeks. . . . Later, when the German children arrived after *Kristallnacht*, can you imagine how they crept away when they had to be shaved bald? They knew all about that from people who had been in a concentration camp."

Eventually she took it upon herself to cut their hair.

She said that the orphanage was very sparsely furnished since the place had to be easy to clean. At first the children had nowhere of their own to keep things, but later each child was given a little chest. This humane policy also led to the development of a library. I asked whether it had been difficult to institute such little changes. She said they could be made, though they did have to be passed by the governing board. Her initiatives resulted from the fact that she had had a respectable upbringing outside an orphanage, and she brought the ideas with her. The director was a nurse, a woman with a good heart, but she knew very little about raising children.

The staff was badly paid, so that few took the trouble to develop personal relationships with the children. She felt able to take the work on, despite the poor wages, only because she saw it as a part of the training she needed for her emigration to Palestine (as it was called then). Night duty was carried out by a night watchman who was paid by a security service. This man had the greatest difficulty in maintaining order and did not hesitate to use brute force. There were two directors. The one who lived in was responsible for the housekeeping, while the deputy director, who lived out, was in charge of education and the general development of the children. Mrs. M. was clear about where the children came from. Those who were not orphans had been sent away from home because their family relationships were disturbed. In general, the families had been respectable but had suffered adversity.[70]

SALOMON AND SIMON: MIRROR IMAGES

Some children were placed in Jewish institutions; others, for one reason or another, could not be. I will give a brief account of two cases—one involving a Jewish institution, and the other not.

SALOMON, THE JEWISH ORPHAN IN THE JEWISH ORPHANAGE

Salomon entered the orphanage as a child. His father had died of tuberculosis and his mother had to go out to work. Before he went to the orphanage, he had not gone to the school for poor children and had been reasonably well clothed. His mother found work with a chocolate company; this forced her half-orphan into an orphanage. He told me about the transition.

"Between 1920 and 1926 my mother set out each day with a suitcase containing sugar, cocoa, tea, coffee, and perhaps also a little butter. She went to people she knew who allowed her to come by, and from them obtained 5 cents more for a pound of sugar than they would have paid in the store. . . . Later she also worked as a housekeeper, but by that time I was in the orphanage. But I know she went off on the infamous line 8 with her suitcase—perhaps I saw her walking with two suitcases." (Number 8 was the tram line that was used for the deportation of Jews.)

At home Salomon was cared for by a grandmother who was over 70 years old. In 1926 the family was broken up. The grandmother went to a home for the elderly, his mother became a housekeeper, and he was placed in the orphanage. He still remembered how awful that was, and repeated Mrs. M.'s story about the *favus* cap.

"In retrospect, I can't really say that I found the moment when I was taken from Nieuwe Kerk Street to the orphanage truly horrible . . . but a couple of nasty things happened right away.

"In those days, when you entered an orphanage, it was apparently assumed that your head was not clean. So for the first fourteen days you had a *favus* cap on your head. A starched cap. And you walked around with that on—the only one among all the children. It didn't make you feel at home right away. I had the advantage that I already knew one of the children there; . . . his father and mother had died. But I had a disadvantage—the moment I met the director, I was overcome by hatred. I hated that woman, and she hated me. I was received in the bathroom, which was also used as an infirmary, where the *favus* cap was put on."

He was not prepared for that. "I had never been there before."

Salomon told how he and this woman were bitter enemies throughout his stay. In a second conversation he was somewhat gentler in his attitude toward her, and his story was gentler as well. He had been thinking about how much he actually had to thank the orphanage for, and did not wish to speak harshly about it. And he was well aware that some of the children found the orphanage pleasant. But Salomon came from a progressive grade school, where highly innovative educational methods prevailed, and he was ahead of his peers in those areas that were not specifically Jewish.

The orphanage was far more old-fashioned and orthodox, with religious services three times a day, and the school was on the premises. It is true that during their free time the children often had to run little errands, such as delivering letters, so that they often got outside the orphanage. Nevertheless, life was centered on just that one place.

He was awakened at six in the morning. All the children had to wash in one large room, and they only had cold water in which to wash. The first religious service, lasting a good half hour, was at half past six. After that came breakfast. The heating had just come on by then, so it was still cold. On the Sabbath they got up at half past seven, and could go off with their families if they had any. Those with no family remained at the orphanage. Salomon told of the long Saturdays:

"I was one of the few children—as I remember it, the only one for several years—who actually stayed at home on Saturdays because I had nowhere to go. My mother was working. The other children went off. Only I stayed."

The food was monotonous because the weekly menu was repeated. On Tuesdays and Thursdays there was always *stamppot* (potatoes mashed with kale or endive). Once or twice he was invited out by families. The orphans wore uniforms; Salomon found that awful when he—one of the very few allowed to do so—went from the orphanage to high school. Winter and summer he was dressed in a black suit with a white collar—the collar was made of celluloid, which was easy to keep clean.

I asked him to describe the orphanage. It was difficult for him to put the images before his eyes into words:

"If you entered on the side of the Amstel River, you went down a couple of steps, and there was a little hallway to the left. To the right a porter's cubicle. Then on the right was the infirmary and on the left, by the street, was the director's office. If I stayed on the right side, then the infirmary adjoined the bathroom and that in turn adjoined a little cubbyhole that was used as a washroom. From the main hallway there was a side corridor that led inside. On the right was the stairwell, which led upstairs, and if you walked past that, you entered the kitchen. To the left was the director's office with a back room, and a coatroom for those who worked there or visited. Once past that, you came to the cupboards for cleaning supplies and then an exit to a small courtyard. Toward the Amstel, there was an area used for solitary confinement."

The little lockers that the boys had on the second floor were often broken into. The playroom was there, the school, and the boardroom.

Punishment was given mostly for insolence, and more severe punishments for running away; a boy might be placed naked in an isolation area. Some of Salomon's experiences still troubled him. Once, when he had gone off without permission, he was given nothing to put on his bread for a whole year.

"In a way, that didn't work, for there were boys sitting all around the table, and you got a little piece of cake from each. And when I spoke once at table on a Friday evening, although you were not allowed to speak at table—I was 16 or 17—she said, 'Now everyone is silent, just you, you stinker, you're still talking.' I answered, 'Well, we'll just have to find out which of us is the bigger stinker.'"

He was immediately sent to bed. When he refused, the chairman of the board was brought in to help.

Throughout the interview, his attitude toward the orphanage and the school that was attached was ambivalent. In the school they were sometimes beaten with a thin board or a whip. In this isolated world, the system of control extended from the school to the domestic part of their lives and back again. Punishment earned at school might be carried out in the home. The smaller children were sometimes thrashed by the larger ones. Once a teacher lashed out at Salomon and beat him badly.

Yet in the end Salomon realized that, despite all the misery, the orphanage defended him against his mother, who wanted him to work rather than attend high school. This comes through in the following anecdote.

"When it came time to move on from grade school to high school, there was a rather serious incident with my mother. When children left grade school and started high school, it was customary to have a conference with the parent who was still living. I don't believe she really had any say in what happened, but that was how it was done. Anyway, there was this evening in the boardroom, and they called your mother in, and you went in, too. You were asked—or rather told—what would happen. I said that I wanted to go on to high school—I was then in the seventh grade. My mother said, and I remember it very well, 'Why do that? Why can't he go and earn something? I have worked my whole life long. I'd like him to go and earn something for me now.' Fortunately the orphanage didn't agree."[71]

With the help of the orphanage, Salomon went on to high school. But his environment made it hard for him to study. There had been one precedent, a doctor who had lived on in the orphanage during his studies; but they really did not want to keep anyone that long. Salomon ended up in an office, found a room with a family, and for the first time lived a normal family life.

Salomon's tale contrasts sharply with that of Simon, who grew up in a far less strict environment and never had a chance like Salomon's. For a boy to enter the Jewish orphanage, his father—the breadwinner—had to be dead; sickness or the death of the mother was insufficient. Simon was therefore placed in a children's home.

SIMON, THE JEWISH ORPHAN IN A NON-JEWISH CHILDREN'S HOME

Until Simon's mother died when he was 12, he did not count as an orphan and hence could not be admitted to the Portuguese Jewish orphanage for boys. While she was alive, he nevertheless needed care, and so at the age of 9½, he was admitted to Jonker, a home for children run by Hulp voor Onbehuisden [Help for the Homeless]. That was not a problem as far as Jewish customs went, since he did not come from a kosher home. What angered Simon was that the Jewish community did not help care for him and refused to get involved. Before he went to Jonker, he said he was always somewhat hungry; after moving to Jonker, that just became worse.

How did he feel when he was sent to Jonker?

"You were brought there. And then you were received by the people in charge. Then you were put with your age group. We hadn't a clue as to what was going on. There was a big room where 50 or 60 children slept. The boys my age were on one side, and then there was a place for the girls and babies. Then you had groups of children where, for example, the father was a widower or was at sea."

Simon is still angry at the way in which, as he sees it, the Jewish community let him down. Because he was not an orphan, he could not go to the orphanage; but the fact that he was just left to manage still smarts.

"At Jonker you got food—they ate bacon, and of course what they cooked you ate, even if it was pork. Sometimes you got ham on your bread, but you ate that, too. At Passover we got matzos. Only while another Jewish family was there besides us [Simon's siblings were at Jonker with him] did they give us kosher food. The rest of the time you had to eat pork. They taught us nothing about Judaism."

"Did the Jewish community just leave you to fend for yourselves in that home?"

"Except on the Day of Atonement."

When Simon arrived at the home they did not give him a *favus* cap, he just took a bath. I asked him if it was strict at Jonker.

"In a way. There was one male nurse, and perhaps it had to do with his illness, for he had tuberculosis . . . he was a big guy, a good man. But there was another who could have been an executioner in a concentration camp."

"How's that?"

"Cruel, and the things he did, he'd creep under the blankets with the boys. During playtime he'd hit out in all directions."

Simon attended a school outside the home on the Nassau Quay. During recess he sometimes helped at the vegetable market nearby and was given an apple or a pear in return. He liked the school, even though it was the first time he was in a class made up entirely of non-Jews. And he was confronted with non-Jewish culture: in the home the nurse on duty prayed before meals, and every Sunday he had to go to church. There was a Jewish teacher at the school who sometimes gave him a little of her own bread. "But I didn't dare ask her, 'Who are you and why are you doing this?'"

A shy child, Simon managed to learn how to stick up for himself. "But what still troubles me is the Jewish community of that time . . . no help . . . nothing, nothing, nothing. . . ." At a certain point he was no longer required to go to church, and he thinks that this was the result of complaints from the Jewish community. "They didn't want to lose those little souls completely, even though they had to eat bacon there." Instead of going to church, he had to polish shoes.[72]

OTHER MIRRORS

The previous two stories are almost mirror images of each other. In the first there is the endless meddling in the strictly orthodox orphanage, and the second is the story of a child who fell through the meshes of the Jewish network of poor relief. The first story contradicts entirely the description of the girls' orphanage in Lea Appel's *Het brood der doden*, in which she claims that:

> In the history of the Jewish orphanage, corporal punishment was never used, as is shown by all the oral and written accounts of former residents going back before 1905. No one was beaten; no child was ever locked up.

And they were never punished by having food withheld. In that respect, those orphanages compare favorably with other institutions of the time.[73]

A woman who did not want to be officially recorded came out with serious criticism of Appel's nostalgic picture. According to her, things were miserable in the orphanages and the girls were beaten. It was a world of treachery and venom, and only the most compliant girls found it a good place to be. I believe I interviewed this woman in a way that was different from Appel's. Appel is a representative of those who paint nostalgic pictures of Jewish proletarian Amsterdam, and it seems as if she was reminiscing about the "good old days" with those she interviewed. However, despite the difference in accounts, there are similarities. Appel writes, for example, of the little orphan girl in her orphanage uniform who went to a non-kosher baker to eat tarts. She was caught by an orthodox gentleman who followed her to the orphanage and reported her to those in charge. They made her change her job, since it was assumed that she must have been under some bad influence, and she was no longer allowed out on Sunday mornings. This is an example of the far-reaching meddling by the Jewish community in the affairs of the orphans who were under their care.[74]

These stories also show how the accounts of eyewitnesses can retouch a nostalgic picture, and how another story is hidden under the layers of nostalgia. It must be obvious that the interviewer plays a crucial role in this, and that the existing literature gives no evidence of any desire to break through the nostalgia to what is beneath it. Jewish institutional homes were strict and intolerant and attempted above all to protect the child from the threat of assimilation. Nothing could be done for children who were admitted to non-Jewish institutions; they had to make the transition to the non-Jewish community as quickly as possible. Those responsible for Jewish poor relief were aware of the misery that this could cause and tried to set up even more institutions.

The children who found themselves within the Jewish network sometimes enjoyed better chances than those in other foundations. That has to be regarded as the beneficial effect of those institutions, while their negative effects lay in the intensive meddling, the social control, and the religious conformity that was enforced to the very last detail.

SOCIALIST YOUTH AND THE APPEAL OF THE FREETHINKERS

The socialist movement provided the most serious competition to Jewish social work. But it reached a different social class from the one just examined. In preceding chapters it was shown how successful the movement was among the Amsterdam Jewish proletariat and how it stood for everything that was new. To be a member of a socialist club in no way precluded a youngster from also taking part in the activities of a Jewish clubhouse—and it certainly did not prevent anyone from falling back on the poor relief provided by Jewish institutions. Nevertheless, joining the socialist movement often did mean a break of sorts, and the youth were sensitive to this, even if it did not imply a real break with Jewish culture.

Socialism offered new values and a new world, and the only youth movement that could compete with it in theory was Zionism. The Zionist movement never truly reached the proletariat. In a certain sense this was true of socialism as well, since it never reached the most impoverished layers of the proletariat. As far as the young people went, it never made an impact on those who still had to be "civilized," reaching only those whose cultural level had already been somewhat raised. Becoming cultured meant distancing oneself from the past, something that the children of the very poor had not yet managed.

The AJC provided an environment that emphasized not only learning but also the importance of school. In his book about the youth and youth movements, *Youth in History*,[75] the historian Gillis described how this emphasis affected the more affluent members of the working class.

> Parents in the upper reaches of the working class valued the school not only for the mobility that it offered their children, but for the social control it represented. Their contempt for the uneducated extended to the undisciplined, with street Arabs and lodging house youth being the targets of particular hostility. Obedience on the part of the children was regarded as an especially important status symbol.[76]

The socialists opened up a whole new world to the young people. It was so different from anything that had gone before, totally different from the Jewish clubhouse activities, which were seen as far more traditional. Here, too, eyewitnesses give an impression of what the experience meant to them.

Joop told me in an interview how, as the son of an SDAP/ANDB man, he automatically became a member of the AJC. I asked if he had ever been approached by other youth organizations, knowing as I did that the Jewish club Nakhalil had attempted to recruit new members on the street where he lived. His answer was clearly that he had not been approached. He did indeed later become a leader in an organization that tried to persuade the working-class youth to embrace Zionism. The AJC in fact functioned for him as a step toward the modern world and assimilation, and hence a step in the direction of adjustment to the broader society around him. This, in turn, was a necessary condition for further advancement.[77]

Herman told me that he was often laughed at in the non-Jewish environment of his high school. His story of a visit to the toilet typifies this:

"I had learned, as a Jewish boy, that after urinating I had to wash my hands and say a *brakha* [a prayer, in this case for purification]. So before I went to the toilet I would take my cap from the hatrack and put it on. I didn't give a thought to the fact that I had my cap on when I came back into class, for I was thinking of something else. The whole class burst out laughing. Such a crazy guy—leaves the class without a cap to go to the toilet and comes back with it on! I had no idea what was up till I realized it was my cap."

He changed schools and came into contact with the AJC.

"I became a member of the Nederlandsche Bond voor Abstinent Studeren-den [Dutch Union of Abstinent Students]. I went around with the AJC, went walking with them. I really began a new life. . . . I used my first allowance to buy a Bible containing the New Testament. I devoured it. I thought, "That Jesus, he sure was a great Jew; how wonderful that Judaism produced someone like that!' " [78]

He wrote in that Bible, "There will come a time when socialism enters the heart of each of us." Socialism was a new religion for him, an expectation, despite his parent's sorrow at his turning against the old religion.

The new ideals did not spread only through the influence of socialism, for there were many freethinkers and artistic circles that attracted young Jews. They, too, had broken with tradition, and to be associated with these groups often led to conflict with parents. Such conflict was often the price that had to be paid for social advancement. I was told how this environment led one person to nurse's training,[79] and in another case the person in question was led to develop the art of debating and to an appreciation literature.[80]

The Boxing Communist

There was yet another, totally different, way in which to escape from poverty—through unusual artistic ability or through sport. Boxing, the Jewish sport of choice, nurtured its own Jewish champions who thereby entered a whole new world. Among the people I interviewed were well-known gymnasts and soccer players, all of them people who had used sport to advance in the world.

It is impossible to deal with all these interviews in the course of this book. I will limit myself to the story of the boxer Beertje who came from Rapenburger Street in the ghetto. The son of a stevedore, he learned early to stick up for himself. The family was physically strong, and his father was accustomed to making use of his strength. Beertje combined artistic and sporting talent, and when illness prevented him from continuing to develop as an athlete, singing took over. But even when he turned from boxing to singing, Beertje sought an outlet for his physical strength and the aggressiveness he felt toward the injustice he saw around him.

"Look here, I was an aggressive guy in the streets. Boxing, that began out on the street. Rapenburger Street had two *wijngaten* or water passages . . . spaces between buildings through which the water ran. Five or six meters across. On the corner of a water passage you had a boxing school where well-known boxers trained. I was always standing around watching. I was 6 or 7 years old, and there stood those boys stark naked. They wouldn't let anyone stand there looking in, but then I'd look in the other door. I was just looking at the boxing. And they said, 'He's going to be a boxer, too.'

"There was a café on a corner where they went to drink coffee. I'd go there, too, and they'd give me a glass of fruit juice. I was a born boxer, and I was very interested in it. But I wasn't allowed to box yet; I was too young for that. You had to be 12 or 13 years old."

Eventually he went to a boxing club with a communist friend. He began to box in competitions and came into contact with the boxing champion Bennie Bril at Olympia. Because he tried to lose so much weight in order to box as a lightweight, he contracted tuberculosis, which meant the end of his career. Still, boxing had brought him in touch with the world outside the ghetto and since he could also sing well, he built up new contacts through that.

Beertje joined the Communist Party, which had a few other members who lived in the old Jewish neighborhood. For them the party meant resistance. His political awareness was originally developed through the socialists, but in his heart he was more attracted to the fierce spirit of the communists. When he met the Christian socialist Banning, he broke with the socialists because, unlike him, they had not turned away from religion. Moreover, he had difficulties in the SDAP because of the situation in the Soviet Union. Beertje favored a pro-Soviet approach. He then met the communist Gerrit Blom, who had originally been a member of the AJC but had joined the communists when fascism began to threaten Europe. He was also much affected by the rhetoric of the party leader David Wijnkoop, himself the son of a rabbi. But it was his fellow boxer Lard Zilverberg who actually signed him up as a party member.

After a long struggle with tuberculosis, he advanced himself yet further through his ability to sing. This brought him to Germany. But his stories about what fascism meant there were not believed in the SDAP. In the interview he showed that he was still disturbed by this:

"I told them about it here. They said that it couldn't be like that. It was unbelievable."

He and his friends began to organize themselves in the neighborhood in case fascism ever came to Holland. Beertje told me about that unwritten story:

"We were guys who could use our hands. We were strong and fast. Guys who were not afraid. When the NSB [the Dutch equivalent of the fascist party] came along, we first drove a Jewish boy into the water."

"Why?"

"He was riding around on a *bakfiets* or carrier-bike with a big campaign poster for the fascists. [In fact, only a tiny number of Jews were members of the NSB.] We drove him into the water, bike and all. Into the Amstel. We got him out again, too. Later he wound up in a camp and was beaten to death.

During the Occupation, when I saw a uniform I went blind with rage. Once when I saw a member of the fascist party out shopping with his wife, I came up and tapped him on the shoulder. He looked round, and I gave him one, right between the eyes. That was still before the war. . . . We yelled out 'Fascism is murder!' and I painted the trams. Once, on Dapper Street, it developed into a real fight. We chucked the paint all over the fascists."[81] Not until the Occupation did Beertje's gang adopt a real strategy.

Boxing was a Jewish proletarian sport just like soccer and gymnastics, and it was a sport of individuals at the same time. Although an organization of sorts was necessary to find an opponent, it was still a sport in which the individual could set himself apart. It was also the sport of the young boys who were used to fighting in the street and using violence. From early childhood on, various neighborhood gangs would fight over turf.[82] Sometimes this involved fighting with the Christian boys from nearby Kattenburg, which was regarded as a fight between Jews and non-Jews. It is difficult to determine whether boxing was not just a sport for individuals but also a sport through which Jews defended themselves. The interviews shed little light on this matter.

CONCLUSION

Poor relief, the struggle to maintain a distinct identity, and social concern were interwoven in the Jewish community. Through a large number of institutions, the community tried to maintain tradition among the young. This serious concern on the part of the community as a whole meant that some of the young people were given an extra advantage. There were two paths to social advancement—one involved attending various Jewish social institutions throughout childhood, the other involved working completely outside Judaism. Where an individual ended up often depended more on background or the social stratum within which one belonged than on conscious decisions.[83]

Certain groups were not reached by the AJC, while for others it was an obvious choice. But for many others who attended high school and had conscious aspirations, this organization was a way of learning about the "other" world and how one had to behave there. This was true both of the social work among the young and the youth movements, which reflected the highly diversified nature of the popular culture.[84]

The enormous changes that occurred in the way of life of the Amsterdam Jewish proletariat brought with them changes in the mechanisms of social control. The social changes could include new services provided by institutions as well as a new involvement in political ideologies. It was only very slowly that the social services provided by a network of (mostly religious) Jewish organizations with Jewish poor relief at their center, changed into a system in which the municipality provided the core material services, while the Jewish organizations filled in the gaps. In addition, new networks arose.

The power of Jewish poor relief made the leaders beloved. The Joodsche Invalide was something people were proud of. In their struggle to maintain a Jewish identity, the leaders became symbols for the Jewish community. At the same time, poor relief, even when it only took the form of providing extra diapers when a child was born, was something real. No matter how poor you were, there were always foundations that could offer help, and a gifted child was seldom left in the lurch.

It would be interesting to find out to what extent the nature of the Jewish leadership that developed during economic hardship and its charisma led the proletariat to continue supporting those leaders during World War II, when a real Jewish ghetto came into existence once again. Perhaps this could explain the fact that—despite the tradition of struggling socialism—the majority of the Amsterdam Jewish proletariat allowed itself to be deported without a struggle. The Jewish proletariat followed the advice of the men who used to lead the various Jewish organizations and who were now members of the Jewish Council, which was under the control of the Germans. Because material assistance had come from these leaders in the past, they were trusted.

Once the deportations began, the Jewish leaders said reassuringly that it would probably turn out better than might be expected, and once again they found provisions for the journey to Eastern Europe. It seemed that their help would once again prove real. When they made it known that they believed the best way out for everyone was obedience and not resistance to the occupying forces, many saw no reason to doubt them. Indeed, most people did not want to doubt, although some did. There was, after all, nothing else to do but to go. Few had any idea how to do anything else.

EPILOGUE

TRUST

Stories about the old Jewish proletariat of Amsterdam never cease. They contradict each other; they can be expanded endlessly; they resemble each other; and each makes the others impossible. Despite their inherent contradictions, I have tried to bring out the patterns, and to interweave the world of remembered experiences with the society of that time. In doing so, one must not forget how people viewed the world then, and how they view it now. I hope that I have done the stories themselves no injustice, and have allowed those who told them to speak for themselves.

The most remarkable thing is the way the Jewish proletariat of Amsterdam trusted the world around it. Even those who were not socialists believed that a new era was dawning, an era that (certainly in Amsterdam) would mean the end of persecution. But persecution did return and all that trust in the world was broken. Because of this, it is extremely difficult to judge the political situation before World War II. Was the hope for a world without persecution justified? And how aware were people of the danger from Germany, which became evident after 1933 and then gradually crept into Dutch society?

The Dutch historian Schöffer pointed out that there was a latent prejudice against Jews, in particular among the middle class, which worked as a mechanism for excluding Jews. The poorer Jews were practically always recognizable as Jews and "were not always treated with respect and courtesy."[1] He warned against exaggeration and overdramatization, but at the same time suggested that:

> The pain that results from anti-Semitic prejudice for those who suffer it is not diminished by the fact that it was always fairly mild in comparison with the anti-Semitism found beyond our borders in the form of discrimination, blind hatred of Jews, persecution, and pogroms.[2]

Schöffer regarded the existing prejudice as culturally based, in particular because of the distinctive characteristics that set the Jews apart. The Depression began in earnest when the Dutch Jews had to deal with a constant stream of refugees from Germany. These refugees were regarded as a threat for both Jews and non-Jews in what was an already very poor labor market. The rise of the Nationaal–Socialistische Beweging or NSB, the Dutch branch of the fascist party, showed how contagious anti-Semitism could be. Schöffer also mentioned the increasing tension between Jews and non-Jews.

The picture is somewhat moderated, according to Schöffer, when one studies the relationships between people on a cultural level, and when one looks at how people interacted. Indeed, among the elite it was unfashionable to discriminate openly, but there were other ways of excluding people. A more glaring picture is obtained by looking at government policies and the attitude of the churches. The official policy of the Dutch government was to close the borders and to send refugees back, and it was strictly enforced. Although this policy showed no compassion for those trying to flee from Germany via Holland, it was not anti-Semitic per se. However, many regarded it as such.[3]

The same is true for some of the reactions in the press, which regularly expressed concern over the increasing numbers of Jewish refugees and their effect on the Dutch economy. Westerbork, the Nazi transit camp in the east of the Netherlands, was originally built by order of the Dutch government, and the expense of caring for the refugees from Germany fell to the Jewish community. The economic burden was heavy and the number of Jewish refugees high. When the money raised by the National Collection held after *Kristallnacht* in 1938 (to raise money for the refugees from Germany) was divided up, the share assigned to the Jewish organizations was far too small, considering the large number of Jewish refugees. That attitude only changed in 1939.[4] The lack of involvement that characterized Dutch society up until then was felt as hostile by a Jewish community in which almost everybody knew someone who had friends or family in Germany.[5]

Was there in fact reason for optimism, in contrast with other countries, because of the centuries-old tradition of tolerance? The stigma of being different had not disappeared, even in the community most friendly to the Jews—the social democrats of Amsterdam. The social democrat Sam de Wolff wrote about this stigma in his *Voor het land van belofte* [For the Promised Land]. He tells how the party faithful from the third district of Amsterdam (the legendary district in East Amsterdam that had many diamond workers as members) came to another district to offer their services during an election.

> Several members of the . . . district could not support house-to-house campaigning by a group that was so heavily Jewish in composition. They feared, perhaps not unreasonably, that the effect of Jewish visitors on a number of the voters would be contrary to what was desired. From both sides, therefore, against their wishes, the Jewish question came to the fore.[6]

In their zeal to raise the cultural level of the Jewish masses, the social democrats were also sometimes guilty of anti-Semitism. Johanna, the child of a Jewish mother and a non-Jewish father, told of her experiences.

"A teacher who was very red [i.e., left-wing], he was a really committed member of the SDAP, but a terrible anti-Semite. . . ."

"How did he express this?"

According to Johanna, he showed his contempt for Yom Kippur, asking if she didn't want to take the time off, but "sort of with a tone of . . . Jews, they're worthless." This teacher always addressed Jewish children at school not by their first names but by their last names. They were not allowed to run errands for him. "You felt it in your bones, like 'You're a Jew' . . . and I could never understand how someone who was a member of the SDAP, someone who was so leftist, could be that way." [7]

And yet optimism dominated the interviews, alternating with sudden shocks when things were obviously not so rosy. For example, Annie took part in the National Collection; she was shocked by the way in which some people responded.

"Now that you ask, that was the interesting part. . . . I collected for the Jewish refugees, as did one of my aunts—later they killed her, as well as her husband. So my aunt also collected, and I came home and I cried. Because I realized just how much anti-Semitism there was and how many NSB members there were. I told my husband, 'We must flee.' I had gone to a restaurant where people were eating lunch—I'll never forget it—and there I was, with my collecting tin. But you had to get permission first, and they all went like this . . . [Annie turns back the lapel on her jacket]. They had NSB pins under their lapels. They didn't say a word and they didn't give a penny."

Annie returned home distraught, and called her aunt. But her aunt was not available; her uncle told Annie that she had gone to bed, worn out with what she had just been through. "She hadn't gone to restaurants, like me, but had collected in the street. I also went to the Bijenkorf [the major department store discussed in chapter 5] that afternoon, but they threw me out. On the second floor they said to me, 'You don't have permission.' But a few people did give money. There was anti-Semitism here, there was a Nazi movement, worse than we thought. . . . I felt it that day; I was devastated."

Even though Annie was aware of what was happening in Germany, it seemed far away. Only when she saw the results of the German crimes first-hand did she realize how serious the situation was, and how close. The shock made her realize that what had happened in Germany could happen to her as well. She tells about this confrontation in the following fragment:

"During the summer I was in Zandvoort. I saw several Jewish invalids there. They were German refugees who had been taken there for a day out. A handsome man, a young man, sat on the beach. They had blinded him, the Germans had; and he had such a noble, beautiful face. I heard his story; I saw all those people, and I became interested. So I asked if they were refugees from Germany. Yes, and the man who had been blinded was an intellectual. I went home and *howled.*" [8]

How secure were people in Holland and how much prejudice was there against the Jews? Were the little jokes told by almost everyone a sign of anti-Semitism? And what about the behavior of the Dutch government? Was that just a matter of keeping foreigners at a distance?

Joop, who had grown up in a leftwing environment and had played in a street where almost everyone was a member of the SDAP, was quite naive about such things. As a small child he did not know what it was to be taunted for being Jewish. He told of the day when he got a pair of spectacles; he was proud of them and went off to show them to his friends. The incident that followed, and his reaction, show how innocent he was:

"When I got back upstairs I told my mother (I remember this very well), 'You know, it's real strange. There were some boys who were shouting after me: Goggle Joop! How did they know I'm called Joop?' Of course they were shouting Goggle *Jood* [Jew], a discriminatory remark, but I interpreted it as nondiscriminatory." [9]

Despite all the hope, the Jewish proletariat was largely excluded from non-Jewish circles. A very few managed to break through as a result of membership in the SDAP or because of their careers. The original optimism, which persisted despite everything, collided with the economic reality of a city hit by the Depression and overwhelmed by refugees, in which certain occupations were not open to Jews. Jews were often turned down by potential employers for "cultural" reasons. Either it was not really acceptable to hire a Jew, or (given the abundant labor supply) the employer preferred to hire one of the unemployed non-Jews.

Occasionally such a refusal was carried out in a rather crude manner, as was attested by a number of interviewees. For example, Jacob applied for a job at a bank:

"I had to earn money, and being a Jew made it difficult to apply. I remember a number of jobs that I didn't get because I was Jewish. . . . There was a bank on the Singel, and about twenty of us turned up at the same time to apply. Twenty or thirty of us were standing there in the reception area. A gentleman came out and looked us over—I felt like I was in a slave market— and he picked one of us. After a while he came back and picked out another. And every time he kept looking at me. But he passed me by. Until all of the others had been picked out. And then he said to me, 'I have nothing for you.' That happened to me a number of times. At one office I was told, 'I don't hire Jews.' It happened several times. . . ." [10]

Apparently it was possible to discriminate openly against the poor, and cultural discrimination also meant economic discrimination.

Marriage to a non-Jew also did not mean entrance to the non-Jewish world, but rather the non-Jewish spouse became part of the Jewish proletariat. Maria married a Jew in the early 1930s, and found herself estranged from her family. Her father absolutely refused to give her permission to marry. Her story shows how great the gulf was between the Jewish milieu and that from which she came. It should be mentioned that she did not come from Amsterdam, and that she was reared in a very religious Protestant family.

"When I met my husband and they said, 'Do you know that he's a Jew,' I asked, 'What is that?' . . . At a certain point I asked him, 'They keep saying you're a Jew; what does that mean?'"

I asked her about the differences.

"It was a totally different way of life. For example, at my home the whole family was there on Sunday and there was meat on the table. But at my husband's family that took place on Fridays."

Her husband's family seemed to be prejudiced against non-Jews. "One said, 'You can't bake a sponge cake,' and another said, 'You can't make pear kugel.'"

She decided to do something about this. "I thought, I'll bake a cake myself. Well, I did that, and they couldn't believe it because it tasted better than theirs. Yeah, . . . the Friday evenings were warm and cozy—*gezellig*—but I missed my Sundays."[11]

Very slowly she became integrated into the Jewish world and forgot her Sundays. Moreover, she felt her parents would have found it far worse if she had married a Catholic.

The question that was asked time and time again—consciously and unconsciously—was whether to abandon the traditional Jewish way of life. The hope for equality, and with it the resulting pressure to assimilate, became less self-evident as events in Germany grew worse. Parents were often shocked to discover how attractive their children found the more frivolous non-Jewish world. Often daughters went dancing at La Gaîté where Rudolf Nelson's company often played, above the Tuschinsky cinema. One of the women I interviewed told how she was embarrassed to stand there among the other girls—until she was asked to dance:

"Sometimes I was ashamed to go there; I thought it was almost like selling myself. It was 'just to dance.' A world like that didn't exist at home, it was a world I didn't know. The unknown. And I loved to dance."

Unfortunately a girl could not refuse when asked, even if the man did not appeal to her. That would create a scandal. You had to dance, whether you wanted to or not. "It was often rather dirty; if the man pressed you close to him, you felt more than you wanted to . . . such a complete stranger, whether you liked him or not, whether or not he had a strong body odor, you danced with him. Because you liked to be asked to dance, and there were some who weren't asked, but you were because you looked pretty. But what you experienced wasn't always pleasant, wasn't always entirely respectable."

Her parents would have been beside themselves with worry if they had known. But in fact it was quite harmless. She paid for her own drinks; that way she never got stuck with anyone.[12]

On the one hand, going out like this was normal; on the other hand, it was taboo. It was understood that such behavior had no place in a Jewish milieu. In the following passage, Leendert's admission that he behaved differently toward Jewish girls is significant:

"Where did you go?"

"We often went to Heilige Road. In the front was a café, in the back a dance hall. If you went there around nine o'clock and you bought a soda (I didn't drink beer), then you could dance right through until 11:30 on that one drink. That cost only 50 cents, plus a 10 cent tip. . . . You danced with as many different girls as possible so you wouldn't have to offer any of them a drink. You didn't want that."

I asked him about his contact with girls, and he was honest. "The non-Jewish girls you tried to seduce, but not the Jewish girls. It's really odd."

"Was that your attitude?"

"You tried to get them to leave with you, but I still don't understand it."

"Were you really serious?"

"I haven't got a clue now." [13]

A great deal was going on in this story, including the breaking of taboos. It is one of many anecdotes that contributes to an increasingly clear picture. People knew they were doing something that did not fit in the old Jewish customs, hence they preferred not to examine it too closely.

The most potent memory of fascism is the war, and beyond that other memories are occasionally visible. Politically, people were against the NSB, although the stories indicate that people felt it was different from German fascism; direct questioning showed that they were well aware of the close ties between the two. One or two people had even known a "good" member of the NSB. These people considered NSB members to be quite different from German fascists. Cases where people had been betrayed by NSB members during the war were brushed off with, "There are always anti-Semites," and in the interviews this memory strengthened the feelings of uncertainty and doubt already referred to.

Those with the clearest view of history were the communists and the members of the Yiddish cultural society of Jews originally from Eastern Europe, Sch. AnSki. The latter had centuries of experience with pogroms and the political ways of countering them, which certainly helped them. Furthermore, they put less trust in Dutch society. David told me that in Manege Street—the "Russian" street—stones had been thrown through windows from time to time, not by anti-Semites but by Dutch Jews. Even they could not be trusted.

There was one other group with a clear perspective on the past—those who had joined the Zionist youth organization at the end of the 1930s. They had learned how to analyze what was going on around them.

These three groups, much as they differed from each other, shared in common a clear and unambiguous view of the world—either one is a victim or one fights. Many members of Sch. AnSki joined the communist resistance during the war. But with regard to the resistance and the Jewish contribution to it, the stories totally contradict one another.

In the following account, the start of the Jewish resistance is associated with Jewish boxers, with Maccabi (the Jewish sports club), and with Jewish solidarity:

"In 1934 and 1935 we held closed sporting competitions. After one of these I met a German Jew who introduced himself as Blazer. 'I am a German from Maccabi in Berlin. . . . We are not allowed to box any longer in Berlin, at least not in competitions, since we are no longer allowed to box against Aryans. Would you be willing to bring your team to Berlin, and give my boys a chance to box in a competition?' "

The group went to Berlin. He continues:

"I saw things there that struck me as unreal . . . and when the Krauts came to Holland I was alarmed. I got a request from Maurits Dekker [a well-known publicist with radical ideas] . . . would I meet with them in a Rotterdam coffee shop to discuss things. . . . It was decided to start a team of Jewish strong-arms [a street gang], and I trained them twice a week." [14]

According to Beertje (cited in the previous chapter), there were strong-arm teams among the communists even before the war, so this story does not fit the facts. And there are other accounts that claim the organization existed before the war. The extent to which this is true could indicate how aware people were of the danger of fascism. Such questions cannot really be answered by interviews. In any case, the Jewish resistance falls outside the scope of this book; it was dealt with only indirectly in the interviews.

"I wanted to leave, but he didn't," said Annie, the wife of a diamond worker. "You could take a grindstone with you wherever you went." That was also true, in a sense, of a peddler's pushcart—you could rent one anywhere. If they had known they would all be killed, they might have fled, but as poor Jews they had nowhere to go. For the time being they considered themselves safe; they had lived in Holland for so long, and everything had gone so well.

And that was true—they were safer in Holland than anywhere in the world. Yet they lived in a city where, despite the existence of a resistance, a large part of the population did nothing to actively resist deportation. A couple of years later, those who had felt so safe sought desperately for somewhere to hide. All too often they received no help, and in some cases they were betrayed and handed over. Such contradictions earmark the memories.

Of the 140,000 Dutch Jews, 80 percent died during World War II. [15] It is generally assumed that the slaughter was worst among the proletariat, although there are no exact figures. The devastation can be seen from the fact that there is no Jewish proletarian culture left at all. In this sense, the history of the Jewish proletariat of Amsterdam is also a study of the consequences of World War II, and of the nature of the destruction brought about by the Holocaust.

This kind of research raises questions about what the past was like and how it can be portrayed. Of course there are many different perspectives on this, but every perspective is colored by the massive slaughter that followed; at the time no one knew what would happen. Every attempt to describe experiences before the Holocaust demands that we temporarily put aside our knowledge of later events, retrieving that knowledge only when memory has provided it with a context.

Louis expressed this in the following:

"You heard rumors, but you said, 'That's impossible,' which was an entirely logical response. We always lived with dignity, and if anyone in the neighborhood was sick or anything, the news traveled like wildfire. I mean, that inhumanity couldn't exist, that could only . . . perhaps this is insulting to animals, but something like that could only happen among animals."[16]

APPENDIX

A BRIEF GUIDE TO DUTCH PLACE NAMES

Because Dutch place names are usually compound words, they tend to be quite long. In order to aid the American reader, place names in the text have been broken down into smaller and more understandable parts. For example, *Kloveniersburgwal* is rendered as Kloveniers City Wall, *Rembrandtplein* as Rembrandt Square, and so on. Below is a list of the Dutch equivalents of the most common terms that have been translated.

alley	*gang* or *steeg*
bridge	*brug*
canal	*gracht*
city	*burg* (originally *burcht* 'citadel, bastion')
gate	*poort*
harbor	*haven*
lane	*laan*
neighborhood	*buurt*
quay	*kade*
square	*plein*
street	*straat*
village	*dorp*
wall	*wal*

The one exception to this in the text is *gracht* or canal, which is familiar to those who have visited Amsterdam.

The diphthong *ij* (as in IJ Harbor) has a pronunciation similar to 'eye' and is treated as one letter.

NOTES

References in these notes are given with abbreviated titles. Full information on titles can be found in the Bibliography.

Chapter One: Methodological Considerations

1. Actually, the original meaning of *vlooien* is probably 'flowing.'
2. S. van den Eewal, *Joodjes-leven*, pp. 7–8. The author's name is probably a pseudonym.
3. C. Reijnders, *Van 'Joodsche Natiën' tot Joodse Nederlanders.*
4. The theoretical part of this book is based on a discussion regarding the use of interviews. See D. Bertaux, *Biography and Society*; *L'illusion biographique*; and L. Niethammer, "Fragen–Antworten–Fragen"; a special issue of the French journal *Annales, Economies, Societées, Civilisations* devoted to the discussion on oral history (1980); L. Passerini, *Torino Operaia e Fascismo*. See also L. Niethammer (ed.), *Lebenserfahrung und kollektives Gedächtnis*. There are two specialized journals, *Oral History* and *International Journal of Oral History*. The proceedings of various international conferences on oral history are also important: P. Thompson (ed.), *Our Common History*; J. Talsma et al. (eds.), *Papers Presented to the International Oral History Conference*; P. Joutard et al. (eds.), *IVe Colloque international d'Histoire orale*; and M. Villanova (ed.), *V Colloqui Internacional d'Historia Oral.*
5. A number of studies, through their manner of handling the material and especially through their perspective, influenced the form of this book. They are, in alphabetical order, Dobroszycki and Kirschenblatt–Gimblet, *Image before My Eyes;* Geisel, *Im Scheunenviertel;* Hyman, *From Dreyfus to Vichy;* Samuel, *East End Underworld;* and White, *Rotschild Buildings.*
6. The destruction of the old Jewish Quarter is perhaps best described by J. Meijer in *Het verdwenen ghetto.* See also Bregstein and Bloemgarten, *Op zoek naar Joods Amsterdam*; M. H. Gans, *De oude Amsterdamse Jodenhoek*; idem, *Memorboek.*
7. This void is described in a literary manner by Siegfried Van Praag in *Jeruzalem van het Westen.*
8. Werkman devoted part of his life to examining the confusion that results from the various methods of looking at a landmark such as Waterloo Square. See his *Waterlooplein.*
9. I dealt with this in my "In Search of the Picture," "Patterns of Cultural Change," and "Nostalgie."
10. According to the Dutch historian Jacob Presser: "Even in May 1943, when the Jewish Council was ordered to select 7,000 people for deportation, the cup

was apparently not yet full, and the Council tried to 'preserve a core.' They apparently had no doubt who constituted it: the intelligentsia and the well-to-do of yore—it was to save this dwindling group, to which they themselves belonged, that an even greater number of sacrifices were fed into the mouth of Moloch." Presser, *The Destruction of the Dutch Jews*, p. 276.

11. J. van der Kar, *Joods verzet*.

12. Sluyser, *Voordat ik het vergeet*; *Hun lach klinkt van zo ver*; *Er groeit gras in de Weesperstraat*; and *Amsterdam je hebt een zouten smaak*.

13. See also his contemporary, the journalist Oznowicz, "Afscheid van de jodenhoek," and "De jodenhoek vroeger," which appeared in the newspaper *Het Vrije Volk*. Oznowicz's work was later collected in *Amsterdam in Naatjes tijd*. See also S. van Praag, *Mokum aan de Amstel*.

14. G. Janouch, *Conversations with Kafka*.

15. Leydesdorff, "The Screen of Nostalgia."

16. See also my "Maakten zij de wereld leefbaar?"

17. See D. Hondius, *Terugkeer*.

18. Interview with Mrs. E.

19. *Fragmenten uit het dagboek van Sam Goudsmit*. Also of interest is an issue of the *Haagse Post* devoted to this topic (5 May 1984). See also J. van Dam, *Poppetje gezien*, pp. 219ff., and the lovely publication *Le-Ezrath Ha-Am, het Volk ter Hulpe*.

20. A. J. van Schie, "Restitution of Economic Rights after 1945."

21. An example is Adorno's magisterial *Was bedeutet: Aufarbeitung der Vergangenheit* in which he compares his own values and historical images to the German assimilation of fascism. Durkheim's detailed studies in *Le Suicide. Étude de sociologie* of how people can respond to the culture around them through, e.g., suicide also springs to mind.

22. Michelet, *Journal, tome I, 1828–1848*, p. 393. See also *The Art of Memory* in which Frances Yates shows how, before the rise of the natural sciences, history was dependent on oral tradition and on the telling of stories again and again from memory. The storyteller, according to Yates, left a trail through the places that (s)he remembered, so that the remembered places and ideas could be recreated afresh again and again with the help of memory. A good example is the lecturer who tells a story while walking through a building. The students recall the story from memory by retracing the tour through the building and remember the relevant ideas in each part of the building. Yates blames the loss of this skill on the rise of modern science, which is oriented toward technology, and on the esteem accorded to it.

23. See Bertaux and Bertaux–Wiame, "Autobiographische Erinnerung."

24. See Halbwachs, *La Mémoire Collective*.

25. A *bedstee* or bed niche is a traditional Dutch sleeping alcove that is built into a wall, much like a cupboard.

26. Interview with Mrs. G.

27. Regarding the February Strike, see my article, "The Mythology of 'Solidarity,'" See also "The Biro Bidzahn Project 1927–1959" by Abramsky for a description of that project.

28. Ginzburg, *Le fromage et les vers*, p. 12.

29. Ibid.

30. Niethammer, "Fragen–Antworten–Fragen." According to Niethammer,

the one who tells the story in an interview is invited to forget the artificiality of the situation and to tell the story in his or her own fashion. Du Bois Reymond formulated it as follows: "(S)he determines the order, the tempo, and the choice of topics. (S)he is not confronted at the start with a long list of questions that have been thought out beforehand. (S)he is regarded as an expert in the area of his or her own life history. As far as possible, the researcher adopts the role of listener, and stimulates the progress of the account with short, undemonstrative gestures and questions" (Du Bois Reymond, "Over de methode van mondelinge geschiedenis," pp. 18ff. In this project I chose to follow this method of taking life histories as far as possible.

31. See Passerini, *Torino Operaia e Fascismo*, and "Work Ideology and Consensus under Italian Fascism." In the latter, she writes: "Oral sources should be regarded as forms of culture and witnesses to its changes through time. But we must try to develop a concept of culture that includes the reality of everyday life" (p. 92).

32. See also my "Geheugen, getuigen en herinneren."

33. Moreau, "Le Memoire, ses blocages, leurs consequences."

34. Hobbs, "Psychological Aspects of Oral History"; Hunter, *Memory, Facts and Fallacies*. For a discussion of the pros and cons of using psychoanalytic techniques, see A. Mitzman, "Het beschavingsoffensief."

35. Leydesdorff, "Nostalgie."

36. Rappaport, *Emotions and Memory*, in particular chapter 5 on psychoanalysis. On repression see S. Freud, "Die Verdrängung" (1915).

37. Freud, "Über Kindheits und Deckerinnerungen" in *Zur Psychopathologie des Alltagslebens*. According to the psychoanalyst Rappaport, the premise that calling up unpleasant feelings is avoided through memories is in fact the psychoanalytic theory of memory. This implies that memory does not lend itself to manipulation; no one is really aware of repressing something. Finally, repression is strengthened when speaking a foreign language, when one is exhausted, or when one is suffering from neurosis or psychosis.

38. Halbwachs, *Les cadres sociaux de la Mémoire* and *La Mémoire Collective*.

39. Williams, *Marxism and Literature*, pp. 115–117.

40. See also Dahmen, "Psychoanalysis and Social Theory."

41. Brecht wrote, "Distancing thus means historicizing, depicting events and persons as ephermal histories. Of course the same can be done with one's contemporaries; their attitudes can be portrayed as time-dependent histories" (*Gesammelte Werke* vol. 16, p. 133).

42. Brecht, *Gesammelte Werke*, p. 517.

43. Macherey, *Pour une théorie de la production literaire*.

44. The French psychoanalyst Jacques Lacan studied what it meant when a life story that was told, in the psychoanalytical sense, was put into language (Lacan, *Le moi dans le théorie de Freud*). People *tell* the stories of their lives, but during the sessions they are not *experienced*. Various experiences and feelings can be expressed in a series of words. It is possible to trace them through semiotics. Terms change meaning when used in different contexts. Every word is given a particular meaning in a specific language system, which in turn is a prerequisite to speech.

The language system dominates the speech of the individual. Because the one who uses language to tell something expects a response from the listener, (s)he will try to use the frame of reference and language system of the listener. Parts of the story may be condensed or may include gaps or voids that reveal subconscious omissions. For this reason, Lacan advocates searching for symptoms throughout the text—readings in which the silences, the untold story, appear. This can provide new clues to what is actually being told. In fact, it is the only way to gain insight into that part of the account which lies outside the symbolic order, because it is improbable and strange—or so weighed down and loaded with unpleasant feelings that it is silenced and repressed.

This use of the concept of "symptomatic reading" was first systematically worked out in Bertaux and Bertaux–Wiame, "Autobiografische Erinnerung und kollektives Gedächtnis."

45. Interview with Mrs. A.

46. This concept was first introduced in the Netherlands by Schwegman in 1981. "Lagen der werkelijkheid."

47. Interview with Mrs. M.

48. Raphael, "Le travail de la mémoire."

49. Due to the intensely personal nature of this interview, I have kept the informant anonymous.

50. The Italian researcher Portelli suggested adding "musical" notations to the transcript, signaling transitions in language. Although a positive addition, it only solves a small part of the problem. Portelli, "Dividing the World."

51. Presser, *The Destruction of the Dutch Jews*, pp. 536–537: " 'the postwar Jewish attitude to life.' The odd thing is that many Jews reflected and talked about this subject, even during the war, wondering whether, after the experiences they had already had or that were still in store for them, they would ever again be able to behave like normal human beings—a question that many of them answered in the negative. After all the fears, all the threats, all the shocks, the panic, the losses—home, family, and even name—how could they hope to find their way back to everyday life, without mental anguish, suspicion, nameless terrors, and nightmares? How could the Jewish woman who had seen her own daughter enter the gas-chamber, ever again face life with her head held high? How could the Jew, robbed of all his children and grandchildren, ever again feel himself an ordinary man among other men?"

52. Bettelheim, *Surviving and Other Essays*, in particular "Trauma and Reintegration"; "The Holocaust—One Generation Later"; and "Schizophrenia as a Reaction to Extreme Situations."

53. This was the case with the researcher Glas–Larsson as documented in *Ich will reden*. Through substantial knowledge of living conditions in a concentration camp, historians were able to help a woman put her memories and her life in order. After a period of intensive cooperation, she was able to find peace of mind. Up till then psychiatrists had failed to help her.

Chapter Two: The Jews and Amsterdam

1. Afdeeling Amsterdam van de maatschappij tot bevordering der Bouwkunst. N. Redeker Bisdom, *Antwoord op de prijsvraag uitgeschreven in het jaar 1865 'Op welke wijze zou Amsterdam het best kunnen worden uitgebreid,'* pp. 7ff.

2. See Brugmans, "Opgaand getij."

3. N. Redeker Bisdon, "Het aanlegen eener aanzienlijke hoofdstraat," p. 8.

4. Idem, "Bouwfantasiën," p. 5.

5. S. E. Kleerekoper, "Het joodse proletariaat."

6. C. Reijnders, *Van Joodsche Natiën.*; H. Brugmans and A. Frank, *Geschiedenis der Joden in Nederland*, part one.

7. A. M. Vaz Dias, "De economische positie van het gros"; "Over den vermogenstoestand."

8. Superficial conversations with old residents quickly brought out the huge differences between the small Portuguese institutions and their larger Ashkenazi counterparts. A number of former residents were extensively interviewed for this study, the results of which are given in chapter 6. See also M. H. Gans, *Het Nederlandse Jodendom*. A similar division seems to have been common in almost all Jewish communities in the eighteenth century. For example, see A. Burgiére, "Groupe d'immigrants ou minorité religieuse?"

9. C. Reijnders, *Van Joodsche Natiën*. pp. 87ff.; E. Boekman, *Demografie van den Joden*, passim.

10. "Statistiek der Bevolking van Joodsen bloede door de Rijksinspectie bevolkingsregisters. 1 oktober 1941" [Statistics on the Population of Those of Jewish Blood by the National Inspection of Population Records. 1 October 1941]. This information is cited in one of the maps with personal annotations by the historian Jacob Presser. The results are the same as those of A. Veffer (*Statistische gegevens*). Veffer cites 79,410 full Jews out of the 800,541 total population of Amsterdam. He based his research on requests for identity cards. In both instances, the estimated percentage is 10 percent.

11. C. Reijnders, *Van Joodsche Natiën*; M. E. Bolle, *De opheffing van de Autonomie.*

12. F. P. Hiegentlich, "Reflections"; J. Michman, "Gothische Torens."

13. *Dr. Meijer de Hond, Bloemlezing*, p. 35.

14. J. Meijer, *Het verdwenen ghetto.*

15. Idem, p. 16.

16. Idem, p. 153.

17. *Dr. Meijer de Hond, Bloemlezing*, pp. 36–37.

18. For example, S. E. van Praag, *Jeruzalem van het Westen* and S. Santen, *Deze vijandige wereld.*

19. S. E. van Praag, *Jeruzalem van het Westen*, p. 17.

20. Chapter 3; pp. 95ff. in the American edition.

21. L. Soloweitschik, *Un prolétariat Méconnu*, p. 15.

22. For centuries many streets had had Jewish names in addition to their non-Jewish names. Henri Polak noted the most important differences in his book on Amsterdam (H. Polak, *Amsterdam die groote stad*, pp. 29–30).

23. E. Boekman, *Demografie van de Joden in Nederland*, pp. 57ff.

24. The *Halacha* is Jewish religious law that regulates lineage, among other things.

25. B. Anderson, *Imagined Communities.*

26. Interview with Mr. V.

27. Idem.

28. M. Vovelle, *Ideologies et mentalités*, p. 27.

29. See R. Roegholt, *Amsterdam in de twintigste eeuw*, passim, and J. de Vries, *De Nederlandse economie*, passim.

30. J. de Vries, *Met Amsterdam als brandpunt* and *De Nederlandse economie*; G. J. Harmsen, *Hamer of aanbeeld.*

31. A large part of this information comes from research done at the Documentatie Centrum voor Nieuwste Geschiedenis. Research topics included social-democratic municipal policy with regard to cost of living, food prices, and what might be described as material life.

32. T. van Tijn, "Geschiedenis van de Amsterdamse diamanthandel."

33. See, e.g., H. Roland Holst–van der Schalk, *Kapitaal en arbeid in Nederland*, part 1, pp. 180ff.

34. G. Harmsen, *Hamer of aambeeld.*

35. H. Polak, *De invloed van den oorlog op de diamantindustrie*, pp. 20–21. See also the earlier publication (probably also written by Polak), *De dreigende verplaatsing van de Amsterdamsche diamantindustrie.*

36. W. A. de Graaf, *Grondslagen*, pp. 22ff. De Graaf specifically names the decline of the garment industry. This industry flourished again with the influx of German Jewish refugees after 1937. Research has not been done on this, although the newspapers of the time reported it. The *Handelsblad* of 27 June 1939 discussed the decline of the Berlin labor market and the manner in which this stimulated prosperity in Amsterdam. On 8 July 1939 this growth was inventoried; the statistics reported that 10,000 immigrants worked in the industry, and one-fourth of the women's garment industry was in German Jewish hands.

See also A. H. Wolf–Gerzon, *Au Bonheur des Dames* and A. H. Pontfoort, "De kledingindustrie in Amsterdam," pp. 203ff.

37. J. C. van Dam, *Sociaal logboek 1900–1960*, p. 105. Centraal Overleg in Arbeidszaken, *Enkele opmerkingen.* The latter discusses wage differences between Brabant and Amsterdam in cigar factories ranging from 10 to 16 percent. This can also be found in the *Jaarverslagen van de Gemeente Amsterdam 1920–1940* (one volume was published each year). See also the *Verslagen van de Kamer van Koophandel 1920–1940.* These statistics were used as a source.

38. J. de Vries, *De Nederlandse economie*, pp. 85ff.

39. These conclusions are based on the annual municipal reports and the reports of the Chamber of Commerce, which in turn were based on the municipal reports. In retail stores and in the markets, the influence of World War I remained strong throughout 1918 and 1919 and only diminished noticeably around the middle of 1920. Complaints that the population of Amsterdam had too little purchasing power persisted until 1926. See *De Amsterdamsche Arbeidsmarkt*, a monthly review of changes and conditions in the labor market in Amsterdam with editorial commentary (1928–1939); *Vijf en twintig jaren samenwerking*; and *Rapport Gemeentecommissie tot bevordering van de ontwikkeling.*

40. "Eenige gegevens omtrent het levensmiddelenbedrijf te Amsterdam."

41. This occurred in 1934–1935.

42. Although the accepted English translation for the Dutch *wethouder* [lit. law holder] is alderman, it should be remembered that this function in Dutch government does not parallel exactly either the British or American govermental positions of the same name. In the Netherlands, *wethouders* are municipal civil servants charged with handling the daily affairs of the municipality. They represent the specific vision of the political parties with which they are affiliated.

43. These observations are from a report by G. van Tijn in the YIVO Jewish Research Institute in New York. This report is among the files from the HIAS, the

Jewish organization that tried to help refugees flee to America. The comments begin on page 9. This document is handwritten and unnamed.

44. C. A. van der Velde, *De ANDB*, Th. van Tijn, "Voorlopige notities"; idem, "De Algemeene Nederlandsche Diamantbewerkersbond (ANDB)."

45. Weinstock uses Soloweitschik as his source.

46. See also S. de Wolff, *Voor het land van belofte*, passim.

47. I analyzed this myth in light of wartime experiences in "Maakten zij de wereld leefbaar?"

48. Such assertions are impossible to verify, but it is enlightening to compare Weinstock's writings, which also report such differences, with those of, for example, Hyman regarding Paris. See Hyman's *From Dreyfus to Vichy*. Members of the Bund organized labor unions among the Jews in France. A similar picture is given of the radicalism of the poor in London's East End by W. J. Fishman in his *East End Jewish Radicals 1875–1914*.

The autobiography of Joe Jacobs, who later became a communist through populism, gives a similar description of recruitment methods used by the neighborhood labor unions for socialism. Throughout his book Jacobs shows that this was a protest against the sweatshops, against working conditions in small factories, and later against fascism. Organizations such as the SDAP or the ANDB are not mentioned.

49. As a hated cultural minority, the Jews were forced to live together in one specific part of Russia (the Pale) and every year or so they were subjected to pogroms in which they were abused and/or murdered. The Pale consisted roughly of the following areas: New Russia, the Ukraine, Belarus (formerly Byelorussia), and Lithuania, those parts of Poland conquered by Napoleon, and a number of Baltic provinces. Jews had to remain inside the boundaries laid down in 1835.

The Jewish *national* movement had already been formulated by Aaron Lieberman during the 1870s. See B. Sapir, "Lieberman et le socialisme russe." The Jewish *workers* began to organize in reaction to the faster pace of industrialization that accompanied the Russo–Turkish war of 1877. Up to that time, Lieberman's ideas were based on the assumption that the lot of the Jewish working class and poor would be improved principally through instruction and education about their own culture. Then, in 1877, the Jewish workers organized a huge strike in Vilnius for the first time. The unrest among the workers and their experience of organized resistance led to a change in the theoretical basis of the movement. The ideas of Jewish nationalism and the goals of socialism were brought together. As a result, socialism spread beyond the confines of the factory and took hold, for example, among the weavers who worked in tiny firms where great numbers of Jews were employed in Central and Eastern Europe.

See also E. Mendelsohn, *Class Struggle in the Pale*. He proposes that Jews were not hired in the new mechanized factories of the time. Despite this, they were exposed to mechanization and influenced by industrialization. The Bund's real foundation of strength was laid after the Jews had slowly but surely infiltrated the real industry. The great masses had Jewish socialism, but the industrial workers left their mark on the organization.

50. There were Jewish social democrats and revolutionaries in Russia who also subscribed to this ideology of equality. They, too, desired one great socialist movement in which differences in origin would be irrelevant. In their personal lives and in their attitudes toward the Jewish workers' organization, it is easy to

see the tension between Jewish nationalism and the goals of the world citizen/socialist—even where this takes the form of simply denying the existence of the problem. The leading socialists demonstrate the extent to which the situation in Eastern Europe differed from that in Holland. Martow, for example, ultimately turned explicitly against Jewish nationalism. Axelrod, who was himself from the Jewish working class, ignored the Bund when he had to make a choice. He was the example of a Jew who chose to live his life in as assimilated a manner as possible, entirely at the service of his goal—a single, undifferentiated socialist party. In this way, his ideas did not differ greatly from those that ruled in the ANDB. See P. Frankel, *Prophecy and Politics*; I. Getzler, *Martow, a Political Biography of a Russian Social Democrat*; and A. Ascher, *Pavel Axelrod and the Development of Menshevism.*

51. N. Levin, *While Messiah Tarried.*

52. S. E. Bloemgarten, "Henri Polak: A Jew and a Dutchman."

53. M. Anstadt and F. Hiegentlich, *De Oost-Joodse Cultuur Vereniging.* See also S. Anstadt, *Een eigen plek.*

54. For the position of the SDAP, see L. Brug, *Het district waar oprees hun burcht.*

55. Various interviews.

56. L. Giebels, *De zionistische beweging in Nederland 1899–1941.* On page 181 she mentions a bourgeois constituency, and on p. 185 she points to efforts to win over the Jewish proletariat of Amsterdam to Zionism.

57. Interview with Mr. B.

58. Interview with Mr. R.

59. G. W. Borrie, *Pieter Lodewijk Tak.*

60. G. W. Borrie, *Wibaut, mens en magistraat.*; R. S. Rodriguez de Miranda, "De economische taak."; P. Hoogland, *Vijf en twintig jaren.*

61. P. F. Maas, *Sociaal Democratische Gemeentepolitiek in katholiek Nijmegen 1894–1927.* The first part discusses politics in Amsterdam.

62. J. Reitsma, "Prijsafspraken en gemeentepolitiek." Social-democratic city administrators had their own publication (*De Gemeente, orgaan van de vereniging van Sociaaldemocratische gemeenteraadsleden*), which often contained articles on the desirability of social-democratic organization of the city from the top down. The policy necessary to achieve this was discussed most by S. Rodriguez de Miranda. Aldermen regularly attended courses in which the policy was explained. Another source was the *Socialistische Gids* (mentioned earlier), in which the advantages and disadvantages of this policy were discussed in detail. See, e.g., D. Groeneveld, "Beschouwingen" and J. Reitsma, "Prijsafspraken en gemeentepolitiek," both of which appeared in the *Gids.*

63. H. F. Cohen, *Om de vernieuwing van het socialisme.*; E. Hueting et al., *Ik moet, het is mijn roeping.*

64. *Het Socialisatievraagstuk.*

65. S. R. de Miranda, "De economische taak van de gemeente"; A. C. de Vooys, "Wijziging in de maatschappelijke verhoudingen."

66. L. Wijmans, "Sociologie, Sociaal-democratie en de middenklasse."

67. P. de Rooy, *Werklozenzorg en werkloosheidsbestrijding.*

68. See Borrie, *Wibaut. Mens en magistraat*; S. R. de Miranda, *In de branding.*

69. P. de Rooy, *Werklozenzorg en werkloosheidsbestrijding.*

70. B. Kautsky, "Haushaltstatistik der wiener Arbeiterkammer 1925–1934."
71. C. H. Wiedijk, *Koos Vorrink.*
72. De Regt elucidated this process in her book *Arbeidersgezinnen en bes-chavingsarbeid.*
73. Idem, p. 199.
74. See chapter 4.

Chapter Three: The Old Neighborhood

1. G. Fülbert, *Proletarische Partei.*
2. H. Heijermans, *Diamantstad*, pp. 103–105.
3. Ibid., pp. 13–14.
4. Ibid., p. 17.
5. In this she differed greatly from other important writers of the 1930s, especially the Querido brothers, who made clear in a number of books how vital socialism was for the Jewish working class—as the bringer of prosperity and modern ways and the tamer of the uncouth masses. The most famous of these books are *Het geslacht der Santiljanos, Levensgang, Roman uit de Diamantbew-erkerswereld* , and *Het Volk God's.*
The first of these books was written by Emanuel Querido under the pseudo-nym Joost Mendes. Against a background of steamy romance, it tells of the coming of a new world to be created by the diamond workers' union. At the same time, Querido clearly recognized the desire to rise above that milieu. Such an attitude can also be found in the work of Heijermans, but in his writings the working person remained in the working class. Moreover, Heijermans's *Diamant-stad* does not end happily—there is a fire in Uilenburg and the loved one dies. In Israël Querido's vision, by contrast, the future becomes steadily rosier—true love runs its course and everyone gains wisdom. In his descriptions of the Jewish milieu of around 1900, a new kind of nostalgia creeps in, a romanticizing of the strong beginnings of the workers' movement. His characters were people whom he believed to represent typical Portuguese Jews.
6. Interview with Mrs. B.
7. Interview with Jacob.
8. Interview with Mr. B.
9. L. Chevalier, *Classes laborieuses*, General Introduction.
10. He uses demographic shifts, immigration waves, and quantitative data along with other evidence. This method of working is set forth in one of the most important books on Jewish immigration to Paris, for which he wrote the introduc-tion. In that book crime is not the central question, but rather the process of acculturation as interpreted from quantitative data. See C. Roland, *Du ghetto à l'Occident.*
11. L. Chevalier, *Classes laborieuses*, p. 62.
12. The name most closely identified with these changes (which had indeed begun somewhat earlier) is that of Sarphati, who was a great stimulus for the beautification of the city during the nineteenth century and whose work continued after his death. L. Brug, *Het district waar oprees hun burcht.*
13. Ibid, pp. 15–17.
14. Jews spread into areas in the Pijp, the Ooster Park neighborhood, that part

of East Amsterdam that bordered on the Dapper neighborhood, the 's Graven-
zande neighborhood, and parts of the Dapper neighborhood itself. C. Reijnders,
Van "Joodsche Natiën" tot Joodse Nederlanders, pp. 81–83.

15. H. Polak, *Amsterdam die groote stad*, p. 30.

16. B. H. Stephan, "Sterfte en ziekte bij Joden en niet-Joden."

17. J. A. Verdoorn, *Het gezondheidswezen in Amsterdam*, p. 62.

18. F. A. Theilhaber, "Die Sterblichkeit der Juden." Cited by Verdoorn, *Het gezondheidswezen in Amsterdam*, p. 438.

19. S. Coronel, "Iets over het verschil in levensverhoudingen tusschen Joden en Christenen," pp. 372ff.

20. R. H. Saltet and P. Falkenburg, "Kindersterfte in Nederland in de jaren 1881–1905."

21. P. H. Pinkhof, "Onderzoek naar de kindersterfte onder de geneeskundig-bedeelden te Amsterdamn."

22. Ibid.

23. J. Sanders, *Ziekte en sterfte bij Joden en niet-Joden te Amsterdam*.

24. Tuberculosis was a danger for diamond workers because of exposure to the dust from cutting and grinding. This dust irritated the lungs, which led to open infection for those with latent tuberculosis. See also H. Heertje, *De diamantbew-erkers van Amsterdam*, pp. 257ff. Heertje reports lead poisoning as another occu-pational illness, due to wetting one's fingers while molding caps (p. 252). He also mentions nervous disorders, which he attributes to fear of unemployment and changing factory conditions. Later he shows how heavily these fears weigh on people (pp. 253–254).

25. J. A. Verdoorn, *Het gezondheidswezen in Amsterdam*, p. 67.

26. Ibid., citing J. H. Korteweg, "Statistiek van difterie en croup," pp. 129ff. and 173ff.

27. J. A. Verdoorn, *Het gezondheidswezen in Amsterdam*, p. 68.

28. E. Boekman, *Demografie der Joden in Amsterdam*, pp. 110ff.

29. Ibid., p. 113.

30. J. A. Verdoorn, *Het gezondheidswezen in Amsterdam*, pp, 229ff.

31. J. H. van Santen and T. van der Brink, "Population Phenomena in Amster-dam," p. 21; E. Boekman, *Demografie der Joden in Amsterdam*, p. 89.

32. This was a first attempt to quantify the social behavior of Jews in compari-son with other population groups. J. Leydesdorff, *Bijdrage tot de speciale psy-chologie van het Joodsche Volk*.

33. Ibid., p. 12.

34. Ibid, p. 39.

35. W. Sombart, *Die Juden und das Wirtschaft*.

36. J. Leydesdorff, *Bijdrage tot de speciale psychologie van het Joodsche Volk*, p. 41.

37. Ibid., p. 95.

38. See chapter 4, pp. 118–120.

39. J. ter Meulen, *Huisvesting van aarmen te Amsterdam*.

40. Ibid., p. 30. Figures for the Jordaan were 1,650 – 6,684 – 729 – 2,540. For the remaining sectors of the old city they were 1,112 – 4,443 – 401 – 1,241.

41. Ibid., p. 36.

42. See also A. de Regt, *Arbeidersgezinnen en beschavingsarbeid*, especially chapter 6, "Armenzorg en disciplinering."

43. According to ter Meulen, her research was possible in part because starting in 1901 the Jewish poor could apply for relief from the municipal authorities.

44. J. ter Meulen, *Huisvesting van aarmen te Amsterdam*, p. 54.

45. Ibid., pp. 68–69.

46. L. M. Hermans, *Krotten en sloppen. Een onderzoek naar de wooningtoestand te Amsterdam.*

47. Ibid., p. 62.

48. Ibid.

49. Ibid., p. 66.

50. Ibid., p. 63.

51. Ibid., p. 71.

52. Ibid., pp. 73–74.

53. Interview with Mr. B.

54. Interview with Mrs. K.

55. Interview with Mrs. B.

56. Interview with Mr. H.

57. A. Keppler, "De krotopruiming in Amsterdam." For a summary of housing policy from a sociogeographic perspective, see also J. Vijgen, *Joden in Amsterdam.*

58. J. Vijgen, *Joden in Amsterdam*, p. 114.

59. H. Heertje, *De diamantbewerkers van Amsterdam*, p. 232.

60. A. Keppler, "De krotopruiming in Amsterdam," p. 134.

61. *Gedenkschrift der Stichting Bouwfonds Handwerkers Vriendenkring.*

62. Research, Handwerkers Vriendenkring 1912, Municipal Archives no. 2327 VM 1914.

63. Ibid., pp. 3–4.

64. Ibid., p. 5.

65. Municipal Archives no. 8482 PW 1914.

66. Gemeenteblad 1915, part II, pp. 843, 867,

67. Gemeenteblad 1916, part II, p. 1294.

68. Gemeenteblad 1916, part I, p. 551; part II, p. 800; part III, p. 149.

69. *Cathalogus van de tentoonstelling: Het verdwijnend Amsterdamsche Ghetto.*

70. J. H. Rössing, *Verdwijnend oud Amsterdam*, p. 20.

71. Ibid., p. 21.

72. Ibid., p. 20.

73. This ended in the Potato Riots in 1919, a hunger uprising organized by the communists and syndicalists as a protest against what they considered to be poor management of food rationing by social democrats, for whom they had no love. The population demanded potatoes, but only rice was available. These riots were the most serious disturbance over food in memory, and indeed they are still talked about.

74. Interview with Mrs. F.

75. Gemeenteblad 1915, part II, p. 710.

76. Gemeenteblad 1918, part II, pp. 2622ff.

77. Gemeenteblad 1919, part II, pp. 2189ff.

78. Research conducted at the Documentatie Centrum voor Niewste Geschiedenis 1978–1980 (unpublished).

79. Gemeenteblad 1923, part II, p. 1809.

80. G. Gimpel, *Amsterdam Oud en Nieuw.*
81. Manuscript of Mrs. D.
82. Interview with Mrs. B.
83. Interview with Mr. S.
84. Idem.
85. Interview with Mr. M.
86. Interview with Mrs. K.
87. Interview with Mrs. B.

Chapter Four: Life in Various Neighborhoods

1. E. Boekman, "De verdwijning van het Amsterdamsche ghetto."
2. Idem, "Oude en enieuwe jodenbuurten in Amsterdam."
3. A. F. Bakhoven, "Het saneren van slechte woonwijken te Amsterdam."
4. Gemeenteblad 1930, part I, pp. 2475, 2481.
5. Ibid., p. 2486.
6. *Gedenksschrift Stichting Bouwfonds Handwerkersvriendenkring*, p. 3.
7. L. Brug, *Het district*; C. Reijnders, *Van "Joodsche Natiën,"* p. 82.
8. Unpublished research done on social-democratic policy with regard to housing policy.
9 See R. Roegholt, *Amsterdam in de twintigste eeuw*, pp. 75–105.
10. G. P. Keers, *De politieke functie van stedelijke structuurplannen*; T. Jansen and J. Rogier, *Kunstbeleid in Amsterdam 1920–1940*, chapter 1.
11. Municipal Archives no. 963 VH 1930.
12. Interview with Mrs. L.
13. In the archives of the Poor Board we find an increase over time in the names of people who came from these streets.
14. Interview with Mrs. E.
15. Interview with Mr. P. (Jerusalem).
16. H. C. van Tiel, *Amsterdam Oost*, p. 23.
17. Interview with Mr. P. (Jerusalem).
18. Municipal Archives no. 753 VH 1929.
19. According to Boekman (*Oude en nieuwe jodenbuurten*) the percentage of Jewish residents in the Lepel Street and surrounding area was 72 percent.
20. Interview with Mrs. S.
21. Interview with Mrs. F.
22. Interview with Mrs. K.
23. Interview with Mr. v. D.
24. Interview with Mr. B.
25. Interview with Mr. M.
26. Interview with Mrs. E.
27. Interview with Mrs. G.
28. Interview with Mrs. G.
29. J. A. Allouche–Benayon, "Mémoires juives et identité."
30. Interview with Mrs. A.
31. In fact, I came to the same conclusion as H. J. Gans in *The Levittowners*. See also his "Symbolic Ethnicity."
32. Interview with Mr. J.

33. M. Zomerplaag, *De groei der Afrikaner of Transvaalbuurt,* p. 3.

34. *De huisvesting van asociale gezinnen te Amsterdam.*

35. F. Smit, "De gemeente als vliegwiel voor volkshuisvesting," p. 22.

36. A. de Regt, *Arbeidersgezinnen en beschavingsarbeid,* passim.

37. Municipal Archives no. 712 VH 1932. Of the 273 apartments around Afrikaner Square, 152 were occupied by people whose old quarters had been condemned; 98 families came from what were classified as bad (*slecht*) quarters, and only 8 families came from "overcrowded" quarters. The majority of those who moved into the Transvaal area came from J. D. Meijer Square (in 1931: 169), others from the Jonker and Ridder neighborhoods (30), and the Weesper neighborhood (13). Only three families moved from the Ooster Park area and the numbers from other neighborhoods in Amsterdam were equally low.

38. Ibid.

39. Municipal Archives no. 407 VH 1933.

40. Municipal Archives no. 922 VH 1931.

41. Municipal Archives no. 997 VH 1931.

42. Municipal Archives no. 167 VH 1934.

43. A. Querido, *Het Zeeburgerdorp.*

44. See also H. J. Reijs, *De husivesting van ontoelaatbare gezinnen.*

45. Municipal Archives no. 1014 VH 1935.

46. Municipal Archives no. 642 VH 1931.

47. Municipal Archives no. 916 VH 1931.

48. Municipal Archives no. 923 VH 1931.

49. Municipal Archives no. 342 VH 1933.

50. Municipal Archives no. 897 VH 1933.

51. Reijs, *De huisvesting van ontoelaatbare gezinnen,* p. 19. See also *De huisvesting van asociale gezinnen te Amsterdam.* The author is almost undoubtedly Keppler, the director of the Housing Department.

52. Reijs, *De huisvesting van ontoelaatbare gezinnen,* p. 37. De Regt tended to be far more neutral regarding the attempts to raise the cultural level of the working classes in his study.

53. Municipal Archives no. 742 VH 1936.

54. Reijs, *De huisvesting van ontoelaatbare gezinnen,* p. 35.

55. Interview with Mr. B.

56. Inteview with Mrs. K.

57. For this reason, memories of the Transvaal neighborhood from that time are often laden with sadness. The most moving of the written accounts is A. Caransa, *Verzamelen op het Transvaalplein.*

58. Municipal Archives no. 193 VH 1933/ 407 VH 1933.

59. Municipal Archives no. 63 VH 1934.

60. Municipal Archives no. 302 VH 1938.

61. Inteview with Mrs. A.

62. Inteview with Mrs. B.

63. S. Goudsmit, *De een zijn dood,* pp. 34–35.

64. G. Pommata, "La storia della donne."

65. R. Ratherford Ruether (ed.), *Religion and Sexism* There is no comprehensive overview. Especially interesting in this volume is J. Hauptman, "Images of Women in the Talmud."

66. Interview with Mrs. A.

67. M. Young and P. Wilmott, *Family and Kinship in East London.*
68. G. Stedman–Jones, "Working-Class Culture and Working-Class Politics in London 1870–1900."
69. E. Ross, "Survival Networks: Women's Neighbourhood Sharing in London before World War I."
70. M. Casciato, F. Panzini, and S. Polano (eds.), *Architectuur en Volkshuisvesting, Nederland 1870–1940;* also D. I. Grimberg, *Housing in the Netherlands 1900–1940.*
71. I dealt with this in my "The Creation of the Modern Family."
72. S. Stuurman, *Kapitalisme. Verzuiling en Patriarchaat.*
73. Interview with Mr. V.
74. Interview with Mr. F.
75. Interview with Mrs. B.

Chapter Five: Working and Living in Poverty

1. E. Boekman, "De wereld der Joden in Amsterdam."
2. *Statistiche mededeelingen,* published by the Bureau van de Statistiek der gemeente Amsterdam, no. 88.
3. Dutch Israelites and Portuguese Israelites were referred to in chapter 2 as Ashkenazim and Sephardim, respectively.
4. Municipal Archives SZ [Sociale Zaken], 157163.
5. A. Veffer, *Statistische gegevens van Joden in Nederland,* volume 1.
6. N. Birnbaum, *Joodsche beroepswizijging.*
7. H. B. J. Stegeman and J. P. Vorsteveld, *Het joodse werkdorp in de Wieringermeer 1934–1941.*
8. H. Heertje, "Het ateliermeisje van Amsterdam."
9. See S. Leydesdorff, *Verborgen arbeid, vergeten arbeid.*
10. A. Mellink, "Roosje Vos (1860–1932)"; PP. de Baar, "Leven en werken van de Amsterdamse ateliermeisjes in de jaren dertig"; PP. de Baar, "Sani Prijes van de Naaistersbond 1876–1933."
11. Interview with Mrs. K.
12. Interview with Mrs. P.
13. Interview with Mrs. K.
14. Idem.
15. H. Heertje, "Het ateliermeisje van Amsterdam," pp. 132ff.
16. Interview with Esther.
17. Idem.
18. F. de Jong Edz., *Van ruw tot geslepen.*
19. Interview with Mrs. G.
20. H. Heertje, *De diamantbewerkers van Amsterdam.* For our purpose, the most important chapters are 8 and 9.
21. Idem.
22. See also O. Montagne, J. Winkler et al., *Dr. Henri Polak.*
23. J. Kroes, *Het paleis aan de laan.*
24. Cited in Kroes, ibid., p. 25.
25. Interview with Mrs. G.
26. Idem.

27. Interview with Mrs. F.
28. Interview with Mr. R.
29. Idem.
30. H. Heertje, *De diamantbewerkers van Amsterdam*, p. 235.
31. Ibid., p. 237.
32. Ibid., p. 239.
33. Ibid.,, pp. 262–264..
34. Interview with Mrs. G.
35. H. Heertje, *De diamantbewerkers van Amsterdam*, p. 302.
36. Interview with Mrs. P.
37. Interview with Mrs. v. A.
38. I. Santcroos, "Interview met S. Rodrigues de Miranda."
39. I. Santcroos, "Het aandeel der Amsterdamsche joden in de straathandel."
40. Idem.
41. Interview with Mrs. B.
42. V. R. A. D. Huberts, *De Amsterdamse venters.*
43. Idem, p. 88.
44. Interview with Mrs. B.
45. Idem.
46. V. R. A. D. Huberts, *De Amsterdamse venters,* p. 35.
47. *Rapport van de commissie voor den straathandel*, p. 7
48. See p. 153.
49. Interview with Mr. A. in Israel. This interviewee's story was also reported in P. Bregstein and S. Bloemgarten, *Op zoek naar Joods Amsterdam*, p. 30.
50. Interview with Mr. H.
51. V. R. A. D. Huberts, *De Amsterdamse venters,* p. 150.
52. Interview with Mr. H.
53. Idem.
54. Gedenkschrift Mercurius.
55. R. Kistenmaker, M. Wagenaar, and J. van Assendelft, *Amsterdam marktstad*, passim.
56. Idem, p. 133.
57. Interview with Mr. S.
58. File no. 22, Municipal Archives SZ, afd. crisis diamant.
59. Ibid., file no. 3326.
60. Ibid., file no. 54.
61. Ibid., file no. 196. This is a lovely letter that gives real insight into the hopeless situation, although probably it was written by a non-Jewish diamond worker. In this instance, the writer's origin does not really matter.
62. File no. 722, Municipal Archives SZ, afd. crisis diamant.
63. Interview with Mr. R.
64. File no. 22224, Municipal Archives SZ, afd. crisis diamant.
65. Ibid., file no. 1454.
66. Interview with Mr. B.
67. Interview with Mrs. A.

Chapter Six: Concern for the Poor, or
Efforts to Preserve the Community

1. L. Frank van Loo, *Den armen gegeven.*
2. Archives Ned. Isr. Hoofdsynagoge, no. 207: *Een ernstig woord.*
3. M. O. Cohen and A. van Praag, *Joodse vereenigingen op sociaal gebied,* pp. 101–102.
4. L. Harveld, F. de Jong Edz., and D. Kuperus, *De Arbeiders Jeugd Centrale,* pp. 108–110.
5. L. Frank van Loo, *Den armen gegeven,* p. 148.
6. H. J. Gans, *The Urban Villagers,* pp. 210ff.
7. This agrees with the findings of Gans, ibid., p. 202.
8. L. Frank van Loo, *Den armen gegeven,* p. 148.
9. L. Appel, *Het brood der dooden.* She wrote about this book: "It is a memorial to the children who were murdered, and in honor of those who worked to care for the children entrusted to them," p. 5. This memorial character can be found throughout the book, and it influences the manner in which she tells about the orphanage. Appel's book deals with both history and what life was like in a girl's orphanage. For this reason, I deliberately chose to interview boys who were orphans for the present book.
10. M H. Gans, *Het Nederlandse Jodendom.* The information and quotations given here are from *De Joodsche Invalide,* vol. 3 (January 1930).
11. "Gestichtszorg voor oude lieden en andere volwassen behoeftigen," *De Joodsche Invalide,* vol. 3 (1930), p. 6.
12. Among those who complained after the Children's Act of 1901 were the management of Hoenderloo. They feared that, due to the government subsidy, they would no longer receive donations from private citizens. The answer they received was, "The burden must rest on the shoulders of the entire community and not only on those of a few." Letter dated November 1917 from the Hoenderloo Directors to the Minister of Justice. (Bijlage op Notulen 25.1.1919 in Archief Algemeen College van Toezicht, Bijstaand en Advies voor het Rijks- Tucht en Opvoedingswezen 1903–1955. ARA, Den Haag.) P. de Rooy pointed out this source, which he and B. Kruithof used for their article in the fall 1986 issue of *Sociologisch Tijdschrift.*
13. M. H. Gans, *Het Nederlandse Jodendom,* p. 92; see also Nederlands Israëlitisch Armbestuur, *Verslag over de jaren 1915–1919,* pp. 50–51.
14. The historian is rarely completely at home with the finer points of theological interpretations. To gain a better understanding of the various nuances and insight into the importance of *tsedaka* in Jewish life, I am deeply grateful to Rabbi A. Soetendorp in The Hague and Prof. N. van Uchelen in Amsterdam. They confirmed my hunch that it is extremely difficult to compare various forms of religious experience. The responsibility for my interpretation of the material, of course, remains with me.
15. M. Weber, *Gesammelte Aufsätze zur Religionssoziologie,* vol. III, *Das Antike Judentum,* pp. 271ff.
16. M. Marrus, *The Politics of Assimilation.*
17. Idem, pp. 77ff.
18. N. H. Snaith, *The Distinctive Ideas of the Old Testament,* pp. 161–173.
19. H. L. Strack and P. Billerbeck (eds.), *Kommentar zum Neuen testament*

aus Talmud und Midrasch, vol. 1, pp. 386–388; H. Bolkenstein, *Wohltätigkeit und Armenpflege im vorchristlichen Altertum, ein Beitrag zum problem 'Moral und Geselschaft'*; K. H. Fahlgren, *Sedaja, nahestehende und entgegengesetzte Begriffe im Alten Testament*; A. van Iterson, *Armenzorg bij Joden in Palestina van 100 v. Chr.–200 n. Ch.*

20. J. M. Hillesum, "Vereenigingen bij de Portugeesche en Spaansche Joden te Amsterdam in de 17e en 18e eeuw," pp. 167ff.
21. M. Cohen and A. van Praag, *Joodse vereenigingen op sociaal gebied*.
22. Interview with Mrs. Asscher–Pinkof.
23. Idem.
24. Clara Asscher–Pinkof, *Star Children*, p. 5.
25. Idem, p. 33.
26. Interview with Mrs. Asscher–Pinkof.
27. J. Gompers and F. Cohen, *Zwerftochten door Klein Jeruzalem*.
28. C. Eitje, "Hoe staan wij tegenover onze jeugd?" p. 30.
29. The Seder is the evening meal celebrating Passover or Pesach, in memory of the Exodus from Egypt.
30. See p. 123.
31. M. H. Gans, *Memorboek*.
32. R. Hoogewoud–Verschoor, *Van zending tot gesprek?*
33. Idem, p. 46.
34. Idem, p. 47.
35. Cited in idem, p. 47; from *Bachoerei*, Siewan 5689 (June/July 1929), p. 3.
36. Archief Ned. Is. Hoofdsynagoge no. 959.
37. J. Gompers and F. Cohen, *Zwerftochten door Klein Jeruzalem*.
38. Idem.
39. Life History of Mrs. M. Unpublished manuscript.
40. D. Koker, "Joodsche buurtverenigingen," p. 40.
41. Minutes of Nachaliel.
42. Interview with Mrs. B.
43. J. Gompers, "Joodsche zwaluwnesten."
44. "Bij het aftreden van den Heer I. Gans."
45. Wereldverbond van diamantbewerkers, *Rapport nopens den toestand in de diamantnijverheid*, p. 46. This can be found in the archives of the ANDB. Membership figures for Patrimonium (Protestant) and St. Eduardus (Catholic) were 44 and 71, respectively. Betsalel and Patrimonium collaborated with the ANDB.
46. "Bij het aftreden van den Heer I. Gans."
47. L. H. Sarlouis, "Joodsche jeugdorganisatie," pp. 10–11.
48. "Bij het aftreden van den Heer I. Gans."
49. Interview with Mrs. P.
50. *Nieuw Israëlitisch Weekblad*, 26 January 1912. All this information is from the archives of the Joodsche Invalide. Mr. M. Gans of Amsterdam not ony allowed me access to this material, but helped me with the organization of this chapter. All cited brochures and newspaper clippings are from this collection.
51. *Centraal Blad voor Israëliten*, 3 Feburary 1911.
52. I. G. Keesing, "Joodsch Sociaal werk," p. 82.
53. S. J. Philips (ed.), *Gedenkboek ter gelegenheid van het honderdvijftig bestaan van het Nederlands Israëlitisch Armbestuur te Amsterdam, 1825–1925*.
54. *Gemeente Blad*, 10 June 1925.

55. *De Rotterdammer*, 22 October 1914.
56. Interview with Mr. M. Gans.
57. Idem.
58. Idem.
59. Idem.
60. Jacob Presser, *The Destruction of the Dutch Jews*, p. 212.
61. Documentatie Sociale Raad. Municipal Archives of Amsterdam 400, no. 542.
62. For an extensive listing, see M. O. Cohen and A. van Praag, *Joodse vereenigingen op sociaal gebied.*
63. *Dr. S. A. Rudelsheimstichting, herinneringsschrift.* In his opening speech, which appears in the annual report of 1932, President Hertzberger argued the necessity of helping the children of the poorest (*Jaarverslag* 1932, pp. 29–30).
64. I. J. Keesing, "Joodsche sociaal werk," pp. 72–93. The Berg Foundation is described on p. 90.
65. Idem, pp. 78–80.
66. J. S. Jessurum Cardozo, "De Joodsche Jeugd."
67. Idem, "Joodsche sociaal werk."
68. *Rapport der commissie tot onderzoek van het Joodsche reclasserings-vraagstuk*, 1931.
69. A. van Ommeren and A. Scherphuis, "De Crèche."
70. Interview with Mrs. M.
71. Interview with Mr. E.
72. Interview with Mr. B.
73. L. Appel, *Het brood der dooden,*, p. 15
74. Idem, pp. 43–45.
75. J. R. Gillis, *Youth in History.*
76. Idem, p. 20.
77. Interview with Mr. V.
78. Interview with Mr. M. For a Jew of his time, reading the New Testament was a giant step, a sign of assimilation. It is not contradictory that he did so because of the influence of fellow AJC members.
79. Interview with Mrs. K.
80. Interview with Mr. M.
81. Interview with Mr. B.
82. H. Safrian and R. Sieder, "Gassenkinder–Strassenkämpfer."
83. In G. Harmsen, *Blauwe en Rode jeugd*, this choice is made more conscious. This does not agree with my findings, including where they concern socialists and communists. People came "by coincidence," but upon closer inspection, the "coincidence" was not so great.
84. This was also the conclusion of J. S. van Hessen in *Samen jong zijn.*

Epilogue: Trust

1. I. Schöffer, "Nederland en de Joden in de jaren dertig," p. 87.
2. Idem.
3. See D. Michman, "De Joodse emigratie en de Nederlandse reactie daarop tussen 1933 en 1940."

4. L. de Jong, *Het Koninkrijk der Nederlanden in de Tweede Wereldoorlog*, Part 1, p. 540.

5. On the attitude of the Protestant churches, see G. van Roon, *Protestants Nederland en Duitsland 1933–1941*.

6. S. de Wolff, *Voor het land van belofte*, p. 79.

7. This interview of Mrs. v. W. was conducted by Evelien Gans, who kindly gave me permission to cite it here. See also D. van Arkel, "De groei van het anti-Joodse stereotype."

8. Interview with Mrs. G.

9. Interview with Mr. V.

10. Interview with Mr. S.

11. Interview with Mrs. K.

12. Because of the nature of the material involved, this interviewee shall remain anonymous.

13. Interview with Mr. H.

14. Interview with Mr. C.

15. *De Joden in Nederland*, 1961, op. cit.

16. Interview with Mr. B.

BIBLIOGRAPHY

C. Abramsky. "The Biro Bidzahn Project 1927–1959." In Kochan (ed.), *The Jews in Soviet Russia* (London 1978).

T. W. Adorno. "Was bedeutet: Aufarbeitung der Vergangenheit" [What Does Dealing with the Past Mean?]. In *Eingriffe. Neun kritische Modelle* (Frankfurt am Main 1963), pp. 125–147.

J. A. Allouche–Benayon. "Mémoires juives et identité" [Jewish Memories and Identity], *IVme Colloque international d' Histoire orale* (Aix en Provence 1982), pp. 531–548.

M. van Amerongen et al. *Voor buurt en beweging, negentig jaar sociaaldemocratie tussen IJ en Amstel* [For Neighborhood and the Movement—Ninety Years of Social Democracy between the IJ and the Amstel] (Amsterdam 1984).

De Amsterdamse Arbeitsmarkt, een maandelijks overzicht omtrent verkeer op en toestand van de arbeidsmarkt Amsterdam [The Amsterdam Labor Market, a monthly review of activity and the condition of the labor market in Amsterdam] (Amsterdam 1928–1939).

Annales, Economies, Societés, Civilisations [Annals, Economies, Societies, Civilizations], vol. 35, no. 1 (1980), pp. 124–200.

B. Anderson. *Imagined Communities. Reflections on the Origin and Spread of Nationalism* (London 1983).

M. Anstadt and F. Hiegentlich. *De Oost-Joodse Cultuur Vereniging Sch. An-Ski, 1921–1979* [The East Jewish Culture Association Sch. An-Ski, 1921–1979] (Jewish Historical Museum, Amsterdam 1979).

S. Anstadt. *Ein eigen plek. Verhalen van een opgejaagde jeugd* [A Place of One's Own. Tales from a Hunted Youth] (The Hague 1984).

L. Appel. *Het brood der doden. Geschiedenis en ondergang van een joods meisjes-weeshuis* [Bread of the Dead. History and Decline of a Jewish Girls' Orphanage] (Baarn 1982).

D. van Arkel. "De grooi van het anti-Joodse stereotype. Een poging tot een hypothetische deductieve werkwijze in historisch onderzoek" [The Growth of the Anti-Jewish Stereotype. An Attempt at a Hypothetical Deductive Method in Historical Research], *Tijdschrift voor Sociale Geschiedenis*, vol. 10, no. 33 (1984), pp. 34–71.

D. Aron–Schnaper and D. Hanet. "D'Herodite au magnétophone. Sources orales et archives orales" [Heroditus and the Tape Recorder. Oral Sources and Archives], *Annales, Economies, Societées, Civilisations*, vol. 35, no. 1 (1980).

A. Ascher. *Pavel Axelrod and the Development of Menshevism* (Cambridge, MA 1972).

C. Asscher–Pinkhof. *Sterrekinderen* (The Hague 1946). Translated into English by Terese Edelstein and Inez Smidt, *Star Children* (Detroit 1986).

PP. de Baar. "Leven en werken van de Amsterdamse ateliermeisjes in de jaren dertig" [The Life and Work of the Amsterdam Sweatshop Girls in the 1930s], *Werken rondom het IJ, vakbondsstrijd in vijf Amsterdamse bedrijfstakken 1870–1940* [Work around the IJ: Labor Union Conflict in Five Amsterdam Industrial Sectors 1870–1940] (Amsterdam 1981).

_____. "Sani Prijes van de Naaistersbond 1876–1933" [Sani Prijes of the Seamstresses Union 1876–1933], *Vijfde jaarboek van de geschiedenis van socialisme and arbeidersbeweging in Nederland* (Nijmegen 1981).

A. F. Bakhoven. "Het saneren van slechte woonwijken te Amsterdam" [Demolition and Reconstruction of the Bad Neigborhoods in Amsterdam], *Tijdschrift for Volkshuisvesting en Stedebouw* (January 1932).

D. Bertaux and J. Bertaux–Wiame. "Autobiographische Erinnerung und kollektives Gedächtnis" [Autobiographical Memory and Collective Memory]. In L. Niethammer (ed.), *Lebenserfahrung und kollektives Gedächtnis. Die Praxis der 'Oral History'* (Frankfurt am Main 1983), pp. 108–123.

D. Bertaux. *Biography and Society. The Life-History Approach in the Social Sciences* (London 1981).

B. Bettelheim. *Surviving and Other Essays* (New York 1952).

"Bij het aftreden van de heer I. Gans als voorzitter van Betsalel" [On the Occasion of the Retirement of I. Gans as President of Betsalel]. Offprint from *Nieuw Israëlitisch Weekblad* [New Israelite Weekly] of 18 November 1927. Provided by Joachimsthal's Printing Works, Amsterdam.

N. Birnbaum. *Joodsche Beroepswijziging* [Change of Jewish Occupation] (1935).

S. E. Bloemgarten. "Henri Polak: A Jew and a Dutchman." In J. Michman (ed.), *Dutch Jewish History* (Jerusalem 1983).

E. Boekman. "De verdwijning van het Amsterdamsche ghetto" [The Disappearance of the Amsterdam Ghetto], *De Vrijdagavond*, vol. 1, no. 21 (18 August 1924).

_____. "Oude en nieuwe jodenbuurten in Amsterdam" [Old and New Jewish Neighborhoods in Amsterdam], *De Vrijdagavond*, vol. 1, no. 22 (22 August 1924).

_____. "De wereld der Joden in Amsterdam" [The World of the Jews in Amsterdam], *De Vrijdagavond* , vol. 7, no. 42, part 2 (16 January 1931).

_____. *Demografie der Joden in Amsterdam* [Demography of the Jews in Amsterdam] (Amsterdam 1936).

M. du Bois Reymond. "Over de methode van mondelinge geschiedenis" [On the Method of Oral History]. In M. du Bois Reymond and T. Wagemakers (eds.), *Mondelinge geschiedenis, over theorie en praktijk van het gebruik van mondelingen bronnen* (Amsterdam 1983).

H. Bolkenstein. *Wohltätigkeit und Armenpflege im vorchristlichen Altertum, ein Beitrag zum Problem 'Moral und Gesellschaft'* [Charity and Care of the Poor in Pre-Christian Antiquity. A Contribution to the Problem of Morals and Society] (Utrecht 1939).

M. E. Bolle. *De opheffing van de Autonomie der Kehillot in Nederland 1796* [The Abolishment of the Autonomy of the *Kehillot* in the Netherlands in 1796] (Amsterdam and Jerusalem 1984).

G. W. B. Borrie. *F. M. Wibaut, mens en magistraat. Ontstaan en ontwikkeling der socialistische gemeentepolitiek* [F. M. Wibaut, Man and Magistrate. The Rise and Development of Socialist City Politics] (Amsterdam and Assen 1968).

_____. *Pieter Lodewijk Tak (1848–1907). Journalist en politicus* [Pieter Lodewijk Tak (1848–1907). Journalist and Politician] (Assen 1973).

F. Bovenkerk and L. Brunt, eds. *De rafelrand van Amsterdam* [The Frayed Edge of Amsterdam] (Meppel 1977).

B. Brecht. *Gesammelte Werke* [Collected Works] (Frankfurt am Main 1967).

P. Bregstein and S. Bloemgarten. *Op zoek naar Joods Amsterdam* [In Search of Jewish Amsterdam] (Amsterdam 1981).

L. Brug. "Het district waar oprees hun burcht" [The District where Their Citadel Rose], in M. van Amerongen et al., *Voor buurt en beweging, negentig jaar social-democratie tussen IJ en Amstel* (Amsterdam 1984).

C. van Bruggen. *Het huisje aan de sloot* [The Little House by the Ditch] (Amsterdam, 1921 edition).

H. Brugmans. "Opgaand getij 1848–1925" [Rising Tide 1848–1925], *Geschiedenis van Amsterdam* (Utrecht and Antwerp 1983, revised edition), pp. 107–121.

H. Brugmans and A. Frank. *Geschiedenis der Joden in Nederland* [History of the Jews in the Netherlands], part 1 (Amsterdam 1940).

J. H. Buiter. *Modern salariaat in wording* [Modern Workforce in the Making] (Rotterdam 1968).

Bureau van de Statistiek der gemeente Amsterdam [Bureau of Statistics of the Municipality of Amsterdam]. *Statistische Mededelingen* (Amsterdam 1930).

A. Burgière. "Groupe d'immigrants ou minorité religieuse? Les Juifs à Paris au XVIIe siècle" [Immigrants or Religious Minority? The Jews of Paris in the Seventeenth Century], *Le Migrant, France terre de migrations internes; France, terre d'immigration* (Colloque d'Aurillac 1985).

S. Burniston and C. Weedon. "Ideology, Subjectivity and the Artistic Text," *On Ideology* (London 1978), pp. 199–299. (A publication of the Centre for Contemporary Cultural Studies.)

S. van Bussum. *Een bewogen vrijdag op de Breestraat in Amsterdam* [A Gentle Friday on Bree Street in Amsterdam] (Amsterdam 1930).

_____. *Het Joodsche Bruidje, een zedenschets uit onze dagen* [The Jewish Bride. A Sketch of Manners of Our Time] (Amsterdam 1932).

I. Calvino. *Invisible Cities*, translated by William Weaver (New York 1974).

A. Caransa. *Verzamelen op het Transvaalplein. Ter nagedachtenis van het Joodse proletariaat van Amsterdam* [Gathering on Transvaal Square. In Memory of the Jewish Proletariat of Amsterdam] (Baarn 1984).

M. Casciato, F. Panzini, and S. Polano (eds.). *Architectuur en Volkshuisvesting,*

Nederland 1870–1940 [Architecture and Public Housing the Netherlands 1870–1940] (Nijmegen 1980).

S. van de Casteele–Schweitzer and D. Voldman. "Historiens et temoins" [Historians and Witnesses], *IVme Colloque international d'Histore orale* (Aix en Provence 1982), pp. 74–82.

Cathalogus van de tentoonstelling: Het verdwijnend Amsterdamsch Ghetto in Beeld, gehouden in het Stedelijk Museum van 29 mei t/m 4 juni 1916 [Catalogue of the Exhibition: The Disappearing Amsterdam Ghetto in Pictures, held at the Stedelijk Museum 29 May to 4 June 1916] (Amsterdam 1916).

Centraal overleg in arbeidszaken voor werkgeversstanden [Central Advisory Committee on Labor Matters for Employers' Positions] *Enkele opmerking over de omstandigheden die van invloed zijn op de vestiging en ontwikkeling van de industrie in Amsterdam* (Amsterdam 1928).

L. Chevalier. *Classes laborieuses et classe dangereuses à Paris, pendant la première moité du XIXe siècle* [Working Classes and Dangerous Classes in Paris during the First Half of the Nineteenth Century] (Paris 1978).

M. O. Cohen and A. van Praag. *Joodse vereenigingen op sociaal gebied* [Jewish Social Organizations] (Amsterdam 1942). Research sponsored by the Jewish Council, 28 August 1941 to 11 February 1942.

H. F. Cohen. *Om de verniewing van het socialisme. De politieke oriëntatie van de Nederlandse sociaal-democratie 1919–1930* [On the Renewal of Socialism. The Political Orientation of the Dutch Social Democracy 1919–1930] (Leiden 1974).

S. Coronel. "Iets over het verschil in levens verhoudingen tusschen Joden en Christenen" [On the Difference in Social Relations between Jews and Christians], *Schat der Gezondheid* (1864).

H. Dahmen. "Psychoanalysis as Social Theory," *Telos*, no. 32 (Summer 1977).

J. C. van Dam. *Sociaal logboek 1900–1960. Spiegel van vooruitgang* [Social Log 1900–1960. Mirror of Progress] (Amsterdam 1959).

_____. *Poppetje gezien, kassie dicht, het levensrelaas van een amsterdamse jood* [Punch and Judy. The Life Story of an Amsterdam Jew] (Amstelveen 1983).

A. M. Vaz Dias. "De economische positie van het gros van de Amsterdamschen Joodsche bevolking voor 1795" [The Economic Position of the Majority of the Amsterdam Jewish Population before 1795], *Nieuw Israëlitisch Weekblad* (7 and 24 August, 7 September 1934).

_____. *Over den vermogenstoestand der Amsterdamschen Joden in de 17e en 18e eeuw* [The Property Assets of the Amsterdam Jews in the 17th and 18th Centuries] (Groningen 1936). Reprinted from *Tijdschrift voor Geschiedenis*, vol. 51, no. 2.

Dittrich and Würzner (eds.). *Nederland en het Duitse Exil 1933–1940* [The Netherlands and the German Exile 1933–1940] (Amsterdam 1982).

L. Dobroszcki and B. Kirschenblatt-Gimblet. *Image before My Eyes. A Photographic History of Jewish Life in Poland. 1864–1939* (New York 1977).

E. Dürkheim. *Le suicide. Étude du sociologie* [Suicide. A Sociological Study] (Paris 1897).

"Eenige gegevens omtrent het levensmiddelenbedrijf te Amsterdam" [Data Regarding the Foodstuffs Industry in Amsterdam], *Statistische mededeeling*, no. 114 (Amsterdam 1940).

S. van den Eewal. *Joodjes-leven, een vertelling uit den Amsterdamschen Jodenhoek* [Jewish Life, a Tale from the Amsterdam Jewish Quarter] (The Hague 1902).

C. Eitje. "Hoe staan wij tegenover onze jeugd?" [What Is Our Attitude toward Our Youth?], *Beis Jisroeil, Joodsche ons thuis. Jaarboekje 1923–24* [Beis Jisroeil, Our Jewish Home. Yearbook 1923–24]. This booklet can be found in the Documentatiearchief van de Sociale Raad (call number 400) of the Municipality of Amsterdam.

K. H. Fahlgren. *Sedaja, nahestehende und entgegengesetzte Begriffe im Alten Testament* [Tsedaka, Associated and Opposing Concepts in the Old Testament] (Uppsala 1932).

W. J. Fishman. *East End Jewish Radicals 1875–1914* (London 1975).

P. Frankel. *Prophesy and Politics. Socialism, Nationalism, and the Russian Jews, 1862–1917* (Cambridge 1981).

L. Frank van Loo. *"Den armen gegeven." Een beschrijving van armoede, armenzorg en sociale zekerheid in Nederland 1784–1965* ["Given the Poor." A Description of Poverty, Care for the Poor, and Social Security in the Netherlands 1784–1965] (Meppel and Amsterdam 1981).

S. Freud. *Zur Psychopathologie des Alltagslebens* [On the Psychopathology of Everyday Life] (London 1941). Various editions.

_____. "Die Verdrängung" [Repression], *Das Ich und das Es* (Frankfurt am Main 1960). Original publication 1915.

S. Friedländer. *Reflets sur le nazisme* (Paris 1982). English translation: *Reflections on Nazism. An Essay on Kitsch and Death* (New York 1984).

G. Fülbert. *Proletarische Partei und bürgerliche Literatur* [The Proletarian Party and Bourgeois Literature] (Neuwied and Berlin 1972), pp. 123–151. Translation in *Te Elfder Ure* , vol. 19, nos. 5 and 6 (Nijmegen 1972), pp. 204–227.

H. J. Gans. *The Urban Villagers. Group and Class in the Life of Italian Americans* (New York 1962).

_____. *The Levittowners* (London 1967).

_____. "Symbolic Ethnicity. The Future of Ethnic Groups and Cultures in America," in H. J. Gans (ed.), *On the Making of Americans. Essays in Honor of David Riesman* (Philadelphia 1979).

M. H. Gans. *Memorboek, platenatlas van het leven der joden in Nederland van de middeleeuwen tot 1940* [Book of Remembrances. A Pictorial Atlas of Jewish Life in the Netherlands from the Middle Ages to 1940] (Baarn 1970).

_____. *De oude Amsterdamse jodenhoek in foto's 1900–1940* [The Old Amsterdam Jewish Quarter in Photos 1900–1940] (Baarn 1974).

_____. *Het Nederlandse Jodendom—de sfeer waarin wij leefden. Karakter, traditie en sociale omstandigheden van het Nederlandse Jodendom voor de Tweede Wereldoorlog* [The Dutch Jewry—The Atmosphere in which We

Lived. Charater, Tradition, and Social Conditions of the Dutch Jewry before the Second World War] (Baarn 1985).

Gedenkschrift der Stichting Bouwfonds Handwerkers Vriendenkring [Memorial Volume of the Building Society of the Friends of the Common Laborer] (Amsterdam 1938).

E. Geisel. *Im Scheunenviertel. Bilde, Texte und Dokumente* [In the Shack Quarter. Pictures, Texts, and Documents] (Berlin 1980).

"Gestichtszorg voor oude lieden en andere volwassen behoeftigen" [Institutional Care for the Elderly and Other Adults in Need], *De Joodsche Invalide*, vol. 3 (January 1930).

I. Getzler. *Marlow, a Political Biography of a Russian Social Democrat* (Melbourne 1967).

Geurts and Messing (eds.), *Economische Ontwikkeling en Sociale Emancipatie II* [Economic Development and Social Emancipation II] (The Hague 1977).

L. Giebels. *De zionistische beweging in Nederland 1899–1941* [The Zionist Movement in the Netherlands 1899–1941] (Assen 1975).

J. R. Gillis, *Youth in History. Tradition and Change in European Age Relations, 1770 to Present* (New York 1981).

G. Gimpel. *Amsterdam Oud en Nieuw* [Amsterdam Old and New] (Amsterdam 1925). Illustrated with drawings from H. Heuff and reproductions from old drawings and paintings; Foreword by R. W. P. de Vries.

G. Ginzberg. *Le fromage et les vers, l'univers d'un meunier du XVI siécle* [Cheese and Maggots. The World of a Miller in the Sixteenth Century] (Paris 1980).

M. Glas–Larsson. *Ich will reden. Tragik und Banalität in Theresienstadt und Auschwitz* [I Want to Speak. Tragedy and Banality in Theresienstadt and Auschwitz] (Molden and Vienna 1981).

J. Gompers. "Joodsche zwaluwnesten" [Jewish Swallows' Nests], *De Vrijdagavond* , vol. 3, no. 6 (7 May 1926).

J. Gompers and F. Cohen. *Zwerftochten door Klein Jeruzalem* [Wanderings through Little Jerusalem], articles from *Nieuw Israëlitisch Weekblad* (Amsterdam 1936). Collected in 1982 in the Bibliotheca Rosenthaliana.

S. Goudsmit. *De een zijn dood* [One Man's Death] (Amsterdam 1938).

_____. *Fragmenten uit het dagboek van Sam Goudsmit, 6 april 1945 tot 13 februari 1946* [Fragments from the Diary of Sam Goudsmit, 6 April 1945 to 13 February 1946] (Assen 1970).

W. A. de Graaf. *Grondslagen voor de stedebouwkundige ontwikkeling van Amsterdam* [Foundations for the City Planning Development of Amsterdam] (Amsterdam 1933).

D. I. Grimberg. *Housing in the Netherlands 1900–1940* (Delft 1977). Unpublished.

D. Groeneveld. "Beschouwingen over het distributiebeleid" [Considerations Regarding the Distribution Policy], *De Socialistische Gids* (1936), pp. 257–269.

M. Grunewald (ed.). *Die Hygiene der Juden* [Jewish Public Health] (1911).

M. Halbwachs. *Les cadres sociaux de la Mémoire* [The Social Framework of Memory] (Paris 1925).

_____. *La Mémoire Collective* [Collective Memory] (Paris 1950).

G. J. Harmsen. *Blauwe en Rode jeugd. Ontstaan en teruggang van de Nederlandse jeugdbeweging tussen 1853 en 1940* [Blue and Red Youth. The Origin and Decline of the Dutch Youth Movement between 1853 and 1940] (Assen 1961).

_____. *Hamer of aambeeld, één en ander uit de geschiedenis van de Amsterdamse arbeidersbeweging ter gelegenheid van het negentig jarig bestaan van de Industrie Bond NVV, afdeling Amsterdam* [Hammer or Anvil. A Thing or Two from the History of the Amsterdam Labor Movement in Honor of the Nintieth Anniversary of the Industrial Union NVV of Amsterdam] (Amsterdam 1979).

L. Hartveld, F. de Jong Edz., and D. Kuperus. *De Arbeiders Jeugd Centrale AJC 1918–1940 / 1945–1959* [The Labor Youth Central Council AJC 1918–1940 / 1945–1959] (Amsterdam 1982).

J. Hauptmann. "Images of Women in the Talmud," in R. Radford Ruether (ed.), *Religion and Sexism. Images of Women in the Jewish and Christian Tradition* (New York 1974), pp. 184–213.

H. Heertje. "Het ateliermeisje van Amsterdam" [The Sweatshop Girl of Amsterdam], *Mensch en Maatschappij*, vol. 10, no. 1 (1934). Reprinted in Bovenkerk and Brunt, *De rafelrand van Amsterdam* (Meppel 1977), pp. 121–143.

_____. *De diamantbewerkers van Amsterdam* [The Diamond Workers of Amsterdam] (Amsterdam 1936).

H. Heijermans. *Sabbath, eene studie* [Sabbath, a Study] (Amsterdam 1903).

_____. *n' Jodenstreek* [A Jewish Trick] (Amsterdam 1904).

_____. *Diamantstad* [Diamond City] (Amsterdam 1906).

L. M. Hermans. *Krotten en sloppen. Een onderzoek naar de wooningtoestand te Amsterdam, ingesteld in opdracht van de Amsterdamschen Bestuurdersbond* [Slums and Alleys. A Study of the Living Conditions in Amsterdam, Commissioned by the Amsterdam Governors' Council] (Amsterdam 1901; reprinted Amsterdam 1974). With drawings by Alb. P. Hahn.

J. Herwaarden (ed.). *Lof der Historie. Opstellen over geschiedenis en maatschappij* [In Praise of History. Essays on History and Society] (Rotterdam 1973).

J. S. Hessen. *Samen jong zijn* [Being Young Together] (Assen 1965).

F. P. Hiegentlich. "Reflections on the Relationship between the Dutch Haskalah and the German Haskalah." In J. Michman (ed.), *Dutch Jewish History* (Jerusalem 1984), pp. 207–219.

J. M. Hillesum. "Vereenigingen bij de Portugeesche en Spannsche joden te Amsterdam in de 17e en 18e eeuw" [Associations of Portuguese and Spanish Jews in Amsterdam in the 17th and 18th centuries], *Eerste Jaarboek der Vereeniging Amstelodamum* (Amsterdam 1902).

S. Hobbs. "Psychological Aspects of Oral History: Content from the Process of

Memory," in P. Joutard et al. (eds.), *IVme Colloque international d'Histoire orale* (Aix en Provence 1982), pp. 110–123.

M. de Hond. *Ghettokiekjes* [Snapshots from the Ghetto] (Amsterdam 1909).

_____. *Kiekjes. Jodenbreestraat–Waterlooplein* [Snapshots. Jodenbree Street–Waterloo Square] (Amsterdam 1926).

_____. *Dr. Meijer de Hond. Bloemlezing uit zijn werk* [Dr. Meijer de Hond. A Selection of His Writings] (Amsterdam 1951/5711).

R. Hoogewoud–Verschoor. *Van zending tot gesprek? De laatste jaren van de Vereeniging voor Israël 1932–1942, en het begin van de Hervormde Raad voor Kerk en Israël 1942–1945* [From Mission to Discussion? The Last Years of the Association for Israel 1932–1942, and the Beginning of the Reformed Council for Church and Israel 1942–1945] (Landsmeer 1982). Unpublished manuscript.

P. Hoogland. *Vijf en twintig jaren Sociaal-Democratie in de Hoofdstad* [Twenty-five Years of Social Democracy in the Capital City] (Amsterdam 1928).

V. R. A. D. Huberts. *De Amsterdamse venters, een sociografische monographie* [The Amsterdam Peddlers. A Sociographic Monograph] (Amsterdam 1940).

E. Hueting, Fr. de Jong Edz., and R. Ney. *Ik moet, het is mijn roeping: een politieke biografie van Pieter Jelles Troelstra* [I Must, It Is My Calling: A Political Biography of Pieter Jelles Troelstra] (Amsterdam 1981).

De huisvesting van asociale gezinnen te Amsterdam [Housing for Antisocial Families in Amsterdam] (Amsterdam 1929). Published by the Gemeentelijke Woningdienst.

J. M. L. Hunter. *Memory, Facts and Fallacies* (London 1975).

P. Hyman. *From Dreyfus to Vichy. The Remaking of French Jewry 1906–1939* (New York 1979).

L'illusion Biographique. Actes de la Recherche en sciences sociales [The Biographical Illusion. Proceedings of Research in the Social Sciences], nos. 62, 63 (Paris 1986).

A. van Iterson. *Armenzorg bij Joden in Palestina van 100 v. Chr.–200 n. Chr.* [Care for the Poor by Jews in Palestine from 100 BC–200 AD] (Leiden 1911).

Jaarverslagen van de Gemeente Amsterdam, 1920–1940 [Annual Reports of the Municipality of Amsterdam, 1920–1940].

T. Jansen and J. Rogier. *Kunstbeleid in Amsterdam 1920–1940. Dr. E. Boekman en de socialistische gemeentepolitiek* [The Art of Leadership in Amsterdam 1920–1940. Dr. E. Boekman and Socialist City Politics] (Nijmegen 1983).

G. Janouch. *Gespräche mit Kafka* [Conversations with Kafka] (Frankfurt 1968).

J. S. Jessurum Cardozo. "De Joodsche Jeugd en het rijksopvoedingswezen" [The Jewish Youth and the National Education of Orphans], *De Vrijdagavond*, vol. 3, no. 1 (2 April 1926).

F. de Jong Edz. *"Van ruw tot geslepen," de culturele betekenis van de Algemene Nederlandse Diamantbewerkers Bond in de geschiedenis van Amsterdam* [From Rough to Polished, the Cultural Meaning of the Diamond Workers' Union in the History of Amsterdam] (Amsterdam 1955).

L. de Jong. *Het Koninkrijk der Nederlanden in de Tweede Wereldoorlog* [The Kingdom of the Netherlands during the Second World War] (The Hague 1969), part 1, "Voorspel."

P. Joutard et al. (eds.). *IVe Colloque international d'Histoire Oral* (Aix en Provence 1982).

J. van der Kar. *Joods verzet, terugblik op de periode rond de 2e wereldoorlog* [Jewish Resistance, a Retrospect of the Period around the Second World War] (Amsterdam 1981).

_____. *De geschiedenis van de markt- en straathandel* [The History of the Open-Air Market and Street Peddling] (Amsterdam 1982).

B. Kautsky. "Haushaltstatistik der wiener Arbeiterkammer 1925–1934" [Household Statistics of the Viennese Labor Chamber 1925–1934], *International Review for Social History*, vol. 2, supplement (Leiden 1937), pp. 1–247.

G. P. Keers. *De politieke functie van stedelijke structuurplannen. Amsterdam van AUP naar Compacte Stad, een politicologisch essay* [The Political Function of City Planning. Amsterdam from AUP to Compact City, an Essay in Political Science] (Amsterdam 1984). Doctoral dissertation.

I. G. Keesing. "Joodsch Sociaal Werk" [Jewish Social Work], *Gedenkboek 50-jarig bestaan Centraal Blad voor Israëliten* (Amsterdam 1935).

A. Keppler. "De krotopruiming in Amsterdam" [Cleaning up the Slums in Amsterdam], *Tijdschrift voor Volkshuisvesting en Stedebouw* , vol. 4, no. 7 (1929).

R. Kisch–Spitz. *Herinneringen* [Reminiscences] (Amsterdam 1952).

R. Kistenmaker, M. Wagenaar, and J. van Assendelft. *Amsterdam marktstad* [Amsterdam Market City] (Amsterdam 1984).

S. E. Kleerekoper. "Het Joodse proletariaat in het Amsterdam van de 19e eeuw" [The Jewish Proletariat in 19th Century Amsterdam], *Studia Rosenthalia*, vol. 1, no. 1 (1967), pp. 97–109.

J. Kocka. "Arbeiterkultur als Forschungsthema" [Working-Class Culture as a Research Topic], *Geschichte und Gesellschaft. Zeitschrift für historische Sozialwissenschaft*, vol. 5 (1979), pp. 5–12.

_____. "Klassen oder Kultur?" [Classes or Culture?], *Merkur*, vol. 36 (1982).

D. Koker. "Joodse buurtvereeniginen" [Jewish Neighborhood Societies], *40-Jaarig bestaan van het Centraal Blad voor Israëliten*, memorial issue (1925).

J. H. Korteweg. "Statistiek van difterie en croup" [Statistics for Diphtheria and Croup], *Nederlandisch Tijdschrift voor Geneeskunst*, part 2 (1885).

J. Kroes. *Het paleis aan de laan. De geschiedenis van het bondsgebouw van de ANDB* [The Palace on the Lane. The History of the Union Building of the ANDB] (Amsterdam 1979).

J. Lacan. *Le moi dans la théorie de Freud et dans la technique de la psychoanalyse* [The Me in Freudian Theory and in the Technique of Psychoanalysis] (Paris 1978).

Le-Ezrath Ha-Am, het Volk ter Hulpe. Het eerste Joodse Blad in 1945 [Le-Ezrath

Ha-Am, the People of Hulpe. The First Jewish Newspaper in 1945] (Amsterdam 1985).

"Leven in de Lepelstraat" [Life in the Lepel Street], *Het Parool* (6 September 1983).

N. Levin. *While Messiah Tarried. Jewish Socialist Movements 1871–1917* (New York 1977).

J. Leydesdorff. *Bijdrage tot de speciale psychologie van het Joodsche Volk* [Contributions to the Special Psychology of the Jewish People] (Groningen 1919).

S. Leydesdorff. *Verborgen arbeid, vergeten arbeid. Een verkenning in de geschiedenis van de vrouwenarbeid rond negentienhonderd* [Hidden Labor, Forgotten Labor. A Reconnaissance of the History of Female Labor around 1900] (Assen 1977).

———. "Patterns of Cultural Change: The Jewish Proletariat in Amsterdam 1918–1940." In P. Joutard et al. (eds.), *IVme Colloque International d'Histoire orale* (Aix en Provence 1982).

———. "Geheugen, getuigen en herinneren. Voorbeelden uit een onderzoek naar het Amsterdamse Joodse proletariaat" [Memory, Witnesses, and Reminiscences. Examples from Research among the Amsterdam Jewish Proletariat]. In du Bois–Reymond and Wagemakers (eds.), *Mondelinge geschiedenis. Over theorie en praktijk van het gebruik van mondelinge bronnen*, pp. 80–101.

———. "In Search of the Picture. Jewish Proletarians between the Two World Wars." In Michman (ed.), *Dutch Jewish History* (Jerusalem 1984).

———. "Maakten zij de wereld leefbaar? Korte geschiedenis van de SDAP in het joodse bolwerk Amsterdam–Oost voor en na de tweede wereldoorlog" [Did They Make the World Better? A Short History of the SDAP in the Jewish Bulwark of East Amsterdam before and after the Second World War]. In M. van Amerongen et al., *Voor buurt en beweging. Negentig jaar sociaal-democratie tussen IJ en Amstel.*

———. "Identification and Power in the Formation of the Romantic Memory," *V Colloqui Internacional d'historia oral* (Barcelona 1985).

———. "The Creation of the Modern Family. Jewish Working-Class Women in the Thirties and the Changes in Their Lives." Paper for the Anglo–Dutch Conference on Working-Class Culture, September 1986.

———. "Nostalgie als droom en werkelijkheid" [Nostalgia as Dream and Reality], *Raster*, vol. 36 (Amsterdam 1986).

P. F. Maas. *Sociaal Democratische Gemeentepolitiek in katholiek Nijmegen 1894–1927* [Social Democratic Municipal Politics in Catholic Nijmegen] (Nijmegen 1974).

P. Macherey. *Pour une théorie de la production literaire* [Toward a Theory of Literary Production] (Paris 1966).

M. Marrus. *The Politics of Assimilation. The French Jewish Community at the Time of the Dreyfus Affair* (New York 1971).

J. Meijer. *Het verdwenen ghetto, wandelingen door de Amsterdamse Jodenhoek*

[The Vanished Ghetto. Walks through the Amsterdam Jewish Quarter] (Amsterdam 1948).

A. Mellink. "Roosje Vos (1869–1932)" (in Dutch). In *Cahiers over de geschedenis van de CPN* (January 1984), pp. 123–135.

J. Mendes (pseudonym of Is. Querido). *Het geslacht der Santeljanos* [The Lineage of the Santeljanos] (Amsterdam 1928).

E. Mendelsohn. *Class Struggle in the Pale. The Formative Years of the Jewish Workers' Movement in Tsarist Russia* (Cambridge 1970).

J. ter Meulen. *Huisvesting van armen te Amsterdam* [Housing for the Poor in Amsterdam] (Amsterdam 1903).

J. Michelet. *Journal, tome 1, 1828–1848* (in French) (Paris 1959). Reprint.

D. Michman. "De joodse emigratie en de Nederlandse reactie daarop tussen 1933 en 1940" [The Jewish Emigration and the Dutch Reaction between 1933 and 1940]. In Dittrich and Würzner (eds.), *Nederland en het Duitse Exil 1933–1940* (Amsterdam 1982).

M. Minco. *Het bittere kruid. Een kleine kroniek* [Bitter Herbs. A Short Chronicle] (Amsterdam 1957).

A. and M. Mitscherlich. *Die Unfähigkeit zu trauern* [The Inability to Mourn].

A. Mitzman. "Het beschavingsoffensief: mentaliteit, cultuur en psyche" [The Push to Civilize: Mentality, Culture, and Psyche], *Sociologische Tijdschrift*, vol. 13, no. 2 (September 1986).

O. Montagne, J. Winkler, et al. *"Doctor Henri Polak." Van het vuur dat in hem brandde* ["Doctor Henri Polak." Of the Fire that Burned in Him] (Amsterdam 1948).

J.-P. Moreau. "Le Memoire, ses blocages, leurs consequences" [Memory Blocks, Their Consequences]. In P. Joutard et al. (eds.), *IV Colloque international d'Histoire orale* (Aix en Provence 1982), pp. 68–74.

K. D. Müller. "De filosoof in het theater" [The Philosopher in the Theater], *Te Elfder Uur 19* , vol. 22, no. 3 (1975).

Nederlands Israëlitisch armbestuur [Dutch Israelite Public Assistance Committee]. *Verslag over de jaaren 1915–1919* [Report on the Years 1915–1919] (Amsterdam 1920).

L. Niethammer (ed.). *Lebenserfahrung und kollektives gedächtnis. Die Praxis der "Oral History"* [Life Experience and Collective Memory. The Practice of "Oral History"] (Frankfurt am Main 1983).

_____. "Fragen–Antworten–Fragen. Methodische erfahrungen und Erwägungen zur Oral History" [Questions–Answers–Questions. Methodological Experiences and Considerations Regarding Oral History]. In Niethammer and von Plato (eds.), *Wir kriegen jetzt andere Zeiten. Auf der Suche nach der Erfahrung des Volkes in nachfashcistischen Ländern. Lebensgeschichte und Sozialkultur im Ruhrgebiet 1930–1960* (Berlin and Bonn 1985).

A. van Ommeren and A. Scherphuis. "De Crèche, 1942–1943" [Daycare, 1942–1943], *Vrij Nederland* (18 January 1986).

G. Oznowicz. "Afscheid van de jodenhoek, de doodsklok heeft geluid" [Goodbye to the Jewish Quarter, the Deathknell Has Sounded], *Het Vrije Volk* (7 January 1956).

_____. "De Jodenhoek vroeger" [The Jewish Quarter in Former Days], *Het Vrije Volk* (2–24 November 1956). Various articles.

L. Passerini. "Work Ideology and Consensus under Italian Fascism," *History Workshop*, no. 8 (Autumn 1979), pp. 82–209.

_____. *Torino Operaia e Fascismo* [The Turin Opera and Fascism] (Rome and Bari 1984).

S. J. Philips (ed.). *Gedenkboek ter gelegenheid van het honderdjarig bestaan van het Nederlands Israëlietisch Armbestuur te Amsterdam 1825–1925* [Memorial Volume for the 100th Anniversary of the Nederlands Israëlite Charity Committee of Amsterdam 1825–1925] (no publisher).

P. H. Pinkhof. "Onderzoek naar de kindersterfte onder de geneeskundig-bedeelden te Amsterdam" [Study of Child Mortality among the Medically Indigent of Amsterdam], *Nederlandsch Tijdschrift voor Geneeskunde* (1907), part 1, pp. 1174–1183.

H. Polak (possibly). *De dreigende verplaatsing van de Amsterdamsche diamantindustrie naar Antwerpen. Een woord aan de burgerij van Amsterdam door het hoofdbestuur van de Algemene Nederlandsche Diamantbewerkers Bond* [The Threat of the Diamond Industry Moving to Antwerp. A Few Words to the Citizens of Amsterdam from the Management of the General Dutch Diamond Polishers Union] (Amsterdam 1902).

_____. *De invloed van den oorlog op de diamantindustrie* [The Impact of the War on the Diamond Industry] (Purmerend 1922).

_____. "Het Amsterdamsche getto" [The Amsterdam Ghetto], *De Vrijdagavond* [The Friday Evening], vol. 1, part 1, no. 19 (1 August 1924). Another part with the same title was published in no. 26 in 1926.

_____. *Amsterdam die groote stad. Een bijdrage tot de kennis van het Amsterdamse Volksleven in de XIXe en XXe eeuw* [Amsterdam That Great City. A Contribution to our Knowledge of Amsterdam Daily Life in the 19th and 20th Centuries] (Amsterdam 1936). With an introduction by W. de Vlugt.

G. Pommata. "La storia della donne, una questione di confine" [The Story of a Woman, a Question of Confinement]. In N. Trafaglia (ed.), pp. 1435–1469.

A. H. Pontfoort. "De kleedingindustrie in Amsterdam" [The Garment Industry in Amsterdam], *Kwartaalbericht Bureau van statistiek der Gemeente Amsterdam* (October–December 1952).

Popular Memory Group. "Popular Memory: Theory, Politics, Method." In *Making Histories, Studies in History-Writing and Politics* (Birmingham 1982), pp. 205–253.

A. Portelli. "Dividing the World: Sound and Space in Cultural Transition," in P. Joutard et al. (eds.), *IV Colloque international d'Histoire orale* (Aix en Provence 1982), pp. 399–415.

_____. *Biografia di una città. Storia e Racconto. Terni 1830–1985* [Biography of a City. Stories and Tales of Racconto, 1830–1985] (Turin 1985).

S. E. van Praag. *Jeruzalem van het Westen* [The Jerusalem of the West] (The Hague 1961).

_____. *Mokum aan de Amstel, een goed huwelijk* [A Jewish City on the Amstel, a Good Marriage] (Antwerp 1976).

J. Presser. *Ondergang, de vervolging en verdelging van het Nederlandse Jodendom 1940–1945* (The Hague 1965). Translated into English by Arnold Pomerans, *The Destruction of the Dutch Jews* (New York 1969).

A. Querido. *Het Zeeburgerdorp. Een sociaal-psychiatrische studie* [The Village of Zeeburg. A Socio-Psychiatric Study] (Amsterdam 1933).

E. Querido. *Het Geslacht der Santeljanos* [The Lineage of Santeljano].

Is. Querido. *Levensgang, Roman uit de Diamantberwerkerswereld* [Life Course. A Novel of the Diamond Workers' World] (Amsterdam 1900).

_____. *Het Volk God's, Van armen en rijken, Amsterdamsch epos* [God's Chosen People. From Poor and Rich, an Amsterdam Epic] (Amsterdam 1930).

F. Raphael. "Le travail de la mémoire, et les limites de l'histoire orale" [The Job of Memory and the Limits of Oral History], *Annales, Economies, Societés, Civilisations*, vol. 35, no. 1 (1980).

D. Rappaport. *Emotions and Memory* (New York 1971).

Rapport der commissie tot onderzoek van het Joodsche reclasseringsvraagstuk [Report of the Commission for Researching the Question of Jewish Reclassification] (1931).

Rapport Gemeentecommissie tot bevordering van de ontwikkeling der plaatselijke industrie [Report of the Municipal Commission for Encouraging Development of Local Industry] (Amsterdam 1937).

Rapport van de commissie voor den straathandel [Report of the Commission for Street Trading] (Amsterdam 1946).

N. Redeker Bisdom. *Antwoord op de prijsvraag uitgeschreven in het jaar 1865 'Op welke wijze zou Amsterdam het beste kunnen worden uitgebreid'* [Competition in the Year 1865: How Can Amsterdam Be Expanded]. Afdeling Amsterdam van de Maatschappij tot Bevordering der Bouwkunst.

A. de Regt. *Arbeidersgezinnen en beschavingsarbeid. Ontwikkelingen in Nederland 1870–1940* [Workers' Families and the Work of Civilizing. Developments in the Netherlands 1870–1940] (Meppel 1984).

C. Reijnders. *Van "Joodsche Natiën" tot Joodse Nederlanders. Een onderzoek naar getto en assimilatieverschijnselen tussen 1600 en 1942* [From "Jewish Nations" to Jewish Dutchmen. A Study of Ghetto and Assimilation Phenomena between 1600 and 1942] (Amsterdam 1969).

H. J. Reijs. *De huisvesting van ontoelaatbare gezinnen in Amsterdam 1915–1945* [The Housing of Unacceptable Families in Amsterdam 1915–1945] (Amsterdam 1979). Dissertation.

J. Reitsma. "Prijsafspraken en gemeentepolitiek" [Price Agreements and Municipal Politics], *Socialistische Gids* (1922), pp. 1124–1133.

Report on the Conditions of Jewish Social Work in Holland (Amsterdam, June 1936).

S. Rodriguez de Miranda. *In de branding van de tijd, een pleidooi voor autonomie en goede financiën der gemeenten door* . . . [In the Breakers of Time. A Plea for Autonomy and Good Finances for the Municipalities through . . .] (Amsterdam, no date). After 1929.

———. "De economische taak van de gemeente" [The Economic Task of the Municipality], *Syllabus cursus sociaal democratische gemeentepolitiek* (Amsterdam 1939). Published by the Instituut voor Arbeitersonwikkeling.

———. *De weg van producent naar consument* [The Path from Producer to Consumer] Amsterdam (1931).

R. Roegholt. *Amsterdam in de twintigste eeuw* [Amsterdam in the 20th Century] (Utrecht and Amsterdam 1975).

C. Roland. *Du ghetto à l'Occident, Deux générations yiddisches en France* [The Ghetto of the West. Two Yiddish Generations in France] (Paris 1962). Preface by L. Chevalier.

H. Roland Holst–van der Schalk. *Kapitaal en arbeid in Nederland* [Capital and Labor in the Netherlands] (Amsterdam 1902).

G. van Roon. *Protestants Nederland en Duitsland 1933–1941* [Protestants in the Netherlands and in Germany 1933–1941] (Utrecht and Antwerp 1973).

P. de Rooy. *Werklozenzorg en werkloosheidsbestrijding 1917–1940. Landelijk en Amsterdams beleid* [Unemployment Assistance and Unemployment Abatement 1917–1940. National Policy and the Policy in Amsterdam] (Amsterdam 1979).

E. Ross. "Survival Networks: Women's Neighborhood Sharing in London before World War I," *History Workshop*, no. 15 (1983), pp. 4–28.

J. H. Rössing. *Verdwijnend oud Amsterdam, met teekeningen van M. Monnickendam* [Vanishing Old Amsterdam, with Drawings from M. Monnickendam] (Amsterdam 1916).

E. la Roy Ladurie. *Montaillou, village occitan de 1294 à 1324* [Montaillou, Village of the Langue d'Oc from 1294 to 1324] (Paris 1975).

De S. A. Rudelsheimstichting, herinneringsschrift ter gelegenheid der opening van haar internaat Beth Azarja te Hilversum, 1925 [The S. A Rudelsheim Foundation Memorial Volume in Honor of the Opening of Her Boarding School Beth Azarja in Hilversum, 1925].

R. R. Ruether (ed.). *Religion and Sexism. Images of Women in the Jewish and Christian Traditions* (New York 1974).

H. Safrian and R. Sieder. "Gassenkinder—Strassenkämpfer. Zur politische Sozialisation einer Arbeitergeneration in Wien 1900 bis 1938" [Street Urchins—Street Struggles. The Political Socialization of a Working Class Generation in Vienna 1900 to 1938], in Niethammer and von Plato, pp. 117–152.

B. Sajet. *Een leven lang Ben Sajet. Verteld aan Hans Fels* [Ben Sajet's Long Life. As Told to Hans Fels] (Baarn 1977).

R. H. Saltet and Ph. Falkenburg. "Kindersterfte in Nederland in de jaren 1881–1905" [Child Mortality in the Netherlands during the Years 1881–1905], *Mededeeling nr. 19 van het Bureau der Statistiek van de Gemeente Amsterdam* (1907).

R. Samuel. *East End Underworld. Chapters in the Life of Arthur Harding* (London 1981).

_____. "History and Theory." In Samuel (ed.), *People's History and Socialist Theory* (London 1981), pp. XL–XVI

J. Sanders. *Ziekte en sterfte bij Joden en niet-Joden te Amsterdam* [Disease and Mortality among Jews and non-Jews in Amsterdam] (Amsterdam 1918).

I. Santcroos. "Interview met S. Rodriguez de Miranda" [Interview with S. Rodriguez de Miranda], *De Vrijdagavond* (31 September 1925).

_____. "Het aandeel der Amsterdamsche joden in de straathandel" [The Share of the Amsterdam Jews in Street Vending], *De Vrijdagavond* (24 October 1930).

S. Santen. *Deze viandige wereld* [This Hostile World] (Amsterdam 1972).

B. Sapir. "Lieberman et le socialisme russe" [Lieberman and Russian Socialism], *International Review for Social History*, vol. 3 (Leiden 1938), pp. 25–89.

L. H. Sarlouis. "Joodse jeugdorganisatie" [Jewish Youth Organization], *Centraal Blad voor Israëliten in Nederland. Gedenkboek ter gelegenheid van het 50-jarig bestaan . . .* (Amsterdam 1935), pp. 10–11.

A. J. van Schie. "Restitution or Economic Rights after 1945." In Michman (ed.), *Dutch Jewish History* (Jerusalem 1984), pp. 401–421.

I. Schöffer. "Nederland en de joden in de jaren dertig in historisch perspectief" [The Netherlands and the Jews in the 1930s in Historical Perspective]. In Dittrich and Würzner,eds.

A. Schwartsbart. *Le dernier des Justes* [The Last Just Man] (Paris 1959).

M. Schwegman. "'Oral History: een kijkje in de keuken" [Oral History: A Peek in the Kitchen], *Groniek*, vo. 12, no. 64 (October 1979), pp. 23–25.

_____. "Lagen der werkelijkheid, Italiaanse en Nederlandse vrouwen tijdens het interbellum" [Layers of Reality. Italian and Dutch Women between the Two Wars], *Tweede Jaarboek voor Vrouwengeschiedenis* (Nijmegen 1981), pp. 110–132.

M. Sluyser. *Voordat it het vergeet* [Before I Forget It] (Amsterdam 1947).

_____. *Het klinkt van so ver* [It Sounds So Far Away] (Amsterdam 1959).

_____. *Er groeit gras in de Weesperstraat* [Grass Grows in Weesper Street] (Amsterdam 1962).

_____. *Amsterdam je hebt een zoute smaak* [Amsterdam, You Have a Salty Taste] (Amsterdam 1964).

F. Smit. "De Gemeente als Vliegwiel voor Volkshuisvesting" [The Municipality as Flywheel for Housing], *Wonen Tabk* (14 July 1973).

N. H. Snaith. *The Distinctive Ideas of the Old Testament* (London 1950).

Het Socialisatievraagstuk. Rapport uitgebracht door een commissie aangewezen uit de SDAP [The Question of Socialization. Report by a Commission Appointed from the SDAP] (Amsterdam 1920).

L. Soloweitschik. *Un prolétariat Meconnu, etude sur la situation sociale et éco-*

nomique des ouvriers juifs [An Unknown Proletariat. Study of the Social and Economic Situation of the Jewish Working Class] (Brussels 1898).

W. Sombart. *Die Juden und das Wirtschaftsleben* [The Jews and Economic Life] (Leipzig 1911).

G. Stedman–Jones. "Working-Class Culture and Working-Class Politics in London 1870–1900: Notes on the Remaking of a Working Class," *Journal of Social History*, vol. 7 (1975), pp. 460–508.

H. B. J. Stegeman and J. P. Vorsteveld. *Het joodse werkdorp in de Wieringermeer 1934–1941* [The Jewish Work Village in Wieringermeer 1934–1941] (Zutphen 1984).

G. Steiner. *Language and Silence. Essays on Language, Literature, and the Inhuman* (New York 1967).

B. H. Stephan."Sterfte en ziekte by Joden en niet-Joden" [Mortality and Disease among Jews and non-Jews], *Nederlandsch Tijdschrift voor Geneeskunde* (1904), part 2, pp. 1631–1654.

H. L. Strack and P. Billerbeck (eds.). *Kommentar zum Neuen Testament aus Talmud und Midrasch* [New Testament Commentaries from the Talmud and the Midrasch] (Munich, no date).

S. Stuurman. *Kapitalisme, verzuiling en patriarchaat. Aspecten van de ontwikkeling van de moderne staat in Nederland* [Capitalism, Religious Segregation, and Patriarchy. Aspects of the Development of the Modern State in the Netherlands] (Nijmegen 1983).

Syllabus cursus sociaal democratische gemeentepolitiek [Syllabus Course Social Democratic Municipality Policy] (Amsterdam 1939).

J. Talsma. "Concept-lijnen voor historische interviews" [Conceptual Lines for Historical Interviews], *Transcript*, no. 3 (May 1980), pp. 1—13.

_____. (ed.). *Papers Presented to the International Oral History Conference* (Amsterdam 1980).

F. A. Theilhaber. "Die Sterblichkeit der Juden" [Mortality of Jews], in M. Grunewald (ed.), *Die Hygiene der Juden* [Jewish Public Health] (1911).

_____. *Die Schädigung der Rasse durch soziales und wirtschaftliches Aufsteigen* [Racial Damage Caused by Moving Up in Society and Economic Improvement] (Berlin 1914).

P. Thompson. *The Voice of the Past* (Oxford 1978).

_____. (ed.). *Our Common History. The Transformation of Europe* (London 1982).

H. C. van Tiel. *Amsterdam Oost tussen Amstel en spoorbaan richting Hilversum* [East Amsterdam between the Amstel and the Train Tracks to Hilversum] (Amsterdam 1967). Published by the Gemeentelijk Bureau voor Jeugdzaken.

Tien jaren arbeid van "Sjaloum Weringous" 1922–1932 [Ten Years of Labor from "Shalom Weringous" 1922–1932] (Amsterdam 1932).

Th. van Tijn. "De Algemeene Nederlandsche Diamantbewerkersbond (ANDB): het succes en zijn verklaring" [The General Dutch Diamond Workers Union

(ANDB); An Explanation of its Success], *Bijdragen en Mededeelingen Betreffende de Geschiedenis der Nederlanden (BMGN)* , vol. 88, no. 3 (1973).

_____. "Geschiedenis van de Amsterdamse diamanthandel en -nijverheid" [History of the Amsterdam Diamond Industry], *Tijdschrift voor Geschiedenis*, vol. 87 (1974), pp. 16–69 and 160–201.

_____. "Voorlopige notities over het ontstaan van het moderne klassenbewustzijn in Nederland" [Preliminary Notes on the Origin of Modern Class Consciousness in the Netherlands]. In Geurts and Messing (eds.), pp. 93–109.

N. Trafaglia (ed.). *Il mondo contamporeaneo. Gli Instrumenti della ricerca* [The Modern World. Research Instruments], vol. 10, part 2

A. Veffer. *Statistische gegevens van de Joden in Nederland,.Deel I. Statistiche gegevens van de Joden in Amsterdam waarin reeds opgenomen enkele voorlopige cijfers van de Joden in Nederland* [Statistical Data on the Jews in the Netherlands, Part I. Statistical Data on the Jews in Amsterdam] (Amsterdam 1942).

C. Vegh. *Je ne lui ai pas dit au revoir. Des enfants de déportés parlent* [I Never Said Goodbye to Him. The Children of Deportees Speak Up] (Paris 1979).

C. A. van der Velde. *"De ANDB." Een overzicht van zijn ontstaan, zijne ontwikkeling en zijne beteekenis* [The ANDB. An Overview of Its Origin, Development, and Importance] (Amsterdam 1925).

J. A. Verdoorn. *Het gezondheidswezen in Amsterdam in de 19e eeuw* [Public Health in Amsterdam in the Nineteenth Century] (Utrecht and Antwerp 1965).

Verslagen van de Kamer van Koophandel 1920–1940 [Reports from the Chamber of Commerce 1920–1940].

Vijf en twintig jaar samenwerking in den Armenraad, gedenkschrift uitgegeven tgv. de 25-jarige werkzaamheid van het Bureau van den Armenraad te Amsterdam [Twenty-five Years of Cooperation in the Public Assistance Committee, a Memorial Volume Published in Honor of the 25 Years of Activity of the Bureau of Public Assistance in Amsterdam] (Amsterdam 1939).

J. Vijgen. *Joden in Amsterdam, assimilatie en segregatie van een ethnische minderheid 1600–1933* [Jews in Amsterdam, Assimilation and Segregation of an Ethnic Minority 1600–1933] (Amsterdam 1983). Dissertation.

M. Villanova (ed.). *V Colloqui Internacional d'Historia Oral. El poder e la Societat* (Barcelona 1985).

A. C. Vooys. "Wijziging in de maatschapelijke verhoudingen" [Change in Social Proportions]. In P. B. Kreukniet, *Bijdragen tot de sociaal-economische verniewing* [Contributions to the Socioeconomic Renewal] (Utrecht and Antwerp 1952), part 14, pp. 28–55.

M. Vovelle. *Ideologies et mentalités* [Ideologies and Mindsets] (Paris 1982).

J. de Vries. *Met Amsterdam als brandput. Hondervijftig jaar Kamer van Koophandel en Fabrieken* [Amsterdam as a Focal Point. 150 Years of the Chamber of Commerce and Factories] (Amsterdam 1961).

_____. *De Nederlandse economie tijdens de 20ste eeuw, een verkenning van het meest kenmerkende* [The Dutch Economy during the Twentieth Century, a

Survey of the Most Distinguishing Characteristics] (Antwerp and Utrecht 1973).

M. Weber. *Gesammelte Aufsätze zur Religionssoziologie* [Collected Articles on the Sociology of Religion] (Tübingen 1976).

N. Weinstock. *Le pain de la misère. Histoire du mouvement ouvrier juif en Europe* [The Bread of Misery. History of the Jewish Labor Movement in Europe], 2 parts (Paris 1984).

Wereldverbond van diamantbewerkers [World Union of Diamond Workers]. *Rapport nopens den toestand in de diamantnijverheid, in het bijzonder aangaande de loonen en tarieven in Duitschland, Zwitserland, Frankrijk, België en Nederland* [Report on the Condition of the Diamond Industry with Particular Reference to the Wages and Tarifs in Germany, Switzerland, France, Belgium, and the Netherlands] (Amsterdam 1924). Present in the archives of the ANDB.

E. Werkman. *Het Waterlooplein* [Waterloo Square] (Amsterdam 1979).

J. White. *Rotschild Buildings. Life in an East End Tenement Block 1887–1920* (London 1980).

F. M. Wibaut. *Levensbouw. Memoires door F. M. Wibaut* [Life Structure. Reminiscences of F. M. Wibaut] (Amsterdam 1936).

C. H. Wiedijk. *Koos Vorrink: gezindheid, veralgemening, integratie: een biografische studie (1891–1940)* [Koos Vorrink: Disposition, Generalization, Integration: A Biographical Study (1891–1940)] (Amsterdam 1986).

L. Wijmans. "Sociologie, Sociaal-democratie en de middenklasse" [Sociology, Social Democracy, and the Middle Classes], *Amsterdams Sociologisch Tijdschrift*, vol. 5, no. 4 (March 1979); vol. 6, no. 2 (June 1979).

R. Williams. *Marxism and Literature* (Oxford 1977).

S. de Wolff. *Voor het land van beloofde, een terugblik op mijn leven* [For the Promised Land. A Look Back on My Life] (Bussum 1954; reprint Nijmegen 1978).

A. H. Wolff–Gerzon. *Au Bonheur des Dames* [To the Success of the Ladies] (Amsterdam, no date).

F. A. Yates. *The Art of Memory* (London 1966).

M. Young and P. Wilmott. *Family and Kinship in East London* (London 1957).

J. H. van Zanten. "Eenige demografische gegevens over de joden te Amsterdam" [Demographic Data on the Jews of Amsterdam], *Mensch en Maatschappij*, vol. 1 (January 1926).

J. H. van Zanten and T. van der Brink. "Population Phenomena in Amsterdam," *Population. Journal of the International Union for the Scientific Investigation of Population Problems*, vol. 3, no. 1 (1939).

M. Zomerplaag. *De groei der Afrikaner of Transvaalbuurt* [Growth of the Afrikaner or Transvaal Neighborhood] (Amsterdam 1973).

INDEX